D0856567

ISLANDS

ISLANDS

From Atlantis to Zanzibar

STEVEN ROGER FISCHER

REAKTION BOOKS

Published by Reaktion Books Ltd
33 Great Sutton Street
London EC1V 0DX, UK
www.reaktionbooks.co.uk

Copyright © Steven Roger Fischer 2012

All rights reserved
No part of this publication may be reproduced, stored in a retrieval
system, or transmitted, in any form or by any means, electronic,
mechanical, photocopying, recording or otherwise, without the prior
permission of the publishers.

Printed and bound by TJ International, Padstow, Cornwall

British Library Cataloguing in Publication Data

Fischer, Steven R.
Islands : from Atlantis to Zanzibar.
1. Islands.
I. Title.
909'.0942-dc23

ISBN 978 1 78023 032 0

Contents

Preface

'*No man is an island*', penned English poet John Donne (1573–1631), articulating the feature's perceived quintessence: that *insularitas* which forever distanced. Yet this 'body of land that is smaller than a continent and surrounded by water' appears only at first blush an isolate and isolator. That inveterate iconoclast and enthusiastic island visitor Mark Twain (1835–1910) noted in nearly every island guestbook he signed that, when he died, he'd rather be transported there than to Heaven. For islands have ever been the venerable hymn's 'Beautiful Isle of Somewhere', too, that all life seems to seek.

This has powerful reasons.

Islands are Earth's crucibles and cradles, bridges and bonds. From fabled Atlantis to mighty Japan, from Minoan Crete to modern Manhattan, from Taiwan to Tahiti, islands have fascinated and empowered, inspired and enriched, delighted and rescued. They have co-enabled, geologically and biologically, the very Earth we know. Forever goals and poles, islands have featured among our planet's primary provenances for plants, animals, hominins. These tiny scraps of sand, these leviathans of stone in oceans, rivers and lakes are veritable worlds that formed the first ferns and feathers and then co-formed *Homo sapiens sapiens*. And so in human history, economy, politics, literature, art, psychology and so many other things islands have been a co-measure of humankind itself.

Islands addresses these things in their, at times, rather surprising multitude of guises. American Surrealist photographer Man Ray (1890–1976) once said there is no progress in art, any more than there is progress in making love – only different ways of doing it. So it is with 'capturing' islands. One can, of course, picture them discretely through the eyes of the individual geologist, botanist, historian, economist, political scientist or other. Innumerable tracks lead to the insular coastline and these have been sailed often. A Man Ray 'different way of doing it' would be to load each of these disciplines onto a single vessel: that is, to attempt an incipient 'nesology' (from Greek *nēsos* 'island') – a comprehensive study of islands. This is the tack *Islands* has taken.

The book is predicated on the recognition that islands take on form through geology, take on life through biology, and take on meaning through culture. Islands are the co-creation of nature (form and life) and culture (meaning). Here, nature is understood to mean the diverse and shifting constructs of the biome humans occupy – or are conscious of – and the dynamics deemed operative upon it, and culture encompasses the beliefs, practices and organization of human societies. The book's first two chapters address island geology and biology. The rest confronts culture: what islands *mean* to us. However, one forgets at one's peril that the trio – geology, biology, culture – are synergetic.

Each of Earth's more than a million islands and islets tells a noteworthy narrative. Yet it's the recurrent constants that fill *Islands*. A particularly cogent one that the author – late of Okinawa, Japan (1956–8); South Island, New Zealand (1975–80); and long-time resident of Waiheke Island, New Zealand (1995–present) – came to appreciate during the researching and writing of this book: all islanders are viscerally attracted to other islands. British poet and novelist Lawrence Durrell (1912–1990), for one, had to confess, 'Islomania is a rare affliction of spirit. There are people who find islands somehow irresistible. The mere knowledge that they are in a little world surrounded by sea fills them with an indescribable intoxication.'[1]

For islands breathe and bleed, embrace and couple, sing and inspire, too. Once one achieves this understanding, goodbye John Donne:

Every man is an island.

one

. . . *of Stone and Sand*

In principio erat insula . . . When ranging islands, we sense time
ever at our shoulder. Unlike mountains, continents and seas, most
islands come and go in 'rapid' succession. One need only think of
the British Isles – hardly 10,000 years of age, a blink in geological
time. If continents are Methuselahs, then volcanic islands, in particular, are mere mayflies. The largest part of today's islands – and
there have been millions over the æons – are quite recent apparitions, products of sea-level change, rifting, volcanism and crustal
rising. Geologists say that the island world we know today is like
yesterday's snow.

Yet islands *as a fact* remain Earth's most timeless feature.

Nobel laureate Jack Szostak (*b*. 1952) has succinctly described
their nursery:

> Imagine Earth four billion years ago. It is a world of oceans, pep-
> pered with volcanic land masses resembling Hawai'i and Iceland.
> The volcanoes spew poisonous gases and the atmosphere is rent by
> the violent impacts of asteroids and comets. Temperatures range
> from the incandescent heat of flowing lava to the frozen ice fields of
> high polar regions. Shallow ponds on the volcanic islands dry out,
> then fill with rain, incubating the fragile chemistry that ultimately
> leads to the emergence of life.[1]

So all life began – on an island.

Around 800 million years ago supercontinent Rodinia experienced great volcanism and rifting – the faulting produced by tension
on either side of a fault plane – which increased weathering and

flooded water-planet Earth with nutrients. By 720 million years ago Earth had been plunged into a glaciation, but when CO_2 levels gradually recovered and the glaciers receded to the poles around 635 million years ago there was new land primed with pioneering green algæ and lichen. These opened new boulevards for chemical and physical rock-weathering and Earth was again flooded with life-prompting nutrients: photosynthesizing bacteria in the seas slowly drove up atmospheric oxygen levels to now-familiar heights. By about 580 million years ago the earliest of all our animal ancestors crawled into the fossil record, soon followed by leafy plants.

The æons rolled on. By 200 million years ago there was only one terrestrial land mass, one 'Earth Island': Pangæa. Tectonic rifting then broke her gradually apart: within 40 million years north and south had split. The south – Gondwana – consisted of what would become Africa, South America, India, Australia, New Zealand, Antarctica and Madagascar: animals could move freely from Argentina to New Zealand and never leave dry land. Then more rifting occurred, prying Madagascar, India, Australia, New Zealand and Antarctica away from eastern Africa. After this, India and Madagascar broke from Australia, New Zealand and Antarctica. Finally, around 70 million years ago, India slipped away from Madagascar and drifted up to collide with East Asia. Madagascar has been abandoned ever since; she is one of Earth's oldest islands.

This process was understood by Roman poet Ovid (43 BC – c. AD 17) already 2,000 years ago:

> The face of places, and their forms decay;
> And that is solid earth, that once was sea;
> Seas, in their turn, retreating from the shore,
> Make solid land, what ocean was before.[2]

Today's oceans cover over 70 per cent of Earth's surface, one billion cubic kilometres of water spread over 360 million square kilometres. That's nearly 300 billion litres (almost 60 billion gallons) *for every person on Earth*. One ocean current alone transports 60 times more water than all the rivers in the world put together.[3] It is indeed a 'water world' on which we live. All the rest? Islands. Continents are merely 'very big islands'. The Pacific, sometimes called the Water Continent in that it encompasses half of our planet, offers the richest assemblage of islands, island groups and island nations.

Our simplest definition would have an island as land surrounded by water. Evidence from planetary science suggests, however, that it might be better to define an island as 'land surrounded by liquid' – as we now appreciate that islands could well populate seas, lakes and rivers of molten rock, liquid methane, liquid carbon dioxide, mercury or more novel concoctions. Many might be happy with the old Scottish definition: an island is 'any place surrounded by water that claims enough pasture to graze one sheep for a year'.

And the geological island? Here complexity takes wing. An island can be a bit of an ancient continent, an accretion of ocean sandbank, the first cooled tip of an erupting volcano, and so much more.[4] She can lie in the sea, in a river, in a lake. She can be as large as Greenland or as small as Loch Lomond's humble Inchmurrin. Some islands are entire countries: Madagascar, Cuba, Malta, Iceland. Other countries are multiple large islands: Japan, Indonesia, the Philippines, New Zealand. Islands can hold two or more nations: Ireland, Borneo, Cyprus, Hispaniola. Some islands sustain one crofter's hut; others host Earth's largest metropolises: New York, Singapore, Montreal, Hong Kong. Hundreds have been notorious penal colonies. A refreshing number are now wildlife refuges.

Islands manifest themselves, or are qualified, in many ways:[5]

ait 'an islet, especially in a river'
archipelago 'an extensive group of islands'
atoll 'a ring-shaped reef or chain of islands formed of coral'
calf 'a small island lying near a larger one'[6]
cay 'a low bank or reef of coral, rock or sand'
eyot 'an islet, especially in a river'
holm 'an islet'
islet 'a small island'
key 'a low-lying island or reef (especially in the Caribbean)'
reef 'a ridge of jagged rock, coral or sand just above or below
   the surface of the sea'
skerry 'a small rocky island' (from the Orkney dialect, from
   Old Norse *sker* 'scar')
tombolo 'a bar of sand or shingle joining an island to the
   mainland'

Celebrated British navigator and explorer James Cook (1728–1779) recognized two island types: high (over the horizon and seen from afar) and low (only a metre or two above sea level and possessing in most cases a coral reef). Today, we prefer to classify islands according to geological composition and original creation. In this way every island is either continental or oceanic. (Political perceptions in the 1800s distinguished a continent from an island: the mighty British Empire's Australia could be a continent, modest Denmark's Greenland could not.)

The presence of a new bridge or causeway does not invalidate insular status: Skye still remains the *Isle* of Skye. Nor does the presence of tidal flats, so Cumbria's Piel Island, 1 km off the southern tip of Furness Peninsula, France's Mont St Michel and Cornwall's St Michael's Mount will remain periodic islands. 'Island' or 'Isle' also lingers in names for erstwhile islands that now comprise mainland: 2,000 years ago England's Isle of Thanet in eastern Kent, for example, served as the Roman legions' *island* port of entry to Britannia; and 14 km southwest of Cardiff, Wales's Barry Island – perhaps also an erstwhile Roman port – was accessible only at the ebb until the 1880s when she was connected to the mainland by a series of docks and a railway.

The geological stage has been crowded with the like. Around 35 million years ago, for example, a thin land bridge called Gaarlandia connected the Caribbean to South America, offering ancient fauna a dry route up to Cuba: it now embraces a sprinkling of innumerable isles.[7] In the last half-million years sea levels have fluctuated between 8 m higher and 150 m lower than today's. During the glacial periods of the Pleistocene – the ice-age cycles that lasted from around 1.8 million to 12,000 years ago – most coasts were some 100 m below present-day sea level. Islands, in this way, have regularly bowed in and out.

Only at the end of the last ice age did the island world we know begin. At the same time coastlines were being reformed by erosion and deposition as well. It was only about 2,500 years ago that Earth's seas reached their present 'near stand-still' (which is anything but, say geologists).[8] Today's islands are only a snapshot of fleeting apparitions. In the very moment we describe them, islands are experiencing further change.

This is particularly evident with coral reefs. Coral production is ancient, but living reefs are infants.[9] Though coral reefs and islands reach back over 400 million years, today's living reefs are only 5,000 to 8,000 years old, as the coral could begin to grow only once the oceans rose again, the coral often building on fossil foundations of earlier growth. Throughout the world most living coral deposits are no more than 30 m thick – paper-thin in geological terms.

All the same, Earth's present stock of over a million islands and islets is something more than impressive. Disregarding Australia, which at 7,682,300 sq km (with Tasmania) arbitrarily counts as a 'continental landmass', our twenty largest islands are:

1. Greenland (2,175,610 sq km)
2. New Guinea (820,660)
3. Borneo (743,330)
4. Madagascar (587,041)
5. Baffin Island (476,560)
6. Sumatra (473,606)
7. Honshū (230,448)
8. Great Britain (229,523)
9. Ellesmere Island (212,688)
10. Victoria Island (212,200)
11. Sulawesi (189,220)
12. South Island, NZ (153,947)
13. Java (132,174)
14. North Island, NZ (114,729)
15. Newfoundland (111,390)
16. Cuba (110,922)
17. Luzon (104,688)
18. Iceland (102,828)
19. Mindanao (94,631)
20. Ireland (84,400)

Islands form from a variety of factors. As Pliny the Elder (AD 23–79) wrote in his *Natural History*:

> For lands are born not only through the conveyance of soil by streams (as the Echinades Islands when heaped up from the river Achelous and the greater part of [coastal] Egypt from the Nile – the crossing from the island of Pharos to the coast, if we believe Homer [in his *Odyssey*, IV, 354], having formerly taken twenty-four hours) or by the retirement of the sea as once took place at Circei . . .[10]

This 'retirement of the sea' is how the British Isles came to be: so-called 'residual islands' which appear as sea levels rise, isolating a resident population from the mainland. In fact, a fill of island forms have come and gone since those first molten seas.

'LIKE A NEWLY VARNISHED CANVAS'

Common as conkers, continental islands are everyman's isles. All of Earth's land masses are surrounded by submerged continental shelves. Their base is granite – not basalt like the sea floor's – and their width can vary from over 1,200 km (off Siberia) to under 1 km (off Peru). Once dry lands, these were flooded when the sea level rose to create, out of their high plains, hills and mountain chains, islands like the Bahamas.[11] This has happened very recently. Most of the Malay Archipelago (Sumatra, Java, Bali, Borneo and others), for example, has comprised islands for only some 12,000 years.

'Calved' islands like Madagascar, the Seychelles or New Zealand are much older. Over æons most continents have calved major islands. A 'microcontinental island' is the term for a great land mass rifted away from the mother continent: Madagascar from Africa, New Zealand from Australia.

Oceanic crust, of silica magnesium rocks, is what always subsides beneath the continental rocks, of lighter silica and alumina. So Earth's surface is more persistently claimed by continental fragments.[12] Geological history is an unending carom board of colliding and fragmenting continental crust. Continents are forever drifting. Their lighter material floats like rafts on the denser crust of the seas. In more 'recent' times – the past 200 million years – Gondwana and Laurasia fragmented into smaller rafting continents surrounded by continental shelves. At the same time, oceans were spreading at rates of between 3 and 10 cm per year; this would date the fragmenting of Gondwana, the Southern Hemiphere's supercontinent, at about 130 million years ago.[13] Such smaller rafting continents that were produced include India (which was an island before it collided – more than 70 million years ago – and fused with the larger Eurasian continent), Hispaniola (Haiti and the Dominican Republic) and Madagascar. Though Australia is often geographically regarded as an island, originally she was the major member of the erstwhile continent of Sahul; Australia's continental shelf still extends to Indonesia.

Continental islands are Earth's largest. They consist of granites, acid volcanics and sedimentary derivatives. Commonly they are also our planet's oldest islands, with a larger and more diverse biota – that is, range of life forms – than oceanic islands could ever claim. Over the past 2 million years, as ice shelves descended and retreated, these 'ephemeral islands' stood apart and again connected. Australia only 'very recently', around 8,000 years ago, lost New Guinea and Tasmania, currently her two neighbouring continental islands, to rising sea levels, 500 years or so after Ireland 'left' Britain and Britain herself 'left' Europe. Only this morning in geological time.

New Zealand tells a similar story.[14] Over 130 million years ago she was still part of Gondwana, attached to South America, Antarctica, Africa, India and Australia. Over the next 30 million years New Zealand's region of the Indo-Australian Plate detached and also isolated itself from Australia and Antarctica. For much of her early history, this newly isolated fragment of continental crust was submerged and the depository of marine sediments; now much of this assemblage is dry land. As a motley collection of continental islands, New Zealand embodies the featural variety of larger fragments of continental crust. The actual 'continent of New Zealand' far surpasses her visible coastlines: from New Caledonia along the Norfolk Ridge and southeastward along the Lord Howe Rise all the way to the far south and east beyond South Island.[15] Today's New Zealand now straddles two of the world's major plates, rendering the country a 'tectonic time bomb': all of North Island and western South Island lie on the massive Indo-Australian Plate, whereas eastern and southern South Island, Stewart Island and the Chatham Islands lie on the enormous Pacific Plate. Location is everything: the Southern Alps, vying with their European namesake at over 3,000 m, are the imposing result, as are active volcanism (North Island's Mt Ruapehu last erupted in 1996) and recurring earthquakes.

Such geological processes were recognized long ago. Again Pliny the Elder:

For another way also in which nature has made islands is when she tore Sicily away from Italy, Cyprus from Syria, Euboea from Boeotia, Atalantes and Macrias from Euboea, Besbicus from Bithynia, Leucosia from the Sirens' Cape . . . Again she had taken islands away from the sea and joined them to the land – Antissa to Lesbos,

Zephyrius to Halicarnassus, Aethusa to Myndus, Dromiscos and Pernes to Miletus, Narthecusa to Cape Parthenius. Hybanda, once an Ionian island, is now 25 miles distant from the sea, Ephesus has Syrie as part of the mainland, and its neighbour Magnesia the Derasides and Sapphonia. Epidaurus and Oricum have ceased to be islands.[16]

One of Earth's richest, and least known, continental island treasuries would have to be British Columbia's approximately 6,500 islands, products of glacial erosion, inundation and sea-level rise. Vancouver Island (32,134 sq km) is breathtaking, the largest on North America's western coast, Canada's eleventh largest and the largest Pacific island east of New Zealand. She hosts many cities, with nearly half of her population of 740,876 (est. 2008) occupying Greater Victoria, British Columbia's capital. (The city of Vancouver is on the mainland.) Indeed, Canada's continental islands are among Earth's largest and most numerous. Alone Baffin Island, largest member of the Canadian Arctic Archipelago, is Canada's largest and the world's fifth largest, yet claims only about 11,000 inhabitants (est. 2007). Newfoundland, Canada's fourth and the world's fifteenth largest island, houses nearly half a million people (2006) and is the site of the only authenticated Norse settlement in North America. Then there is pastoral Prince Edward Island in the Gulf of St Lawrence, which ranks as Canada's smallest province in both area and population: 5,656 sq km that support some 141,000 residents (est. 2009).

Further continental islands include the Bahamas, whose reefs started forming perhaps as early as 350 million years ago when algæ and coral collected on the windward edge of an expansive continental shelf created by sedimental erosion from North America.[17] Sands on the leeward side consist mainly of shattered coral strewn over wide reaches of shallow sea, now called the Bahama Banks. This was dry land only 12,000 years ago before the sea rose, yet isolated from the North American mainland by the up to 800-m-deep Florida Strait. At times of maximal glaciation life forms there, including humans, enjoyed land access to South America.

The continental islands of Britain share the Bahamas' age, for they, too, were isolated from Europe at the end of the last glaciation. Folk wisdom has it that there are as many islands around Scotland's coast as days in the year, around England's coast as weeks in the year, and around Wales's coast as months in the year. Actually,

Britain can claim more than 1,000 islands and islets. The Isle of Man is the largest, followed by the Isle of Wight and then Wales's Môn (Anglesey). Though now 'attached' to the Welsh mainland by highway and railway, Môn will forever remain a holy isle in the Welsh psyche. Her largest town, Caergybi (Holyhead), Great Britain's major port serving Ireland, is situated on Ynys Gybi (Holy Island) which is an island off an island (Môn) off an island (Britain).

Throughout the world one finds many such thrice-removed isles. Tiny, renowned Iona in the Inner Hebrides lies just 1.6 km off the coast of Mull, herself just 2 km off the Scottish coast. Sheep station and now vineyard-strewn Pōnui broods a mere 1.4 km southeast of Waiheke Island – where this book was written – herself only 17.7 km east of Auckland on New Zealand's North Island. In future, many more 'double-calves' will appear, particularly in Scotland and the Baltic where the land is still rebounding from the last ice age.[18]

Before the Pleistocene, Crete was the summit of a grand chain of mountains curving from the Peloponnese in the west to Asia Minor in the east. Then the Ægean plateau submerged, the mountains rose, and Crete found herself isolated from the western and eastern mainlands. Now around 250 km long, with three main mountain groups lying west to east (the highest peak being central Mt Ida at 2,500 m), Crete boasts fertile coastal plains and valleys; her lower upland plains are occupied year-round, her higher ones only in summer.[19]

The Greek islands and islets in general – and there are some 6,000 of them – are rocky and mountainous. The mountain areas are chiefly limestone; in the valleys clays and sandstone predominate. Here one finds all the geological periods, from the Neotriassic to the Pleistocene, with modern alluviums as well. The climate of the Greek islands is temperate. Rainfall differs markedly from one island to another. The Ionian Islands between Greece and Italy are wetter and more wooded; Corfu has Greece's greatest rainfall (but for the mainland's Ioannina region in some years).

Lawrence Durrell loved the Greek isles. He wrote passionately of the 'island' of Calavria on the northeast coast of the Peloponnesos in the Gulf of Athens, saddled between Ægina in the northeast and Poros in the southeast. Calavria is connected to the mainland by a narrow isthmus. She was once famous for her sanctuary dedicated to Poseidon. Plutarch, Durrell tells us, once related how Demosthenes (384–322 BC), the Athenian statesman and orator, fled here

A courtly vessel plying the Japanese isles during the Heian period (794–1192).

before the invading Macedonians, certain they would never violate Poseidon's sanctuary, but then poisoned himself at the god's altar once he realized his error. 'The whole island', Durrell writes, 'smells and shines like a newly varnished canvas – the green of olives and yellow of lemons; and stealing softly across the waters, come the steady drizzle of *bouzouki* music and the higher, more febrile drizzle of sun-drunk *cicadas*.'[20]

Djerba, at 514 sq km North Africa's largest island, with a population of around 140,000 (2004) Berbers, Arabs, Jews and black

Africans, lies in Tunisia's shallow Gulf of Gabès which is underlain by the continental shelf of the African Plate. The island, joined to the mainland by a 6-km causeway built on a Roman foundation, is an oasis covered with more than a million date palms and nearly as many olive trees. Now a popular tourist destination, Djerba finds that half of her 600,000 annual visitors are Germans.

The world's third strongest economy and greatest island economy, mighty and majestic Japan comprises a continental archipelago of no fewer than 6,852 islands – 97 per cent of whose area is claimed by Hokkaidō, Honshū, Shikoku and Kyūshū. The mostly mountainous islands hold the world's tenth largest population (over 127 million). Tokyo, with more than 30 million residents, is Earth's largest metropolitan area. Like Britain, Japan embraces many groups of islands and archipelagos. In the expansive Bay of Sagami, for example, south of Tokyo, lie the Izu Islands, the most distant of which is located some 250 km southeast of the Japanese mainland: including Hachijō, Mikura, Miyake, Kōzu, Niijima, Tōshima and Ōshima, all erstwhile summits of the Izu mountain range. Stretching south and southwest of Kyūshū to within 120 km of Taiwan are Japan's Ryūkyū Islands, the largest of which is Okinawa. Differing in climate from northerly Japan, the subtropical Ryūkyūs enjoy mild winters but suffer hot, humid summers. They are also more vulnerable to violent typhoons: the author will never forget the 1957 monster that, howling like Godzilla, all but ripped off the red roof tiles of his family home.

Just north of Japan's Hokkaidō lies Russia's largest island, Sakhalin, the world's 23rd biggest at 72,492 sq km. Like Japan a mountainous insular world with two parallel ranges traversing her from north to south, Sakhalin is separated from the Siberian mainland in the northwest by the shallow and very narrow Mamiya Strait. During the Miocene era, from around 23 million to 5 million years ago, Sakhalin was included in a continent that comprised northern Asia, Japan and Alaska. Never very populated, the island registers a present population of a little over 500,000, mostly ethnic Russians; of Sakhalin's indigenous peoples, only some 2,000 Nivkhs and 750 Oroks survive.

In the South China Sea, Hainan, the smallest province of the People's Republic of China, is a Belgium-sized island of 33,920 sq km boasting a population of 8,640,700 (2009), 83 per cent of whom are Han Chinese. Hainan is separated in the north from the Leizhou

Peninsula by the narrow and shallow Qiongzhou Strait. In this province one finds some 200 islands linked in three different archipelagos, yet Hainan claims 97 per cent of the total area. Eight major cities dominate the island, whose climate is tropical and moist. Like Okinawa, eastern Hainan suffers intermittent typhoons which often cause major flooding. Her economy predominantly agricultural, Hainan is also a popular Chinese tourist destination: in 2008 over 20 million visited, with one out of twenty coming from overseas. Hainan is also home to China's strategic nuclear submarine fleet, harboured in 18-m-high caverns built into hillsides around a major military installation.

The largest Chinese-inhabited island, at 35,980 sq km, is of course Taiwan, between the East China Sea and the South China Sea, 120 km from the Chinese mainland. Her population is nearly three times that of Hainan, at 23,046,177 (2009), now 98 per cent of whom are Han Chinese. Much of Taiwan was formed through complex tectonic activity, as the island is situated between several major plates, with uplifting, as a portion of the Eurasian Plate detached itself and was subducted beneath residue of the Philippine Sea Plate. Eastern and southern Taiwan comprises a complex system of belts formed by the North Luzon Trough section of the Luzon Volcanic Arc colliding with South China continent. Taiwan's seismic status stands at 'most hazardous' for nine-tenths of the island; earthquakes are common and can be violent. Taiwan's climate is also tropical and subject to ferocious typhoons. An economic powerhouse with great industrial development, Taiwan suffers from a magnitude of pollution seldom witnessed on Earth's islands, though in recent years the air quality has markedly improved as a result of new environmental regulations.

Brazil is home to hundreds of islands, most of which are continental and virtually unknown to the outside world. Ilha Grande, for example, lying off the coast of Rio de Janeiro state, is 193 sq km of mostly undeveloped beauty, enticing tourists to enjoy her pristine beaches, luxuriant vegetation and challenging landscape: a remnant of Brazil's Atlantic rainforest, she hosts one of the world's richest ecosystems. Connected to the 0.5-km-distant mainland by three bridges (one has remained closed since 1991), Santa Catarina island on Brazil's south coast – 424 sq km supporting 315,000 (2006) – houses the Santa Catarina state capital of Florianópolis; Santa Catarina is actually the largest island in an archipelago of more than 30 isles. Similarly, Vitória Island is both an island and an archipelago, this time in Brazil's Espírito Santo state; Vitória is the main island, with an area of 89 sq km and a population of some 300,000 (2010), and also houses the state capital.

Few outsiders know that the city of Stockholm, Sweden's capital, sits on fourteen continental islands – downtown Stockholm is actually lapped by water. There used to be far more islands around Stockholm, but over the centuries they have disappeared due to land elevation, reclamation and fill-in. The Baltic is replete with islands of enormous historical importance. Sweden's Gotland is the undisputed king of the Baltic, with 57,221 inhabitants (2009) on 2,994 sq km. Sweden's Öland is the Baltic's noble queen, with 25,000 inhabitants on 1,347 sq km. And Denmark's Bornholm is the shining crown prince, with 42,154 (2010) living on 588 sq km, many of whom speak *Bornholmsk*, an official dialect of Danish. Denmark claims around 406 islands, not including the Faroe Islands and Greenland; only about 70 of these are populated, though, and more and more of them are losing their young people to the main cities, like Copenhagen. Copenhagen herself, with a metropolitan population of 1,901,789 (2010), stands on the two islands of Zealand and Amager and is, like Stockholm, very much an island capital.

Finland's almost entirely Swedish-speaking Åland Islands, the nation's smallest region, include the main island of Fasta Åland, 1,010 sq km of rocky and lean-soiled bleakness 38 km east of Sweden, with a total population of 27,700 (est. 2009); historically guarding one of the main accesses to the Swedish port of Stockholm, the now demilitarized continental archipelago consists of 1,527 sq km of more than 300 habitable islands, only 80 of which are occupied. Some 6,000 skerries lie scattered about as desolate sentinels. Not too far away to the southeast lies Saaremaa, Estonia's largest island at 2,673 sq km, part of the West Estonia Archipelago, a group of islands totaling 4,000 sq km; Saaremaa, with over 39,000 inhabitants, has been inhabited for over 5,000 years and forms the main defence between the Baltic Sea and the Gulf of Riga. Just a few kilometres north lies Estonia's second largest island, Hiiumaa (989 sq km), which supports a population of 11,087 (2009). Both islands rose out of the Baltic Ice Lake some 10,000 years ago when retreating glaciers effected an enormous uplift of the Earth's crust; all of the archipelago's islands are still rising, at the rate of around 2 mm per year. As Baltic Sea islands continue to rebound from the last ice age many will disappear, too, as they rejoin the mainlands of Sweden, Finland and Estonia.

Only a handful of Arctic islands are oceanic. Most are near-shore, abutting a mainland. Of course, this means that during an ice age, with much lower sea levels, most Arctic islands were not islands at all but lay under thick ice or formed part of a continent. The entire Arctic region is geologically very young, the product of stupendous forces over several eras of glaciation. The 14 million-sq-km basin about which all major northern land masses are situated – the Arctic Ocean – is home to massive, mostly ice-dominated islands, which include Svalbard (Spitsbergen), Severnaya Zemlya, Novaya Zemlya, Franz Joseph Land, Wrangel Island and New Siberian Islands; and Canada's Ellesmere, Baffin, Banks Island, Devon, Victoria and many smaller islands. In winter, ice and snow obscure more than two-thirds of the region, erasing all land-or-sea distinctions and linking the islands. Some areas, like North Water between southern Ellesmere and Greenland, hardly ever freeze over, and these shoreleads and 'polynias' (a space of open water in the midst of ice) are crucial to sea animals. Further south of the Arctic islands lie the more temperate Commander group, Aleutian chain and Kuril Islands in the Pacific; and Iceland, the Faroes and others in the Atlantic.[21]

A unique island 'community' lies scattered in the Southern Ocean as well, between 45°S and 59°S, as isolated from the continents as they are from one another. The eight small islands and island groups are found between the most southerly shores of South America, Africa, Australia and New Zealand: Macquarie (200 sq km), Heard/McDonald (368), Kerguelen (6,500), Crozet (400), Prince Edward/Marion Islands (52/300), Bouvet (50), South Sandwich (618) and South Georgia (3,755). These straddle the Antarctic Convergence, where warmer northern currents meet cold Antarctic waters. Free of ice and snow most of the year are the islands at Kerguelen or just north of the Convergence, hence Macquarie, Crozet and Prince Edward and Marion islands. The islands south of this are mostly snow-covered and widely glaciated: Heard, South Georgia, South Sandwich and Bouvet. Despite appearing in a common ring each island displays a different geological history, from upturned oceanic crust to strato- and shield volcanism. Some are as old as 130 million years (South Georgia) or as young as 40,000 years (part of Kerguelen). Like Scotland and the West Estonia

Archipelago, their relative altitudes have altered with rises in the sea floor, and, since the last maximal glaciation, sea has risen while glaciers have retreated, exposing ever more land.[22]

Most of the Malay Archipelago is actually the remnants of the earlier Sunda subcontinent that once separated the Indian Ocean from the South China Sea. The region only became islands once the sea rose following the last ice age. Continental and oceanic both, Indonesia – which, together with island Malaysia (part of Borneo), Brunei and East Timor, makes up the vast archipelago – holds the record as Earth's most island-studded nation, with around 18,000. She is also the world's fourth most populous country, with approximately 238 million inhabitants (2009).

Greenland, part of the North American continent, is a tectonic superchild. The world's largest island – albeit one of the least-populated nations or dependencies (56,452, est. 2010) – measures nearly 2,200,000 sq km, only about 19 per cent of which is not permanently covered by the Greenland Ice Sheet. Only along her coastal rim, interspersed with huge crumbling glaciers, can one enjoy ice-free regions that are either rocky outcrops or heaths of dwarf shrub stretching over 2,600 km from the Arctic down to subarctic waters. The far north, above 0°C for only two months of the year, begrudges few flowering plants, whereas the southern interior – with seven months above freezing – larders willow copses and beech forests. Greenland's ice sheet is second only to Antarctica's in size.[23]

Often continental and oceanic islands are forced to dance 'the tectonic tango'. As undersea subduction zones account for 90 per cent of all seismic energy released worldwide, it is little wonder that islands are earthquake traps. Once tectonics calves islands, climate-conditioned erosion and rock composition then fashion them, the protracted erosion working on different rock types in manifold ways. Glacial erosion is particularly industrious: it loves to carve up mountains into monstrous troughs that, when inundated by rising seas, paint a palette of profound island fjords, such as Fiordland on South Island, New Zealand. The glacier-carved and sea-filled valleys have fashioned many an Alaskan and western Canadian island (including massive Vancouver Island, in 1946 the site of a 7.3-magnitude earthquake, the greatest experienced on Canadian soil), Scotland's Hebrides, the Lofoten Islands off the northwest coast of Norway, and many of southern Chile's coastal islands.

When glaciers chew up lowlands, leaving behind irregular outcrops of rock, the sea can rise around these to form skerries. Such skerries typify the coasts not only of the Orkneys, but also of Norway's Skjærgård and of Finland, too.[24]

'SUDDENLY SHOT UP A GREAT FLAME'

Oceanic islands are those not on continental shelves. Nearly all are volcanic, with notable exceptions (like tectonic islands lifted above sea level by plate movement). Plate subduction produces a volcanic island arc, such as most of the Tongan Islands, the Marianas in the Pacific or some of the Lesser Antilles in the Atlantic. An oceanic rift, too, can rise above sea level to produce volcanic islands; there are only two examples of this having happened, both in the Atlantic – Iceland and Jan Mayen. Volcanic hotspots also form islands, such as the Pacific's Hawaiian Islands and the early Tuamotus. An atoll is an eroded and submerged volcanic island fringed by a coral reef that has risen above sea level, usually ring-shaped with a central lagoon: one need only picture the Tuamotus in the Pacific or the Maldives in the Indian Ocean.

As with Taiwan, many oceanic islands issue from a complex kitchen. Rupture is a further island recipe: take one large land mass – isolated over æons through tectonic activity – and let it simply 'calve' like a fragmenting iceberg. An archipelago of 115 islands totalling 451 sq km, the Seychelles in the Indian Ocean were served up in just this way: some 1,500 km east of the African mainland, they are neither volcanic nor coral but, like the Scillies and the Channel Islands, granite (though they do display, here and there, coral attachments), tiny fragments of 700 million-year-old continental crust that broke off, one from the other, possibly around 66 million years ago.[25]

All land masses owe their origin to volcanism. And almost all volcanos are either in the sea or no further than 200 km from a coast, the simple dictate of plate tectonics. Earth's outer crust and the mantle's solid part – that is, the lithosphere – appear to comprise around twelve large chunks that are in constant motion relative to one another.[26] When plates drift apart or collide, they surge semi-liquid magma upwards. Under the seas the lithosphere is younger and thinner than ancient continental crust which has had more time to thicken, so it is in the seas (or near them) where most volcanism occurs and where most islands are created.

From Africa to the Pacific, various hominins have competed alongside volcanos for millions of years. But the race runs on rock time: just like our predecessors, we *Homo sapiens sapiens* experience only few eruptions, if any, during one lifetime, and always find plenty of time to flee, adapt and rebuild. The author's island of Waiheke, just 17.7 km off Auckland, overlooks no fewer than 50 volcanos around which New Zealand's largest city has risen, the world's richest urban volcanic field. Between Waiheke and Auckland's North Shore, prominent Rangitoto Island shot up out of the sea only around 700 years ago – an event witnessed by New Zealand's earliest Māori settlers.

It appears that almost all of Earth's volcanos – both submerged and exposed – belong to one of three classes: *mid-ocean ridge*, *island-arc*, or *hotspot*.[27]

Mid-ocean ridge volcanos feed on a constant, robust, magmatic plume that can form veritable leviathans. 'Iceland represents such a plume-driven volcano located astride the northern end of the Mid-Atlantic Ridge, and is an excellent example of how sea-floor spreading works on the ocean floor. Iceland is in a state of east–west tension, one half located on the Eurasian Plate moving eastward.'[28] Many of the Atlantic's oceanic islands lie on, or originate from, the Mid-Atlantic Ridge where, approximately 150 million years ago, North and South America began pulling away from Europe and Africa at the pace of one's nails growing – 2 to 7 cm annually. (The East Pacific Rise, in contrast, is fast-spreading – 10 to 18 cm.) Astride the northern terminus of the Mid-Atlantic Ridge, Iceland is Earth's largest mid-oceanic island and closer to our planet's elemental creative force than any other place. Here one can actually see Earth's largest open wound, where her crust is being literally ripped apart. Little wonder that it was here that Jules Verne located his *Journey to the Centre of the Earth*.

The Azores, Ascension, Tristan da Cunha – all were born in this way, too. 2,500 km from any neighbour and midway between South America and South Africa, four islands – Tristan da Cunha, Inaccessible, Nightingale and Gough – comprise Earth's most isolated group. Tristan, a near-circular island averaging 12 km diameter, at 98 sq km is the largest member, lorded over by her central volcano, Queen Mary's Peak (2,062 m), whose flanks fall precipitously into the sea. The volcano last erupted in 1961, when Tristan's entire population of 264 was briefly evacuated to Britain.

In the island's northwestern corner, on a small plateau under the volcano's towering cliffs, lies the single settlement of Edinburgh, in 2011 home to the same number of residents as 50 years earlier.

Island arcs – curved rows of islands – are often created when one earth plate slides under another, the resultant friction causing various degrees of eruption over a wide area. Hotspots are violent island makers, relatively stable eruption points over which a plate drifts; the most illustrious example is the Hawaiian chain, still being generated by a hotspot after more than 30 million years. As the sea floor drifts away from the hotspot, it subsides naturally and automatically at the same time as coral reefs occupy the volcano's sagging flanks, growing ever higher. Often the original volcano sinks below the sea and disappears entirely, leaving as its legacy only its former reef: a coral island is born, resting on volcanic foundations. For the Pacific's Kure, Midway, and Pearl and Hermes reefs, these foundations now lie more than 150 m under water.

Jeju-do, South Korea's largest island and a special autonomous province since 1946, with around 565,000 inhabitants (2009), rose up out of the sea about 2 million years ago to form a 1,845-sq-km isle of basalt dominated by the 1,950-m-high volcano Halla-san. A subtropical island, she's warmer than the mainland, with cool dry winters and hot humid summers. Today a popular tourist destination and conference site, which accounts for much of her economy, Jeju-do features some of the world's longest and most fascinating lava-tube systems. (Over the centuries the island has also developed her own distinct Korean culture and language.)

Indonesia is as equally oceanic as she is continental, claiming more volcanos than any other nation on Earth.[29] Beneath her more than 18,000 scattered islands, the Indo-Australian Plate, slowly moving northeast, is being drawn beneath the thicker Eurasian Plate. The subduction zone has produced a chain of vigorous volcanos, with nearly a thousand eruptions having been recorded. Because of the region's high population density, 85 of these eruptions have caused fatalities, including the latest at central Java's Mt Merapi in 2010. (At the time of writing, Mt Merapi continues to erupt, while two others remain on high alert; eighteen further Indonesian volcanos are showing signs of activity, including Krakatoa.) Indonesia lies on the 'Ring of Fire' circling the Pacific, Earth's most seismic region.

A land of superlatives, island Indonesia stretches 1,760 km from north to south and 5,120 km from west to east. In area she measures

2 million sq km, geographically Earth's eighth largest nation.[30] Indonesia features four major island regions. On the sub-oceanic Sunda Shelf – Asia's former eastern subcontinent – lie, among many other smaller islands, Sumatra, Java, Borneo (Indonesia's claim is Kalimantan) and the smaller Bali. East of Bali lies the Lesser Sunda island chain in deeper seas, from Lombok to West Timor and crossing the Wallace Line (the acknowledged boundary between the Oriental and Australasian zoogeographical regions). Indonesia's third island region, at the border of the Indo-Australian and Eurasian Plates, comprises the Moluccas (Maluku), which are volcanic islands and tectonic uplifts in deep waters. The western half of New Guinea is regarded as Indonesia's fourth region: Papua and West Papua. Linked to Australia under the Arafura Sea, this rests on the Sahul Shelf – ancient Australia, New Guinea and Tasmania – rather than on the Sunda Shelf.

Concerning hotspot volcanos: literally thousands of islands in the Atlantic, Indian Ocean and within the Pacific Basin (not the Pacific Rim) were forged in these geological furnaces. Some of the hotspots have been proper 'island fountains', spewing for up to 70 million years, and entire island chains have formed in this way. The Pacific Plate, for example, moving over hotspots north then northwest created the Hawaii–Emperor, Marshall, Marquesas, Tuamotu, Austral, Society and Cook chains of islands.[31] Midway Island, a 6.2-sq-km atoll between Tokyo and Honolulu, was formed by submarine volcanism around 28 million years ago at the geographical site of the Lō'ihi Seamount, 35 km off the southeast coast of the Big Island of Hawai'i; since Midway was formed, she has drifted atop the lithosphere in a northwesterly direction – and this for a distance of almost 2,600 km.[32] In fact, the Hawaiian Ridge is Earth's longest chain of seamounts, coral reefs and volcanic islands. Also known as the Hawaiian Seamount Chain, it extends northwest from the Big Island of Hawai'i for some 2,900 km in total, and the seamount Lō'ihi, still submerged, promises to become its very next island.

The eighteen Hawaiian Islands, stretching from Hawai'i in the southeast to Kure in the northwest, are the most isolated major island group in the world. In the northwest, one finds low coral islands; in the southeast, eight major volcanic islands. Here the nesoscape stretches from shoreline desert to rainforest, from lava flows to bogland, from flat atolls to snow-covered peaks. One of the wettest places in the world is Mt Wai'ale'ale on Kaua'i, which in 1982 achieved a record-breaking rainfall of 17,300 mm for a single year; it is also the only mountain on Earth with a swamp on its summit, accessible only by helicopter when the perennial cloud cover briefly clears. There are three active volcanos within the present Hawaiian hotspot: Mauna Loa and Kilauea on the Big Island of Hawai'i, and the Lō'ihi submarine volcano. Mauna Loa, which is not only the highest volcano on Earth's surface but also the world's highest mountain when measured from its sea-floor base, erupted throughout the twentieth century on average every 3.7 years.[33] Since 1956 its summit has housed the Mauna Loa Observatory, one of the world's most important.

In the Atlantic, similar hotspot activity formed the Azores, Canaries, Cape Verde, Tristan da Cunha and St Helena.

Hotspot volcanos, as well as other volcanic islands, can also experience 'gravitational collapse' due to inherent instability.[34] Built mainly of loose fragmented material and lava flows, they are often destroyed by simple pull of gravity, exacerbated by the outward pressures of internal magma. Such forces produce Earth's most spectacular landslides, in which whole territories the size of small nations start shifting. All of Hawai'i's volcanos, for example, are literally crumbling to pieces. Kilauea, one of Earth's most active volcanos (it has been erupting almost non-stop since January 1883), is disintegrating in landslides and gigantic slumps, due to gravitation and magma pressure pushing seaward. The magnitude is awesome – a volume of more than 16,000 cubic kilometres. In the past, entire sections have broken off and slid, with calamitous results. Part of Mauna Loa collapsed 100,000 years ago and sent a tsunami 280 m high crashing up the side of neighbouring Lāna'i. Such events are extremely rare, however. (The sometimes observed open breaks in newly developed fringing reefs and also in young atolls – often used as channels by vessels – could well represent the scars of ancient submarine subsidence.)

Over time, island volcanos invariably ride with the plate, away from their magma source, and so become extinct, sink and erode. Midway Island, for example, has eroded right down to sea level. As they sink, many volcanos develop fringing coral reefs, and once a volcano's summit is submerged the remaining coral reef is called an atoll. In the immensity of the world's oceans, atolls are mere motes. The world's largest chain of atolls, the Tuamotus, comprises 78 coral atolls supporting 15,862 Polynesians (2002 census, together with the Gambier Islands), and covers a land area of only about 885 sq km. Further west in the Pacific, Tuvalu – the world's fourth smallest nation with only 26 sq km of six atolls and three reef islands – is the second least-populous sovereign state in the world, with only 12,373 inhabitants (est. 2009). Volcanos that have sunk below sea level and lost their coral reef are flat-topped seamounts, also known as guyots. In 1831, a volcanic island broke the surface of the sea southwest of Sicily, rose to about 100 m in height and several kilometres in circumference, and then within two years disappeared again: today she's another guyot.

The Galápagos Rift, some 900 km west of Ecuador, releases magma almost continuously as well. This has created an archipelago of islands which one could call Earth's volcano and earthquake capital: with due respect to Indonesia, some say eruptions are more frequent here than anywhere else on the planet. The entire chain is a mere infant, perhaps no older than 5 million years for the oldest island and less than one million for the youngest.

Island-arc volcanos populate the Antilles, Aleutians, Malay Archipelago (such as Indonesia's Krakatoa), Mediterranean (Santorini), eastern Indian Ocean and Pacific periphery (the infamous Ring of Fire). In all, there are some 22 such long island chains, commonly featuring narrow deep-sea trenches and explosive volcanism. They result from one plate of the Earth's crust plunging beneath another – the process called subduction. The oceanic crust then remelts 700 km deep but, already at around 100 km, it also heats and only partially remelts. 'The mixture of remelted basalt and melted oceanic sediments overlying the subducted crust forms a siliceous, gassy magma that migrates to the surface and erupts in the form of lava.'[35] More siliceous – that is, containing silicon dioxide – than basaltic lavas, lavas from island-arc volcanos are lower in temperature, more gaseous and potentially much more explosive than submarine and basaltic hotspot volcanos. These form steep-sloped, cone-shaped, angry volcanos, like the Mediterranean's Stromboli and Etna and those in Japan's southern Izu-Bonin Islands.

History is replete with accounts of islands emerging from the sea or blowing their tops and vanishing. Once more Pliny the Elder:

> The famous islands of Delos and Rhodes are recorded in history as having been born from the sea long ago, and subsequently smaller

ones, Anaphe beyond Melos, Neæ between Lemnos and the Dardanelles, Halone between Lebedos and Teos, Thera [Santorini] and Therasia among the Cyclades in the 4th year [197 BC] of the 145th Olympiad; also in the same group Hiera, which is the same as Automate, 130 years later; and 2 stades from Hiera, Thia 110 years later . . .

Before our time also among the Æolian Islands near Italy, as well as near Crete, there emerged from the sea one island 2500 paces long, with hot springs, and another in the 3rd year [126 BC] of Olympiad 163 in the bay of Tuscany, this one burning with a violent blast of air . . . So also the Monkey Islands are said to have risen in the bay of Campania, and later one among them, Mount Epopus, is said to have suddenly shot up a great flame and then to have been levelled with the surface of the plain.[36]

Rhyolitic lava eruptions are horrifically explosive. They produce incandescent billows of superheated particles, mixed with steam, that rush down slopes at up to 100 km per hour. Such a nasty struck Santorini (Thera) around 1470 BC, decapitating the towering volcano and weakening the Minoan thalassocracy as a result, perhaps transforming the entire power basis of the eastern Mediterranean. Greek geographer and historian Strabo (*c*. 63 BC – *c*. AD 23) tells of a new island emerging there in 196 BC; Santorini's Mikra Kaumene appeared in 1570 and then Nea Kaumene in 1770. In 1815 Tambora on the Dutch East Indian (modern Indonesian) island of Sumbawa blasted 150 cubic km of pumice and ash into the upper atmosphere: the year 1816 in Europe, northern Asia and North America was an endless winter. Krakatoa off Java, in 1883, ejected 20 cubic km of pumice and ash and caused 36,000 immediate deaths. Such an eruption also struck Mont Pelée in Martinique in 1902, the pyroclastic flow snuffing out more than 30,000 lives at St Pierre; only two men survived – one a prisoner who had been locked in a subterranean cell. Such near-shore island-arc volcanos of rhyolitic and andesitic magmas are still very active in the Pacific Rim, Malay Archipelago and Mediterranean.

Coral animates our planet's 'biological islands'. Coral is 'the most successful form of life that has inhabited the Earth. It is the oldest and the largest and the most enduring.'[37] At the bottom of Bikini's lagoon a shroud of coral growth even adorns 21 radioactive wrecks. Most coral islands reflect the cooperation of geology and biology over millennia. Algæ living inside most coral tissues feed the coral animal which then secretes a limestone skeleton at the rate of about 1 cm each year. The time scale is stupendous: 'Uplifted mountains over 300 metres (1,000 feet) high in Australia and China ... consist entirely of reef skeletons laid down during the Palæozoic era over 250 million years ago.'[38] Coral islands are still commonly classified as 'high' or 'low' islands. Usually, high coral islands are young, reef-fringed volcanos; however, they can also be continental fragments crowned with coral reefs, like the Seychelles. Low coral islands, consisting wholly of the skeletons of coral and other living calcareous (that is, containing calcium carbonate) matter, are almost at sea level. To grow, coral needs a sea temperature normally above 20°c, so coral islands are limited to the tropics: 30°N to 30°S. Most have developed on the peaks of subsiding and submerged volcanos, extinct and vanishing.

Atolls are coral islands which comprise a lagoon surrounded by islets and one or more barrier reefs. Some atolls and reefs can reach down as much as 1,600 m. Eminent British geologist Charles Lyell (1797–1875) had been the first to suggest that such 'lagoon islands' formed through coral growth along the rims of the craters of submarine volcanos. Using this idea, British naturalist Charles Darwin (1809–1882) was the first to describe the process. Scaling the towering slopes behind Pape'ete, Tahiti, in 1835, Darwin regarded neighbouring Mo'orea's lagoon and barrier reef and comprehended that if Mo'orea were to sink beneath the sea her coral barrier reef, in time, with further upward growth, would create an atoll. It was more than a century later that scientists testing at Enewetak Atoll in the Marshall Islands finally proved Darwin right: 49 million years of 1,000-m subsidence of Enewetak's erstwhile volcano together with perennial upward growth had indeed created the atoll. The central volcano had simply sunk beneath the waves, through either erosion or subsidence of the crustal plate beneath it.

But coral reefs don't really require a volcano to form. In the Malay Archipelago, for example, thousands of minor high islands offer perfect shelf environments to produce Earth's richest coral reefs – over 80 genera and 500 species of reef-building corals which then foster a treasure house of tropical flora and fauna.[39] Individual coral colonies coalesce to comprise 'patch reefs' which, on reaching sea level, proceed to grow outwards as the perimeter calcifies and the centre dies. Only a few metres in diameter, a micro-atoll like this often repeats for kilometres along a coast, first turning into a shallow fringing reef allowing waves to wash over it then enlarging to halt them, defining a barrier reef. 'Thus a ranking of reef structures from youngest to most mature would be: coral colonies, micro-atolls, patch reefs, fringing reefs, barrier reefs, and atolls.'[40] With the last, we finally have an island. In Earth's seas lie 261 coral atolls, most of them gracing the Pacific's tropical latitudes.

Coral reefs even form on shallow continental shelves, so long as the critical temperature range is maintained.[41] On plate margins, islands and their associated reefs can be uplifted tens or even hundreds of metres by tectonic forces. This has happened on some of the Loyalty Islands east of New Caledonia, Papua New Guinea's Trobriand Islands and Makatea in French Polynesia's Tuamotus. All of New Guinea has known violent tectonic uplift, as she comprises the forespit of the Indo-Australian Plate intruding into the western rim of the giant Pacific Plate: some coral-reef terraces on the Huon Peninsula there, for example, reach higher than 600 m. Such uplifting can also 'eliminate' islands by reattaching them to other islands or to their continental land masses.

Island reefs enjoy a prodigious longevity, as they grow at about the same rate at which their parent volcanos subside and slip ever deeper into the depths.[42] At the end, where earlier there had been a fringing reef, we see only a circular atoll. The same applies to Australia's Great Barrier Reef which has, only 600 m away, an ancestral reef reaching 110 m down and 169,000 years back. Here it appears that, as sea levels rose at the end of the last ice age, some coral larvæ migrated to shallower waters nearby and seeded a new reef which then thrived, while the much older reef lost its necessary light in ever deeper water and died.[43]

FROM PARIS TO LONG ISLAND

In Earth's family of islands, continental and oceanic isles are the parents. Then come the many children:

eyots (also called aits)
morainic islands
barrier islands
depositional islands

deltaic islands
floating islands
artificial islands
'vanished' islands

Not just oceans but large rivers and deltas form islands, too. When currents deposit sediment which accumulates over time, this commonly yields eyots or aits, usually understood to mean an islet in a river. Most are ephemeral (see 'depositional islands' below), making river navigation difficult, especially when, as in a braided channel, several form; this used to be a common feature on the Mississippi, and still plagues navigation on the Amazon and Burma's Irrawaddy and many other major rivers. Where the current is relatively constant, however, such river islands can last for millennia.

Paris was born on an eyot. Over 2,000 years ago a small Gallic tribe called the Parisii lived on the Île de la Cité, a low-lying eyot in the Seine used as a ford and fortress (though some scholars identify a now-submerged eyot instead). Along with neighbouring Île Saint-Louis she became the nucleus – Celtic settlement, temporary Roman camp, Merovingian capital – for modern Paris. Today, majestic Notre Dame still crowns this most historic eyot in the world, now overwhelmed by the megalopolis she spawned. The eyot remains not just the heart of Paris, but of all France: each of the nation's road-distance markers are calculated from the 'mother marker' on the Place du Parvis, facing Notre Dame's glorious west facade.

London, too, once featured a prominent eyot: Thorney, or the Isle of Thorn (-ey is an ancient suffix for 'isle'), just upstream from medieval London, was originally fashioned by the currents of the River Tyburn where this entered the Thames. In ancient times Thorney was a ford, then a favoured residence as she was surrounded by fertile fields but not too far from the walled squalor of the city. Over the centuries the land rose, the various rivulets were built over with underground channeling then conduiting, the Thames itself was fully embanked, whereupon as an island Thorney ceased to exist. On this ancient eyot rose Westminster Abbey and the Palace of Westminster, now the Houses of Parliament. In this regard one might hazard to say that all of the British Isles are still ruled from a smaller island, Thorney. Today the former eyot also boasts England's oldest garden: the 1,000-year-old College Garden.

The world's most populous eyot is the Island of Montreal, with 1,854,442 inhabitants (2006) on 499 sq km. Lying at the confluence of the Saint Lawrence and Ottawa rivers as one part of an island chain of over 70 isles, the Island of Montreal is a dominant part of the city of Montreal. She is also the world's most populous island situated in fresh water. Her access includes some of the busiest bridges in the world: over 100 million vehicles annually use the Champlain Bridge and the Jacques Cartier Bridge.

Other notable eyots include Germany's thirteenth-century Burg Pfalzgrafenstein in the middle of the Rhine, a fortress incarnation of a 'river tollbooth'. There is Bamberg's Altes Rathaus built in 1386 in the middle of the Regnitz River and accessible by two bridges. Scotland's Eilean Aigas, a romantic and historic lodge on a holm of the River Beauly in the Highlands, was home to the fraudulent 'Sobieski Stuarts' who, in the 1800s, attempted to revive an imaginary Highland civilization. And still today the clan Macrae maintain their war memorial and museum at the thirteenth-century Eilean Donan Castle erected on a western Highland holm – in this case the conjunction of lochs Duich, Alsh and Long; a footbridge lets the holm's total population of one access the mainland.

Morainic islands are those formed when rising seas isolate old glacial moraines along a coast; seafronts are then shaved and trimmed by waves and often display barrier beaches with intervening lagoons.[44] Earth's most famous is probably Long Island in New York, which, stretching 190 km from Manhattan Island to Montauk Point, represents the longest and largest island in the contiguous US. Rising to 120 m, Long Island actually comprises three terminal moraines from the last ice age whose southern exposed shore is flanked by wave-formed barrier beaches with inland mudflats and marshes. Long Island's northern shore, facing Long Island Sound, enjoys sheltered sandy bluffs, inlets and bays. Already in the early 1600s the Dutch began reclaiming the western salt marshes; eastern Long Island remains an important agricultural producer and her many southern state parks and beaches attract large numbers of visitors annually.

Over several ice ages, glacial deposits that were laid down and only partially stabilized atop sedimentary rock outcrops have, with rising seas, created Germany's North Frisian Islands. Largest and most famous is narrow Sylt, 99 sq km and nearly 40 km from north to south. Rising to only 52 m, some 40 per cent of Sylt – since 1855 a popular seaside resort – lies below the high tide mark and so is vulnerable to flooding. She used to claim a robust moraine ridge but wave erosion has dispersed Sylt's substance north and south where winds have also blown up series of giant dunes, especially popular with tourists. Sylt faces serious ecological problems: northwest Germany is subsiding in general and, as a result, Sylt's beaches annually lose some 1.5 m to the sea; she's vulnerable to increasingly powerful North Sea storms; global warming presages a further sea-level rise; and morainic erosion is on the increase. Breakwaters, sea walls and large concrete 'tetrapods' have been effective measures to hold back the sea and discourage erosion. Simple pumping of sand from offshore to replenish natural loss has, however, proved to be the most effective measure.

Barrier islands present a similar situation. Waves that approach a shoreline obliquely and carry sediment along in a parallel direction – in a process known as 'longshore drift', using sand from earlier exposed continental shelves – may form offshore spits and sandbars that, increasing in mass, can eventually become barrier islands. These are also found everywhere on Earth.[45] The most researched barrier islands are those on the Texan coast of the US and those in the Frisian Islands (Netherlands' West Frisian Islands and Germany's East Frisian Islands). Such islands create straight coastlines in the back of which the sea carves out a highly indented secondary coastline. Barrier islands can stretch more than 100 km in length, and between them – as they tend to form archipelago-like – yawn unstable tidal inlets. On the lee side, away from the open ocean, brood large expanses of mangroves or salt marshes which, in the northern hemisphere since the last ice age, have risen to consolidate into thick deposits of peat.

Some barrier islands are truly impressive. Those of Australia's southeastern Queensland – fed by strong swells, river and continental-shelf sands, and high continuous winds – can create dunes higher than 300 m. Lagoonal 125-km-long Moreton Bay, for example, on the eastern coast of Australia, 45 km from Brisbane, claims around 360 offshore barrier islands of sand that restrict the flow of oceanic water and determine the ecology of the internal zone. Moreton, Bribie, North Stradbroke and South Stradbroke enclose the vast bay, their land-facing lees rich with mangroves. A bit further north, Fraser Island is simply awe-inspiring, the largest sand island in the world: 120 km long, 24 km wide and up to 240 m in height –

mostly dunes and beach aggregate that have been collecting over 2 million years. She's by now so old and rich that vegetation, including ferns and even rainforest, abounds, along with perched lakes. (A 'perched lake' forms when a perched water table – created by impermeable layers of cemented sand trapping groundwater – is intercepted by the ground surface.) Fraser Island's 40 perched lakes include both the world's largest (Lake Boemingen, 200 ha) and highest (the Boomerangs, at 130 m).

Where ocean and temperature conditions are optimum, barrier reefs will develop a fair distance offshore and so provide for islands and mainlands a critical defence from eroding wave action.[46] Such is the service of two of Earth's greatest barrier reefs: the 2,000-km-long Great Barrier Reef off Australia's northeast coast, and Central America's enormous formations off eastern Honduras and Nicaragua. And when barrier reefs steadily subside they can also produce coral islands; Pohnpei in Micronesia is a classic example.

Depositional islands are often barrier islands, too (as with Fraser Island above). Here, erosion can entail simple weathering in a process that can create wholly new islands when dunes and beaches collect large amounts of sand, as well as when – through currents, winds and tides – sediment accumulates. These islands of deposition are frequent in large rivers like the Amazon, Mississippi and Irrawaddy (though also occurring in oceans) but are commonly short-lived, mobile and highly vulnerable to climate and erosion. Perhaps the planet's most spectacular example is Canada's Sable Island (from French *sable* 'sand'), 300 km southeast of Nova Scotia. A very narrow sandbar of 34 sq km extending over 42 km in length, Sable is the infamous 'graveyard of the Atlantic', home today to some 300 feral horses which water at several freshwater ponds and one brackish lake. In an attempt to stabilize Sable's soil, the Canadian government in 1901 planted over 80,000 trees, but none survived. Because of the island's scientific importance, experts from varied disciplines regularly occupy the permanently manned Sable Island Station. Since 1920, two children have been born on the slowly shifting depositional island.

Deltaic islands result when rivers bring more sediment into seas than waves, winds and currents can redistribute.[47] This occurred where northern Italy's Po river entered the Adriatic, creating the deltaic isles of Venice, and where the Mississippi entered the Gulf of Mexico, creating many types of islands which are especially vulnerable to subsidence and erosion – a single hurricane can shift such islands several hundreds of metres. (Fragmented islands then become shoals, like the Trinity and Tiger shoals in the Mississippi delta.) Deltaic islands are also found throughout the world, often comprising substantial land masses, like the Brazilian Amazon's striking *ilhas* of Grande do Gurupá, Queimada, Caviana, Mexiana and Janaucu.

Floating islands are in a league of their own, known in various guises since antiquity. They fascinated Pliny the Elder:

> Certain islands are always afloat, as in the districts of Cæcubum and of Reate . . . and Modena and Statonium, and in Lake Vadimo, the dense wood near the springs of Cutilia which is never to be seen in the same place by day and by night, the islands in Lydia named the Reed Islands which are not only driven by the winds, but can be punted in any direction at pleasure by poles, and so served to rescue a number of citizens in the Mithradatic war. There are also small islands at Nymphæum [a promontory in Illyria] called the Dancing Islands, because they move to the foot-beats of persons keeping time with the chanting of a choral song. On the great lake of Taquinii in Italy two islands float about carrying woods, their outline as the winds drive them forward now forming the shape of a triangle and now of a circle, but never a square.[48]

A common phenomenon in lakes, marshlands and wetlands, floating islands are in fact compactions of mud, peat and aquatic plants that can range in thickness between several centimetres and many metres. Some are manufactured to serve as temporary or permanent domiciles, retreats or refuges, and can encompass hectares. They are commonly made of bundled reeds, when available. Prominent modern examples of such floating islands are those of the Uros tribe of Lake Titicaca and the papyrus islands of Lake Kyoga in Uganda. The floating garden islands on Inle Lake in Burma are simply stunning: one-third of the open water area has been lost to natural silting and plant growth, but especially to floating garden agriculture since 1935; in some places along Inle Lake's western shore the floating gardens first seem like, then actually turn into, terra firma.

Artificial islands have been known since time immemorial. Pliny the Elder writes of the channels of ancient Leucas, a long peninsula off the western coast of central Greece's Acarnania along the

Ionian Sea that was made into an island by the Corinthians in the seventh century BC.[49] Human societies have created islands and archipelagos for a variety of reasons – connecting holms, building on submerged reefs or raising structures in shallow lakes, rivers and estuarine waters. Long after the lakeside inhabitants of Germany's and Switzerland's Lake Constance, some 5,000 years ago, constructed entire pole villages that could swiftly be converted into artificial islands for defence purposes, the Celts of Ireland and Scotland were still building wooden crannogs – as individual dwellings and even as complete settlements – well into the medieval era. In Micronesia the ceremonial centre of Nan Madol off the eastern coast of Pohnpei – artificially constructed islets first started in the eighth or ninth century then converted into megalithic complexes as of the twelfth or early thirteenth century – became the political capital of the Saudeleur Dynasty, home and mortuary precinct alike to Pohnpei's nobility; perhaps 500 to 1,000 people resided on these artificial islets, which fell into ruin after the dynasty's fall around the year 1500.

The Aztecs' fourteenth-century, 12-sq-km, insular capital of Tenochtitlan, on the western side of shallow Lake Texcoco (one of five interconnected lakes), was already supporting over 200,000 when the Spaniards arrived in 1519. By this time it was one the world's major cities, surpassed in Europe only by Paris, Venice and Constantinople. Indeed, connected as it was to the mainland by broad causeways Tenochtitlan appeared quite the 'Venice of the New World'. For the island city was divided into four zones, each zone subdivided into twenty precincts, each precinct defined by wide separating transport canals – very much like Venice – whose wooden bridges were removed each night. The city was also encircled by hundreds of artificial *chinampa* islands: rectangular wattle fencing, much like the floating isles of Burma's Inle Lake. Measuring some 30 by 2.5 m and layered with sediment, mud and decaying vegetation to create similar 'floating gardens', these were actually embedded in the lake floor and cultivated to feed the overpopulated island's inhabitants. (In even earlier times such *chinampa* were mainly used in nearby lakes Xochimilco and Chalco.) Providing up to seven crops a year rather than the customary one or two, the artificial isles enabled the Aztecs to rise to empire in the 1400s.

During their Edo period (1603–1868) the Japanese constructed the artificial island of Dējima in Nagasaki Bay to contain the Dutch merchants forbidden direct contact with city-dwellers. From 1782 to 1838, India's Mumbai (Bombay) arose on the artificial Salsette Island that had been created by connecting several smaller islands and leveling hills to infill shallows; bridging causeways were later also filled in. Salsette Island – which is Mumbai herself – is today Earth's fourteenth most populous (13 million) and fourth most densely populated isle. In 1827 Parisians created the 850-m-long and 11-m-wide Île aux Cygnes ('Isle of Swans') in the Seine to protect the city's port of Grenelle; a tree-lined promenade, the Allée des Cygnes, now extends the length of the isle, which is spanned by three bridges. Land reclamation created small Ellis Island alongside New York City to serve as an immigration centre in the late 1800s and early 1900s: she quickly became the illustrious portal to the United States of America. To celebrate Canada's centennial, Montreal's Expo '67 constructed the artificial island of Île Notre-Dame, which rose alongside Montreal Island in the St Lawrence River over ten months in 1965 out of 15 million tonnes of rock excavated for the city's underground rubber-tyred metro system. Today, Dubai has several artificial island projects underway: the three Palm Islands, The World and the Dubai Waterfront. Only one of the three Palm Islands is currently inhabited, Palm Jumeirah, already the world's largest artificial island – actually an archipelago, fashioned from land reclamation in the shape of a palm measuring 5 by 5 km and connected to the mainland by a 300-m bridge. Over 500 families have already moved onto the isles.

'Vanished' islands are of assorted types: those submerged by rising seas, those which have subsided, those covered by glaciers, those eroded away, and many more. Mythical Atlantis is supposed to have vanished in a natural cataclysm. Countless islands along the Netherlands' and Germany's Frisian coast, many of them inhabited, succumbed to wave action and flood tides throughout the Middle Ages and up to the present. All over the world builders have connected nearshore isles to the mainland, thus erasing insularity. Lebanon's Tyre, for example, was once a great Phoenician trade centre that 'vanished' in this way as an island. One of the best harbours in the eastern Mediterranean, famous for her purple dye and for being the birthplace of Europa and Dido, Tyre was originally located on just such an offshore isle, dependent for her fresh water and supplies on neighbouring Ushu on the mainland. Alexander the Great built a causeway then destroyed the old city to reuse her cut stone. Sediment built up over the centuries and the causeway turned into permanent mainland. Modern Tyre now covers most of the ancient island site as well as the greater part of the much enlarged causeway.

Great Tenochtitlan, the Aztec capital, 'vanished' as islands, too. Conquered by Spaniard Hernán Cortés (1485–1547) and his conquistadors in 1521, the hundreds of isles were refashioned entirely to suit the conquerors' new needs. After this, centuries of land reclamation saw Lake Texcoco disappear and Mexico City – Mexico's capital and at 8,846,752 inhabitants (2010) the largest city in the Americas and Earth's third largest metropolitan area by population – rose in its place.

Thorney, London's 'Isle of Thorn', vanished, too, over the centuries. And the Isle of Thanet, erstwhile Stone Age settlement and Romans' island gateway to Britannia – once separated from mainland Kent by the over 600-m-wide Wantsum Channel – disappeared as the channel became flat marshland. In the mid-1700s there was still a ferry running to Thanet from Sandwich, but when a drawbridge was built the ferry service ceased.

*I*slands suffer greater erosion by wind and wave per square kilometre than do mainlands. With finite land at their disposal growing island populations also place greater demand on limited resources, accelerating erosion. Islands are also much more vulnerable than mainlands to earthquakes, volcanos and tsunamis. As global warming heats and expands Earth's oceans, these weigh more heavily on the planet's plates, causing greater tectonic activity: that is, more frequent and more violent earthquakes. Sometimes the magnitude of these events is awe-inspiring. In the autumn of 1996 at Europe's largest glacier, the Öræfa, the Vatnajökull ice field blasted open to form an ice canyon 150 m deep and 3 km long, which then filled with magma that melted the ice and created a gigantic crater lake. This burst on 5 November, producing a new river that flowed under the glacier with the magnitude of the Congo River, the planet's second largest. It then emerged with such force nearly 50 km away that it 'calved' from the glacier ice blocks of 1,000 tonnes each. What this natural cataclysm left behind can best be compared to the boulder-strewn fields of Mars. Since the beginning of the ninth century AD, 60 such catastrophic floods have occurred in Iceland alone.[50]

Islands also feel the force of Earth's meteorological bluster: hurricanes in the Atlantic and eastern Pacific; typhoons in the western Pacific; cyclones in the Indian Ocean and southern hemisphere. (The three classifications hold no meteorological difference.)

The greater lesson? – That insularity may protect from man but never from nature.

Islands of stone and sand, from Paris to Long Island and from Taiwan to Tenochtitlan, will continue to accrete and erode, to quake and explode, to vanish and sink below somnolent lagoons. And as they do, they will ever demonstrate a geological variety, indeed opulence, rivalled only by breathtakingly balanced ecosystems, regal realms of ferns and feathers.

two

... of Ferns and Feathers

Island biology flaunts itself in the unfurling frond of New Zealand's endemic silver fern (*Cyathea dealbata*). Found on New Zealand's main islands and in the Chathams as a medium-size tree fern up to 10 m in height, it bears a dense crown of characteristically looping *koru* fronds that are usually 1 to 2 m long with silver-white coloration on their undersides.[1] Used in art, carving and tattooing as the Māori symbol for new life, peace and strength, the *koru* is Air New Zealand's logo and also figures in the country's coat of arms. Most importantly for Kiwis, the *koru* is also the official emblem of the All Blacks rugby team.

Similarly, insular vitality is replete in the 'bare Christmas tree' that is the imposing Norfolk pine (*Araucaria heterophylla*), a conifer that grows up to 65 m which is endemic to Norfolk Island, just north of New Zealand. Only recently has it flown its cradle to adorn gardens from Australia to southern Florida.

It's all about living constants. Island life takes hold and grows, exploits all available space, then moves on, sometimes to the very ends of the Earth. Our planet is a macrocosm of the same process. If not seeded from space, says one theory, terrestrial life probably originated in a volcanic eruption – the intense heat and electricity common to volcanism provided the energy required to synthesize the complex proteins that comprised the precursors of primitive life. This would surely have taken place in a shallow pond. And the pond most likely lay on a volcanic island.

Once the supercontinents had finally filled with flora and fauna, subsequent 'calving' sent species drifting to evolve separately from those on the mainland. Unique island environments fashioned distinctive island species, the isolation spawning exotic life forms while preserving those that had become extinct back on the mainland.[2] In New Zealand, for example, 85 per cent of all species are found nowhere else. With continental islands, the biota developed on the original continent then evolved independently after separation – explaining, for one, New Zealand's differing biology from Australia's. Recently calved islands similarly stranded species – accounting for the two prehistoric mammoth tusks, each measuring 2 m in length, that were discovered on San Miguel Island off California's coast. Continents can host millions of species, islands as few as 30. The further one goes from a mainland, the poorer the biota. This is perhaps one of islands' most telling constants.

Island evolution possesses its own dynamic. Take insular dwarfism, for example. This occurs when a population's gene pool must draw from a restricted environment. Several species of dwarf dinosaurs thus evolved on Haţeg Island, Romania. Dwarf ground sloths thrived on Hispaniola, Puerto Rico and Cuba. Small woolly mammoths flourished on Alaska's Saint Paul Island. Dwarf stegodons once ranged the Philippines and many of the islands of the Malay Archipelago (Sulawesi, Flores, Sumba, Timor).

Then there's the other extreme, insular gigantism. Some animals, especially birds and reptiles, can grow to enormous sizes in the absence of larger predators. Consider New Zealand's several extinct species of moa and also the extinct Haast's Eagle; Madagascar's extinct elephant bird; Fiji's extinct giant pigeon; Mauritius's extinct broad-billed parrot; the Seychelles' and Galápagos' giant tortoises; or Indonesia's Komodo dragon, still found on several islands. It's possible that many of these, of even all of them, derived from species of giant birds or reptiles that were widely distributed on the supercontinents Laurasia and/or Gondwana. Equally plausible is independent converging evolution. Here, the jury is still out. New Zealand's moas, like Hawai'i's honeycreepers and the Galápagos' finches, displayed remarkable species radiation: that is, they evolved variations in feeding mechanisms and body shape and size because of isolation, climate and environmental modification over time.[3] The eleven species of moa in six genera ranged in size from 1 to about 3 m, and could weigh as much as 200 kg. New Zealand's moas were Earth's largest birds. (Their end came by around AD 1400 when the Māori torched habitats and overhunted.)

Island insights are crucial for biologists and zoologists. 'The simplified ecology of an island reveals principles of evolution that would be much more difficult to understand by studying the vastly more complex history of life on the continents.'[4] It would of course be no exaggeration to claim that it was islands that gave us evolutionary science. Fascinated by islands, Charles Darwin wrote of the Galápagos: 'The natural history of these islands is eminently curious and well deserves attention.'[5] It's now common knowledge how Darwin came to his understanding of evolution by natural selection while there on the *Beagle*. Not only the islands of the Pacific but also many elsewhere have turned out to be the proving ground for natural selection as well as for an understanding of its intricate operations.[6]

What Darwin saw and comprehended in the Galápagos in 1835, Welsh naturalist Alfred Russel Wallace (1823–1913) saw and comprehended in the Malay Archipelago in the mid-1850s, arriving at very similar conclusions about the formation of new species by observing island life. It was Wallace who, in 1858, first put to paper a precis stating the central concept of the theory of natural selection. (Which action finally spurred Darwin to publish his own detailed exposition.) It was Wallace, too, who recognized the biological boundary later named Wallace's Line that, between Bali and Lombok in what is today Indonesia, divides the fauna of Asia from that of Australia and Oceania: 'The strait is here fifteen miles wide, so that we may pass in two hours from one great division of the earth to another, differing as essentially in their animal life as Europe does from America.'[7]

How did larger animals arrive at isolated islands? In September 1995 one of two strong hurricanes that struck the Caribbean island of Guadeloupe carried fifteen large iguanas on some unrooted trees over 300 km to tiny Anguilla, which had no iguanas. By March 1998 one of these was pregnant – and with this, a successful iguana colony was established. The case is now celebrated, for it is clear evidence for 'rafting' of new species.[8] After introduction, there appear to be two main reasons for differing biota on adjacent islands. First, group occupation: since single birds, for example, cannot colonize, it requires a flock to find a favourable ecological niche, a task which is most difficult, as it happens. And second, emigration of the weak: great land masses favour dominant groups of co-adapted species which spread out from a centre, with the least successful members occupying the periphery – that is, forced into inhabiting islands, which can accommodate fewer species. Here, the least successful elsewhere remain, evolve and proliferate, discouraging subsequent intruders.

Islands alter new biota in ways that, given specific conditions, remain constant worldwide. Many bird species, for example, lose the ability to fly.[9] It is mostly rails – small, crane-like, wading marsh birds – that turn flightless on Atlantic islands, but other seas ground geese, ducks, pigeons (including Mauritius's dodo), ibises and many others. In most instances they need fear no mammalian predator and so, to conserve energy, they reduce breast muscle and weight to maximize available resources, with a corresponding lowering of metabolic rate. As testified by the fossil record this has occurred for æons on islands throughout the world. Sadly, the human introduction of mammalian predators (earlier: dogs, rats, pigs; later: cats, possums, weasels, ferrets, stoats and many more) has sealed the fate of almost all flightless birds. Even rigorous conservation measures barely sustain viable breeding populations.

Another island constant: the further one distances oneself from a mainland – so long as it is not along a common sea route – the greater one's chance of finding an intact ecology, *if* there's been no earlier settlement by man. This holds true for all of Earth's islands, including the Arctic and subarctic, as well as the Antarctic and subantarctic. Yet even where humankind has lived and thrived for tens of thousands of years – be it in the Malay Archipelago's more than 20,000 islands, the world's greatest collection of 'lands surrounded by liquid'; or among British Columbia's more than 6,500 isles, one of Earth's most opulent, and least known, insular treasures – island life can still be awe-inspiringly rich and informative.

PACIFIC ISLANDS

Eighteenth-century European voyagers, tentatively probing the vast Pacific, discovered new birds like the kiwi, honeycreeper and toothed pigeon. They came across tree-dwelling snails and marvelled at unknown cultivated plants like the breadfruit. Entire collections of such were brought back home to bulge cabinets that later proved cornucopian to the burgeoning sciences of biology and zoology. Soon Europeans were capital observers of nature and recognizing larger patterns hitherto unsuspected. Having participated in Cook's second voyage to the Pacific (1772–5), German Johann Reinhold Forster (1729–1798) came to realize: 'The countries of the South Sea . . . contain a considerable variety of animals, though they are confined to a few classes only . . .'.[10] And Adelbert von Chamisso (1781–1838), German naturalist and poet aboard Russia's 1818 *Rurik* expedition, observed of the Pacific's plant life: 'This rich Flora seems to have become more scanty in the islands of the Great Ocean, from the west towards the east.'[11] Both were fundamental insights of huge import to biology, whose significance for Pacific islands became clear only later.

The high islands of the central Pacific – those east of the western fringe – comprise Micronesia's and Polynesia's thousands of volcanic islands rising steeply from the ocean floor. North of the equator there is Guam and the other Marianas, the Caroline Islands' Chuuk, Pohnpei and Kosrae; and south of the equator the Samoan Islands, Tongas, Societies (with cosmopolitan Tahiti), Marquesas, Cooks, Australs and lonely Easter Island. All are called high islands to distinguish them from low limestone islands that are frequently neighbours. Many exceed 300 m in height. Tahiti's Mt Orohena is 2,237 m, its neighbour Mt Aora'i, 2,067 m. As in the west, here one finds mangroves, palms, pandanus, woody plants, jungle climbers and forest ferns – though far fewer species, just as von Chamisso noted. Guam can count around 356 native plant species, Samoa 320, the Marquesas fewer than 200.[12] Fruit bats are the only mammals and there are no reptiles or amphibia. Land birds, molluscs and insects predominate. Tahiti claims two species of kingfisher, the Marquesas two of pigeon. Two islands in Samoa are home to the rare tooth-billed pigeon (*Didunculus strigirostris*), a big fruit pigeon resembling a dodo. Guam has a flightless rail, the reef of the Marianas an endemic crow. Each high island (except barren Easter Island) supports her own subspecies of fantails, fly-catchers, reed warblers and fruit doves.

Insects, however, fail to distribute into those large groups, families and orders common to all continents. One can hardly find any ants between Samoa and Easter Island. East of 170°E all anopheline mosquitoes – that is, those that can transmit the malaria parasite to man – are missing. (Captain Cook encountered no mozzies at all on Tahiti and Easter Island.) Most of the insects on these isles happen to be weevils. On the Pacific's high islands are comparatively few genera, though some of them have disproportionately large numbers of species.[13] Land snails are the only group in which entire families are endemic to the Pacific.

Pacific low islands tell a different story. Between Palau in the west and the Tuamotus in the east lie more than 300 islands. Most of these are low islands – atolls or raised coral isles – characterized by limestone geology and sparse biota. Their beach plants are those found throughout the Pacific – beach heliotrope, morning glory, scævola, pandanus and so on. But that's all the plant life on a low island: beach plants *are* the flora. Variety alone distinguishes island from island, for each represents a unique ecosphere. If there's little water, there is scrub. If plenty, a jungle. A flora of only nine species inhabits the semi-arid, northernmost atoll in the Marshall Islands, for example, yet some 60 native species occupy an atoll in the rainy south of the same chain.[14] Low-island birds are mostly nesting sea birds that absent themselves much of the time. But there is also a large number of land birds, many of them endemic to certain islands, like the Makatea fruit dove (*Ptilinopus chalcurus*); the flightless, now-extinct Wake Island rail (*Gallirallus wakensis*); or the Henderson fruit dove (*Ptilinopus insularis*) endemic to Pitcairn.

How did life first arrive on Pacific islands? Through accident, by rafting on floating pumice, logs and trees; drifting as current-driven planktonic larvæ; wafting as propagules on air currents; and flying as seeds and tiny animals with arriving birds. It was again Darwin who first argued that such chance dispersal functioned as a filter, weeding out those too weak to colonize distant islands. Thus the remoter the ocean habitat, the sparser the genera and families. What we observe in the Pacific islands is, to a large extent, the result of the filtering out of most continental species and of the vicissitudes of incremental chance dispersal.

It's tough to colonize oceans. The further Nature tried, the worse – that is, the more harrowed and frugal – she ended up. New Guinea is a veritable cornucopia of flora and fauna, the distant Marquesas an impoverished garden. Still, once arrived, limited species can rapidly flourish. For example, for Hawai'i biologists estimate that, over several million years, more than 1,000 species of indigenous flora evolved from only 272 colonists; that 10,000 insect species arose from only 300 arrivals; and that the 1,000 land snail species came from only 22 to 24 founders.[15] Similarities from island to island are attributable to like carriers – the frigates, terns, boobies and so on that figure from New Guinea to Easter Island.

However, variations defy simple migrations. Island isolation disrupts the gene flow.

Indeed, the diversity of the floras and faunas of Pacific islands is inversely proportional to the distance between an island and the Malayan region to the west: there is more endemism in the Hawaiian Islands and southeastern Polynesian islands which are further from the Malayan archipelago.[16]

As Forster and von Chamisso suspected, Pacific island biology has certain basic rules:

the species that inhabit Pacific islands are few in numbers compared with those on equal continental areas; there is a gradual elimination of major groups of plants and animals from west to east across the Pacific; there are diminishing numbers of species from west to east; many islands have species that are endemic, or unique to them; and the animals and plants of Pacific islands are, for the most part, related to those of the west rather than the east.[17]

The Solomons boast one marsupial mammal and various rodents and seventeen bat species, for example, whereas Fiji supports only four bat species and east of Tonga and Samoa all fruit bats disappear. East of Fiji all frogs and snakes vanish. New Guinea has more than 250 land birds, the Marquesas only seven. East of New Guinea and Australia, all freshwater fishes disappear; east of Fiji and New Zealand, all amphibians. There are no indigenous conifers, bamboos or rhododendrons east of Fiji. Shoreline fruit trees and mangroves made it to the Marshalls, but not to Hawai'i. Though as many as 28,000 species of flowering plants can be found in the Malay Archipelago (Indonesia, Malaysia, Brunei and so on), New Caledonia and Vanuatu show fewer than 1,000.

Islands of the Pacific's western fringe – the seven major island groups of New Guinea, Palau, the Solomons, New Caledonia, Fiji, Vanuatu and New Zealand – are continental and volcanic both. A few are ancient, like New Zealand (once home to dinosaurs). All share the plants and animals of Southeast Asia, the Malay Archipelago and Australia, frequently with some important family or order absent or some life forms found nowhere else. New Guinea boasts spiny anteaters, birds of paradise, cassowaries and tree kangaroos. New Zealand still has the unique tuatara and flightless kiwi, and Fiji an iguana. New Caledonia hosts the chicken-sized kagu, a flightless ground bird like the kiwi. Palau, the Solomons and Vanuatu are home to the incubator bird that lays its eggs in sand or piles of leaves to be incubated by the heat of decomposition. While Fiji still has frogs and snakes, New Zealand has three frogs but no snakes. Kauris, araucarias, breadfruits (not in New Zealand, however), durians (native to Malaysia, Indonesia and Brunei), palms, climbing vines and several species of pandanus fill the tropical rainforests, while mangroves populate the shorelines. Even subtropical and temperate New Zealand preserves many tropical forest dwellers, alongside non-tropical fuschias and southern beech. These western islands comprise a biological montage of lack and luxury.

New Zealand is a stunning treasure. Continental drift separated New Zealand from Gondwana about 100 million years ago, isolating her flora and fauna.[18] Forty million years later, the Tasman Sea claimed roughly its present width, meaning that all subsequently colonizing species had to fly, float or fin. Though rich in bird life, and not lacking bats, New Zealand is Earth's only great land mass that never hosted native land mammals. Also, more than four out of five of New Zealand's vascular plants are unique – a walk through a New Zealand native forest is a life-altering experience. Her tropical rainforests number species of native trees in their hundreds, each a flowering plant. New Zealand's vegetation is characterized by 'divaricating shrubs': cushion-like in form, densely interlaced, with wiry stems and quite small leaves. One theory postulates that these evolved as a defence against attack by New Zealand's giant ostrich-like moa. Polynesians arrived around 700 years ago and their hunting, forest clearance, dogs, pigs and rats led to mass extinctions of several ducks, the complete order of moas, the giant Haast's eagle, a swan, a large goose and some fourteen other birds.

A second and far more virulent wave of ecological depredation in New Zealand came with European settlement, especially as of the 1840s. Even today, the Pacific nation can claim around 150 native and endemic bird species on her two main islands and many smaller offshore islands, several of which are now important Department of Conservation sanctuaries. Some New Zealand bird species have even made a secondary successful colonization in a process known

Māori bird-woman Kurangaituku, with *koru* fronds
and her pet birds and tuatara lizards.

as 'double invasion': an endemic black stilt, for example, that had originated in Australia as a pied stilt and is now endangered, within the last century and a half is being replaced in New Zealand by another invasion of pied stilts.

Still, the current situation is not encouraging. Despite her pristine image New Zealand suffers serious contamination of fish (mercury, crop spraying, poison drops), of rivers and lakes (mostly from dairy run-off), and of wide tracts of farmland and forest (crop spraying, cattle effluent and anti-pest drops). The 'clean green' image that is internationally touted is all too often a tourist ploy – the country has been neither clean nor green since the 1840s. More recently, corporate dividends from the agrochemical revolution – especially in the exaggerated use of the agricultural chlorines DDT, 2, 4, 5-T, 1080 and more – have too frequently defied both common sense and respect for nature.

The biology of the Hawaiian Islands fascinates. More than 90 per cent of their insects, land snails and flowering plants are endemic. Yet their biota is quite unbalanced, lacking figs, mangroves, bromeliads and gymnosperms (conifers or related plants). There is only one genus of palm, two genera of butterflies and four orchids. The islands support only one endemic family, the land snail Amastridæ; and one endemic subfamily of birds. The unique flora includes tarweeds, lobelia and several legumes. Enormous bird and insect speciation has occurred here, remindful of the Galápagos: for example, the islands' 500 endemic species of drosophilid flies surpass that of anywhere else on Earth.

Diversity in island biology can also come from 'adaptive shifts': daughter populations occupy a different island habitat, then evolve there into, or with, adaptations that render them sometimes unrecognizable from the parent species.[19] In this way the small Hawaiian inchworm turned carnivorous, preferring spiders, flies, leafhoppers and other tasty fare. Sometimes several such shifts have taken place on one island, yielding a large group of descendant species populating a range of habitats. Over millions of years – as one volcano after another will drift over a hotspot – evolving species from the old will colonize then adapt to the new, as is witnessed so spectacularly in the Hawaiian archipelago.

Another major cause of diversity of plant and animal life is the tremendous range of island habitats determining evolutionary change. Most endemics develop on high islands' inland areas where valleys and ridges experience abrupt climate changes. 'In Hawai'i it has been said that each ridge and valley has its own land snail.'[20] In the past such appearances happened slowly. It has been estimated that before the arrival of humans in the Hawaiian Islands one new species appeared every 35,000 years; now, with human intrusion and modern mobility, Hawai'i registers 50 new species each year. With some notorious exceptions – like Bikini Atoll, Enewetak, Christmas Island, Moruroa – the Hawaiian Islands have probably suffered most egregiously from man's interference. Polynesians brought pigs, chickens and dogs; but their most insidious cargo was the Polynesian rat, the Hawaiian *'iole* (*Rattus exulans*). Later Europeans and Americans introduced goats, sheep, cattle, other pigs, mongooses, domestic cats and the axis deer from India. The result? – a massive devastation of flora and fauna. The introduction of alien plant species to mitigate the damage only exacerbated it. Australian casuarina trees were planted to halt erosion and be a windbreak, but their needles poisoned the soil; the thick stands crowded out native vegetation. The guava trees imported for their fruit and flowers were soon choking the natives, too. However, not all introductions were bad. Polynesians had imported the *kukui* or candle-nut tree (*Aleurites moluccana*) – Hawai'i's 'official state tree' (a twentieth-century US custom) – that can grow to over 25 m and furnishes dye, oil, canoe wood and fish floaters. The swamp mahogany that later European settlers introduced to prevent erosion and protect the watershed accomplished this well and provided excellent construction lumber, too.

The Galápagos present a similar living laboratory.[21] At 972 km west of continental Ecuador and 5,600 km east of the Marquesas, with their island fauna dominated by reptiles (iguanas, tortoises, lizards) and birds, they register a low diversity of organisms: only 500 native plant species, for example, compared to Ecuador's 10,000. There are ten main islands and several smaller ones. Darwin's visit of 1835 during his voyage on the *Beagle*, observing the variation between populations of tortoises, mockingbirds and plants on discrete islands in the group, led him to postulate that species are mutable – that is, over time they can experience change in their morphology in response to different environmental conditions. This was of course the foundation of the theory of evolution based on the principle of natural selection. 'These early discoveries in Galapagos made a lasting contribution to the development of evolutionary theory, and the islands continue to provide scientists with information about the ecological factors that shape evolution.'[22]

In the Galápagos' isolation one seed-eating finch, Darwin found, had eventually generated fourteen species, each adapting to a specific island environment and food supply: some eating seeds, others fruit, berries, cactus, grubs or insects. The birds' diet and habitats determined their size and bill shape. More recent studies have shown that the chief evolutionary determinant is food limitation, also affecting feeding behaviour and, in turn, mating behaviour, leading to reproductive isolation and reinforcement of the diversity. 'Darwin's finches have evolved in response to alterations in their physical environment and to indirect changes caused by their competitors.'[23] Similarly, the marine iguana *Amblyrhynchus cristatus*, unique to the Galápagos, has evolved to become mostly herbivorous, preferring marine algæ; for this, it has evolved long claws and an abbreviated snout for rasping algæ from rocks.

Coral islands throughout the world, not just in the Pacific, are in a class of their own biologically, displaying common constants but with astounding variation. 'Coral islands and reefs harbour some of the most complex and diverse ecosystems in the world', claims eminent American oceanographer Richard W. Grigg.

There are between 500 and 1,000 species of tropical reef fishes, and if all number and kind of algæ, invertebrates, and microbes on the reef were to be fully enumerated there could be over 50,000 in any one major zoogeographic province.[24]

The importance of coral islands and reefs lies in their resilience over hundreds of millions of years, surviving continental drift, mountain formation, asteroid strikes, mass extinctions, tropical storms and various ice ages. Nearly all of today's living coral reefs and the coral islands that survive on their ecosystems find themselves in some stage of recovery from disease, starfish predation, storms or river run-off sedimentation. Humankind's impact has seemingly been even greater than nature's: operating beyond coral reefs' and islands' limits are human plundering, destruction of habitats, exploitation, overfishing, pollution, dynamite fishing and human-induced global warming that is now overheating the oceans. 'Resources are being depleted at an alarming rate.'[25] Coral reefs and islands are commonly the jurisdiction of small, impoverished nations whose overpopulation, corruption, weak governance and subsistence economy bode ill for local ecology. Adequate steward-ship costs, and at present the money and will are not there. 'Here is another example of the "Tragedy of the Commons" where technology may not provide a solution.'[26]

The great variety of coral islands is breathtaking – from Holly-wood idyll to sun-baked desert. Australia's Great Barrier Reef, for one, offers the whole spectrum. One would expect uniformity in one region, but 'time and stability' dictate against this. Whereas continental islands, having once been part of the mainland, isolated flora and fauna when they became detached (as early Britons were isolated when the English Channel filled), coral islands' biota were water- or airborne. A new island will be quickly colonized by robust species – like little children, young islands are great acceptors – and then post-colonized by the reluctant stragglers, commonly once the island has developed sufficiently to support them. A stable island will accommodate a smooth transition between old and new species, an unstable island will pit each against nature's more fre-quent vagaries, making island survival that much harder. Honey conditions for some are vinegar for others.

A general evolution of a sandy coral island will be: bare sand > initial vegetation > central vegetation > shrub ring > parkland > forest > erosion.[27] An island will revert to an earlier stage – includ-ing bare sand – depending on the caprice of waves, winds and plant and animal colonization. Greater events such as human invasion, global warming, ice ages, even Earth's precession, will of course exacerbate life's already precarious hold.

Most destruction is part of a natural process, a fine balance of island life and death.[28] Humans have, of course, introduced an un-precedented and unparalleled dimension to this. Mining, farming, introduction of alien species, human waste and so much more have tipped the sanity cart, it seems. Eradication of native species leads to accelerated erosion of coral islands and their reefs, with large tourist developments the most egregious perpetrators.

Yet the positive pursuit of even one interloper can sometimes reverse the trend. Lady Elliot Island on the Great Barrier Reef, for example, was the most ravaged in the region, munched and crunched away by goats and guano miners since around 1900 and finally lacking all vegetation and soil. Now, because of one man's reforestation programme, she supports shady groves of the coastal oak *Casuarina equisitefolia* which invite seabirds to nest. This has been achieved 'by a private citizen wishing to establish a modest, comfortable holiday resort in natural surroundings'.[29]

Compared with Pacific islands, those of the Atlantic are clearly second-division: in number, life variety and palm-fringed aquamarinity. Yet they can charm and teach, too, in their own way. And they claim a history nearly as old as Earth. Such big islands as the British Isles and Newfoundland, for example, being post-ice-age 'continental calves', support the vestigial plant and animal life of their adjacent land masses. Yet most Atlantic islands are not like this: their plants and animals had to cross vast seas to arrive and survive, and only a handful were robust enough to colonize successfully.[30] All of these oceanic islands are volcanic, but for the St Peter and St Paul Archipelago – fifteen Brazilian islets and rocks in the Northern Atlantic that support several insect and three seabird species. Many lie on, or originated from, the Mid-Atlantic Ridge where, some 150 million years ago, North and South America began pulling away from Europe and Africa.

The Atlantic's oceanic islands derive their plants and animals mostly from their respective adjacent land mass. So St Helena's and Ascension's flora and fauna most closely resemble Africa's; Fernando de Noronha's and Trindade's, Brazil's. In so-called Macronesia – the Azores, Madeira, the Canaries and Cape Verdes – all plants and animals are linked with northern Africa's and southern Europe's biota. Bermuda displays affinities with North America. Though closer to Africa, Gough Island and the Tristan da Cunha group possess a land bird assemblage more similar to that of South America, doubtless because of prevailing westerlies. In the Gulf of Guinea, west of Gabon, where volcanism created the chain of islands of Bioko (Fernando Póo), Príncipe, São Tomé and Annoboón (Pagalu), only Bioko is continental, whereas the others are oceanic islands that support several unique species: a grosbeak, a pigeon, a dwarf ibis and more.[31] Equatorial Africa has clearly been the progenitor for most of these islands' biota. Islands in the extreme north and south display respective Arctic or Antarctic wildlife.

Because the Bahama islands were probably connected to South America during epochs of maximal glaciation, their flora and fauna

relate more closely to Central and South American than neighbouring North American species: the Florida Strait was simply too
harsh a racist. So one can find cuckoos, bullfinches, parrots, banana
quits and orange tanagers, but no bluejays, cardinals or pelicans.

The Falkland Islands – that British Overseas Territory of 778
islands east of mainland South America – flaunt both South American and Antarctic features. Charles Darwin found the Falkland
wolf (*Dusicyon australis*) – the archipelago's only native land
mammal, by 1833 confined to the island of West Falkland and
already in decline – so tame that he collected his own exemplar with
a hammer! Perhaps unsurprisingly, the species is now extinct.

It was Atlantic island seabirds that suffered human impact most
severely. With islands few and far between, seabirds depend on them
for nesting: no island habitat – no nesting nor birds. Atlantic isles
tend to be small; habitat for nesting, when an island does occur, is
scarce. Most celebrated of insular seabirds was the flightless auk
(*Pinguinus impennis*) – a kind of northern penguin – which once
nested on islands from the British Isles to the Gulf of St Lawrence.
Sailors slaughtered all they found for food and oil; the last known
pair was butchered in 1844. St Helena once supported millions of
seabirds, at least six species of which have disappeared since human
arrival, with the rest now decimated and exiled to offshore islets.
Millions of cahow petrels (*Pterodroma cahow*) bred on Bermuda
for millennia; devoured by colonists and their cats, dogs, pigs and
introduced rats, only a few dozen survive today. Bermuda also supported several flightless rails, an owl, a finch, a heron, a woodpecker
and more; today, there's not one endemic land bird species left there.
The Azores no longer claim even one endemic bird species.

Only a few Atlantic species have flown off into the sunset. All
the rest have otherwise crashed: 'Millions of petrels, terns, frigate-
birds, boobies, and other efficient surface predators were removed
from the oceanic environment.'[32] It has left many a 'ghost island'
behind. Doubtless this has had an incalculable effect on the fish and
squid that once were their prey, as well as on the offshore nutrient
recycling and the birds' onshore habitat contribution.

Madeira, for example, was uninhabited and densely forested
when discovered by Portuguese sailors in 1419. Subsequent settlers
burned off nearly all woodland. Madeira still has the Trocaz
pigeon (*Columba trocaz*); the Madeira firecrest (*Regulus madeiren-
sis*), a very small, plump passerine; and the small gadfly petrel

(*Pterodroma madeira*) – all endemic. Yet her fossils reveal she once had finches, thrushes, a rail and two quail species as well that perhaps were flightless.[33]

Over the last 12,000 years in the Caribbean, mammals have suffered Earth's highest extinction rates.[34] No primates, for example, now occupy the region: it used to host primitive vestiges – just as Madagascar did, whose lemurs still belong to a rare African species. And a primate skull recently found on the island of Hispaniola yet resembles South America's ancient monkey, with the Caribbean primate having evolved special features for its long isolation, just as Madagascar's monkeys did. Now extinct, with rodent-like incisors the Jamaican monkey was actually very much like Madagascar's aye-aye lemur (*Daubentonia madagascariensis*). And the limbs of the Cuban monkey, in another case, suggest that it was partly ground-dwelling, something unique among New World monkeys.

Onto all of the Atlantic islands settlers introduced goats and rats. Later came their mice, cats, dogs, pigs, horses and cattle that further plundered the vegetation. European colonists in particular – whose burning of forests and bushland for agricultural use and introduction of insects and noxious plants wreaked untold havoc – dug the graveyard with especial industry: large populations of land snails, land birds, seabirds and several species of mammals and reptiles soon vanished.[35] Fossils of now-extinct species have been discovered on most isles (but for Trindade, which geologically disfavours fossil deposition). The Canaries, for example, have turned up fossils of a finch, a tortoise, rodents and lizards; all are now extinct.

Atlantic islands' erstwhile living treasuries were not depleted: they were devastated, and chiefly by humankind. Perhaps one shouldn't curse but rather clap with approval when dive-bombed in Shetland by those infernal gannets and skuas, while thanking heaven – as one lifts a stick topped with a handkerchief to shield one's skull – that they are still there.

MEDITERRANEAN ISLANDS

One must only marvel in contemplation of the verdant, teeming opulence of the Mediterranean islands of old: that is, before the last major climate change and before man arrived with axes of stone and bronze. What we find there today is of course only a dry, poor shadow of that past splendour. Still, there is much to extol in this saddening sea.

Beginning in the far west, Spain's Balearics – Majorca, Minorca, Ibiza, Formentera and many minor isles – still support a rich biome of wildflower species, many of them endemic, as well as being a veritable haven for orchids. Butterflies abound on Minorca, with 30 species thriving there. But reptiles and amphibians are few: only toads, frogs, lizards, two species of geckos and several of snakes. The Balearics are centrally placed on bird migration routes and so many migrants call; natives include Audouin's gull (*Ichthyætus audouinii*), the sedentary Thekla lark (*Galerida Theklæ*) and the blue rock thrush (*Monticola solitarius*). Large mammals are missing, but among the smaller mammals are mice, rats, rabbits, the European pine marten (*Martes martes*) and the North African hedgehog (*Atelerix algirus*).

To the northeast, France's Îles d'Hyères – Porquerolles, Port-Cros and Île du Levant, measuring only 26 sq km in total – mostly reproduce the flora and fauna of the immediate mainland. The superb botanical conservatory on Porquerolles, for one, does preserve some rare varieties of olive trees, as well as fruit, mulberry, fig and palm trees, emphasizing heritage to provide a gene reserve. Three vineyards also dignify the island. In 1971 the French government purchased four-fifths of Porquerolles to rescue her from imminent property development; with this France saved a national treasure.

Further to the east, France's volcanic Corsica – the Mediterranean's most mountainous island, with 8,680 sq km – has only 20 per cent forest cover. Her natural vegetation comprises woodlands and shrubs, with Holm oak (*Quercus ilex*) and cork oak (*Quercus suber*) in lowland abundance; various oaks, pines and deciduous trees adorning the montane zone, up to 1,800 m; and sparse vegetation and even small glaciers hiding in the alpine zone, up to 2,700 m. Nearly half of the island is now dedicated to various nature reserves, preventing destructive development. Corsica is rich in birdlife and often marks, with Sardinia, a species's southern range: the hooded crow (*Corvus cornix cornix*), for example, cannot be found in more southerly latitudes than these two islands. The island is home to two endangered subspecies of hoofed mammals: the endemic Corsican red deer (*Cervus elaphus corsicanus*) and the mouflon (*Ovis aries musimon*). For much of the Pleistocene,

Corsica and her southern neighbour Sardinia were joined and both shared a teeming fauna – an endemic insular dog species, a dwarf megaloceros (like a small elk), a shrew, a native pika (like a giant tailless rabbit) and others – most of which vanished when humans arrived.

Just south of Corsica looms Italy's great, earthquake-proof Sardinia. As old as 500 million years, she's one of Europe's most ancient geological bodies, and with 23,821 sq km the Mediterranean's second largest island after Sicily. Sardinia still supports several species of mammals, like the Corsican red deer; endemic Sardinian long-eared bat (*Plecotus sardus*), first discovered in 2002; mouflon; Sardinian fox; Giara's horse; wild boar; Sardinian sheep; and others. The Sardinian skink (*Chalcides ocellatus*) also occupies Sicily and the Maghreb. Four bird subspecies are endemic, while another ten are shared with Corsica. Still, many common European species are not to be found here, such as the marmot and viper. One-fourth of Sardinia's territory, over 600,000 ha, is now environmentally protected in three national and ten regional parks. The island also hosts 60 wildlife reserves, 25 natural monuments, five World Wildlife Fund Oases and a UNESCO-backed Geomineral Park.

The largest island of the Tuscan Archipelago, Italy's Elba – 224 sq km situated only 20 km from the mainland – once formed part of the ancient land bridge that connected the Italian boot to Corsica. Her plants and animals closely resemble those of coastal Italy. Mouflon and wild boar still thrive on the lofty slopes of Mt Capanne (1,018 m).

Sicily is Empress of the Mediterranean, with 25,708 sq km. An autonomous region of Italy, she once courted a wealth of endemic and native plant and animal species, some exhibiting insular dwarfism, such as a dwarf hippo (*Hippopotamus pentlandi*) and dwarf elephant (*Elephas mnaidriensis*). A rich treasury of Quaternary mammalian fossils has been discovered there, suggesting that Sicily once held a post-Tertiary connection with the African continent. Many of these mammals vanished with the arrival of humans around 8000 BC. Sicily's wealth of floral species is stupendous, yet endemism is relatively infrequent, with the insular vegetation closely resembling that of the Italian mainland – after all, Calabria is only 3 km distant.

Like that of so many Mediterranean islands, Sicily's biota has been greatly altered by introductions within more recent human history. Also, intense deforestation has significantly warmed and desiccated the island. Her dense population has also meant intense cultivation. Irrigation determines here the presence or absence of many floræ: the near-treeless plain of Catania contrasts enormously with the north and northeast coasts' orchards so redolent of lemons, citrons and oranges, and heady with vines, mulberries, pistachios, figs, carob trees, pomegranates, almonds and especially olives. Dwarf palms grow more profusely in some regions of Sicily than anywhere else on Earth. Forests, on the other hand, cover barely 3 per cent of the island. A famous landmark – the Chestnut Tree of One Hundred Horses – is the largest and oldest chestnut in the world; in 1780 its still-intact circumference measured 57.9 m.

The Sicilian deer (*Dama carburangelensis*) has been extinct for several centuries. Sicily's wolves are nearly gone now, yet foxes abound. Rabbits are ubiquitous, but hares are rarely seen. As on other Mediterranean isles, migratory birds frequent Sicily's coastal regions in great numbers and variety. Eagles and falcons inhabit the higher slopes; partridge, quail and grouse occupy the interior cultivated areas. A recent reintroduction has been the purple swamphen (*Porphyrio porphyrio*). In Mt Etna's national park and in some of the remoter protected areas, wildcats still thrive. In the woods of the Madonie or Nebrodi, squirrels and even beaver are seen. A Sardinian wild boar has been reintroduced to the island, and the boar-like Nebrodian swine is now more of a domesticated pig. Nocturnal hedgehogs and porcupines are infrequently seen. Many species of toads and frogs inhabit the wetlands, and geckos are plentiful. Hermann's tortoise (*Testudo hermanni*) finds Sicily a perfect habitat. Eels are still fished from island streams, but the once plentiful freshwater fish are now mostly extinct.

Italy's seven Æolian (or Lipari) Islands northeast of Sicily – Lipari, Vulcano, Salina, Stromboli, Filicudi, Alicudi and Panarea, which measure 1,216 sq km in total – are all volcanic in origin and apparently were never joined with Sicily, separated by a 200-m-deep channel. Some 900 typically Mediterranean plant species grow here, only four of which are endemic. Again like Sicily's, the Æolian Islands' vegetation has been almost entirely modified by humans since the Neolithic, with many abandoned vineyards and olive groves. Migratory birds also favour Æolian coastlines. Around 40 bird species inhabit the archipelago; ten of these figure in the Sicilian Red List of endangered avian species. There are seven species of bat and one endemic subspecies of garden dormouse (*Eliomys quercinus leparensis*). The archipelago hosts seven reptile species as well as four subspecies of Æolian wall lizard (*Podarcis raffonei*) and two subspecies of Italian wall lizard (*Podarcis siculus*). There are over fifteen endemic species of invertebrate animals in the isles.

Italy's fascinating Pantelleria island, 100 km southwest of Sicily and only 70 km east of Tunisia, displays on her 83 sq km a prevailing vegetation of evergreen woods (maritime pine, Aleppo pine), maquis (most commonly heather), *gariga* and herbaceous Mediterranean steppes. There are, in all, some 570 different plants on the island. Due to long geological isolation her fauna is characterized by extreme conservatism and endemism. The birdlife – featuring a wide range of migratory, native European and African species – is astonishingly rich: the isle is quite the birdwatcher's paradise. Among the rare endemic vertebrates is the talpa mole (*Talpa europæa*). Pantelleria shares with Sardinia a horseshoe-shaped coluber snake (*Coluber ippocrepis*), known for its fantastic colouration; further reptiles include the rare spur-thighed tortoise (*Testudo græca*), lizards, geckos and eyed skinks (*Chalcides ocellatus*). The native goat is nearly extinct now, and the native donkey – the venerable 'tractor' serving the isle's many vineyards – is trotting towards the sunset. Wild rabbits (*Oryctolagus cuniculus*) and wildcats (*Felix silvestri*) range Pantelleria's mountain slopes each night.

East of Pantelleria, 218 km away, mighty and magnificent Malta – like Cyprus a proud island nation – is in fact a 316-sq-km archipelago of three inhabited islands (Malta Island, Gozo, Comino) and numerous smaller islets and rocks. Of the approximately 4,500 identified species on Malta, 23 plants and 55 animals are endemic. Among the endemic flora are Malta's national plant, the flowering Maltese rock-centaury (*Cheirolophus crassifolius*); Gozo's flowering plant, the Maltese everlasting (*Helichrysum melitense*); and the flowering perennial Maltese hyoseris (*Hyoseris frutescens*), common on Gozo but rare on Malta Island. Much of the archipelago's animal life is common to, or also resident in, the Mediterranean, like the Sicilian shrew (*Crocidura sicula* ssp. *calypso*) that also inhabits Gozo. Yet Malta displays a rich endemic assemblage as well. The Maltese wall lizard (*Podarcis filfolensis*), also found in Italy, has four subspecies endemic to Malta. The Maltese palpigrade (*Eukoenia christiani*), belonging to a primitive order of arachnids, was discovered in 1988 in a cave in the Girgenti Valley on Malta

Island. The Maltese ruby tiger moth (*Phragmatobia fuliginosa* ssp. *melitensis*), with dark brown forewings and reddish-pink back wings, is common throughout the archipelago. The ten-legged, greenish-grey Maltese freshwater crab (*Potamon fluviatile* ssp. *lanfrancoi*), found only in certain areas, is now quite rare due to desiccation, pollution and capture.

Malta's birdlife is most impressive, the object of dedicated ecological monitoring. Of the 384 bird species registered in the archipelago, 21 breed regularly and a further seventeen only infrequently or erratically; 170 species are recurring migrants; the rest are seen only rarely. Two nature reserves – Ghadira and Is-Simar, wetland areas that comprise Malta's most expansive free-standing water sources – are managed by BirdLife Malta. The two reserves are vital to the migrating waterbirds – herons, waders, waterfowl and many others – that find refuge on Malta between their wintering and breeding grounds.

Claiming over 6,000 islands and islets, Greece is Europe's foremost 'island nation'. As with much of the Mediterranean, in ancient times the Greek isles were redolent of aromatic plants . . . which then fell to goats' hooves and charcoal burners' zeal. Spring's wildflowers can still be rather inspiring, though: cyclamen, asphodel, anemone, iris. And most culinary herbs are yet savoured: sage, rosemary, lavender, garlic. But the grasslands, forests, rivers, brooks and springs are mostly gone – mainly through deforestation but also due to climate change. In Greece, the erstwhile subtropical Ægean is, in many places, all but desert now. Today's isles host a wholly different ecology, with new natives: palms, cacti, citrus fruits, loquats, eucalypti and tomatoes. Perhaps even the cypress and olive are immigrants.[36]

Cephalonia is celebrated for Mt Ainos's (1628 m) forest of Cephalonian fir (*Abies cephalonia loudon*). Chios has profited from her thousands of mastic trees (*Pistacia terebinthus loudon*), exploited since the Middle Ages for a sort of chewing gum. The Mediterranean cypress (*Cupressus sempervirens*) abounds, as does the Aleppo pine (*Pinus halepensis*) which is replaced in Crete and the southeast Dodecanese by the *Pinus brutia* – straight-trunked, thick-leafed. Also abundant in the isles are the elm, white poplar and eastern plane. Now that the white poplar has been attacked by various fungi, its place is being taken by the introduced Canadian poplar (*Populus canadensis*). Also common is the so-called 'tree of heaven' (*Ailanthus altissima*), first imported to France from north China around 1751 and now found throughout the Mediterranean: actually, Greek peasants cannot stand it – its seedlings intrude into vineyards and plots, they claim – and call it the 'stinking tree'.[37] Scientists, pointing out its swiftly growing, anti-erosion root system, encourage its maintenance.

The Greek isles favour almond, lemon, orange and other fruit trees and vineyards in nearly every locale. Native bush chiefly comprises laurel (*Laurus nobilis*), myrtle (*Myrtus communis*), the Judas tree (*Cercis sili-quastrum*), lentisk (*Pistacia lentiscus*) and Christ's thorn (*Paliurus spina-christi*), but there are many others. Scores of these would grow into large trees but for the ubiquitous goats and locals' need for fuel for brick kilns and pottery ovens.

On the larger islands with sufficient water amphibians are copious: the common toad (*Bufo bufo*), green toad (*Bufo viridis*), Greek newt (*Trituris vulgaris græca*) and others. Among the many frog types are the Greek frog (*Rana græca*), agile frog (*Rana dalmatina*) as well as the marsh frog (*Rana ridibunda*) whose call Aristophanes (*c*. 448–*c*. 380 BC) immortalized in *The Frogs*. Very common is the lovely, small tree frog (*Hyla arborea*) that spends the summer in trees before returning to autumnal ponds.

Freshwater fish are rare on Greek isles and include the minnow (*Leucaspius stymphalicus*), roach (*Rutilus pleurobipunctatus*) and dace (*Leuciscus peloponensis*). Introduced just before and after the Second World War – to fight malaria – was the Central American mosquitofish (*Gambusia affinis*) that feeds on mosquito larvæ, now perhaps the most widespread fish of all. In larger streams one finds the common eel (*Anguilla anguilla*).

Invertebrates include southeastern Europe's normal insects, crustacea, spiders and so on. Of note is the Oleander hawkmoth (*Daphnis nerii*), a pink-and-white marbled green moth with a wingspan of 12 cm. Streams high up in the mountains contain the freshwater crab; in the Ionian Sea, this is the *Potamon fluviatilis*, in the Ægean the *Potamon potamios*.

All Greek islands display a varied but unplentiful bird population, with common European species and a variety of migrants. In the mountains you'll see the golden eagle (*Aquila chrysætos*) and griffon vulture (*Gyps fulvus*). Widespread are the little owl (*Athene nocturna*), Scops owl (*Otus scopa*), magpie (*Pica pica*) and raven (*Corvus corax*). The nightingale (*Luscinia megarhynchos*) thrills island gardens. Many gull species call the isles home, as do common swallows, swifts, doves and pigeons. Goldfinches (*Carduelis carduelis*) fly in small flocks, particularly in summer at thistle seeding time. Migrant birds include the white pelican (*Pelecanus onocrotalus*), great white egret (*Egretta alba*), bittern (*Botaurus stellaris*), purple heron (*Ardea purpurea*), grey heron (*Ardea cinerea*), woodcock (*Scolopax rusticola*), mallard (*Anas platyrhynchos*) and snipe (*Gallinago gallinago*). All are losing their habitats to cultivation, and most game birds are disappearing.

There is one poisonous Greek snake, the horned viper (*Vipera ammodytes meridionalis*), while all others are harmless: the leopard snake (*Elaphe situla*), ringed snake (*Natrix natrix*) and tesselated snake (*Natrix tesselata*). But the angry snake (*Coluber viridiflavus carbonarius*) will bite and hang on like a bulldog after darting out javelin-like from the bush. There are many types of lizards, some quite large, like the agama lizard (*Agamo stellio*) which grows up to 30 cm. Widespread is the disc-fingered gecko (*Hemidactylus turcicus*) that hunts insects along smooth walls, much to the fright of superstitious islanders who call it the *molintiri* or 'defiler'. There is the land tortoise (*Testudo hermanni*) as well as two freshwater terrapins: the European pond tortoise (*Emys orbicualris*) and Caspian terrapin (*Clemys caspica*). In the Ionian Sea one can sometimes see the false-hawksbill turtle (*Caretta caretta*) that can reach 1 m in length.

Larger animals are getting scarcer in the Greek isles, a constant of all islands. The jackal (*Canis aureus*) still haunts the larger islands, such as Corfu. The fox (*Vulpes vulpes*) ranges most isles. Delos claims both the brown hare and wild rabbit; north of Delos there are only hares, south only rabbits. The weasel (*Mustella nivalis*), hedgehog (*Erinaceus europæus*), pine marten (*Martes martes*), mole (*Talpa cæca*) and a type of nocturnal dormouse (perhaps *Dryomys nitedula*) dwell among island pines. Crete's towering mountains still host the ancient *agrimi*, the long-horned ibex (*Capra hircus cretensis*), now rare.

Among the Greek isles' marine animals, the monk seal (*Monachus monachus*) is now also rare – in the Ægean it's wholly absent, resentful fishermen having killed it off. Rare too is the bottlenose dolphin (*Tursiops truncatus*). Common dolphins (*Delphinius delphis*) and porpoises (*Phocæna phocæna*) still abound.

In the far eastern Mediterranean – one of Earth's most islandless coasts – colossal Cyprus looms large in lonely isolation, like some overgrown orphan. 'The island of Cyprus probably took its name from the tree', claimed Lawrence Durrell, though others have suggested this derives from the early Greek word for 'copper' or 'henna'.[38] With 9,248 sq km the third largest of the Mediterranean islands, by around 1,500,000 years ago Cyprus was home to hippos and elephants, both excellent swimmers, which evolved into endemic dwarf species. Today the island is a floral and faunal wonderland, unparalleled anywhere in the Mediterranean. For her array of habitats – as Cyprus lies at the junction of Europe's, Asia's and Africa's floral zones – and her wide-ranging geology and microclimate, some 8 per cent of her indigenous plants are endemic, tallying around 128 of the roughly 1,800 plant species. Major species include maquis of rock rose (*Cistus creticus*) and Phoenician juniper (*Juniperus phoenicea*) as well as forests of Aleppo pine (*Pinus halepensis*) and collages of all these in discrete communities. Cyprus is the Eden of the Mediterranean.

Her fauna is no less impressive, though the island is relatively sparse of mammals, with only 21 known species. The over 380 sighted bird species include millions of migrants that seek out and rely on Cyprus – in particular her two major wetlands, the salt lakes of Larnaca and Akrotiri – during long flights between the continents. Among the more majestic that visit are the imperial eagle (*Aquila heliaca*), common flamingo (*Phoenicopteridæ*) and Eleonora's falcon (*Falco eleonoræ*). The largest of the wild animals still to be found here is the rare wild sheep, the Cypriot mouflon (*Ovis orientalis ophion*). And one of the smallest must be the endemic Cypriot mouse (*Mus cypriacus*), seen mainly in the Troodos Mountains and recognized as a new species only in 2004 – the Mediterranean islands' only remaining endemic rodent. There are eleven species of lizards and ten of snakes. Regularly breeding on the Akamas Peninsula's sandy beaches are the green turtle (*Chelona mydas*) and loggerhead turtle (*Caretta caretta*). Amphibians are few. Much of Cyprus's biome is under threat, mainly because of robust urbanization, rabid tourist development and extensive forest exploitation since the Second World War – only 18 per cent of Cyprus's original habitat remains.

ISLANDS OF THE INDIAN OCEAN

Pacific islands may be far more numerous, but those of the Indian Ocean are both geologically and biologically far more diverse.[39] Relatively few suffer human occupation, while archipelagos are rare, with only two main island groups: the twin Maldives/Laccadives and, further south, the Chagos. In contrast, individual coral atolls are legion. Quite large islands also feature, the two most imposing being Sri Lanka and Madagascar. In the far east, just north of Western Australia, lie the uninhabited Rowley Shoals and many other atolls offering little terrestrial yet spectacular submarine life – some of the world's best diving sites.

Between Australia, Sri Lanka and the Chagos lie the Cocos Islands (or Keeling Islands) which support a marine life similar to that of the Malay Archipelago. Since first settlement in 1826, the Cocos bird and turtle populations have crashed; the group's main island is nearly birdless now, victim of introduced predators, alien flora and human spoilage. Yet 24-km-distant North Keeling, which has been spared continuous human occupation, is today a celebrated seabird rookery boasting healthy colonies of frigate birds; common, sooty and white terns; red- and white-tailed tropic birds; and many more.

Madagascar – Earth's fourth largest island, 400 km off Africa's southeast coast and a 'nation island' like Sri Lanka – is a continental fragment with a varied climate and topography. She claims very distinctive communities of flora and fauna, too, the island's southwest being mostly arid desert, her east humid and wooded.[40] 'Madagascar as we know her today harbours Earth's highest percentage of endemic species: 85 per cent of her flora and fauna evolved here. French naturalist Philibert Commerçon visited Madagascar in 1771 and called her "the naturalist's promised land".'[41] The island's wonders will never cease, it seems: in 2010 alone fourteen new species of palm were discovered, for example. Madagascar's flora is more like the western Pacific's than Africa's and includes an extraordinary number of endemics notable for their miniaturization (insular dwarfism, an adaptive strategy).

Most celebrated among Madagascar's fauna are her lemurs, saucer-eyed primates comprising 40 per cent of the island's mammals.[42] The ring-tailed lemurs – such as the *Lemur catta*, with long limbs, a long bushy tail and fox-like face – generally prefer rocky crevices in arid territories. Most other lemurs choose tree habitats on the island's wet, eastern side. Madagascar also hosts half of Earth's chamæleon species; iguanas whose closest kin reside in South America; and tenrecs, primitive hedgehog-related insect eaters. Carnivores number only eleven species, such as the fox-like *fanaloka* or Malagasy civet (*Fossa fossana*) and the larger cat-like fossa (*Cryptoprocta ferox*).

Unhappily, Madagascar is also one of the planet's ecological disaster areas, her flora and fauna seemingly in free fall. Austronesian settlers continued a slash-and-burn method of farming over some 1,500 years which might have functioned well for small mobile populations but proved catastrophic for the large settled population which eventually flourished there. The island's soil is now exhausted, her forests vanishing, her eroded hillsides slumping into denuded valleys, her rivers flowing crimson as wasted topsoil bleeds life itself out into the sea. Unique species of plants and animals are vanishing at an alarming rate. There are no freshwater fish, poisonous snakes or toads (yet over 150 species of frogs). Only 82 bird species – unusually small for such a large island – can now be found, half of these endemic. The Malagasy still cannot comprehend the environmentalists' warnings: life has always been a battle waged against the forest, never a partnership with the forest. 'A baobab tree or a child – which is more valuable? Stated in these terms, it is hard to convince the people that by destroying their environment they are committing suicide.'[43]

North of Madagascar lie the Seychelles, an archipelago of 115 islands. Eighteenth-century settlers had planted coconuts for copra, but since the 1980s jet travel has veritably drowned the islands in tourist dollars. Before this they had enjoyed 66 million leisure years of sundry species of flora and fauna arriving by both air and sea – ultimately to render the Seychelles a 'living natural history museum', as British biologist Julian Huxley (1887–1975) once described them.[44] The islands' fauna is still impressive, laying claim to fifteen endemic bird species, including the Seychelles kestrel (*Falco aræa*), the world's smallest falcon. Among the endemic amphibians is the earthworm-like, burrowing cæcilian *Hypogeophis*, which should exist also on neighbouring Madagascar, yet does not.[45] Cousin Island, a 27-ha bird sanctuary, is now protected by law; her Seychelles warbler (*Acrocephalus sechellensis*), the islands' smallest bird at half the size of one's thumb, numbered only twelve in 1973 but now over 2,500 thrive on Cousin, Denis, Cousine and Aride islands. Aride's 68 hectares, managed by the Seychelles' Island Conservation Society, host the archipelago's largest collection of seabirds, some 1,250,000, including the world's largest colony of Audubon's shearwater (*Puffinus lherminieri*).

The Seychelles' flora is no less impressive. In the densely wooded vale of Vallée de Mai on 38-sq-km Praslin Island, for example, stands of the famed coco de mer palm tree (*Lodoicea maldivica*) tower higher than 30 m and bear Earth's largest and heaviest fruit: a double coconut – resembling a woman's buttocks, islanders claim – weighing up to 42 kilos, the only genuine case of island gigantism among the Seychelles' flowering plants. Equally naughty are the stout catkins of the male plant: Seychellois aver that the female and male trees tryst at night.[46]

Roughly 900 km east of Madagascar lies Mauritius, whose loss of forest cover – from land clearance and felling for fuel and timber (homes, boats, waggons, tools) – has destroyed or endangered many species. Of particular concern at present are the Mauritius kestrel (*Falco punctatus*) and pink pigeon (*Columba mayeri*). During the 1970s, owing to DDT use, habitat loss, and egg predation by mongooses, monkeys and rats, the kestrels – a large, dark-brown, hawk-like bird of the falcon family – were down to two breeding pairs. Still, an imaginative programme by the dedicated Mauritian Wildlife Fund, that saw British and American ecologists scaling high cliffs to collect precious eggs for controlled hatching and rearing, had some 40 kestrels breeding in the wild by 1996.[47] Foreign ecologists then also rescued the pink pigeon from imminent extinction, chiefly through artificial insemination; by the year 2000 there were over 50 pink pigeons on the island, nearly the threshold to be self-sustaining.

Sad tales emerge, too. The domed Mauritius giant tortoise (*Cylindraspis triserrata*) and saddle-backed Mauritius giant tortoise (*Cylindraspis inepta*) were slaughtered for food by Dutch and French sailors and settlers in the 1600s and 1700s. And Mauritius's dodo (*Raphus cucullatus*) – a flightless bird resembling a pigeon but twenty times bigger – is today emblematic of island extinctions everywhere. Its flightlessness might have evolved in either of two ways: with no predators on Mauritius, it lost the need to fly and to stay light; or it had never been a flying bird at all but always a ground bird, which had rafted to Mauritius in a typhoon and subsequently evolved there in isolation. The dodo's discoverers, the

Portuguese, called it *dodou* or 'simpleton', owing to the bird's absolute trust in humans. Indeed. Living exemplars were even sent to Europe in the 1600s . . . just before the Dutch extinguished them on Mauritius herself. Human-introduced rats, however, were proliferating exponentially by the 1800s, ultimately threatening the island's harvests and birdlife. This prompted the then-ruling British to import mongooses from India to eradicate them. Yet by the early 1990s Alain O'Reilly, managing the wildlife refuge on Mauritius, was declaring that he and his team had caught and post-mortemed thousands of mongooses: 'We find [in their stomachs] toads, birds, lizards, but we've never found that they've eaten a rat.'[48]

Christmas Island, a high island (360 m) of only 135 sq km with surrounding coral reef, is part of the same volcanic chain shared by the Cocos Islands. A haven for birds, she features the golden bosun (*Phæthon lepturus fulvus*), the Christmas Island frigate bird (*Fregata andrewsi*), Abbott's booby (*Papasula abbotti*) and other endemic species. Most famous for her big land crabs that thrive in the absence of large predators, Christmas supports more than twenty species of these, the most common being the Christmas Island red crab (*Gecarcoidea natalis*), robber crab (*Birgus latro*) and blue crab (*Cardisoma hirtipes*). Numbering approximately 120 million, the red crab is everywhere: roughly one each square metre. As a result, forest or garden debris is almost nonexistent.[49]

Befitting Sri Lanka's magnitude and location, her flora flaunts diversity and endemism: 3,210 species and subspecies of flowering plants belonging to 1,052 genera, endemic being 916 species and eighteen genera. Alone the island's ferns tally some 350 species. And Sri Lanka's fauna is no less daunting: around 90 species of mammals (41 threatened), 16 of which are endemic (14 threatened); as well as 30 species of bats and 26 species of cetaceans. Of the 171 species of reptiles (56 threatened) – most of these being snakes – 101 are endemic. With over 106 species of amphibians and more than 90 of these endemic, Sri Lanka offers one of the planet's richest ranges. There are well over 250 species of birds (46 threatened) and 82 species of freshwater fish (28 threatened).

Indonesia, Earth's greatest island nation in terms of insular inventory and population, reveals a breadth and diversity of plant and animal life that is simply breathtaking. Characterized by tropical rainforest, enjoying warm temperatures and heavy rain year-round with no significant dry period, the greater Malay

Archipelago features roughly 28,000 species of flowering plants, Earth's second largest biodiversity. Broadleaf evergreen forests dominate Indonesia's flora on less densely populated islands; cultivated vegetation marks Java and Bali, with swamp, mangrove and nipa palm (*Nypa fruticans*) forests describing coastal regions. With lower rainfall the Lesser Sunda Islands nourish grasslands. Mountain areas support alpine and subalpine growth. Over the past 200 years Java's, Bali's and much of Sumatra's primary forest was felled for timber as populations soared.[50] Though 45 per cent of Indonesia still comprises tropical rainforest, deforestation now takes an annual toll of 2 million ha. Many secondary forests have recently been burned and replanted in vast palm plains for biofuel. The stench of burning forests and dark palls of smoke and ash have been polluting many Indonesian islands for years on end, one of Earth's worst cases of ecological mismanagement, rivalling that of ancient Greece and prehistoric Easter Island.

Indonesia's fauna is no less notable, with a commensurate biodiversity in respect of insular size, location and geological history. In the west, Asian fauna flourishes; in the east, Australasian. Of the 381 mammal species in Sundaland alone – that is, Sumatra, Java, Borneo and their immediate islands – 173 are endemic, including the Bornean orangutan (*Pongo pygmæus*), Sumatran orangutan (*Pongo abelii*), Javan rhinoceros (*Rhinoceros sondaicus*), Sumatran rhinoceros (*Dicerorhinus sumatrensis*) and Bornean proboscis monkey (*Nasalis larvatus*). Some 771 bird species abound, 146 of them endemic. Sundaland's reptiles and amphibians number a remarkable 449 species in 125 genera. The region's swamps, lakes and rivers host no fewer than 1,000 species of fishes.

Wallacea – that is, the transitional islands to the east, between Sundaland and western Australasia – displays a similar wealth of biodiversity: 223 native mammal species (126 of which are endemic); 650 bird species (265); 225 species of reptiles and amphibians (99); and 310 species of freshwater fishes (75). Further east, in Indonesia's West Papua, New Guinea, the predominately Australasian fauna reveals a similar wealth of variety and number, much of which differs markedly from that in the west.

By 2009 greater Indonesia could pride herself in possessing no fewer than 50 declared national parks. Nonetheless, continued deforestation, unchecked pollution, soaring population growth, increasing industrialization and sustained wildlife plunder make for alarming statistics. Indonesia's plant and animal life, still so incredibly rich, warrants ever more vigilant attention by every nation, lest a whole planet suffer the consequences.

ARCTIC AND SUBANTARCTIC ISLANDS

In chilling contrast to that of the Malay Archipelago, the Arctic's island biome is hardly distinguishable from that of the nearest mainland and there are hardly any endemic species of plants or animals at all – the very 'polar opposite' of that tropical splendour.[51] Arctic islands were 'life rings' for imperilled species. Many grabbed at them; few survived. Plants and animals had better chances on islands that managed to stay ice-free, like much of the Bering Strait area, parts of the Yukon and a few islands of the Canadian Archipelago. There are no trees here; conditions are simply too harsh.

Still, a broad spectrum of flora and fauna obtains. Nearly all plant species are shared in common among the Arctic islands. The same holds with mammals: continental Arctic foxes, hares and polar bears occupy all nearshore islands when winter ice reconnects them. Seals and sea lions are fully at home on many northern groups and further south. But it's birds above all which are the true denizens of the Arctic islands. When summer food is abundant, hundreds of millions migrate there to breed: gulls, terns, ducks, geese and many more. Great populations of some southern shearwaters migrate to the northern Pacific and Bering Sea in April and May at the onset of the Southern Hemisphere winter, then return in October or November to the southern oceans to breed. Permanent Arctic island residents include gulls, ducks and auks: birds that prefer shallow, nearshore situations.

Below the Arctic's southern reaches, in more temperate climes, some species select small offshore stacks on which to breed in preference to all other rookeries. Nearly all North Atlantic gannets (*Morus bassanus*), for example, choose these to breed on, often close to the mainland. Bonaventure Island in Canada's Gulf of St Lawrence hosts some 18,000 pairs; Bass Rock in Scotland's Firth of Forth around 14,000 – both together comprising about one-seventh of the world's population of breeding pairs for this species.[52]

Subantarctic islands' position, relative to the oceanographic boundary of the Antarctic Convergence, is critical for their terrestrial flora and fauna.[53] The lower slopes of the treeless northern islands support herbaceous plants and tussock grasses. With far less land free from snow and ice, the southern islands begrudge only lichens and mosses, the southernmost a handful of flowering plants. The floral range is very limited: with sixteen ferns, 32 herbaceous plants and 24 grass species these isles seem a long way indeed from Java and Bali: 'The scarcity of the subantarctic flora is due to the remoteness of the islands, the direction of the prevailing winds, the area of available land for colonization, and the climate.'[54] Though a fossil record exists on a few of the northerly islands, it appears hardly anything survived glaciation, including vegetation.

So most plant and animal life on Arctic and subantarctic islands arrived by wind dispersal, avian transport and sea currents less than 8,000 years ago – Earth's youngest island biota. Growth was then limited by extreme cold, little sunshine, harsh climate and poor adaptability. Some settlers were tough cookies: Ellesmere Island's woolly bear caterpillar (Gynæphora groenlandica), for one, hibernates in temperatures of minus 70°C, only surviving by allowing its intestinal load, blood and all extracellular liquid to freeze inside. Such harsh conditions also foster longevity: Earth's oldest-known living animal is a marine clam of the species Arctica islandica which, estimated to be at least 400 years old, fetched up off Iceland's coast.

Otherwise, animal life on subantarctic islands – apart from seabirds and sea mammals – comprises small invertebrates like insects, spiders, molluscs (snails and slugs), nematodes and worms. Microscopic organisms like protozoans and tardigrades also survive. There are no freshwater fishes, reptiles or amphibians. Of the vertebrates, only seven bird species endure, among these ducks, sheathbills and a pipit. Macquarie Island was once home to a parakeet (Cyanoramphus erythrotis) and rail (Gallirallus philippensis macquariensis). At summer, seals and seabirds of course breed here in enormous numbers, safe from humans. Among the most common seabirds are petrels of various sizes, grey-headed albatrosses (Thalassarche chrysostoma), light-mantled sooty albatrosses (Phoebetria palpebrata), wandering albatrosses (Diomedea exulans) and black-browed albatrosses (Thalassarche melanophrys). And there are many penguin species in large numbers throughout the island ring, particularly the king (Aptenodytes patagonicus), macaroni (Eudyptes chrysolophus), rockhopper (Eudyptes chrysocome) and gentoo (Pygoscelis papua) penguins. Since breeding sites are small and finite in number, seabird colonies turn into proper ornithopolises.

A few islands of the Southern Ocean have been spared human interference: Heard Island had her penguins and seals once hunted, yet suffers no introduced species; and the McDonald, South Sandwich and Bouvet islands might even be called pristine. Still, most have seen their flora and fauna egregiously impacted within the past two centuries.[55] Most lack resources for sustainable human occupation and so were forced to tolerate visitors and settlers who brought their own resources with them: pigs, rabbits, goats, sheep and, on the larger islands, even horses and cattle. The consequences were devastating. Well over a century ago sealers knowledgeable of the Southern Ocean islands were warning: 'It would not be well to introduce pigs to the southern islands as they would destroy the birds, the main support of chance castaway mariners.'[56] Yet alone on fifteen of the Antarctic's islands or island groups mammals were introduced as a source of protein; today, thirteen suffer continuing depredations, though the human intruders themselves – but for those manning scientific or conservation stations – have left. Norwegian whalers in the early 1920s introduced eleven reindeer onto South Georgia Island; now she tallies several thousand that destroy barely viable vegetation. Mice and rats were accidentally introduced onto all the islands, whereupon cats were brought to combat them: ever since, such pristine rookeries as Macquarie Island and Marion Island have festered with feral cats.

Island floral and faunal extinctions have always occurred, chiefly because of changing climate. Periodic ice ages especially wreaked havoc everywhere, causing massive sea-level fluctuations that could simultaneously create and destroy islands:

> Bermuda, for example, shrank to around a tenth of its present size when the seas rose to their maximum extent some hundreds of thousands of years ago, but at the height of the last glaciation, about 18,000 years ago, when sea levels dropped precipitously, Bermuda was 10 times larger than it is now. At that time, we know from fossils, a crane, a duck, and four different species of flightless rails existed on Bermuda that have since disappeared.[57]

St Helena's oldest fossils are the only evidence that she once supported a pigeon and shearwater – both extinct because of environmental change thousands of years before the first human interloper.

Yet man has been the chief island-slayer, at least within the recent
past. No other animal – not even the ubiquitous rat – has been so
rabid or toxic. It's that an island biota is far simpler than a mainland
biota, and thus more vulnerable. Even one alien introduction – a
kelp, pig, rat, cat – can confuse and destroy an entire ecosystem. The
islands of Vanuatu, for example, nurtured half-tonne meiolaniid tur-
tles until roughly 2,800 years ago, just 200 years after Austronesian
voyagers settled there from the west and started hunting them for
food.[58] The planting and cultivating of sugar cane for so many
centuries in the Caribbean decimated the islands' natural flora and
so also the fauna that relied on it. The Indian mongoose (*Herpestes
auropunctatus*) introduced to Fiji in 1833, to Hawai'i in 1883 and to
several other islands was meant to eradicate rats, but also devoured
rat-eating snakes and nestling birds, creating an even greater problem
in the end. Rats which abandoned the deliberately beached
Makambo on Lord Howe Island between New Zealand and Australia in 1918 had within two years nearly wiped out all the island's
songbirds; the rats still plague Lord Howe today. In 1949, 1951 and
1952 the barn owl (*Tyto alba*) was introduced to the Seychelles in a
series of controlled releases to contain rats, but the owls all but
annihilated the local white terns (*Gygis alba*) instead; today, the rats
remain as rife as before. Goats are second only to rats in thwarting
regrowth of unique trees, bushes and plants, sometimes denuding
entire islands – as Greeks have complained since antiquity.[59]

Introduced birds often rule the roost now: doves and starlings,
sparrows and blackbirds, mynahs and thrushes have overwhelmed
native populations on many colonized islands. Organizations
formed to promote such introductions thrived into the 1920s: for
sport, food or merely a touch of Home. Ancient Pacific voyagers
had done just the same, carrying the Southeast Asian domestic
chicken, for example, everywhere they sailed, even as far as distant
Easter Island. Such indigenous introductions have adapted well,
whereas more recent European introductions have tended to cluster
in urban and semi-rural areas, avoiding rainforests and dense bush.

A new dimension has now exacerbated the problem of alien
introductions. It all started in 1837 when the British introduced
possums to New Zealand to create a market in skins. Since then,

possums have infested the land, proving catastrophic especially to flightless birds. With the development of organochlorines since the Second World War, New Zealand's government began aerial drops of these synthetic chemicals to poison the possums and conserve rare birdlife. However, the agent they have selected for this in recent years of aerial treatment – the highly lethal brodifacoum – has impacted devastatingly on a wide variety of other wildlife, leaving poisoned carcasses of many untargeted species to rot on native alpine slopes. Such modern poisons have revealed themselves to be modern mongooses.

And it gets worse. The organochlorine pestacide lindane, for example, has been found in Guam, Tasmania and the Marshall Islands – islands where lindane has never been used commercially – so potent is its atmospheric dispersal.[60] The worldwide use for decades of halocarbon refrigerants (CFCs, freons, halons) has also allowed, through the depletion of the ozone layer, ultraviolet rays on sun-blessed and palm-fringed beaches to increase rates of basal cell carcinomas and melanomas: skin cancers that are not only disfiguring but, with the latter, frequently lethal, especially in southern latitudes like New Zealand's.

Insular isolation itself encourages genetic inbreeding, resulting in an island where colour blindness or cleft lips, for example, are alarmingly frequent. Genetic inbreeding – a doubling of recessive alleles – can harm a species or, when combined with other factors, lead to extinction. Insular extinction seems to occur once a breeding population falls below 50. The larger the population above this, the greater the chance for island survival. 'Five hundred has been suggested as the number of individuals that would provide sufficient genetic variety.'[61] Similarly, an island's size and location determine the number of species she can support: huge Sri Lanka in the warm Indian Ocean is species-rich, small Macquarie Island in the subantarctic species-poor. Understandably, extinctions of endemic species have occurred far less frequently on large than on small islands.

What benefit lies in protecting insular ecology? Southern Madagascar's periwinkle (*Catharanthus roseus*), for one, is merely a tiny pink flower, hardly noticed, seemingly insignificant. Yet it holds a substance that, when extracted, can arrest children's leukæmia. Madagascar hosts nearly 10,000 flowering plants, including further species of periwinkle.[62] *Very few have been tested for their value to humankind*. Perhaps many of these, too, bear the gift of life.

three

... *of First Footprints*

It is Europe's first literature. It hails from an island. And it heralds war:

> Hear ye, Cretans and Greeks:
>   my great, my quick.
> Hear ye, Danaïdans:
>   the great, the worthy.
> Hear ye, all blacks, and
> Hear ye, Pudaan and Libyan immigrants.
> Hear ye, waters, yea Earth:
>
> Hellas faces battle with the Carians.
>
> Hear ye all.
> Hear ye, Gods of the Fleet, aye
> Hear ye all:
>
> Faces battle with the Carians.
>
> Hear ye all.
> Hear ye, the host of black people,
>   and all.
> Hear ye, lords, yea freemen:
>
> To Naxos!
>
> Hear ye, Lords of the Fleet:

To Naxos!

Hear ye, ye immigrants,
  the great and the small.
Ye countrymen
  skilled, most stalwart.
Lords Idaian.
All Cretans:

Strike ye out with the Greeks, and
Smite the Carians, mine enemy, and
Succour my stricken.

Safeguard me, Idaians,
I am sore afraid:
  Loose me now.
My night, my great:
  Ye loose me now.
These afflictions so terrible and so great,
Verily so molestful:
  Ye loose me now.

Down to the sea, everyone!

Yea, deliver me of my great afflictions![1]

Imprinted on both sides in Minoan Greek, the Phaistos Disk, a hand-sized artefact of baked clay unearthed on Crete in 1908, is the world's first known example of printing with movable type. Fashioned around 1600 BC, it also conveys Europe's first voice, possibly that of Crete's Minos himself: 'Minos was the first who fought a battle with a fleet', Pliny the Elder tells us.[2] And the outcome of Europe's first documented war? – 'Minos is the earliest of all those known to us by tradition who acquired a navy', penned Thucydides (*c.* 460–*c.* 395 BC), father of European history.

> He made himself master of a very great part of what is now called the Hellenic Sea, and became lord of the Cyclades islands and first colonizer of most of them, driving out the Carians and establishing his own sons in them as governors.[3]

In saving the Ægean from the Carians, Minos laid the keel for Hellenic history. Thus it is to him and his great island of Crete that we owe the Greek civilization on which Europe is founded.

A constant of human history is that water connects. Rivers and seas have forever invited exploration, settlement, trade and, as with Minos of Crete, conquest. Though island size counted for resources and growth, location counted even more – islands that punctuated main routes of migration, voyaging and trade were forges which fed, shaped and inspired the cultural history of the planet. Islanders then became history's boldest sailors, ceaselessly seeking out new isles to exploit and settle. Later settlers arrived and mixed, then great peoples and societies either seized or held stewardship over Earth's most remote islands and archipelagos: Austronesians, Minoans, Phoenicians, Greeks, Romans, Chinese, Polynesians, Japanese, Indians, Malays, Vikings, Venetians, Portuguese, Spaniards, Dutch, Danes, French, British, Americans.

A further constant: islands exist to be exploited. Hominoid islanders have always modified and degraded their environments, chiefly through tree felling and depletion of fauna.[4] It all began around 1,810,000 years ago with *Homo erectus* on the banks of the Solo River in East Java. But this was still the Sunda subcontinent – Java was not yet an island. Sometime between 900,000 and 800,000 years ago, a small flotilla of migrants deliberately crossed Wallace's Line to settle the island of Lombok and then Flores where they caused the extinction of pygmy stegodons (bony-plated quadrupeds). Discovered on Flores in 2003 were the remains of what appeared to be diminutive humans, since named *Homo floresiensis* – otherwise 'hobbits'. Fossil hominins between 90,000 and 18,000 years old, these hobbits can be explained by one of three hypotheses: that their very small heads were the result of a congenital condition; that they were dwarf *Australopithecus* or early *Homo*; or that island dwarfism evolved them from *H. erectus* or even from *H. sapiens*.

Around 60,000 years ago Sunda's *H. erectus* population had been joined by intruding *H. sapiens* from the west, many of whom remained on the Sunda subcontinent while others crossed Wallace's Line to the eastern islands and continent of Sahul (later Australia, New Guinea and Tasmania). This arriving Papuan people were the earliest-known modern humans to occupy the Malay area and points east. The first Australians arrived at least 50,000 years ago, participating in this spread of early peoples from Asia and Sunda along the eastern archipelago to New Guinea's great isles. The Huon Peninsula of Papua New Guinea, for example, was occupied as early as 40,000 years ago. 'Within 12,000 years (and perhaps considerably earlier) groups of people had crossed the 160 kilometres (100 miles) of open water that lie between New Britain and the Solomon Islands.'[5] Papuan communities were occupying West New Britain 35,000, New Ireland 32,000 and Buka 26,000 years ago.

Between 700,000 and 130,000 years ago hominins of some sort, probably Neanderthals, were also inhabiting south-coast shelters on Crete in the Mediterranean, which had been separated from the mainland some 5 million years earlier – Greek and US archæologists announced in 2011 that they had unearthed rough axes and other primitive tools from this time. It's Greece's oldest-known human island habitat.

On Luzon, largest and northernmost island of the Philippines, a French team recently unearthed a hominin foot bone at least 67,000 years old, the earliest date for a hominoid presence on any Southeast Asian island. Bone size suggests either *H. habilis* or *H. floresiensis*.[6] Not only does this confirm very early seafaring technology, but also the sophisticated language that planning for such a voyage requires. These island occupations occurred during so-called 'depletion-and-search' migrations, whereby small tribes would migrate at the rate of around 50 km per generation. Once arrived at a shore, they would construct small bamboo-and-vine rafts capable of bearing 1,000 kg which they would then paddle or let monsoon winds drive to hardly visible shapes on the horizon. (There were no sails at first.) An absolute minimum of 25 couples can – biologically, socially, psychologically – settle an island successfully and permanently.

The earliest evidence of the presence of man in Britain comes from Boxgrove in Sussex, which has revealed artefacts dated to around 500,000 years ago. This Neanderthal people of the Lower Palæolithic age were no islanders, however, for Britain was not an island in her entirety until around 6000 BC. (Only intermittently were various parts of Britain an island.)

Some 50,000 years ago Sri Lanka was settled by a tribe arriving from India, most likely 'island-hopping' from the mainland. Within 10,000 years seaborne settlement became a cultural necessity there and it continued well into the nineteenth century AD when the last deserted islands were colonized.[7] All human and avian movements in the Indian Ocean have forever been at the mercy of the region's unique monsoonal wind systems.

During the Upper Palæolithic, perhaps as early as 40,000 years ago, humans were arriving on the main islands of Japan, doubtless from the Korean peninsula. Further north, two separate times over the past 38,000 years lowering seas have allowed the appearance of a 'land bridge' – now called Beringia by geologists – across the 85-km passage of the Bering Strait west of Alaska. It is likely that early humans entered North America from Siberia using this route; others might have drifted along the coasts in primitive rafts. Around 30,000 years ago the first humans were colonizing Taiwan, 120 km off the Chinese mainland.

Back in the Mediterranean, such Greek islands as Corfu, for example, were being settled as early as 35,000 years ago, probably by Neanderthals, to judge by unearthed stone tools of the Levallois-Moustier type. Around 12,000 years ago the ice wall of the last glaciation began its final (until now) retreat and the temperature continued to rise until around 3000 BC when northern Europe, for one, was 2.5°C warmer than today. This had a revolutionary impact on the environment. Many more islands – Cyprus, Corsica, Sardinia, Sicily, Malta – were deliberately colonized at this time by a variety of non-related tribes.

In the Far East, giant Sakhalin became inhabited by around 12,000 years ago. At the same time on California's Channel Islands, Native Americans were crafting uniquely barbed spearheads and possibly trading technologies with mainland Clovis tribes.

Britain's Star Carr house, a neolithic structure built on the edge of a now-vanished lake in North Yorkshire 10,500 years ago and discovered only in 2008, housed a family when Britain was still attached to continental Europe. When Britain became an island around 8,000 years ago as the ice melted and climate warmed, the reindeer, bison and mammoths vanished and an altered environment welcomed red deer, boar and oxen, to which the land's ancient inhabitants had to adapt. The Palæolithic economy – that peripatetic relationship between hunter and wild – disappeared once herds did and woodland replaced open grassland. By 3000 BC agriculture and horticulture had become the new economy: numerous settled communities of permanent round houses encouraged food surpluses and storage, creating security, trade capital and leisure to teach, learn and invent. Populations soared. Societies were born. The first, substantial, permanent constructions of humankind – almost 1,500 years before Egypt's earliest pyramids – are the *cromlechs* of the British Isles, most often chambered tombs frequently in the vicinity of megaliths and stone circles.

Whereupon Britain's prehistoric farmers decimated their extensive forests, an ecological disaster from which the islands have never recovered. Today's Britain is less than 4 per cent woodland, with almost all of the deforestation having occurred before the Romans arrived. (The clearance was chiefly a later Celtic enterprise, leaving the land far less wooded than the erstwhile Celtic homeland – Germany, northern France, Belgium and Holland – is today.) 'Clearance of the thinner woodlands of the northern and western uplands caused the soil to deteriorate and become acidic, resulting in the formation of exposed wet heathlands useless for farming.'[8] It was a prehistoric crime surpassed only by today's destruction of island rainforests.

At last separate from what had become the island of Britain, Ireland managed to maintain her unique ancient cast. Though the indigenes later adopted the Celtic tongue of eastern intruders, the Irish preserved their genetic difference from all other Europeans, even from their closest Celtic neighbours – the most surprising revelation to emerge from the first sequencing of an Irish person's genome. The representative genotyping study has shown that 'the Irish genome inhabits a hitherto unsampled region in European genome variation', says team leader Brendon Loftus of University College Dublin.[9]

As the sea rose, the Papuan peoples of the Sahul continent found themselves becoming New Guineans, Australians and Tasmanians. The latter, present on Tasmania as early as 35,000 years ago, were long believed to be a 'separate race', as the island's nine major ethnic groups displayed no obvious cultural links to mainland Aborigines. Then early nineteenth-century documents were found which revealed that there still had existed into historical times unmistakable similarities – though there had been no tribal contact since the land bridge between Australia and Tasmania had been lost around 8000 BC.

A plethora of new societies then populated Earth's lesser remote regions, the new islanders sharing much in common: above all, an immediate appreciation of sea, resource limitations and self-sufficiency. And one and all they teased their children at eventide camp-fire, too, with the timeless conundrum: 'Why is the ocean always near the shore?'

'IN THE MIDST OF THE WINE-DARK SEA'

Europe's most complete Neolithic village, an assemblage of ten houses occupied from 3180 to 2500 BC, graces the west coast of Mainland in Scotland's remote Orkneys. Yet Skara Brae and similar excavated sites comprise less than one-hundredth of what is yet to be properly addressed. Here in Britain's north – in some cases long before Stonehenge and Egypt's pyramids – human societies were teeming with activity. Relatively secure, dynamic, interactive communities of like ethnicity and tongue, in a region that, for them, was anything but remote, were making history.

Shetland, for one, measures 1,466 sq km of roughly 100 islands, only fifteen of which are inhabited today. The chief island, also called Mainland, is Scotland's third and Britain's fifth largest. Shetland has been populated at least since 3400 BC, the islands' inhabitants pursuing subsistence agriculture and cattle farming. Around 2000 BC, with cooling climate, the islanders favoured coastal areas. As of the Iron Age, around the sixth century BC, Shetlanders were taking to the construction of stone fortresses, indicating an era of increased intrusion with accompanying aggression.

Around 3000 BC, at the mouth of the Nile in Egypt, an 'island' of a different ilk was being created. According to the legend narrated by Egyptian historian Manetho in the third century BC, Menes, the pharaoh who united the lands of the Upper and Lower Nile, formed an artificial eyot in the river when he diverted it with dykes made of enormously high, thick, rock walls meant to protect the terrain from annual flood. And it was on this 'walled artificial island' (if only during flood) that Egypt's first great capital, Memphis, arose. Whether or not the legend is true – and many scholars have questioned its authenticity – something similar did occur on two small islands much further up the Nile, just above the First Cataract: on Philæ's two islands, honoured by Egyptians and Nubians both, at once holy and commercial. Several temples to Egypt's gods rose here, as well as a robust marketplace for those commodities traded along the river. Two thousand years later Philæ would become the centre of the great Temple of Isis, and the two isles were regarded as one of the burial places of Osiris, brother and husband of Isis and god of the afterlife; consequently, Philæ was regarded as one of later Egypt's chief pilgrimage centres and adorned with antiquity's most inspiring architecture. Featuring prominently on the Nile was also Elephantine Island in Upper Egypt on the southern border to Nubia, measuring only 1,200 by 400 m but venerated in the second millenium BC as the residence of the cataract god Khnum to whom a temple was erected on the fortified eyot; today, flaunting many imposing ruins including a third-dynasty stepped pyramid and a sixth-dynasty shrine, Elephantine forms part of the modern city of Aswan.

Around 6,000 years ago a distinct Asian population who were settled along China's southern coast sailed 130 km of open ocean to occupy Taiwan where, over subsequent centuries, their culture and language(s) developed into Proto-Austronesian. Descendants then sailed south to recolonize the Philippines around 5,000 years ago, then west and southwest to establish settlements in eastern Vietnam and Cambodia; on the Malay Peninsula; and on the islands of Borneo, Sumatra and Java. Other Austronesians sailed directly south of the Philippines to colonize Sulawesi, Timor, southern Halmahera and Western New Guinea (modern Papua and West Papua). Speakers of a proto-language which, in time, would become the Oceanic languages of the Pacific were probably settling regions of Papua New Guinea's northern coast beginning around 4,500 years ago. They finally settled on the islands of New Britain and New Ireland in the Bismarcks around 4,000 years ago. Here, the Austronesians colonized coastal regions, generally keeping apart from the indigenous Papuans.[10]

Also around 4000 BC farming and animal husbandry arrived in the islands about Copenhagen and Stockholm, whose Neolithic settlers with their polished flint axes and earthen pottery began burying their dead in megalithic tombs. By the Middle Neolithic period, 3100 to 2700 BC, Ajvide on the island of Gotland in the Baltic Sea had developed into an enormous settlement of 200,000 sq m, whose inhabitants, too, had all but given up their earlier dependence on seal, porpoise and fish to concentrate instead on cattle, sheep and pig farming – a trend witnessed on many Baltic islands at the time, no doubt the consequence of a major climate change.

The earliest Maltese who, as Neolithic hunters or farmers, had first settled the Mediterranean island around 5200 BC, were by around 3500 BC erecting megalithic temple complexes at Mnajdra, Ħaġar Qim, Tarxien and also at Ġgantija on Gozo Island. Demonstrating a similar communal enterprise, Britons were hauling Stonehenge's first bluestones into place around 3000 BC.

The earliest Greenlanders appear to have been seal and musk-oxen hunters from Canada who, around 2500 BC, sporadically occupied coastal areas but did not permanently settle for the brutal climate and unreliable game. For all of her history Greenland has been sparsely populated (she counts only around 55,000 islanders today). Farming is all but impossible here. Hunting and fishing have sustained tiny ephemeral settlements for nearly all of Greenland's history. Around 4,000 years ago early North Americans also arrived on Wrangel Island in the Arctic Ocean where it appears they caused the extinction of Earth's last mammoths – isolated there since the ice sheets had melted and the sea level had risen 5,000 years earlier.

Also by about 2000 BC Wales had received the bulk of her original folk, those who would later be speaking the Brythonic language of the Celtic family that would eventually advance into Welsh.[11] As of around 1000 BC, because of competition for land due to a sudden population increase that occurred when the now-deteriorating climate rendered less tillage available, the Welsh began constructing hill forts, many of which housed quasi-urban communities. Of all the other Atlantic islands only the Canaries have revealed a similar prehistoric settlement. Colonized by the Guanches – apparently an ancient Berber tribe – perhaps as early as 1000 BC, the Canaries were subsequently visited by, and mixed with, Numidians, Phoenicians and Carthaginians.

Modern humans arrived on Crete from Asia Minor before 6000 BC, settling as agriculturists in the Knossos area. Back then, Crete was a woodland redolent of oak, cypress, cedar and fir, fertile at all altitudes. By around 2500 BC a number of 'Eteocretan' settlements adorned particularly the island's central region. Olive groves dignified lowland slopes, vineyards favoured sun-blessed valleys, and in all upland plains wheat thrived. Intensive sheep farming dotted hillsides, and salted mutton and wool abounded – Crete was quite the New Zealand of the ancient world. All of these activities produced copious surpluses for profitable export to mainland Hellas. Villages were large, indulging the characteristic 'add-on' architecture that had stone structures ultimately sporting dozens of rooms.

It was perhaps around this time that mainland Proto-Hellenic speakers were also establishing trading centres on Crete, marrying into the local aristocracy, or even invading. For by about 2000 BC the island's rulers were speaking a very early form of Greek; within centuries, these were the *Kouretes* of legend, the Hellenic Minoans mentioned on the Phaistos Disk. Crete was valued from Troy to Egypt for her fine pottery, bronze work and statuettes, gold jewellery, ivory carvings, stone seals and signets, and the Mediterranean's choicest wine. Syllabic writing was used – Europe's first writing and literature – introduced from the cosmopolitan Levant around 2000 BC. The Kouretes (called Minoans only as of the 1900s AD) created, between around 1900 and 1450 BC, Europe's first high civilization, with Knossos as Europe's first capital. Their ship-builders having developed the keel, bestowing mastery over the Mediterranean, their 'thalassocracy' or island empire by around 1600 BC came to dominate the Ægean and beyond, their goods exported to the ends of the known world, but mainly to Hellas, the Canaanite Levant and glorious Egypt.

Dynamic trade with other island Hellenes was only achieved once the eastern Carian intruders were conquered in the 'Battle of Naxos', commencing a robust commerce with Rhodes, then Kos, Samos and mainland Miletus in Asia Minor, as well as profitable custom with eminent Cyprus in the east. The Kouretes colonized, exploited and dominated most eastern Mediterranean islands at this time, assuring a monopoly on valued goods. Their Minoan culture influenced many peoples, with historic ripple effects that would eventually yield later Classical Greek culture. Not without signifi-cance was it believed in antiquity that it was in Crete – 'in the midst of the wine-dark sea', as Homer tells us – that Zeus was born. For Crete was Europe's island crucible.

What caused her demise? Egyptians write of the cessation of Cretan imports of olive oil and cedar – substances they required in the mummification industry – around 1500 BC. They also tell of floods and days of darkness when 'the sun appeared in the sky like the moon'.[12] This could well point to the eruption of Santorini's volcano, situated 110 km north of Crete. Around 1456 BC – a date suggested by radiocarbon analysis of a tree growing on Santorini when the cataclysm occurred – the volcano known as Stronghyli self-destructed in prehistoric Europe's most catastrophic eruption, devastating Santorini, burying the cliffside town of Akrotiri, and covering wide swathes of sea and land south and southeast in tephra, pumice and ash. (The explosion was four times greater than Krakatoa's.) The event doubtless weakened Minoan Crete's economy, though any immediate destruction would have been rather localized and limited.

Yet around 1450 BC most Cretan palaces (but for Knossos) and landed villas were also torched, indicating some sort of violent takeover coming from Knossos. Mainland Mycenæan Greek invaders may have been responsible in some way, as Mycenæan replaced Minoan culture nearly everywhere on the island. Some palaces were rebuilt but the economy and population collapsed. In unprecedented fashion, a militant society rose, centred at Knossos. One can assume there was an influx of mainland Greeks in large numbers. Knossos herself was destroyed by fire around 1375 BC, perhaps due to an earthquake. Soon the Mycenæans lost hold and the Cretan economy collapsed once again, this time beyond repair. It was the age of the 'Sea Peoples': Viking-like Danaans and their confederates who plundered and established new colonies on the islands and in the Levant.

During all this time, however, Crete's celebrated '100 cities' remained culturally active: the legendary Idomeneus of Crete is said to have raised many ships for the Troy campaign of approximately 1198 to 1188 BC. Trade continued, though the seas remained unsafe so long as no central authority like a Minos presumed to police them with a standing fleet. Gradually, Crete became a backwater, away from Phoenician trade routes now controlled from Syria. True prosperity didn't return until the first century BC when Crete became central to new Roman routes, whereupon she grew ever more important as trade increased between Egypt, the Levant, Cyprus, Asia Minor and powerful, wealthy, ravenous Rome. The dynamic continued until North Africa was lost to Arab hegemony, at which juncture Crete was even more prized by new trade demands: the island was contested in turn by Saracens, Byzantines, Genoese, Venetians, Turks, Greeks, even Germans. Crete's incorporation into the Greek nation occurred only in 1913.

BEYOND THE PILLARS OF HERCULES

As of the first millennium BC – soon after a group of Austronesian pioneers in double-hulled canoes had sailed east from Melanesia to settle Fiji, Tonga and Samoa and initiate a new culture that would eventually come be to known as Polynesian – Phoenicians were zealously colonizing North Africa's coastline; parts of the islands of Sicily and Sardinia; and southern Iberia (Spain). Having profited from the Assyrian empire throughout the ninth century BC – then at the height of its power, which secured its resources (especially silver, by then the main international medium of exchange) from the Phoenician Levant – by around 770 BC the Phoenicians were founding Gadir on an Atlantic island just off Iberia's mainland. With some historians suggesting she could even have been a trading port serving the British Isles and Atlantic seaboard already in the second millennium BC, Gadir rose to a great trading centre. Gadir's primary settlement stood on the northernmost island of Erytheia, but eventually ranged over three islands. (The earliest site is now Cádiz's old quarter; because of silting and sea-level change the three islands merged with the mainland, forming a large terrain just below the modern urban sprawl.)

Here the Phoenicians dominated the trade in tin, essential for the manufacture of bronze. Most tin came from the so-called Tin Islands – known in antiquity as the Cassiterides – which lay somewhere off the Atlantic coast. It's possible that the term denotes Britain's southwest and the Scillies: British tin deposits were being extensively worked throughout the second and first millennia BC.[13] Later, Greeks accessed a number of small marts on the southwestern coast (like Mount Batten in Plymouth Sound) where they traded for tin, copper and possibly gold. However, nothing in ancient sources or modern archæology supports the frequent claim that Cornwall was buzzing with Phoenician or Greek merchants.

These western and northern isles of Europe fascinated antiquity's voyagers and writers. It seems that even Iceland was sporadically visited at least from around 1000 BC.[14] The Greek Pytheas of Massalia (modern Marseille) claimed to have sailed six days north of Britain 'to the edge of the cosmos' and visited Thule – which some experts believe means Iceland – to witness the astronomical marvels there. Such a voyage was well within the technological capabilities of Orkney and Shetland sailors of around 300 BC.

At the time, Greeks knew little about what lay beyond the Pillars of Hercules – today's Strait of Gilbraltar – whence flowed much of their tin, amber and gold. It was Pytheas who introduced them to this unknown world, providing history's earliest writings about

Brittany, the British Isles and the North Sea's eastern islands and coasts around 300 years before the birth of Christ. Later Romans were equally rapt. Pliny the Elder: 'The historian Timæus says there is an island named Mictis lying inward six days' sail from Britain where tin is found, and to which the Britons cross in boats of osier covered with stitched hides.'[15] Pliny is drawn to isles yet more distant:

> The most remote of all those recorded is Thule, in which we have pointed out there are no nights at midsummer when the sun is passing through the sign of the Crab, and on the other hand no days at midwinter; indeed some writers think this is the case for periods of six months at a time without a break.

Three Roman coins were found on Iceland, at different times; it lends credence to the notion that Romans, too, might have landed.

For Romans possessed an astounding geographical knowledge. Pliny writes further of the '40 Orkneys, separated by narrow channels from each other, the 7 Shetlands, the 30 Hebrides, and between Ireland and Britain the Islands of Anglesea, Man, Rackling, Whitehorn, Dalkey and Bardsey . . .'.[16] Listing Pytheas as one of his sources, Pliny mentions the 96 islands of the 'Gallic Ocean' (probably the North Sea). Though the Frisian coastline of the Netherlands and Germany – antiquity's amber mart – lost many settlements during the third century BC because of a rising sea level, still at the time of Pliny roughly three centuries later the region lay scattered with hundreds of islands; many of these were to disappear over subsequent centuries with draining, reclamation and resettlement.

In the Indian Ocean during the first millennium BC, the indigenous Vedda people of Sri Lanka, with other ethnic groups, suffered several incursions of Sinhalese from southern India. The intruders settled Sri Lanka's northern plains and established there large city-kingdoms, mixing with the Veddas and others to create a separate Sinhalese identity. Vastly improved irrigation techniques rendered the region a breadbasket and society flourished. In the third century BC India's emperor Ashoka deputized his son Mahinda to convert Sri Lanka's Sinhalese ruler to Buddhism: Mahinda met the king on the island's holy mountain of Mihintale. After the ruler's conversion, Mahinda sent him several holy relics of Buddha's, among which were a footprint, eye tooth and branch from Buddha's sacred bo tree – the latter was immediately planted at the capital of Anu-radhapura alongside Mihintale. (The direct descendant of this bo tree, a venerated goal of pilgrims, still stands today, it is claimed.)

Over a period of many centuries Anuradhapura waxed to stupefying magnitude, one of Earth's largest and most extravagant complexes of shrines: one *dagoba* alone, the one constructed to house Buddha's footprint, was said to have measured some 80 m in height and 90 m in diameter. Sri Lanka's wealth, power, location and holy relics rendered the island one of the richest and most frequented in the first millennium AD. (Because the ruins of many of these great cities and shrines abound, the island is an archæo-logical treasure trove.) In later centuries the Tamil – Hindus from southern India – invaded in several waves and pugnaciously warred against the island's Sinhalese Buddhist rulers, destroying most of the island's rich patrimony. Long centuries of internal conflict then destroyed the irrigation systems, ruined the infrastructure, hindered trade and collapsed the society in general. Sri Lanka never regained her former glory.

By 3200 BC the Egyptians, principally in order to navigate against the Nile's current, had invented sails. The innovation allowed them also to access and trade with the isles of the eastern Mediterranean. One of the first goals was a small island just off the coastline of the Nile Delta, which became a modest port that worked in conjunction with the sheltered harbour behind it. Doubt-less frequented by the Minoans, later by the Phoenicians and others in their robust commerce with mighty Egypt, the small island yielded eventually to the Greeks, who assumed more of this trade and made the isle, Pharos, as well as the mainland port, one of their chief overseas stations. For his admiration of the northern island of Rhodes – then the wealthiest and most peaceful in the Ægean – Macedonian Alexander the Great (356–323 BC) renamed a much smaller inner-harbour islet Antirhodos after his conquest of Egypt in 331 BC. (The mainland port he made his Egyptian capital, which he renamed after himself: Alexandria.) On the much larger island a substantial, wealthy, smaller version of the mainland capital arose as an urban centre, connected with the mainland by an artificial causeway called the Heptastadion. And on a long and narrow spit of land jutting out east towards the rising sun, Alexander's Mace-donian successor in Egypt, Ptolemy Soter (367–283 BC), ordered the construction of an enormous lighthouse of stone: the Pharos.

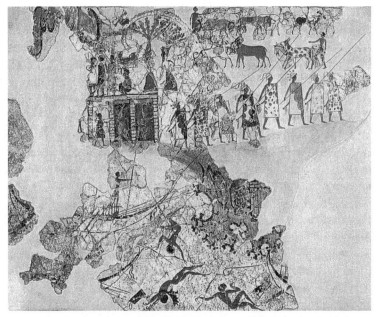

Shipwreck and armed warriors on an Ægean isle in the first half
of the second millenium BC.

It was Ptolemy I's son and successor, Ptolemy Philadelphus
(309–246 BC), who had his chief engineer and architect Sostratus of
Cnidus complete his father's dream between 280 and 247 BC – after
which the Pharos, the celebrated Lighthouse of Alexandria, came to
command the Egyptian capital's harbour. Around 130 m in height
and costing some 800 talents to construct, it served 'in connection
with the movement of ships at night, to show a beacon so as to give
warning of shoals and indicate the entrance to the harbour', as
Pliny wrote nearly 2,000 years ago.[17] The lighthouse was one of the
Seven Wonders of the Ancient World and it was claimed in antiquity that from 47 km away at sea one could see its fire. Greatly
damaged by two earthquakes in the 1300s, the Pharos's ruins disappeared in 1480 when Egypt's Sultan, cannibalizing the rubble,
constructed a fort on the terrain.

Ibiza had been established as a Phoenician centre by traders
from Gadir (modern Cádiz) around 750 BC – part of that island
network known as far as the Levantine coast, where Isaiah was
proselytizing for the Judæan god: 'Let them give glory unto the
Lord, and declare his praise in the islands' (42:12). A century later

Jeremiah would echo: 'Hear the word of the Lord, O ye nations, and declare it in the isles far off' (31:10); and Zephaniah repeated the call: '. . . and men shall worship him, every one from his place, even all the isles of the heathen' (2:11). By the sixth century BC, however, it was Carthage that was controlling Corsica, Sardinia and the Balearics, for in 574 BC Tyre on the Levantine coast had fallen to the Babylonians under Nebuchadnezzar and other rich trading cities there soon followed, meaning that the Phoenician colonies in the west were cut off, allowing Carthage to assume leadership over the western isles. Carthage now seized Ibiza, too, for her own empire. Taking control of all important trading routes in the western Mediterranean, Carthage then finally seized Gadir herself. From the sixth to the third centuries BC Carthage defended her control of Mediterranean trade, much of it island-based, against expanding Magna Græcia: the Greeks of southern Italy could never quite beat them.

Surely in antiquity the greatest island phenomena were the 6,000-odd isles and islets of the Greek homeland herself. Their history would be paradigmatic of island occupation in general. As Lawrence Durrell so poignantly attested, 'We shall never know, presumably, who the Greeks really were or really are; and any brief history of the ancient world only deepens the mystery.'[18] Product of the Ionian islands and coasts, Homer's *Iliad*, for one, sees life's primeval entity to be water – Oceanus – whose consort, Tethys, bore all subsequent gods. (A creation myth that differs significantly from mainlander Hesiod's.) Homer looked to the sea as both source and future, for this was the Greek island way.

'MANY FIRES BURN BELOW THE EARTH'

Prince Theseus of Athens was Hellas's first 'island retiree'. He had fought the Minotaur at Knossos, run off with Minos's virginal daughter Ariadne only to abandon her, then indulged a career of abducting one pretty damsel after another, from Helen to Persephone. In old age, however, he was allowed by King Lycomedes of Skyros in the central North Ægean to retire there. Yet Lycomedes was finally forced to have Theseus thrown into the sea once he tired of hearing those bawdy boasts of antiquity's Don Juan. A dangerous place, the Ægean: one of petty passions and bloodletting, of incomparable crimes and intoxicating charms. It is the island matrix.

Homer himself went to tiny Ios in the central Cyclades to die, they say. Many islands and mainland towns claim his birthplace; only Ios his deathplace. His 'tomb' adorns the northern flank of Mt Pirgos . . . 'a marvellous site where the wild grass rustles in the north wind and the weary climber, unpacking his lunch, turns his eye towards the East, towards Asia and the distant plains of Troy'.[19] Greek utopias often involved islands. Indeed, it became a classical commonplace. Much of this had to do with the commercial expansion of Miletus in Asia Minor with her many trading colonies at all points of the compass.

> Along these strands commodities flowed and with them knowledge of all kinds gleaned from the ends of the world – ancient mathematical and astronomic wisdom from the civilizations of Babylon and Egypt and a new awareness of anthropology and geography from the more barbarous regions. The Ionian Greeks were in a unique position to begin to piece together a new world view based not on myth but on natural science.[20]

Pythagoras (*c.* 570–*c.* 495 BC), greatest of the early philosophers, was born and raised on the eastern Ægean isle of Samos. The father of Western medicine, Hippocrates (*c.* 460–*c.* 370 BC), was born on Kos in the Dodecanese, just 4 km off Asia Minor's coast. Through the Dodecanese ranged the pre-Socratics, 'who first posed questions we are still trying to answer satisfactorily'.[21] To Metrodorus (*fl.* fourth century BC) from 904-sq-km Chios is attributed the aphorism, 'It is unnatural in a large field to have only one shaft of wheat, and in the infinite universe only one living world.' In the far west, Empedocles (*c.* 490–*c.* 430 BC) – hailing from Agrigentum, a Greek city in Sicily, only 130 km from Europe's greatest volcano, Etna – was among the first to acknowledge the creative importance of volcanism. Not fearing it as a destroyer but lauding it as a builder of lands, Empedocles taught that the coming together and parting of four primary substances – air, fire, earth, water – underlay the physical world's great diversity: 'Many fires burn below the earth', he declared.[22]

Further islanders excelled. Aristarchus of Samos (310–*c.* 230 BC) placed the sun at the centre of the known universe. One of the Library of Alexandria's most famous directors was Apollonius of Rhodes (*d.* after 246 BC), a Macedonian Egyptian who had lived on

Rhodes for some years; another was Aristarchus of Samothrace (*c.* 220–*c.* 143 BC) from this famous island in the northeast Ægean. Ænesidemus of Knossos from Crete, lecturer and philospher at Alexandria around 44 BC, wrestled with the relativity of mortal perceptions and the impossibility of true knowledge; he was one of Cleopatra's favourites.

Only 18 km off the Asia Minor coast, Rhodes held one of the Wonders of the World – the Colossus, a statue of the sun god Helios. Erected by the conquering Macedonian Demetrius to commemorate his successful siege of Rhodes, his architect Chares of Lindos, starting in 302 BC, took twelve years to raise it. Wholly in bronze to a height of 35 m, it became a landmark for all vessels, an icon of Rhodes. Its exact location and stance still a subject of debate, the Colossus stood around 60 years until an earthquake in 227 BC felled it – onto land, not into the harbour. (So it probably never straddled the entrance.)

> According to rumours and legends Helios was supposed to have been displeased with the statue, and his oracle forbade any attempt at restoration. No Rhodian therefore dared touch it once it fell and the huge thing lay there for nine hundred years until AD 635, when it was taken off by Saracen marauders and sold to the Jewish merchants of the Levant.[23]

Another Wonder of the World, the Temple of Hera once blessed Samos; today, only a single column remains. Another of Samos's most famous sons was Polycrates, who enthroned the island as 'queen of the seas' in 535 BC. A pirate-king who warred for the fun of it, and a great patron of the arts, Polycrates assembled a fleet of 150-oar galleys and a standing army of 1,000 archers. Always victorious, he had the Temple of Hera erected in honour of his patron goddess, the sister-wife of Zeus. Polycrates was finally lured to Ionia, where his enemies and victims flayed then crucified him.

The small 'home island' of Ægina in the Saronic Gulf, only 27 km from Athens, once rivalled the celebrated metropolis in seapower and riches. She only submitted to Athens in 458 BC, never to regain her erstwhile status; Athens's destruction of Ægina was complete and all inhabitants were deported. Athens left behind a ghost island. Once part of the Minoan thalassocracy, Ægina then slumbered for many centuries. (But history would call on Ægina again.)

Cyprus, 'that most Greek of Greek islands', the essential link between the cosmopolitan Canaanite culture of the early second millennium BC and ancient Hellas, was first part of the Hittite Empire then home to merchant Minoans and settling Mycenæans who came to dominate.[24] She then experienced Phoenician settlement on her south coast as of the eighth century BC. A century of Assyrian rule followed, then domination by Egypt and finally by Persia from 545 BC onwards. Greek rule over the island was finally secured two centuries later by Alexander the Great, and the Macedonian Ptolemies who had assumed control from Alexandria then allowed Cyprus to enjoy the full benefits of eastern Mediterranean Hellenization until the island was subsumed into the Roman Republic in 58 BC. In AD 395, with the division of the Roman Empire, Cyprus came under the administration of the Eastern or Byzantine Empire where she would remain for many centuries until the crusades of the Middle Ages.

Rome inherited by conquest the island legacy of Carthage, Magna Græcia and Britannia – by the first century BC Rome was controlling all the isles of the Mediterranean and many of those in the North Sea. On many the Romans integrated, their customs being similar. On others they changed island culture profoundly. Over the centuries on Britannia, for example, not only did Rome reform all society into one of planned towns, walls, roads, stone architecture and organized administration with writing and coinage, but the Romans most likely also brought the first oats and apples and certainly introduced parsnips, turnips, carrots, leeks, cherries, walnuts, vines and sweet chestnuts.

The military use of small islands was appreciated by some wary generals. For one thing, isles could guarantee personal safety, away from a bow's reach. In November of 43 BC, for example, Octavian (63 BC – AD 14), Marc Antony (83–30 BC) and Lepidus (*c.* 89–*c.* 13 BC) met on an eyot in Bononia (Bologna) – 'to exchange enmity for friendship' in full view of their respective armies – where they spent two days in historic discussion, agreeing on dividing the Empire among them.

Islands were the favoured turf of many Roman rulers. Emperor Augustus, the former Octavian, had fallen in love with Capreæ (Capri) and preferred to holiday there; he had twelve ornate villas, each on a balconied cliffside, constructed for himself, with gardens of ilex and olive trees, and he dubbed the island *Apragopolis* or

'Bumsville' for its indolent lifestyle.[25] Augustus's stepson and successor Tiberius (42 BC – AD 37) was so enamoured of this island that he made Capreæ the capital of the Roman Empire from AD 27 to 37. Roman explorers also went in search of island realms. In the first century AD Julius Agricola (AD 40–93) sent his personal fleet on a voyage around Scotland, during one stage of which Demetrius of Tarsus, a Greek scholar, accompanied the explorers then met the Greek biographer and philosopher Plutarch (c. AD 46–c. 120) later at Delphi to whom he related his adventures in the remote Caledonian waters. Plutarch's published version thrilled young and old alike and sold like hot cakes.

LATE ANTIQUITY

By at least 1,600 years ago Barbados, the easternmost island of the Caribbean archipelago, was home to Amerindians from South America. In the Pacific, the Japanese were forming a more unified society as descendants of the indigenous Jōmon and immigrant Yayoi peoples. Immediately north of Japan, the great island of Sakhalin supported indigenous Ainu in the south, Oroks in the central region, and Nivkhs in the north. Melanesians had settled most islands of Near Oceania, Micronesians had occupied the far-flung islands and atolls north of the equator, and Polynesians were beginning their early forays to more distant isles in their great double-hulled canoes.

Inhabited since ancient times, the 33 islands of the archipelago that comprises Bahrain in the Persian Gulf – where there were always plentiful fish, fresh water, rare shells and pearls for trading – had been taken over by the Parthians, who then began constructing military garrisons to secure the rich southern trade route. In the third century AD the Sassanids replaced the Parthians and held the islands until the advent of Islam three centuries later.

Settlement of the islands of the Indian Ocean commenced at least 40,000 years ago, and would continue well into the nineteenth century when the last few deserted isles were occupied.[26] Around AD 400, Austronesians sailing from Java arrived at hitherto uninhabited Madagascar by way of Sri Lanka and the Maldives, both of which had already been settled for centuries by southern Indian migrants. They brought with them their breadfruit, banana and taro, staples which survive today. The Malagasy are black, but their features are Austronesian: they resemble Polynesians more than they do the Africans only 300 km away. By then all the largest Indian Ocean islands were settled. Some of the small chains of islands, like Socotra (four continental islands lying around 240 km east of the Horn of Africa), had known occupation for tens of thousands of years, yet now were enjoying a robust mercantilism that was transforming hitherto remote islands into dynamic trading centres. Africa's east-coast islands had been settled by Bantu speakers, who would go on to occupy Madagascar's west coast. And the Nicobar Islands and Andaman Islands in the far northeast, south of the Bay of Bengal, had been settled by primitive hunter-gatherers who resisted all contact with the outside world (and would do until the 1800s).

Islanders on large islands – Madagascar, Sri Lanka, Sumatra, Java – lived off the land. Those on small islands lived off the sea. Yet for all islanders the sea was a vital food source and link to the outside world. Throughout history, until the advent of modern road, rail and air travel, sea routes have been far more important than land ways. And Indian Ocean populations – whether on islands or a mainland – always found maritime trade easier and far more profitable than hinterland trade. Over time this created a robust and dynamic synergism of mercantile voyaging and migration, similar to the Pacific's. Coastal dwellers looked out to the sea for sustenance, engendering networks of insular and continental intercourse that connected and shrank the Indian Ocean's vastness. Monsoon winds sped lateen-rigged vessels through the Maldives and Laccadives to Africa's Comoros and the Seychelles, or to Sumatra and her western archipelago of Simeulue, Nias, Kepulauan Batu, Kepulauan Mentawai, down to tiny Enggano before reaching Java.

By late antiquity, long-distance trade between east and west was thriving, as extensive seafaring enlivened the coastlines of Southeast Asia, the Malay Archipelago, Burma, India and Sri Lanka. 'India was the natural link between these two great spheres of marine activity.'[27]

Only 35 km off the coast of northern Tanzania lies Zanzibar, the tourists' 'dream island', clearly visible from the mainland: a green, fruit-filled tropical isle rich with copra and cloves and embraced by coral reefs in clean aquamarine waters.[28] A main attraction for millennia has been the island's store of fresh water in deep limestone caverns. For as long as 2,500 years Arab dhows would sail with seasonal winds south bearing beads, copper utensils, carpets, cloth, tiles, salted fish and china to trade there – east Africa's island emporium – for ivory, rhino horns, spices and sturdy mangrove poles (for construction). Then, after two to three months of refitting in the heat and humidity, the Arab crews would sail home again, riding the vigorous southwest monsoon. It is assumed that Zanzibar's earliest settlers were mainland Africans. Zanzibar and her northeast neighbour Pemba are first recorded in a Greek text from AD 60. Persians established there the first non-African settlement in 701.

As antiquity drew to a close, islands and eyots were assuming more centralized roles in the new societies developing in western Europe. The Celtic Parisii's eyot hub of Île de la Cité in the middle of the Seine was replaced by a temporary Roman camp which, in turn, was superceded by a higher and healthier Left Bank settlement that became Lutetia (modern Paris). When attacked by Huns, however, subsequent Roman rulers moved back onto the isle. Later Merovingian ruler Clovis (c. 466–511) built a fortified palace on the eyot which in the year of his death became the capital of the Merovingian realm of Neustria. It was from this small island that all of northern France was ruled.

The Celts of Scotland were doing much the same: the Strathclyde kingdom – the Brythonic Ystrad Clud in the Hen Ogledd or 'Old North' – had their capital at illustrious Dùn Breatainn (Dumbarton Rock) on a mountainous crag of an eyot at the east-bank mouth of the River Leven where it flows into the Clyde estuary. Tiny Iona, only 1.6 km off the coast of the island of Mull in the Inner Hebrides, hosted as of 563 the exiled Irish monk Columba's monastery which eventually brought about the Christian conversion of Scotland's Picts in the late sixth century and that of Northumbria's Anglo-Saxons in 635. In this archipelago, too, the sea unites, and from the landing of Ulster Scots in Argyll in the late fifth century the west of Scotland – separated from the east by mountains – identified with and looked to Ireland, not to lowland Celts or later Saxons, Danes and Normans. Culturally and ethnically, the western Highlands and all the Western Isles long remained an Irish colony.

In Wales, the island of Môn (later Anglesey, from Norse 'Ongull's Isle'), which had been the Druidic capital of most western Celts, felt the full force of Roman might, then came to profit from the empire's civilizing ways – its termination in the fifth century AD only brought invasion by Irish pirates who attempted permanent colonization. Three kilometres off Wales's Llyn Peninsula lies Enlli (Bardsey), inhabited since the Neolithic and, as of the fifth century AD, a refuge for Christians, who erected a small monastery on the 1 by 1.6 km isle; St Cadfan arrived from Brittany in 516 and built St Mary's Abbey, whose holy relics enticed pilgrims from throughout the British Isles for centuries. The tidal isle of Lindisfarne off the northeast coast of England, like Iona in Scotland an early Christian centre, was originally called Medcaut in Old Welsh, probably 'Healing (Isle)' for her renowned medicinal herbs; her monastery, founded by the Irish St Aidan in 635, became the chief centre for converting England's north as well as parts of Mercia. St Cuthbert, Northumbria's patron saint, was first a monk there and later became the Lindisfarne monastery's abbot. All these small islands exerted a great influence on the culture and subsequent history of the British Isles. All suffered tremendously from later Norse raids, too, beginning at the end of the eighth century, and from subsequent Danish colonization, mixing peoples and altering ancient ways and trade routes – ever the fate of vulnerable isles. The sustained island warfare that lasted far too long also brought settlers, traders, merchants, a new people . . . Scandinavia's legacy to Britain and Ireland.

In the Pacific, after more than a 1,000-year hiatus, Samoans set off around AD 300 to cross 3,000 km of open ocean to colonize the Marquesas Islands in eastern Polynesia. Here the founding population prospered, and about AD 500 their descendants left to colonize the eastern Tuamotus, the Gambiers (Mangareva), Pitcairn, Henderson and then, around 700, Rapa Nui (Easter Island). Over these two centuries the first Marquesan departees had transformed themselves into a distinct Southeastern Polynesian people.[29] Back in the Marquesas Islands, however, the founding population was developing into Central Eastern Polynesians, who had already begun further voyages: northwest to Hawai'i and southwest to the Society Islands, including Tahiti.

'THRONED ON HER HUNDRED ISLES!'

From the nucleus of a Viking capital in the Baltic Sea, Gotland had become a great trading centre. Plying Russian rivers, Gotlanders followed the Volga, Don and Dneiper to the Black Sea and from there to Constantinople – founding along the way both Kiev and

Smolensk. All through the Middle Ages, Gotland was an independent state, a German and Scandinavian marketplace for merchants who traded skins for Eastern gold and jewellery. The island of Gotland became the King of the Baltic, her high-walled city of Visby with its many towers and churches an expression of insular power and wealth.

As long-distance trade developed further in the Indian Ocean, certain islands, by virtue of location, assumed new economic and cultural importance.[30] In religion, Sri Lanka became in the first millennium AD the principal junction of Islam, Hinduism and Buddhism and created a unique culture as a result: not only spices were carried on vessels powered by the monsoon winds, but also life-changing ideas. Further west, by the 1200s, the trade between the Middle East and the Maldives and Laccadives, which for well over a thousand years had a culture determined by Hinduism and Southeast Asian Buddhism, had grown so influential that Islam now replaced both these faiths there. Islam also displaced all native beliefs from Socotra to the Comoros Islands, due to active trade with the Persian Gulf, the wealthy and powerful Arabian Peninsula and the Red Sea. Out of this developed, by around 1100 if not earlier, a wholly new Afro-Asian culture conveyed by the hybrid Swahili lingua franca. Persians, Arabs and, most importantly, Africans themselves – through island and coastal trade and settlement – altered traditional economies, introduced a new prosperity, embraced a new faith and created a new oceanic society.

In the Malay Archipelago, tribal groups had yielded in time to the first island kingdoms, which came to be called the 'Indianized States' since they closely resembled India's governance. On Sumatra, from the seventh to fourteenth centuries, the Buddhist kingdom of Srivijaya flourished, eventually controlling the Malay Peninsula and West Java, but the Hindu kingdom of Majapahit in eastern Java wrested away control and came to claim nominal allegiance from most other kings in the archipelago. By the twelfth century Islam had arrived, and by the end of the 1500s this had largely replaced Hinduism on Sumatra and Java. Some islands – notably Bali – never replaced Hinduism with Islam, but today Hindus represent only 2 per cent of the Indonesian population. (Today, 88 per cent of Indonesians are Muslim, 9 per cent Christian.)

The Arabian Sea had been well known to the ancient world, from Africa's Horn to India's southern tip. After Rome's decline it fell to the Arabs, and from this body of water – especially with Islam's rise in the seventh century – the great Muslim religious and economic expansion took sail. Arab merchants plied their dhows to India, Burma, Malaya, Indonesia and even China. They also ranged the East African coast, not only bringing, as early as the ninth century, tales celebrating the island exploits of legendary Sinbad the Sailor, but also imbuing all Africans they encountered with their own reverence for the word of Muhammad. But long before them, other traders had brought word of the tale of Jesus of Nazareth, and this had soon inspired the same sort of island monasticism one could find from Greece to western Ireland. As early as the first millennium AD Ethiopia's largest lake and the source of the Blue Nile, Lake Tana, boasted perhaps over 30 islands on which as many as nineteen Christian monasteries were housing treasures of the Ethiopian Church. About these isles were spun fantastic tales of the Virgin Mary and early Church Fathers, and still today all Ethiopians revere the isles deeply as pilgrimage sites. Until the twentieth century most were unknown to the outside world.

In the North Atlantic, islands of legend were becoming islands of fact. Already in the early sixth century AD Irish monk St Brendan had undertaken an expedition in a hide-covered *curragh* in which he and his hearty Celtic companions, searching for solitude in a 'promised land of the saints', came upon Iceland and perhaps sailed even further to discover distant Newfoundland.[31] Irish monks eventually settled on Iceland around 700. Some 160 years later, when Norsemen island-hopping through Orkney, Shetland and the Faroes arrived at Iceland only to find that the Irish monks had vacated shortly before, they settled and remained.

When Erik the Red was banished from Iceland in 982, he sailed with a small group westwards and came upon Greenland's southern fjords, where he remained in exile for three summers before returning to Iceland to boast of this 'Green Land' – so the legend – in order to encourage settlement.[32] At the same time, his son Leif Eriksson had been told of the Icelandic trader Bjarni Herjólfsson, who had been caught in a storm and blown west of Greenland in 981 where he discovered a hitherto unknown land. It took Leif around twenty years before he was able to purchase Bjarni's vessel and set off to retrace the route, voyaging along the coasts of the mainland and islands of North America until arriving first at Labrador. He settled on Newfoundland's northern coast, which he

named Vinland for the wild grapes he claimed to have found growing there – which might or might not have been true. (Today's
northern Newfoundland is far too cold for viticulture.) Several
settlements resulted. In 1963 archæologists located the site of one
of these Norse settlements at L'Anse aux Meadows near Newfoundland's northern tip. For unknown reasons it had been
abandoned after only a few years of occupation.

Subsequent centuries had discrete groups of Norse cattle- and
sheep-farmers occupying Greenland's southern fjords and the
southwest coastland around Nuuk – Godthaab, today's administrative capital – where they would also fish and hunt. (Some of these
same farmers were later the ones who briefly settled Labrador and
Newfoundland.) In this way, Greenland was integrated into the
Danish-Norwegian realm. Roughly when the Norse were settling
southern Greenland, the Inuit from Canada were occupying northern Greenland – descendants of the 'Thule' culture who, over the
following centuries, ranged southwards along both coasts to
become the ancestors of all native Greenlanders. By the 1400s the
Norse colonies had expired because of the Little Ice Age, worsened
communication with the homeland and soil degradation and
erosion due to overgrazing. Only the Inuit remained, who for two
centuries pursued in harsh peace their caribou, whales, seals and
fish. At the same time, northwestern European whalers began
frequenting Greenland and bartering with the Inuit for their walrus
and narwhal tusks.

The deltaic isles of Venice – 117 small islands in the Venetian
Lagoon along the Adriatic Sea in Italy's northeast – were now ac-
complishing what Crete had accomplished before and what Britain
would achieve from the sixteenth to nineteenth centuries: an island
empire, which Lord Byron (1788–1824) would later laud: 'Where
Venice sat in state, throned on her hundred isles!'[33] Venice's traditional foundation is dated to the dedication of the church of San
Giacomo on the Rialto islet in AD 421. By the eighth century, after
growing trade with Constantinople, the island dwellers elected their
first *dux*, who here came to be known as the Doge. Charlemagne
(*c.* 742–814) agreed with Constantinople's Nicephorus I in 810 to
acknowledge Venice as Byzantine territory, bestowing trading rights
along the Adriatic that enriched the city further. By 828 Venice had
secured from Alexandria the relics of St Mark, which were now
deposited in the new basilica dedicated to the evangelist: pilgrims

flocked to Venice from far and wide and the city's fame and prestige soared. Once the Adriatic's Dalmatian pirates were expunged – just as Minos of Crete had crushed the Carian pirates 2,600 years earlier – island Venice was free to rule the seas and she soon developed into a rich and powerful city-state. The new Republic of Venice began appropriating foreign towns, first along the Adriatic, then further afield, to guarantee her trade routes, acquire essential wheat and continue her course of self-enrichment. The Fourth Crusade in 1204 veritably drowned Venice's coffers when Constantinople herself was sacked and plundered. As the Byzantine Empire weakened, Venice thrust forth to assume an even greater role in the Mediterranean.

By the end of the 1200s – when, in island Japan, the Kamakura Shogunate was successfully repulsing the two attempted Mongol invasions of 1274 and '81; when, west of Taiwan, Han Chinese of the Southern Song Dynasty began settling the 90 small islands of the Penghu Archipelago; when Hainan under the Yuan Dynasty became an independent province; when, in the Caribbean, chiefs of the native Taino and Ciboney peoples were receiving and distributing tributes in communities as large as 3,000; and when New Zealand, the Kermadecs, Lord Howe and Norfolk Island were receiving their first Polynesian settlers – the Republic of Venice was the region's superpower, Europe's most prosperous city. Commanding a fleet of over 3,300 ships and 36,000 sailors, Venice had each wealthy family now vying to erect the most sumptuous palace on pilings in this man-made archipelago, and medieval 'skyscrapers' filled with gold, silver, tapestries and paintings became the talk of all Europe. Her culture, architecture, administration and finances were emulated from London to the Levant. Venice was the New York of the Middle Ages: indeed, the greatest island power since Minoan Crete.

Sicily had been an important, if disunited, insular force to reckon with in the Mediterranean since her colonization by Greeks around 750 BC, home to many of Magna Græcia's greatest heroes, philosophers, poets and scientists, and later the local granary of Rome. Conquered by Arabs in AD 965, the island was in Norman control by 1072 and by 1130 the Kingdom of Sicily was united, prosperous and politically potent – indeed, it is claimed that she was then even richer than the Kingdom of England. The extinction of the Norman line led to Sicily's crown being passed to German

Hohenstaufens. The Holy Roman Emperor Frederick II – king of Germany, Italy, Burgundy and Jerusalem (by virtue of marriage) – maintained his royal court in Palermo from around 1220 until his death in 1250; it was one of Europe's wealthiest, most powerful and most cultured courts. The Hohenstaufens' continual conflict with the Papacy, however, led to the Pope crowning the French prince as king of both Sicily and Naples. A succession of wars to expel the French lasted until 1302, when Hohenstaufen Frederick III finally regained the crown as sole king of Sicily. The island remained an independent kingdom until 1409, when she became part of the Crown of Aragon, the powerful Mediterranean thalassocracy that ruled from eastern Spain and southwestern France.

On the other side of the globe, China was discovering islands at last. Of course the Chinese had been using coastal vessels for millennia, but their earnest voyaging began only around the time Charlemagne was ruling much of western Europe. By the ninth century, Chinese navigators were familiar with the Gulf of Aden and coast of Somalia. It is evident that Zanzibar and even Madagascar were known to Chinese sailors in the eleventh century. In the 1290s the Venetian Marco Polo (1254–1324) was amazed by the size of China's ocean-voyaging merchant vessels that, with a crew of 300, could carry up to 6,000 baskets of pepper. China never waxed a great maritime power, however, staying centralized, inward-looking and distrustful of foreigners and their ways. Only in the early 1400s, two generations before Columbus's birth, did China embark on major exploratory expeditions. Admiral Zheng He (1371–1435) of the fleet of Ming emperor Yung Lo (1360–1424) and two successors, between 1405 and 1433, led seven separate expeditions that visited 37 countries: along the coasts of Indochina, the Indian Ocean, Persian Gulf, Red Sea and East Africa. But Yung Lo's later successors didn't share his vision and so potential trade routes fell into the hands of western visionaries, enriching Portuguese, Spaniards, Dutch, French and Britons instead and changing the course of world history.

'THERE WERE SO MANY ISLANDS'

In the 1400s – when 800 km east of New Zealand the Māori finally completed the Polynesian settlement of the Pacific with their occupation of the Chathams – the history of islands took a fateful twist.

Europe had generally ignored the Atlantic, until then the purview of isolated Celtic and Norse traders, settlers and monks. Mainland Europe looked south and east for markets and profit – their 'true' ocean was still the Mediterranean. All trade before the late 1400s remained eastern trade: through the *Mare Nostrum* to the inland Silk Road, or east and southeast to the Arab lands and India. Sailing west to reach the east had been tried several times, however, and it now seemed a sensible recourse in the face of violent opposition to Christian merchants intruding on a perceived Muslim monopoly.

It was therefore the more aggressive Muslim empire of the 1400s that was compelling enterprising Europeans to seek – using new maritime technology – safe trade routes to India and points east, now unencumbered by powerful China which had withdrawn from exploration nine years after Yung Lo's death. Already in 1416, Portugal's King John I (1357–1433) and his son Prince Henry 'the Navigator' (1394–1460) had set up a school of navigation, then two years later had sent explorers João Gonçalves Zarco, Tristão Vaz Teixeira and Bartolomeu Perestrelo to explore the western ocean. Some 965 km southwest of Lisbon they came across Porto Santo Island and then, under a massive cloud 43 km away to the southwest, a large island filled with enormous trees – so many that Zarco named the island after them: Madeira, Portuguese for 'wood'. (The Madeira group were probably Pliny the Elder's 'Purple Islands', only rediscovered in 1418 and 1419.) Wishing to establish a settlement on Madeira, Zarco encharged one of his lieutenants to burn a clearing, whereupon the officer proceeded to torch the entire island; the conflagration raged for seven long years. Colonization commenced in 1425 and thus, long before Christopher Columbus's (1451–1506) historic first voyage to the west, Madeira was already a major sugar importer for Europe.

By 1487 Portugal had reached the Cape of Good Hope. Whereupon it all opened up. 'Only after 1492 can we speak of planetary empires, spanning whole oceans.'[34] Cartographer and navigator Columbus, too, realized that Europe would be cut off forever from Eastern markets unless she turned her attention westward, across the unknown Atlantic, to reach the riches of the East by a route over which the Muslim empire had no control. Only once he had made this clear to Spain's King Ferdinand V (1452–1516) and Queen Isabella (1451–1504), with promises of untold riches, did he get his backing to 'discover' these western isles. Christian proselytizing also played a crucial role, especially for Isabella who personally financed Columbus's three ships in a celebratory wave of encouragement for having just 'cleansed' Spain of her heathen Moors and Jews.

It took several centuries to depopulate, repopulate and then overpopulate the islands of the Caribbean. A tale of bravado and bravery, yes, but mostly of bloodshed – with a fair portion of greed, power and passion thrown in. In the end, individual island fates flourished and fell under the famous and fiendish who came to call them home.

The Bahamas, first settled by the Taíno people around 500 years before Columbus's fateful arrival, over time had yielded to the Lucayans who, by the end of the fifteenth century, numbered some 20,000 to 30,000 souls. Europe's first footfall occurred here – most experts believe it happened on San Salvador – on 12 October 1492. The Lucayans were peaceful, gentle and handsome of features and proportions. They occupied all of the Bahamas, and the related tribes of Arawaks and Taínos filled Cuba, Jamaica and Hispaniola. In contrast, the Caribs to the east and south were cannibal warriors.

> They frequently raided the Bahamas, arriving secretly by night, carrying off men, women, and children in canoes. The males were mutilated, tortured, and eaten. The women were kept for breeding purposes. At any time without warning this terrible danger could descend on the Lucayans from the sea.[35]

Yet who embodied the greater danger? Within 25 years of Spain's intrusion not one Lucayan remained alive – for almost immediately Columbus had enslaved all he had found, who then died of their harsh treatment and the Old World diseases against which they had no immunity.

Still believing he was in the Indies – that is, the Malay Archipelago – Columbus sailed from the Bahamas south to Cuba and Hispaniola (modern Haiti and the Dominican Republic) in search of gold, his chief objective. Hispaniola was volcanic – which the Bahamas are not – and did contain gold, the Taíno there being much like the Lucayans, gentle and peaceloving. Columbus and his successors worked, starved and whipped them to near-extinction. Perhaps around 300,000 Taínos had welcomed Columbus's arrival; by 1550 fewer than 500 remained. The Spaniards also raided the Lucayans of other Bahamian islands to work the gold fields of Hispaniola – they died just as quickly. In the end, a ship was despatched to scout the islands for any sign of life at all: after three years of searching only eleven islanders had been found.

Columbus was all but oblivious to his intrusion's effect on the Caribbean peoples. He raved about their isles instead, calling them

> very lovely and green and fertile . . . The singing of little birds is such that it seems that a man could never wish to leave this place; the flocks of parrots darken the sun, and there are large and small birds of so many different kinds and so unlike ours, that it is a marvel. There are, moreover, trees of a thousand types, all with their various fruits and all scented, so that it is a wonder.[36]

Columbus couldn't fathom the sheer plenitude of one group: 'There were so many islands I scarce knew to which one I should go.'[37] So he named them for St Ursula and her 11,000 devotees: the Virgin Islands.

Between 1499 and 1505 as many as eleven small Spanish fleets followed Columbus, commencing colonization. The Portuguese-designed caravels left Spain with summer winds south to the Canaries, then west to the Caribbean; when homeward bound, they would ride the winds to the northern Azores, then cross back to Spain. After this, Spain sought her gold from the Aztecs of Central America and Incas of South America. By the mid-1500s the capitalistic, imperialistic and missionary enterprise – one of history's greatest and bloodiest – had elevated Spain to Europe's richest and most powerful nation. By then, however, the Caribbean islands were as good as forgotten, mere ports of call for gold-laden galleons on their way home. Many lay silent as the grave – true ghost islands.

Five years after Columbus had embarked on his first voyage, Vasco da Gama (c. 1469–1524) sailed from Lisbon to India – eastwards, opposing Columbus's route, and opening up at last to his Portuguese patrons the resources not only of Africa and the Indies, but of the islands further east, the 'Spice Islands', as well as the Far East, including Taiwan (which in 1544 the Portuguese named *Ilha Formosa* or 'Beautiful Island') and Japan. Sailing westwards in 1499, the Italian Amerigo Vespucci (1454–1512) extolled in terms similar to Columbus's the Atlantic seaboard and islands of South America, which he was exploring until 1502 for King Manuel 1 of Portugal: 'I thought I must be near the Earthly Paradise'.[38]

England had hardly ignored this maritime expansion. In 1497 Giovanni Caboto of Venice (John Cabot, *c.* 1450– *c.* 1499) left Bristol on commission from King Henry VII 'to sail to all parts, regions and coasts of the eastern, western and northern sea' and here, having followed Erik the Red's route to Greenland, he rediscovered the island of Newfoundland. Soon Newfoundland's abundant fisheries were being robustly exploited by Europeans, especially the Basques, the Old World's most intrepid fishermen.

1500S AND 1600S

The floodgates burst open. In the Dodecanese – that group of twelve larger and 150 smaller isles west of southern Asia Minor – where the Venetians, Genoese and Knights Hospitaller had ruled for two centuries or more, the Turks seized Rhodes in 1522 and the rest of the group one year later, forcing the Knights Hospitaller to flee to Malta – which Charles I of Spain (1500–1558) then deeded to them in 1530. (The Hospitallers held Malta until Napoleon's invasion in 1798.) Under the Turks the Dodecanese flourished and even came to be known as the 'Privileged Islands' because of generous tax exemptions and other privileges bestowed by Suleiman the Magnificent (1494–1566). In stark contrast, in 1537 the Turks landed 30,000 troops on Corfu to murder and ravage, departing with 15,000 slaves.

Even more radical island changes befell those of the New World, Indian Ocean and Malay Archipelago. Portugal and Spain controlled Europe's foreign trade well into the seventeenth century, their galleons loaded to the gunwales on six- to eight-month voyages to the Philippines, Japan, China and especially the East Indies (modern Indonesia). But England, the Netherlands and France finally made their move. England incorporated her East India company in 1660, followed two years later by the Netherlands.

European expansion on this unprecedented global scale was a product of new maritime technology and navigational knowledge, combined with the psychological and economic imperatives of developing nation-states in search of new domains, particularly the riches of India and China. At heart, however, lay the 'search for Eden' – a phenomenon whose roots lay in a complex of European, Arabic and Indian philosophical traditions.[39]

During the 1500s the Indian Ocean had still been a Muslim demesne. But gradually here, too, Portuguese, English, Dutch, French and Danes began exploratory navigations, followed by more active trade in the 1600s.[40] At first, Europeans discreetly dominated the East African islands and coasts, hardly influencing the deep-rooted Islamic and Swahili cultures of the locals. France then assumed the most aggressive role in the remote islands, colonizing by the end of the 1600s the uninhabited Seychelles, Diego Garcia, Rodrigues, Mauritius and La Réunion. European settlers brought their slaves with them from India, the Comoros, Madagascar and Mozambique, and within two generations these slaves – far out-numbering their mostly white French masters – converted to Christianity as they developed various African-French Creole languages particular to each island or group. Likewise, as of the 1600s in India, Sri Lanka and the Malay Archipelago, the Portuguese and Dutch were similarly active, but wanting France's so egregious cultural impact: for Portuguese and Dutch colonists were far out-numbered by native Indians, Ceylonese and Malays. No new languages arose here – though some pidgins briefly flourished – and only isolated Christian churches rose. Sri Lanka felt Portugal's power most keenly, as did India's Goa and Kerala where local tra-ditions integrated Christianity and Portuguese music, vocabulary and proper names – still evident in the twenty-first century.

In the early 1500s the Portuguese had claimed both Zanzibar and Pemba, then stayed for almost 200 years. Finally they were evicted by Arabs from Oman who then held dominion for two cen-turies. Zanzibar's main economic attraction was her slave market, and the island grew rich on human flesh. The French and Spanish, for example, populated Mauritius as well as South American plan-tations with Zanzibar-bought chattel, a trade that ceased only in 1873 because of British objections. (Britain felt her competitors were enjoying an unfair economic advantage.) Once the slave mar-ket crashed, Zanzibar fell back on her cloves and prospered further: the nineteenth century saw clove plantations established throughout Zanzibar and Pemba and most of the world's cloves today still come from these two islands in the Indian Ocean.

Discovered by the Portuguese in 1505, Mauritius was used as a convenient calling for fresh water and food on long voyages to the East Indies, yet she was never settled. Annexed by the Dutch in 1598, she was eventually abandoned in 1710, and several years later the French East India Company announced here their new 'Île de France'. France now founded a colony and, using slaves from Madagascar and Africa, began clearing the forests in order to establish sugar cane plantations. Forever after, sugar was king. In 1810 the British attacked and stole France's investment, then carried on producing sugar. When the plantation owners were compelled to free their slaves in 1835, to maintain production indentured Indians were imported on terms hardly better than slavery – a wage of roughly one US dollar a month. (The same was happening on Pacific islands at this time.) Before the 1600s Mauritius had been uninhabited; today, her French, Indians, Chinese and Creoles reside in one of the planet's most densely populated nations.

Spain began her occupation of the Philippines in the 1500s and ruled until the US attacked and claimed the islands for itself in 1898. The Spanish influence – on language, religion (Roman Catholicism) and general culture – has been overwhelming, creating a hybrid people who have forged an island world of unique cast. In the southern Philippines, however, on Mindanao and in the Sulu Archipelago, the Muslim fervour that flushed the Malay Archipelago in the 1500s found fertile fields and flourished over the centuries. (Here, ethnic groups who have ever since identified more with Indonesian Muslims now threaten the national unity.)

Portugal established ports on the islands of Taiwan and Japan, too. Many exploratory voyages were effected in the spirit of evangelism. Spanish navigator Álvaro de Mendaña de Neira (1542–1595), who thought he had found Terra Australis – the long-sought Great Southern Land – in 1568, bestowed on the islands the biblical name of 'Solomon'. And when Portuguese navigator Pedro Fernándes de Queirós (1565–1614) hailed the New Hebrides (modern Vanuatu) in 1605, he had found his 'New Jerusalem'. Such discoveries were as much evangelical missions as capitalistic ventures, in fact, harking back to Eden but with New Testament fulfilment.

In the northeastern Pacific a Portuguese explorer sailing for Spain, João Rodrigues Cabrilho (c. 1499–1543), first encountered the Chumash of the Channel Islands off California's coast, a gentle and honest people. When one of Cabrilho's Catholic priests forgot his metal crucifix on one of the islands, the next day 'at daybreak it was discovered that one of the little canoes of the island was coming to the ship, and that one of the heathen [sic] was carrying in his hand the staff with the holy cross'.[41] For this deed the Spanish visitors at once named the place Santa Cruz ('Holy Cross'). Nearly all the names they bestowed on these islands reflect an equally important Christian mission: in the Santa Barbara Channel the islands of San Miguel, Santa Rosa and Santa Cruz (only Anacapa has a Chumash name); further south and further apart lie the islands of Santa Barbara, San Nicolas, San Clemente and Santa Catalina. Today, three are nature reserves (San Miguel, Anacapa and Santa Barbara), two are restricted Naval zones (San Nicolas and San Clemente), and only one has a village – Catalina's Avalon.

At the great Mexican island metropolis of Tenochtitlan, captured by the Spanish in 1521, a native killer virus (much like modern ebola) struck in the middle of the sixteenth century and slew sixteen out of every twenty inhabitants, fatally weakening the ancient culture and exacerbating the European incursion. Within decades, the hundreds of man-made isles there disappeared and within a couple of centuries no trace of the original Lake Texcoco – the largest of five interconnected lakes – remained. Once the capital of the mighty Aztec empire, Tenochtitlan was no more.

Some 1,000 km from the east coast of the US, Bermuda, discovered in 1505 by Spanish navigator Juan de Bermúdez (c. 1480–1570), was finally settled by Britain in 1609; three years later St George's, the island's capital, was founded, only the second town established by Britons in the New World and today the oldest continuously inhabited town in the Americas.

In the early 1600s voyagers from Britain and France were claiming this and that island of the Bahamas, without effect. But in 1648, seeking religious freedom, a group of British settlers from Bermuda hailed a long, narrow island they named Eleuthera, Greek for 'free'. Having wrecked on her reef and near starvation, they sent eight men in a small boat for help and these managed to sail to British Virginia and secure food, equipment and seeds. Over the following years several settlements on various Bahamian islands succeeded and thrived. Earlier a graveyard, the Bahamas had finally come to life again. Africans were imported in great numbers to work the sugar plantations; soon, they outnumbered the white British settlers. In the 1770s and '80s, in order to flee a revolution they couldn't condone, many loyalist British Americans emigrated to the Bahamas in particular, once again altering its demographic.

As of 1666 the Virgin Islands had become a profitable colony of Denmark. Barbados, that easternmost island of the Caribbean, was one of Britain's oldest overseas colonies.[42] By at least 1,600 years ago she had become home to the Saladoid-Barrancoid people, and about 800 years later migrant Arawakan-speaking Caribs from South America were settling. From the middle of the 1500s into the 1610s the Portuguese intruded and may have blackbirded most of the resident Carib population for slave labour. (Some Arawak still live on the island today.) British voyagers arrived in 1625 and the first settlers landed in 1627 when the island was claimed by the Crown. She became Britain's first 'sugar island' and virtually wrote the textbook on colonial ruthlessness. In time Barbados grew into one of Earth's most densely populated nations, nearly all of her residents being transported West Africans. (Until the granting of independence in 1966 Barbados remained resolutely a British colony, the only Caribbean island not to change hands during many centuries of capricious colonialism.)

The island of Manhattan began her European incarnation when the Dutch established a fur-trading settlement in 1624. Within a year Fort Amsterdam was rising, with the participation of several Dutch colonial families as well as assorted Germans, Swiss, Italians, Spaniards, Irish, Britons, Danes, Swedes and some Africans from the Caribbean. From its earliest days, though nominally Dutch, the island settlement was remarkably cosmopolitan. The Dutch remained firmly in control, however, incorporating the burgeoning township of New Amsterdam in 1653. But then the British attacked in 1664 and appropriated the lot, renaming the town New York. The Netherlands retaliated with a fleet of 21 ships in 1673 and won back the settlement, which the Dutch renamed New Orange. But at the end of the following year, in return for certain treaty concessions the Dutch ceded to Britain their wide-ranging colonial province of New Netherland (later divided into New York and New Jersey). Whereupon New York went on to become the globe's wealthiest, most famous and most cultural eyot.

At that time, France and Britain were vying to establish settlements on many of North America's islands and eyots, especially at the junction of new trade routes. The Island of Montreal, for example, 499 sq km at the confluence of the St Lawrence and Ottawa rivers, began as a primitive fur-trading post in 1611 under French explorer Samuel de Champlain (1567–1635), the 'Father of New France'; today's Montreal is one of the great eyot metropolises, home to Earth's 37th largest island population. Situated just southeast of Massachusetts, Martha's Vineyard – at 231 sq km the largest disconnected island of the East Coast of the US (accessible only by boat or plane) – was still home to the indigenous Wampanoag people when the British settled at Great Harbor in 1642. The island is now perhaps the US's most famous insular colony, the preferred haunt of the loaded and lauded.

St Pierre and Miquelon, claiming a total of 240 sq km only 24 km south of Newfoundland, is France's oldest and smallest (and only 'white') overseas colony. There are actually three islands here: St Pierre, Grande Miquelon and Langlade, with various cays and rocks. In the early 1500s, Norman, Breton and Basque fishermen set up temporary camps here, but not until around 1670 did they finally establish more permanent stations. A truly stable colony was still not assured, however, until expelled Acadians from British Nova Scotia arrived in the early 1700s, whereupon the islands' forests were almost obliterated for fuel and what remained were peat bogs, unsuitable for agriculture. Ever since then, the islanders have regarded fishing as the group's principal occupation. Britain was forever attacking, seizing, occupying and withdrawing, causing great human anguish in these isles. In the wake of the failed War of 1812–14 with the new United States, Great Britain agreed with France in 1814 to drop all claims to St Pierre and Miquelon, on condition that France pledge not to fortify these as military garrisons. This agreement held until Canada's Constitution Act of 1867 which created 'one Dominion under the name of Canada', yet through new treaties Canada has continued to acknowledge the islands' French sovereignty.

'A KIND OF SECOND PARADISE'

Though Greenland's resettlement in 1721 brought tobacco, tea and firearms, native Greenland life hardly altered.[43] The Inuit there still followed their seasonal game from campsite to campsite, while the Danish-Norwegian trading posts – occupied almost entirely by Danes – developed into proper towns that also enticed small numbers of Inuit. However, official government policy discouraged mixing.

In the Caribbean, fought over and traded and ravaged and repopulated for nearly two centuries now, the triangular rum trade had come to dominate the economy as it forever altered demographics. For in the 1600s and 1700s not beer, wine or whisky but rum was Britain's and America's leading alcoholic beverage. In Britain's North American colonies the first rum distillery, established in 1664 on Staten Island (today a borough of New York City), thrived, and the industry soon became all of New England's most prosperous. But with such success came also a growing demand for the sugar required to manufacture the molasses used in rum production. So sugar plantations multiplied, worked by slaves imported from Africa. Within a century, a robust trade based on slaves, sugar and rum was circulating money, men and mayhem between West Africa, the Caribbean isles and British North America. Many believe that the Sugar Act of 1764 that eventually disrupted this capitalistic dynamo underlay the colonial discontent which led to the American Revolution.

By the eighteenth century Britain and France were friends and foes alike in the Caribbean, depending on the stakes and circumstances, with all the attendant and inevitable tensions. St Kitts, for example, was jointly occupied by both nations, who now united to ambush and annihilate the island's true owners, the Carib people. As soon as this was accomplished, 8,000 French troops besieged the 800 British manning the nearly 100-year-old fortress there on Brimstone Hill, and within a month the British were forced to surrender. (Later they returned, but then abandoned the enormous defence complex to nature, appreciating after a century of construction that the position was militarily untenable.) Jamestown, capital of Nevis Island, was struck by cholera then destroyed by either an earthquake or tsunami; a new capital, Charlestown, had to be erected not far away – and it was here that Alexander Hamilton (c. 1755–1804) was born, one of the Founding Fathers of the us, son of a Scots father and Creole mother.

Yet the 1700s was the century of Pacific island discovery, too, the opening up not only of new markets but also of new concepts of colonization and of humankind itself. The Caribbean story had prefigured the Pacific one by three centuries: the Caribbean being discovered and exploited by Catholic southern Europe with gold and conversion in mind, the Pacific chiefly by Protestant northern Europe with selling, science and settlement as goals. The first invasion was bloody, cruel and utterly devastating; the second largely pacific, eventually beneficial and ultimately revelational. For in

Europe's transformation of, and changing through, the Pacific islands, she changed the world.

Since 1571 the Pacific had been regularly crossed by Spain's galleons, from Manila in the Philippines to Acapulco in Mexico, along what came to be known as the 'Acapulco Run'. But it was largely still an unknown ocean by the eighteenth century when, above all, lords in London and Paris concluded that anyone who discovered and colonized the Terra Australis would win strategic advantages over Spain. The Pacific could well be crossed, but it needed to be *mapped*. Advances in maritime technology and navigation now made this possible, and various voyages – under Byron, Carteret, Wallis and Bougainville – sailed off in search of the Great Southern Land only to discover an embarrassment of unknown South Atlantic and Pacific isles instead. Yet it was the three voyages of Britain's James Cook that revealed the true wonder of Pacific islands, chiefly through careful observation, recording and extremely popular publishing. On the *Endeavour* voyage from 1768 to '71, naturalist and botanist Joseph Banks (1743–1820) enthused about the new world they encountered:

> [We] walked for 4 or 5 miles under groves of Cocoa nut and bread fruit trees loaded with a profusion of fruit and giving the most grateful shade I have ever experienced, under these were the habitations of the people most of them without walls: in the short the scene we saw was the truest picture of an arcadia of which we were going to be kings that the imagination can form . . .[44]

Of the Arcadia they discovered in Tolaga Bay, New Zealand, Banks's illustrator, the Scot Sidney Parkinson (*c.* 1745–1771), penned that its forest and waters were 'agreeable beyond description . . . [and] with proper cultivation, might be rendered a kind of second Paradise'.[45] French admiral Louis-Antoine, Comte de Bougainville (1729–1811) raved of Tahiti:

> One would think himself in the Elysian Fields. I thought I was transported into the Garden of Eden; we crossed a turf covered with fine fruit trees, and intersected by little rivulets, which kept up a pleasant coolness in the air.[46]

Bougainville fancied the isle to be La Nouvelle Cythère, Venus's abode: 'the very air the people breathe, their songs, their dances, all conspire to call to mind the sweets of love, and all engage to give themselves up to them'.[47]

Europe's reaction might have been anticipated, as the explorers found only what they had brought with them. A concept of a 'Paradise Island' is traceable throughout history, informing Sanskrit mythology, Persian poetry, the Jews' Garden of Eden, the Greeks' Arcadia and Elysium – also eventually what the Judæo-Christian tradition mixed of Arcadia's sensuality and Elysium's afterlife to create 'Heaven' itself. Hadn't Dante in his *Purgatorio* presented a redemptive paradise that he accessed 'through the Devil's anus at the center of the earth, set on an island in the southern hemisphere, directly opposite Jerusalem'?[48] Such heavens on earth were even purposely built: one need only recall the botanic gardens of medieval India, Egypt and Arab lands, to be later copied in Spain, then throughout western Europe as of the late Middle Ages. The Renaissance renewed the fancy, yielding the opulent landscaping of sixteenth- and seventeenth-century Europe in order to create a terrestrial paradise since no actual biblical Eden was to be found, it seemed.[49]

Islands had long been settings for political utopias – a word coined by Sir Thomas More (1478–1535) in his *Utopia*, a fictional island – for isles are reckoned small, visible, manageable and surrounded by a sea that 'could have physical and moral cleansing and redemptive characteristics, and of course a journey was always required to get to an island thus connotating the elements of pilgrimage and adventure'.[50] And historical 'seekers of paradises' linked such islands to the fancy to concoct the 'island paradise'. In earlier centuries the hybrid notion was applied to the Caribbean, as we have seen, then to West Africa's offshore isles (the Canaries, Madeira, St Helena) and also to the Indian Ocean (especially Mauritius). But the new isles of the Pacific now trumped them all.

This was because of the age and its rare observers. German naturalist Johann Reinhold Forster (1729–1798), for one, also aboard HMS *Endeavour*, as a Linnaean scholar understood what Polynesian islanders might contribute to the understanding of humankind in general: Forster sought and found both climatic and cultural (educational) explanations for the incredible variety of cultures witnessed in what he judged to be the childhood or savagery stage of human ascendance. Forster's speculations went on to inspire the founding of the social sciences.

Others couldn't care less, to be sure, and saw only what they wished to see. Accompanying Bougainville in 1766–9, French naturalist Philibert Commerçon (1727–1773) noted with Gallic exuberence:

> Tahiti is perhaps the only country in the world where men live without vices, without prejudices, without necessities, without disputes. Born under a most beautiful sky, nourished on the fruits of an earth which is fertile without tillage, ruled by patriarchs rather than kings, they know no other god but Love.[51]

Not one word of which was true, of course.

Horrible endemic diseases, unseen by brief European visitors, haunted all island communities.[52] Domestic violence, territorial conflict, tyrannical kingships, cannibalism and many further 'anti-Eden' practices hid themselves beyond European blinkers. Numerous island environments did enjoy a certain protection – because of small human populations they encouraged better hygiene and cooperation, in contrast to the mass populations of Asia, Africa or Europe that generally knew only crowding, disease and warfare. And their climates and fertility surpassed anything yet experienced by Europeans. Still, some prescient observers recognized the danger they themselves represented. James Cook, for example:

> We debauch their Morals already too prone to vice and we introduce among them wants and perhaps diseases which they never before knew and which serves only to disturb that happy tranquillity they and their fore Fathers had injoy'd.[53]

An unrecognized European *superbia* also intruded: all assumed a fundamental moral and biological weakness of the Polynesians, one that had doomed them even before Europeans had arrived – or would certainly doom them now that Europeans had contaminated them. 'Because of the way in which they had been molded by nature, they were assumed to be fatally flawed.'[54]

Western missionaries, administrators, scientists and scholars reported back to Europe about Pacific island morals, customs, geology, flora and fauna – raw data that fed a nursery of burgeoning sciences from Dublin to St Petersburg. It was the Pacific that directly inspired the new anthropology of Friedrich Max Müller (1823–

1900), Edward Tylor (1832–1917) and J. G. Frazer (1854–1941).[55] It was the Pacific, too, that became 'one of the single most important laboratories for the natural sciences. Investigations of the nature of icebergs and coral reefs and into the distribution, boundaries, and variety of plants and animals led directly to evolutionary theory.'[56]

And all this while Pacific island discovery still continued apace. British Royal Navy officer George Vancouver (1757–1798), who had sailed with James Cook, explored the northwest coast of North America from 1792 to '94 and encountered, among hundreds of others, the largest island east of New Zealand, subsequently named after him: Vancouver Island. And on the other side of the Pacific, in Westernport Bay just off modern Melbourne, Phillip Island and Churchill Island were 'discovered' by a doctor in a rowing boat. With a handful of crew in an 8-m whaleboat, Ship's Surgeon George Bass of HMS *Reliance* explored in 1798 around 1,000 km of coast, a journey that explorer Matthew Flinders (1774–1814) hailed as having 'not perhaps its equal in the annals of maritime history'.[57] The two islands lay at the western extremity of the voyage, huddled before what Bass reasoned had to be a strait leading to the open ocean. He was correct and Bass Strait has borne his name ever since. Fifty-hectare Churchill Island has hardly changed since Victoria's first colonists arrived 200 years ago; holding one working farm, the island now connects through a narrow causeway to Phillip Island, and since the Second World War a bridge has joined Phillip to the Victoria mainland. With over 3.5 million visitors each year, 10,000-ha Phillip hosts holiday homes and retirement cottages, and many of today's more than 7,000 permanent islanders commute to Melbourne each day. Discovered by *La Naturaliste* in 1802, nearby 17,000-ha French Island – originally 'Île de Françoise' – is now accessible by suburban train and ferry. With 40 km of gravel roads, one small general store and post office, and only generators for electricity for her farming and tourist-oriented population of around 90, she celebrated when in 1997 the Australian government set aside 70 per cent of her land as the new French Island National Park.

The islands of the Bering Strait had been discovered as early as 1728 by the Danish explorer Vitus Bering (1681–1741), sailing for Imperial Russia. In 1806 the Englishman William Scoresby (1789–1857) explored Greenland's Arctic east coast. In 1818 Scottish rear admiral Sir John Ross (1777–1856) explored Greenland's west coast and ventured up into Baffin Bay by Baffin Island; then, from 1829 to '33, ranged the Canadian Arctic's islands and seaways. Between 1819 and '21 German explorer Fabian von Bellingshausen (1778–1852), also sailing for Imperial Russia, circumnavigated Antarctica and fetched up off 49,070-sq-km Alexander I Island – one of Earth's last islands to be discovered and, until 1940, believed to be part of the Antarctic mainland.

THE CENTURY OF ISLANDS

With the 1800s methodic island colonization commenced. Up till then no such business existed: islands were to conquer, pillage and plunder. Now, great numbers of cosmopolitan nations were sending their citizens to settle already occupied islands and multiply there, especially in the Indian Ocean and Pacific. In time, the demographic intrusion evolved into hybridization, creating new island peoples: in Mauritius, La Réunion, New Zealand, Hawai'i and many others. With colonialism, some islands suffered horribly. In the first half of the 1800s British settlers either hunted for bounty or moved to offshore islands thousands of aboriginal Tasmanians who had occupied their island for tens of thousands of years. Born of greed and ignorance, the ethnic replacement approached genocide. Yet native Tasmanians survive today and take enormous pride in the remarkable story of their people. Most other islanders, however, experienced a new social stability and affluence, the end of tribal warfare, and the introduction of disciplined governance. Offering fragile island economies a similar stability, colonizers' gunboats oversaw flourishing markets.

The Indian Ocean changed profoundly.[58] The region's most aggressive player was also Britain. Asserting herself everywhere, she seized violently most of France's islands there, then prized away Sri Lanka, Cape Town and Malayan Malacca from the Netherlands. (It was then that much of India was 'appropriated' as well.) In the early 1800s these new acquisitions fed the Industrial Revolution's enormous appetite for raw materials, rendering Britain even richer and more powerful. In 1819, Sir Thomas Stamford Raffles (1781–1826) founded a port on a small island at Malaya's southern tip in order to permit the British East India Company to control local sea commerce in imitation of Dutch Batavia (modern Jakarta): his new Singapore quickly grew into Britain's Southeast Asian capital, the 'Emporium of the East', rivalled only by Hong Kong Island in the Far East.

In 1833 Parliament abolished slavery throughout Britain's foreign possessions. The economic repurcussions were immediate and immense. Indian Ocean plantations were only sustainable if one imported hosts of cheap Indian and Chinese labourers. Both were used in Malaya and tiny Singapore, but indentured Indians also laboured in rice fields and plantations from Uganda to South America, including the islands of Sri Lanka, Mauritius, La Réunion and, in the Pacific, Fiji. Indian labour made possible Sri Lanka's tea and Mauritius's sugar exports. Malay and Chinese labourers mined phosphate on uninhabited Christmas Island, while in the hitherto unoccupied Cocos Islands a Scots mercantile family established a private 'corporate state' with indentured Malays.

There were profound social repercussions. French-speaking islanders everywhere now had to side either with the new majority Muslims and Hindus or with the minority whites and African Christians. Mauritius's French speakers, for example, gradually yielded to the evolving Bhojpuri of the island's now-permanent 'guest workers' from northern India. Chinese labourers eventually inherited all of Singapore. Northern Sri Lanka now became almost wholly Hindu Tamil; the Tamil had occupied the Jaffna Peninsula for over 2,000 years, but their British resettlement to highland tea plantations saw their numbers and distribution encroach upon native Sinhalese. (The British Raj favoured the Tamil, sowing a discontent that would lead to violent war in the following century.) A new Malay-Muslim culture, product of the Scots' 'corporate state', eventually evolved in the Cocos Islands, while on Christmas Island a private phosphate company held feudal sway over indentured Chinese and Malays who were inventing a new, similarly oppressed society there.

Under British rule, East Africa's coastal islands similarly assumed the cast of hierarchical British colonies – those ruled by white administrators, merchant traders and plantation managers with only minimal military or naval presence. Madasgascar had generally been spared but for marauding pirates, yet France invaded in 1883 then annexed Earth's fourth largest island in 1896. However, French language and culture failed to take root in Madagascar and the Comoros, though Christianity at last overwhelmed Madagascar (and Moroni in the Comoros). From the African coast to Singapore, English and French were now the *lingua francas* among island elites, merchants and traders.

Europe's colonization of the Pacific saw sealers, traders and whalers landing on New Zealand, Tahiti and Hawai'i.[59] The sandalwood trade flourished first in Fiji, then in the Marquesas Islands and New Hebrides (modern Vanuatu). Soon missionaries from Britain, France and the US were descending. For the first time in more than 3,000 years a different people were beginning to call Pacific islands home, whereupon foreign stations and settlements grew into European townships. Having acquired islanders' lands, settlers grew bolder and challenged not only islanders' authority but also their identity. New Zealand turned British. Most of eastern Polynesia – the Societies, Marquesas, Tuamotus, Gambiers, Australs – were seized by France. Tonga's and Hawai'i's indigenous monarchies, however, were strong enough to attain international recognition and prevail.

The depopulation of many islands through the introduction of Old World diseases, against which islanders had no immunity, not only altered ancient ways forever: it exacerbated the ethnic replacement. Losses could be staggering. In the Australs, Ra'ivavae's population in 1826 fell from 3,200 to 120. Easter Island tallied some 3,000 Rapanui in 1863, but only 111 in 1877. The 142,000 native Hawai'ians counted in 1823 were down to 39,000 by 1896. All the New Hebrides lost half their population. Many Western Melanesian isles lost as much as 90 per cent of their people. In Micronesia the overall loss approached 50 per cent, though some islands also experienced 90 per cent. Kosraeans, for example, numbered around 3,000 in the 1820s but only 300-odd by the 1880s. Nevertheless, Pacific population decline is now regarded by historians more quantitatively: significant declines cannot be denied, but some islands – Tonga and Samoa, for example – remained relatively, though not wholly, unaffected. A few islands even increased their populations.[60] Many losses might have been exaggerated by foreign observers, as the extinctions of seeming 'inferior peoples with barbarous customs and gods' were regarded by many Europeans as fulfilling a natural law – indeed, as modern historians now understand, the conceit was even actively promoted as 'the destiny of Western nations in the Pacific'.[61]

All the same, colonial governments were concerned. Didn't their justification for insular annexation rest, at least publicly, on humanitarian grounds? – that is, to mitigate the consequences of an unregulated colonial presence? Also, such mortality robbed capitalists of essential labour, wiping out profits and thwarting economic growth. As late as 1921 concerned Britons were heralding that the islanders *need not die out . . .* No, *if the natives are given their chance*, they can increase, and can be made good and useful citizens – an asset to the Empire – and the matter lies in our hands.'[62] Others were anticipating the other extreme: that islanders might one day be replacing Old Europe's tribes, perceived then as being in decay themselves. The question was posed as early as 1800 – in the wake of the great era of island exploration –

> when New Zealand may produce her Lockes, her Newtons, and her Montesquieus; and when the great nations in the immense region of New Holland [Australia] may send their navigators, philosophers, and antiquaries, to contemplate the ruins of *ancient* London and Paris, and to trace the languid remains of the arts and sciences in this quarter of the globe.[63]

The British poet, historian and politician Thomas Babington Macaulay (1800–1859) imagined in 1840 a New Zealand Māori 'standing on the remains of London Bridge sketching the ruins of St Paul's'.[64]

As with the settlement of the Greek isles in the third and second millennia BC, the colonial economic systems in the Pacific ravaged island biota chiefly through deforestation, here exacerbated by cattle and sheep farming, mining, plantations and overfishing. European nations then invented in the post-colonial Pacific the 'protectorate' as a mask for the now unpalatable truth of 'colony'. Only when old-style colonialism was drawing to a close did Portugal, in imminent danger of losing her African colonies to England and Germany, resolve to establish a systematic settler presence in her far-flung empire, which included the island of Timor in the Malay Archipelago. And in a similar thrust, at the eastern terminus of the Pacific, Chile annexed Easter Island, which was briefly settled and then abandoned; Chile then leased the isle instead as a sheep farm to a string of venture capitalists.

Off the Californian coast, the Channel Islands remained home to the Chumash (north) and Tongva (south) peoples until the 1800s when they were slaughtered by invading Aleutian Islanders who had been recruited by the Russian-American Fur Company to hunt seals and sea otters there: the atrocity obliterated an ancient society of islanders who once numbered in their tens of thousands. The few Chumash and Tongva who miraculously survived were later transported to the mainland by the Spanish government to labour at Catholic missions. Most died within a year or two.

Contested by so many nations for centuries, the Caribbean was home to a new majority population who, against all odds, now began opposing their white oppressors. It was the first time that transported slaves or their descendants had revolted. Miraculously, a small number succeeded. In the western half of Hispaniola, for example, Toussaint Louverture (1743–1803) – freed slave, property owner and brilliant military leader – by 1798 had evicted Spain, Britain and then even his ally France. One year after his death the new nation of Haiti was proclaimed, the first in Latin America to achieve full independence and the first in the world to be led by blacks. The island nation of Haiti was also the second independent republic in the Americas, after the us.

A similar struggle engaged Greek islanders, eager to cast off the centuries-old Turkish yoke. The crucible of this campaign was the island of Ægina, just 27 km south of Athens – an irony as it happened, as Ægina had been occupied since the Middle Ages by Venetians, not Turks. It was under the Venetians, too, that the people of Ægina had built their forts, churches and chapels, and had transformed their island into an important trade centre. The Venetians had withdrawn in 1718, but within one century the Æginans were claiming centre stage in the war against the Ottoman Empire, their capital of Paleochori the seat of the provincial government of an embryonic Greek nation. It was from here and the neighbouring islands of Spetsæ, Hydra and Poros that the Greeks launched their victorious naval campaign against the Turkish fleet in the early nineteenth century.

The late 1800s and early 1900s saw whalers from Europe setting up seasonal stations on hitherto uninhabited islands in the southern Indian Ocean – like Amsterdam, McDonald, Heard and Saint Paul Islands, as well as on various isles in the archipelagos of Prince Edward, Crozet and Kerguélen.

It was then that New Zealand's offshore isles were settled by white farmers, who bought up great tracts of land for sheep runs, now that most of these isles – especially in the Hauraki Gulf just east of Auckland – had been denuded of their glorious stands of kauri trees to construct the colonial metropolis. By the end of the century the world's first official air-mail delivery system was implemented there when, in 1897, a regular pigeon-post operated between Auckland and Great Barrier Island.

It was also at the end of the 1800s that the US finally resolved to acquire island colonies of her own, and this at a time when that bitter colonial pie had long been digested and was threatening evacuation. After the Alaskan Purchase of 1867, US territorial expansion meant island expansion – mostly, but not exclusively, at Spain's cost. As a result of the Spanish–American War, the Treaty of Paris in 1898 liberally granted the US temporary dominion over Cuba and open-ended authority over the Philippines, Guam and Puerto Rico. In response to the Philippine War of Independence which then raged from 1899 to 1902 – the First Philippine Republic's attempt to expel the new foreign occupiers and achieve sovereignty – American troops depopulated wide areas of the country. Perhaps as many as 20,000 Filipinos died in the now-forgotten struggle.

In Hawai'i in 1892–3, the US consul secretly encouraged a small group of American revolutionaries to force Queen Lili'uokalani (1838–1917) to capitulate, after which the revolutionaries announced their self-styled 'Republic of Hawai'i' and sought annexation from Washington. On 12 August 1898 the US Congress approved the Newlands Resolution accepting the 'Republic of Hawai'i's' cession of sovereignty to the US and establishing a US territorial government there. The US then annexed Tutuila and Aunu'u in Samoa in 1900, then included the Manu'a group in 1904 when the Tu'i Manu'a, Eastern Samoa's highest-ranking chief, was the last to sign a cession agreement with the US government. (The act of annexation was not formally ratified by Congress until 1929.) Of all these islands today, only Cuba and the Philippines are independent of the US, though it appears Puerto Rico might soon hold a referendum on independence or statehood.

In a similar campaign of acquisition Meiji Japan annexed the Ryūkyū Islands in 1879, then acquired Taiwan from China's Qing Empire after the victorious First Sino–Japanese War of 1894–5. The resultant Treaty of Shimonoseki – which heralded independence and autonomy for Korea – forced China to cede to Japan 'in perpetuity and full sovereignty' not only the important island of Taiwan but also the 90 small islands and islets of the Penghu group off Taiwan's western coast. Here Japan ruled until 1945.

1900s

Unlike the African continent the world's islands experienced the end of colonialism as the start of stable local governance, with only infrequent regressions to tribal infelicities. Erstwhile colonizers were themselves becoming New Islanders, no longer expatriates from Britain, France, the Netherlands or Portugal but a special breed sensitive to unique island climes, topographies and needs. By the 1900s most indigenous islanders were regarded as 'tamed', their ancient cultures essentially moribund. 'This near universal belief offered a potential human void in the Pacific', to highlight one region.

> This was to be filled with a new race of Pacific men – the Britons of the south, that is, the European peoples of Australia, and especially New Zealand, who, from the 1880s, regarded themselves as an advanced, reinvigorated version of their Old World forefathers and represented the 'coming man'.[65]

After the 'Kaiser's War' (1914–18, see chapter Five) most island emporiums met new commercial challenges and thrived. Take Singapore – that diamond-shaped island at the tip of the Malay Peninsula, developed by Sir Stamford Raffles in the early 1820s and considered Britain's greatest fortress east of Suez – which the booming automotive industry of the 1920s and '30s veritably gilded because of international demand for Malaya's rubber. Singapore even had her own Ford factory, Southeast Asia's only car manufacture plant. Around Singapore's commercial hub rose shanty towns redolent of cinnamon, nutmeg, tamarinds, incense, frying fish and rotting fruit. Great fortunes were made here, mostly for British investors. Without a sizable Royal Air Force contingent, however, by 1940 Singapore was, as seasoned military observers frequently complained, all too horribly 'naked'.

Not only Singapore suffered the consequences. The Second World War altered island life throughout the world in hitherto unimaginable ways, from Iceland to Crete and from Japan to Bora Bora (see chapter Five). Over Britain a great battle was fought in the skies, something new in human history. In the Mediterranean thousands perished in the streets of Malta, the vineyards of Crete, the olive groves of Sicily. In the Pacific, war meant almost exclusively island war. But not only islands suffered. All Earth bled and suddenly grew old; whereupon a new nightmare descended when the atomic age exploded over two island cities.

Following the war, Britain's historic divestment of her overseas colonies brought independence for most of her Indian, Caribbean and Pacific Ocean islands. In the Indian Ocean, nationhood was granted to Ceylon (which became Sri Lanka), Mauritius, the Seychelles, the Maldives, Madagascar, Singapore and most of the Comoros. Coastal East African islands were mostly incorporated into nearby mainland nations, since they, too, now achieved their independence. As India herself became a nation, she assumed international jurisdiction over the Laccadives, Andamans and Nicobars. The Malay Archipelago, chiefly Dutch, now became Indonesia, Malaysia, Brunei and East Timor. Australia took over Christmas Island and the Cocos group. Britain retained the Chagos group. Resisting decolonization, France absorbed La Réunion and Moroni in the Comoros as *départements*.

Through the Treaty of San Francisco in 1945 Taiwan and her Penghu group were finally taken from Japan and granted to the fledgling Republic of China. Four years later, however, the entire Republic of China comprised only these islands, for it was to here that the Kuomintang government of Chiang Kai-shek (1887–1975) fled after losing the Chinese Civil War against the communist forces of Mao Zedong (1893–1976). Two to three million Mandarin speakers then imposed themselves on five to six million Fukienese (Min) speakers whose ancestors had occupied these islands back in the 1600s; it led to great social tension.

Among the more than 7,000 islands of the Caribbean, 27 sovereign states, overseas departments and dependencies have come into being since the Second World War. Though Britain has shed most of her dominion here, the US, France and the Netherlands still uphold neo-colonial structures throughout the area (see chapter Five).

The 1960s and '70s saw many Pacific colonies under British, Australian and New Zealand administration gain their independence: Western Samoa, Fiji, Tonga, Papua New Guinea, the Solomon Islands, Vanuatu (formerly the New Hebrides), and Kiribati and Tuvalu (both formerly the Gilbert and Ellice Islands Colony). Alone Pitcairn Island of *Bounty* fame today remains a British Pacific colony. Cook Islanders and Niueans enjoy independence only in free association with New Zealand; Tokelauans prefer New Zealand citizenship over independence. All French territories in the

Pacific islands – New Caledonia, Wallis and Futuna, and the many groups comprising French Polynesia – possess internal autonomy under local French officials not accountable to respective Territorial Assemblies. Easter Island (Rapa Nui) remains Chile's prized jewel, with Sala-y-Gómez and the Juan Fernández Islands. Papua and West Papua (Western New Guinea) still cower under Indonesia's stern administration.

American Samoa is as fully American as is Guam. In 1959 Hawai'i was made the fiftieth, and last, state of the United States; she is now an inseparable part of the us. By 1976 the Mariana Islands had become a commonwealth of the us, thereby relinquishing any future claims to independence. Whereupon the remaining Trust Territory of the Pacific Islands, a legacy of the earlier Japanese Mandate, was partitioned and renamed the Federated States of Micronesia (formerly the Caroline Islands), the Republic of the Marshall Islands, and the Republic of Palau. Micronesia's nominal 'independence' is a new incarnation of colonialism – that is, island nations are allowed to be what their former trustee, the us, requires them to be. In such a guise, they remain generally divorced from the truly independent and freely associating nations of the Pacific islands.[66]

Such constructs can have chilling repercussions. Consider 2.7-sq-km Johnston Atoll, an unincorporated territory of the us. Her phosphate deposits exhausted since 1908, the island was designated a bird sanctuary in 1928. During the Second World War Johnston became an important fueling base for flights to further islands, then a strategic us Air Force base. In the 1950s and '60s the us detonated nuclear bombs there. Then, as of 1971, Johnston became a prime dump for decommissioned biological weapons – chiefly mustard and nerve gases, in their thousands of tonnes. Only in the 1990s was an incineration facility finally installed. 'Dioxin and furan are sometimes released into the air, and all personnel on the island are required to have their gas masks ready.'[67] Leaking storage containers were discovered in 1998.

Having upheld the Empire for over two centuries Britain's Royal Navy all but retired before the us Air Force and Navy, with the hegemonic supersession almost exclusively an insular phenomenon. In the main a us campaign, air and missile power effectively supplanted naval power already by the mid–1900s. As Rome once dominated the islands of *Mare Nostrum* – the Mediterranean –

through her triremes, quadriremes and quinqueremes, the US now controls a global network through her ICBMs, Tridents and satellite arrays. In the process Britain has not shied from mass expulsion. The more than 60 tropical islands of the Chagos Archipelago in the Indian Ocean, for example, officially part of the British Indian Ocean Territory, experienced between 1967 and '73 the eviction of indigenous Chagossians in order to enable the US to construct a 'joint defence and naval facility' on Diego Garcia. Since 1971 this atoll alone of the entire archipelago has been inhabited, and solely by US military personnel and their civilian contractors. (A British administrator is not even present.) When the British government proposed in 2009 that the entire region be designated the world's largest marine reserve, it soon came to light that behind this manoeuvre lay the preclusion of any return by Chagossians to their homeland – this in order to perpetuate the special security agreement with the US. Today, Chagossians still languish in exile on Mauritius and in the Seychelles.

That most insular of all nations, Indonesia – with nearly 238 million people (2010), Earth's fourth largest nation and greatest Muslim country by population – has suffered most grievously and injured most egregiously. Heavily forested, the interior areas of the outer islands are still home to a small number of hunter-gatherers, whereas most rural Indonesians are farmers or fishermen. The isolated highlanders trade downriver and with coastal peoples, and these in turn trade with other islands. Because of robust inter-island trading over millennia most coastal communities resemble one another yet retain local customs and languages. Indonesia's seas and difficult terrain have discouraged migration and encouraged localized conservation and conformity, leading to a rich palette of cultures through the archipelago, one seen nowhere else to such a degree. Change has always come first to coastal dwellers.

For over 350 years the Dutch were in control here, who developed the Malay Archipelago as one of the world's most profitable colonial holdings.[68] In the early 1900s Indonesians began agitating for independence and they never ceased their struggle, even during Japan's occupation. Finally, on 17 August 1945, only three days after Japan surrendered, Sukarno (1901–1970), leading a small group, proclaimed the independent Republic of Indonesia. At once the Dutch tried to re-establish their own administration and control, and they fought brutally against Sukarno's forces, but lost. In 1949 the Netherlands officially recognized the new Republic's sovereignty, yet still retained dominion over Western New Guinea. In the 1950s and, above all, the '60s, Sukarno battled armed Islamic and anti-communist groups led by Suharto (1921–2008) who was backed by the US, Britain and Australia; the conflict led to the slaughter of over a million Indonesians (see chapter Five).

When the Dutch finally withdrew from Western New Guinea, Indonesia invaded (the region is home to wholly dissimilar ethnic groups). Full sovereignty over Western New Guinea was then formally transferred to Indonesia in 1969, who renamed the land Irian Jaya (today Papua and West Papua). When the Portuguese finally decolonized East Timor in 1975, Indonesia invaded there, too, then officially annexed East Timor the following year as Indonesia's 27th province: the subsequent occupation cost as many as 180,000 Timorese lives. Indonesia's rule of terror ended only in 1999 under enormous international pressure. (East Timor became the twenty-first century's first sovereign state, on 20 May 2002.) Though vying with Japan, Britain and Manhattan as one of the four insular powerhouses, Indonesia remains deeply troubled:

> The country's leaders face such problems as the economy's declining but still considerable overreliance on petroleum, the great income inequality among its people, overpopulation, major regional differences in popular access to the political process, and the incomplete development of civilian institutions independent of the military.[69]

The Mediterranean islands, too, have entered a new age. Take the Greek Dodecanese. Under Turkish rule these had long been known as the 'Privileged Islands' because of those tax exemptions and other privileges first bestowed by Suleiman the Magnificent. In 1908 the islanders had banded together to cast out their Ottoman overlords and within four years had achieved this and were planning to join the Greek nation. But the First World War broke out and Greece was informed by European powers that she would be able to subsume the Dodecanese only once hostilities had ceased; whereupon at the Treaty of Sèvres between the Allies and the Ottoman Empire in 1920 the Dodecanese were given to Rome, not Athens, as Italy's reward for services to the victors. Only in 1948, following Italy's defeat as Germany's ally in the Second World War, were the Dodecanese incorporated into the Greek nation.

The issue of sovereignty challenged even the Channel Islands between Britain and France. An archipelago of British Crown Dependencies geographically much closer to France than Britain, the Channel Islands can be regarded as a family, with grandmother and grandfather Guernsey and Jersey; parents Alderney, Sark and Helm; grown children Brechou, Lihou, Burhou and Jethou; and grandchildren groups of Les Écréhous, Les Minquiers and Les Casquets. One French cousin skulks: Chausey. Channel roots, culture, even language at times are Norman through and through. Yet each island prizes her own climate, topography and character, and each islander is 'home' only on the *île mère*.

Lying around 17 km off the French coast, Chausey, for one, with a permanent population of around 30, is actually a group of some 50 islets, only eight of which have some grass and a few trees on them. Britain claimed Chausey for herself in 1950, but France refused to budge. Finally, in 1953, the International Court found in France's favour. Chausey's neighbours, however – the island groups of Les Écréhous and Les Minquiers – were apportioned to Jersey, 10 km to the southwest. La Marmotchiéthe in Les Écréhous even has a 'town' on it that consists of one short street and a customs office. In 1993 and '94 French nationalists 'invaded' the isle from mainland Normandy, pulled down the Union Jack and raised Norman flags before lunch was enjoyed by all and a French priest held a historic mass.

Only following the Second World War did Greenland, Earth's largest island, come of age.[70] Denmark was determined to industrialize Greenland, eliminating the traditional villages of under 100 residents and forcing all Greenlanders to concentrate in towns and mostly labour in fishing and fish processing, the mainstays of the economy. In exchange, modern amenities – hospitals, schools, public services – would be provided free. Soon all Greenlanders were granted full Danish citizenship. One generation later, on 1 May 1979, Greenland's status was redefined as a distant nation within the Kingdom of Denmark and home rule now allowed Greenlanders to regulate their own affairs, but for Copenhagen's foreign representation and defence. Generous grants still today maintain otherwise unaffordable social services. Of the island's population of 56,452 (est. 2010), 80 per cent identify Inuit, 20 per cent Dane ethnicity. Four out of five Greenlanders live in only seventeen towns, fifteen of which are situated on the western and southern coasts.

Lead, zinc and cryolite have been mined to exhaustion; there now remains only small-scale mining of platinum, gold and other minerals. Cod catches plummeted when western waters cooled, perhaps due to ice melt-off; now shrimp top the harvest, followed by cod, halibut and salmon. Sheep farming is pursued by a handful of hardies. The University of Greenland now instructs in the local Inuit language as well as Danish. While island art proves popular and sometimes profitable, tourism is only a meagre financial option. Greenland's government hopes more tourists will soon be visiting Earth's largest national park.

The salvo for the twenty-first century actually sounded on 11 September 2001 – '9/11' – the island atrocity that shocked the world. Surveying all the island changes since the Second World War – nationhood for so many, Chinese emigrating to Taiwan in their millions, Cubans fleeing to Miami, Pacific islanders flocking to Tahiti, Hawai'i, Auckland, Melbourne and Sydney – we are once more reminded how islands have forever been fuses and floodgates. One cannot forget the 'Battle of Naxos' that saved the Hellenic world in around 1600 BC, or that of Salamis south of Athens over a thousand years later. Then there was the *kamikaze* or 'Divine Wind' that rescued Japan from two Mongolian invasions, the Spanish Armada that nearly took England in 1588, and all those island flashpoints of more recent memory: Guadalcanal (1942), Quemoy and Matsu (1954–5, 1958), the Cuban Missile Crisis (1962), the Cyprus invasion (1974), the Falklands War (1982), Grenada (1983), 9/11 on Manhattan (2001) – and now new anxieties about Taiwan.

As island isolation disrupts the gene flow, leading to biological variation through speciation, so too does it disrupt the culteme flow, leading to cultural variation – the creation of new tribes, new customs. Unique island cultures have distilled under the constraints of isolation, time and adaptation – some isles settled twice, even thrice, by waves of indigenous intruders and by floods of foreign colonials. Take the Caribbean's St Barthélemy. Once home to the Ciboney, Arawaks and Caribs, she was 'discovered' by Columbus in 1493, then finally resettled by Bretons and Normans from France. But Louis XVI (1754–1793) deeded the island to Sweden in 1784 in exchange for berthing and warehouse facilities at Gothenburg, whereupon Sweden renamed the capital of Carenage to 'Gustavia' after Sweden's monarch, declared this a free port, and stayed for

nearly a century. After suffering hurricanes and a terrible conflagration that destroyed most of Gustavia, the island reverted to
France. She remains French today: very French, in fact, as slavery
failed to prosper here like on most of the Caribbean islands. Of St
Barthélemy's erstwhile Carib population, however, there is no trace.

Cubans and most Tasmanians failed to survive one century of
contact with outsiders. Other islanders accepted and adapted:
Hawaiians, Māori, Maltese, Malagasy, Easter Islanders and so
many more. Island size has often dictated the dynamic. The histories of Britain, Japan, Madagascar and New Zealand occupy a
dimension different from that of Hawai'i, Crete, Skye and Corsica,
and these in turn from that of Martha's Vineyard, Waiheke, the Isle
of Wight and Phillip Island. A further constant: the greater the
isolation, the 'smaller' the story: Greenland's saga could be that of
a small island resort, and Canada's Ellesmere Island – ninth largest
in the world – has hardly a history at all. Location, location. One
need only contrast small Singapore, Hong Kong and especially
Manhattan.

Just like some people, islands change identities over time.
Moloka'i in the Hawaiian Islands was a Polynesian mainstay, then
an international station, then a Catholic leper colony (in one part),
and now headlines as an American tourist paradise with hotels and
golf courses. Norfolk Island, east of Australia, was for centuries a
Polynesian outpost, then a British settlement and penal colony
(1788–1814, 1824–55), a refuge for Pitcairn Islanders, then finally an
Australian retreat and retirement haven. Islands also lose identities:
Bikini Atoll in the Marshalls hosted a thriving Micronesian society
for well over 2,000 years until her people were evacuated by the US
in 1946 when the island was blasted by 23 atomic bombs; testing
ceased in 1958, leaving only a haven for strontium-90 and cesium-
137.

Some regions were more successful – or less exploited – than
others. In general one can view Pacific islands as a 'successful
Caribbean'. There occurred here no mass extinction and racial replacement, but by and large a gradual integration and assimilation
through hybridization. Today's New Zealander, for example, represents the best of both worlds – the robustness of an indigenous
vigour mixed with the sophisticated technology, economy, infrastructure and education of any modern European or North American society. Such a hybrid, as known from biology, creates a

stronger strain, more adaptable and thus viable. Pacific islands in general have demonstrated a melding of peoples and cultures that might stand as exemplary for the twenty-first century.

Island history is humankind's own. When Minos of Crete cried 'Hear ye, Cretans and Greeks' 3,600 years ago he was creating an island empire that would span the Mediterranean. Millennia later Britain created another, spanning the globe. It's unlikely there will be a third. For empires are now measured in megadollars and giga-bytes, both as landless as they are ephemeral.

It's all a question of 'tin and tans'.

four

... of Tin and Tans

If there is one economic constant that determines island cultures, then it's *location*. Britain and Japan, Hong Kong and Singapore, Taiwan and Java – economic titans all – occupy dynamic trade routes; Canada's giant Ellesmere remains a cultural dwarf. The world's leading financial centre is currently London, followed by New York: both island metropolises. Basic subsistence is all any island offers humankind. But if, like ancient Crete, the island animates trade, she will grow; and if, like modern Indonesia, she routes resources, she will flourish. And where subsistence is lacking, location alone will often create culture: the arid atoll of Wake Island between Japan and Hawai'i, for example, was an uninhabited wasteland until Pan American Airlines constructed 'PAAville' there in 1935 to refuel flights on the new US–China route, elaborating an instant economy. A capricious commerce will then rule: if trade fails, if relief crashes, if the human connection vanishes – 'ghost islands' are the result.

These are familiar throughout the world, abandoned isles whose past inhabitants are whispers in the wind. Some might have been settled for hundreds, perhaps even thousands of years, like so many in the Ægean, then deserted for any number of reasons. A range of difficulties assails the settlement of smaller islands in particular: shortage of water and food, internal conflict, natural disasters, pandemics, psychological isolation. Lying in the Pacific are some 27 known 'Mystery Islands' which, archæological evidence suggests, survived as sustainable cultures only so long as their voyaging spheres lasted: once active exchange and disaster relief ceased, populations sailed away or perished.[1] Among the more prominent of these are Pitcairn, neighbouring Henderson, Hawai'i's Necker and Nihoa, the Cooks' Palmerston and Suwarrow, the Kermadec Islands north of New Zealand, and Australia's Norfolk Island. (Several of these have since been resettled.) Most appear to have been abandoned by around AD 1500 or slightly earlier, though the Little Ice Age of the sixteenth to nineteenth centuries might have caused the desertion of others.

A veritable archipelago of island economies has materialized over the millennia, shifting too with the sands of world history. Almost all islands – but for rare exceptions like Wake Island – began as subsistence settlements. Trade then made or broke an insular culture, with such variables as piracy, slavery, whaling or fishing sealing an island's fate. Novel social phenomena can intrude: since the Second World War air tourism has affected island cultures more greatly than anything previously in history. Whereupon tourism-spawned offshore banking then transformed some isles into the wealthiest plots on the planet, reproducing on a global scale what Knossos had attained in the ancient Ægean, Venice in the medieval Mediterranean, Tonga in the Central Pacific, and Sumatra in the Malay Archipelago.

SUBSISTENCE

On the world's largest islands within reasonable reach and clime – Madagascar, Sri Lanka, Sumatra, Java, Luzon – agriculture came to engage most settlers; only a minority turned to fishing, net-making and boatbuilding, even fewer to maritime trade. On smaller islands, however, the sea has always been food and ford: the source of life, the link to the larger world. Yet unless the smaller island lay on a well-travelled route or crossroad, her early inhabitants mostly struggled in a backwater. The most fortunate islanders were those whose home's size and location meant they could feed themselves from sea and land both, while regularly augmenting supplies from passing merchants.

Among the latter were the early Cretans.[2] They enjoyed a diet of fruit and nuts, several beans and root vegetables, grains, grapes, olives, and perhaps some wild grasses, bulbs and vegetables. Then there was fish of all kinds, birds, game in forested hills and mountain ranges. Sheep and goat herds were extensive, and so milk and milk products graced each meal. Honey and wild herbs delighted the palate. The island's salted mutton, famed wine and olives were exported to the Levant (Ugarit, Byblos, Sidon, Tyre), Egypt (Tanis and Avaris), Libya and Putaya (northern Cyrenaica) – often via Cyprus. Trade flourished with Asia Minor, the Cyclades, the Peloponnese, Mycenæ, Pylos, Athens and many more, perhaps as far as Troy, Italy, Sicily, Iberia and beyond the Pillars of Hercules (Strait of Gilbraltar). Crete lacked most minerals, but timber for the Minoan fleet and for housing filled mountain forests. Limestone, schist and gypsum galore built impressive cities of stone, and extraordinary palace complexes rose all over the isle.

And all this at a time when most of the world's islanders hardly survived 30 years of fishing or hunting game, of picking scarce fruit and berries, of tending tiny plots lashed often by Caribbean hurricanes and Pacific typhoons.

'THE ENDS OF THE EARTH'

Around 9,000 years ago New Guinean highlanders were trading with coastal regions, and by 2,500 BC vying in polished stone tools and pottery. At the same time Austronesian traders and explorers, Earth's premier mariners, were arriving from northern and western islands. They were the people who would take Pacific trade as far as it could go, first bringing New Britain's Talasea obsidian to the Solomon Islands by 2000 BC, firing their characteristic pottery in the Bismarck Archipelago, then transporting their goods throughout Near Oceania. Soon, early Lapita ware was appearing through Island Melanesia (with the exception of the contiguous Solomons) and as far afield as Samoa – more than 4,000 km away. During the 'Lapita Millennium' – the era of principal pottery activity that lasted from around 1500 to 500 BC – obsidian still remained one of the Pacific's most valuable trade items, used chiefly for fashioning cutting tools. The Talasea site on New Britain continued to be an important source for Pacific islands obsidian, its stock traded in Vanuatu, New Caledonia, the Santa Cruz Islands and even in remote Fiji. Both Lapita pottery and Talasea obsidian, above all, prove that long-distance trading was indeed taking place, though far less frequently than inner-archipelagic trading.[3]

By the third millennium BC northern Europeans had already voyaged to Shetland with domesticated animals and seed corn. Within 2,000 years Ireland's and Britain's metallurgists were regularly voyaging through the isles – from Aran off the Galway coast to just off Norway – loaded with beeswax, refractory clay and bronze scrap in order to work makeshift foundries and cast whatever bronzes islanders were willing to trade for.[4] In 2005 a Mediterranean or Iberian boy, aged around fourteen or fifteen, was discovered buried with an amber necklace 5 km southeast of Stonehenge on Boscombe Down: apparently around 1550 BC he had arrived in Britain as part of a larger family group involved in trading who were also visiting the 'temple' of Stonehenge, doubtless by then a celebrated tourist site. Some historians claim that Helston in far western Cornwall, now inland, was once the chief port for the export of the famed Cornish tin, perhaps sourced already by Minoans in the second millennium BC.

Also by the third millennium BC maritime trade between the Persian Gulf and the Indus had been pioneered in stout vessels. The sea fairly invited exploration, settlement and, above all, trade: for there was yet no 'Empire of Roads', not until the Persians ruled the Middle East around 500 BC and the Xin Dynasty tyrannized China's Middle Kingdom 250 years later. Nothing on the planet facilitated trade like the sea, and so islands became both harbour hubs and embryonic empires. So it was with Crete once again.

Minoan Crete of the Hellenic Kouretes 'ignited' chiefly because of the island's already established robust trade with the Levant and Egypt. It was no coincidence that Zeus himself was believed to have been born in a Cretan cave: Crete was the economic focus of the Mediterranean and Knossos was the New York of her era. We have mentioned Crete's prized wares – her salted mutton, olive oil, wine, pottery, and bronze and ivory statuary – but we need to regard saffron in particular. Perhaps the world's most alluring, exotic and expensive spice, saffron thrilled the ancient world. Believed to have originated in Kashmir in northern India, its cultivation spread to the Middle East and then to the Mediterranean islands: saffron-gathering priestesses feature in a mural from Santorini (Thera) dated to around 1500 BC. Saffron is also mentioned in the Song of Solomon. As one can gather from later Greek and Roman usage, the Minoans would have perfumed their baths, theatres and halls with saffron, and actively encouraged trading partners to do the same. A tenth-century AD codex from England lauds saffron's healing properties. Derived from the purple crocus, saffron is prepared from three stigmas hand-picked from each flower then dried over charcoal fires. Its chief uses, however, were as a food flavouring and dye. Some 2,000 years ago saffron became the institutionalized colour for the robes of Buddhist priests. Its rarity and high cost are due to the extremely small yield from each crocus.[5] Like with certain poppies today, Minoan fortunes would have flowed from the flowers.

Just north of the Pillars of Hercules, Phoenicians focused on Gadir (modern Cádiz) perhaps as early as 1000 BC.[6] Within 300 years this magnificent port was trading in large amounts of tin and amber from the islands of northern Europe. Around 460 BC the Greek historian Herodotus (c. 485–c. 425 BC) described both imports as coming from 'the ends of the earth' and, in the same text, refers to the 'Tin Islands' which some historians claim to be the tin-rich Cornish peninsula.[7] Phoenicians also brought beer to island Celts, an import of paramount significance, some would say. Perhaps Minoans had brought wine earlier, but the islanders couldn't cultivate vines in their colder climate; sprouted and dried grain, however, they could use to produce malt in abundance. Trade flourished between Britons, Cypriots and Hellenes, with the Hellenes, largely an island people, financing and defending Bronze Age fortresses with copper from one island (Cyprus) and tin from another (Britain).

Around 700 BC Etruscan traders were bringing eastern Greek pottery and amphoræ of wine and olive oil, as well as bronze flagons, cauldrons and other metalwork to the British Isles for tin, amber, gold and slaves. A hundred years later, setting out from France's oldest city of Massalia (Marseille) – founded by Greeks from Anatolian Phocæa in 600 BC – Greek merchants were working in partnership with these Etruscan traders before establishing a series of their own branch colonies, from Nice westwards to Iberian Emporion (Ampurias). For centuries the Greeks then dominated the island commerce.

In the classical era, it was island trade above all that made Greece Europe's most advanced society, raising great city-states of Parian marble – from the island of Paros in the central Cyclades. (Used for centuries, this translucent blonde stone was the marble of choice for Greeks and Romans alike.) Among them rose glorious Rhodes, 18 km southwest of Anatolia (modern Turkey). Rhodes held a special place in Mediterranean commerce, renowned for her spices, resins, ivory, silver, wine, oil, fish and amber 'from every point of the compass'.[8] The Rhodian fleet was the sea's best, though it probably numbered no more than 50 ships of the line. Then came Rhodes's decline: jealous of the isle's fame and wealth, Rome in retaliation declared 3.4-sq-km Delos in the Cyclades a free port, crushing Rhodes's monopoly; whereupon in 42 BC Gaius Cassius Longinus destroyed Rhodes the city, located at the island's northern tip, and slaughtered most of her residents: 'Of her thousands of statues, buildings, and harbours, nothing remained – or hardly anything. The invaders left no stone upright upon another.'[9]

Miniscule Delos herself, runt of the Cyclades, then waxed into an emporium extraordinaire – it would be difficult to name an ancient god who didn't take up residence there. For each and every mariner and trader, from Massalia to the Levant, was welcomed here as a native and Delos's religious tolerance was legendary. With this the island became one of the Ægean's wealthiest. And the view over Delos today, more than 2,000 years later? 'Everywhere the eye turns there is desolation; nothing whole, nothing erect, nothing complete . . . A whole brief civilisation was swallowed up here, battered to pieces.'[10]

Naxos – where Theseus had abandoned Ariadne after fleeing with her from Crete, poor Ariadne sleeping on the beach, then capturing the heart of youthful Dionysus, god of wine, who then chose to make the island his own – became in antiquity the headquarters of the Cycladean wine trade. (When newly arrived in Greece, Lord Byron fancied he would purchase Ithaca, but then saw Naxos and resolved to settle there instead.) Yet it was Lesbos which claimed the title as the Ægean's premier winegrower. When Aristotle, so the story goes, needed a new teacher for his school and his choice lay between Menedemus of Rhodes and Theophrastus of Lesbos, he asked both men to serve their islands' wines to him: declaring both excellent, he nonetheless declared Theophrastus his appointee, as the wine of Lesbos had more body.

Chios prided herself on the juice of the mastic plant (*Pistacia lentiscus*) with which the island's residents distilled a liqueur that today's Chiots attribute to St Isidore of Chios (*d.* AD 251). They also made this into a 'pistachio chewing gum' which later proved very popular in Turkish harems as a breath-freshener and digestive-tranquilizer. Chios cornered the Mediterranean's mastic market. Calymnos, on the other hand, was famous in antiquity for her sponge-divers, but the sponge capital was the small Dodecanese island of Astypalea. In Homer's *Odyssey* servants wiped the tables with sponges; all artists used sponges to paint; each soldier's kit held a sponge as a drinking 'vessel' – the crucified Christ was offered vinegar on a sponge. In the Middle Ages, burned sponge was a proven medication; prostitutes applied olive oil to a sponge as a contraceptive pessary; and island Venice won herself a monopoly in Dodecanese sponges in the 1200s, a sponge then known as a 'Venetia'. Today sponges are still used, but the market is fickle. Surgeons still prefer high-quality Dodecanese sponges, but the natural sponge beds are nearly exhausted and foreign artificial sponges have inundated the market.

By sheer necessity the Roman Empire was a maritime economy. It was all a question of transport. It's been calculated that the ratio of land–river–maritime costs in the Empire was a remarkable 55:6:1.[11] Luxury items dominated imports, with the balance of trade against Rome as overseas suppliers demanded payment in hard currency – usually silver denarii. For their imports the Romans also supplied other precious metals, as well as Spanish oil, Italian wine, pottery, emeralds, wool, copper, asbestos and particularly prized glassware.[12] A favourite with trading partners, especially Indians, was red coral, which the Romans harvested at Sicily, Sardinia, Corsica, the Balearic Islands and elsewhere. Chinese craved Rome's liquid storax, a resin. With such payment, out of Africa and her isles came ivory, cassia and tortoiseshell; out of the Arab lands and isles came myrrh, frankincense and aloes; and out of India and Sri Lanka came spices, drugs and pepper. Azurite arrived from Armenia. Pliny the Elder tells us that he had personally seen the emperor Caligula's (AD 12–41) wife Lollia Paulina at an ordinary betrothal banquet garbed in 40 million sesterces' worth of emeralds and pearls – not 'presents from an extravagant emperor, but ancestral possessions, acquired in fact with the spoil of the provinces'.[13] Most of these items arrived in Rome from the east, through the islands of Cyprus, Crete and the Ionian Sea. In the north there was trade as far as the island of Gotland in the Baltic: at Havor in 1963, a storage jar was discovered which contained Roman wine ladles, strainers and also a contemporary gold ring from the Crimea.[14]

In the British Isles, trade with the Roman Mediterranean had by now become so vigorous that all traditional trading routes had been quite overturned. (Until then, Scotland, Wales and Ireland, in particular, had focused their activities on a natural western, not eastern, market.) Once the Romans pulled out, more traditional sea routes and exchange systems resumed, albeit infrequently. 'The pottery and glass were probably exchanged for leather and skins, for coinage virtually vanished from Britain within a few years of the end of Roman rule.'[15]

On the tops of isolated peaks of the Moluccan, or Spice, Islands south of the Philippines and west of New Guinea, special evergreen trees had evolved that grow nowhere else: clove and nutmeg. Very early on, it was found that the seeds or flower buds of these trees possess highly flavoured, aromatic spices that could enrich the taste of any food. 'Although this may not seem to be of great importance in human affairs, at one time these spices were worth more than their weight in gold!'[16] As early as 200 BC, envoys from Java to China carried cloves with them to sweeten their breath when they were granted an audience with the Han emperor. It was recognized as well that these and similar spices preserved fish and meat in an age and clime with no natural refrigeration; rendered spoiled fare palatable; cured or assuaged all sorts of illnesses; and could embalm, perfume and otherwise de-stench in an era of the foulest smells imaginable.

Island spices of all kinds have been known and treasured for millennia, filling the holds of trading ships plying all seas. Sri Lanka, for one, was celebrated for cinnamon and pepper (just like mainland India). Cinnamon, from an evergreen tree of the angiosperm family (like nutmeg and cloves), is harvested in the wet season; the young shoots are stripped of their bark, then wrapped into long quills and dried; medieval Europeans fancied it as flavouring and also used it in Christian rites. Pepper was the prime meat preserver and a favourite food flavouring; indeed, it is pepper – and not the Crusades or inflation – that some historians have blamed for the sudden demise of Europe's feudal aristocracy in the High Middle Ages: their indulgence poisoned them. Frankincense and myrrh, well known from the Nativity but otherwise all but obsolete today, were long prized as incenses and perfumes. Frankincense also served as a medicinal plaster; myrrh was a tonic and ointment, and is still applied today as a mild antiseptic. It was Arabs who traded these throughout the ancient world; medieval island ports grew wealthy from their export. If anything, demand only increased over the centuries. Trade in spices was the oil economy of the past – the wealthiest market on Earth.

In time this trade was challenged by the Portuguese and Dutch, both contesting to wrest the markets, ports and even resource islands away from Arab merchants and Malay kings and tribal chiefs. European nations sought alternative shipping routes when Arabs fought back – it was in search of a quicker, safer route to India and the Spice Islands that Columbus sailed west in 1492. The nation that held the monopoly on the island spice trade, it was firmly believed, would control Europe's destiny and steer Christianity's future. Portugal made the most robust early bid. In 1512 she seized Ambon Island in the Banda Sea just west of New Guinea, built a fort there, and controlled the spice trade from this base. Profits were phenomenal. 'It is said that one of the ships of Portuguese navigator Ferdinand Magellan, after its circumnavigation of the globe in 1519–1522, brought back a load of cloves, which was sold in Europe for more than the entire cost of the three-year trip.'[17]

Thousand-sq-km Ambon Island hosted possibly the world's greatest treasury of cloves. Her neighbouring islands – Ceram, Buru, Mangole, Obi, Misool and others – were scented with clove trees, nutmeg and pepper vines. Here Portugal throned for nearly a century.

Then the Dutch invaded, over and over, usually in cover of night, finally seizing Ambon's fort and driving out the Portuguese in 1609. Whereupon the Dutch devastated the biota to keep the spices rare and prices artificially high: an adumbration of later Manhattan tactics. It was now the Dutch East India Company that controlled one of history's most lucrative markets. Much of the Netherlands' subsequent wealth stemmed from this treasure house of spices; from Ambon the Dutch held most of the Moluccas in sway, dispatching their treasure ships back to Amsterdam and Rotterdam and enabling Holland to challenge Britain for control of the seas. It was they alone who now pocketed the phenomenal profits – until the eighteenth century, that is, when France shattered the Dutch monopoly.

It's a fascinating tale.[18] An administrator of Île de France (modern Mauritius) in the Indian Ocean named Pierre Poivre (French 'pepper', an amusing historical irony), while visiting Dutch Ambon thousands of kilometres to the east, surreptitiously purloined clove and nutmeg seeds. Once returned to Île de France, Poivre successfully cultivated the seeds and descendants of these spread to other Indian Ocean islands, where they flourished. So it was that the Spice Islands – and the Dutch – were toppled from their throne of spice.

(Today, for example, the world's greatest producer of cloves is an island off Tanzania: Zanzibar.)

Smaller Indian Ocean isles also rendered rare resources.[19] Bahrain in the Persian Gulf was a pearl treasury. Socotra yielded valuable resins. Maldive cowries counted as currency from southern China to western Africa. Eastern African islands provided rare timber, ambergris and ivory. The storehouses of small eastern Malay islands bulged not only with nutmeg and cloves but also with the aromatic sandalwood so prized in India and China.

By nature and isolation many islands are 'single-ware' places dependent on one resource for sustenance and revenue. Iceland, for example, sources 75 per cent of her export earnings from fishing, which is central to nearly all of Iceland's treaty and trade negotiations with foreign states; fishing also underlay Iceland's infamous Cod Wars of the 1950s and '70s. (Today, Iceland's cod are all but gone.) Single-crop agriculture also strangles many island economies for being so succeptible to disease and fluctuating markets. When Caribbean islands trading in tobacco in the 1500s and 1600s discovered they were losing markets to the superior plantations of British America, they gave up tobacco for sugar. But planting and harvesting sugar required a larger labour force and so black Africans were imported to this end, which altered the demographics of the West Indies forever – with a soaring population also placing unsustainable demands on nature.

On Barbados, for example, sugar, rum and molasses came to rule. Barbados had begun as a colony of small British farms, but over one generation the island was transformed by her pioneer settlers into a major sugar exporter, with extensive plantations.[20] In the mid- and late seventeenth century Europe's taste for cane sugar had grown exponentially: greater tracts were cleared for production; further islands were settled and cleared; the smallholders had to yield to a coterie of privileged venture capitalists who, residing in Britain, let managers run their estates with slave labour from West Africa. Successful despots to a man, the managers produced profligate profits, enriching the – almost exclusively – English absentee owners. By the 1700s nearly all of the Caribbean economy was based on sugar production with its grand support network of shipping and slaves.

It was then that Barbados lost her lead to Jamaica when the 'Rum Trade' completed the network. Yet by around 1820 each 'sugar colony' of the Caribbean found itself in decline: those huge profits of the mid-1700s to early 1800s, while slavery thrived, dwindled once the labour force dissolved. (The same obtained on the Indian Ocean's plantations.) Today, with rocketing labour costs, Barbados, for one, has limited sugar production; like many smaller islands she cannot afford to mechanize and so cannot compete with big-island competitors like Cuba. Barbados's sugar industry now brings in less than half of the country's export revenues. Enticed by tourism's quick profits, with little economic diversification Barbados chose at her peril the path of the tourist mecca.

Madeira, in the eastern Atlantic, flaunted her eminence as Portugal's wealthiest sugar-producing colony, but this was short-lived. Settled in 1420 and already exporting sugar by the 1450s, Madeira was upstaged in this role a century later by American competitors, especially Brazilians. One reason for her decline was that Madeira never fully exploited that cheap slave labour which was to facilitate the sugar industry of the New World. Once Madeira lost her lead, she never fully recovered. By the mid-1500s vines were replacing Madeira's cane and soon wine was the island's chief export – 'madeira' is still enjoyed throughout the world. As of the 1980s Madeira, too, became a preferred destination of jet-age beachcombers.

In the Indian Ocean, Sri Lanka grew into one of Earth's great tea centres. The British had first planted coffee in the central highlands, but in the early 1870s the plantings were devastated by a leaf disease – the coffee rust or *Hemileia vastatrix*. Tea became the substitute, with more than 100 varieties cultivated. The island's tea is regarded as among the finest in the world. Though Sri Lanka's lowlands still produce rice, which has been cultivated there since ancient times, tea is emperor. Almost all of the labour – in both the tea plantations and rice fields – is performed by women, who also have to cook, clean, sew, mend, and bear and rear the children. 'Sri Lanka may be a second Garden of Eden for Adam, but not for Eve.'[21] Many men spend their days fishing from the shore or outrigger canoes. Or they go 'toddy tapping': collecting nectar from palm blossoms along high tightrope walkways suspended between the treetops. Sri Lanka is also a treasure house of many of the planet's precious and semi-precious gems – rubies, sapphires, topaz, garnets, aquamarines and tourmaline 'litter' the land, spilling out of riverbeds. Already thousands of years ago gem mines were operating there. Under her red clay Ratnapura – the 'city of gems'

– still prizes the deposit which furnished ancient Greece and Rome with jewels.

A bangle of another ilk has been prostitution. Many mariners sought solace in this trade, while islanders took in rare goods and even rarer genes (crucial for islands with high in-breeding). Chios, fifth largest of all the Greek isles, was once infamous for her easy women. Scottish traveller William Lithgow (1582–1645) experienced for himself how

> The women of the city of Scio [on Chios] are the most beautiful dames or rather Angelical creatures of all Greeks upon the face of the earth, and greatly given to venery. Their husbands are their panders, and when they see any stranger arrive, they would presently demand of him whether he would have a mistress; and so they make whores of their own wives.[22]

But it was the Pacific, above all, that was notorious for perceived meretriciousness. On each Polynesian isle, it seemed, young girls would offer themselves for a piece of cloth, a hat or even a nail, with their fathers and brothers grinningly encouraging the trade. From Hawai'i to Easter Island, European and American tars and masters alike failed to comprehend the plain economics of the intercourse: it wasn't European prostitution at all, but island survival.

Apart from rare incursions, Pacific island economies were still mostly based on agriculture and fishing, with occasional trade in pottery, obsidian, fish hooks and adzes, often over many thousands of kilometres. With growing European intrusion, however, the dynamic changed entirely. European staples – potatoes, dairy products, beef and pork – became the unwonted purview of indigenous islanders now eager to cash in on the alien commerce, as ever more foreigners descended to trade, purchase land and wield dominion. The whaling industry then brought an increased demand for goods, alcohol and women, and coastal settlements thrived, metamorphosing into 'European' towns. There were great success stories. New Zealand became prime farmland once her dense mountain forests were cleared for sheep runs. The sugar industry appropriated the Fijian islands, its success dependent on indentured labourers brought from India by the British. Both flourished.

There were failures, too. Nauru in Micronesia was once a mountain of rich guano. This valuable source of phosphate was mined as of 1907 and by the late 1960s and early '70s Nauruans enjoyed the highest per capita income of any sovereign state. But once the phosphate was exhausted in the 1980s many Nauruans found emigration to be their only recourse. A similar fate befell the islanders of Johnston Atoll, southwest of Hawai'i; Makatea in the Tuamotus; the Chincha Islands off the coast of Peru; and Banaba Island in the Republic of Kiribati (formerly Gilbert Islands).

In most Pacific societies, and for varied reasons, 'there was generally an enthusiastic participation in new commercial activity, whether sandalwood gathering or involvement in the infrastructure of nuclear testing'.[23] As with those ancients of the Outer Hebrides, Malta or Minoan Crete, Pacific Islanders could easily adapt themselves to the larger world that came with delicacies and demands, offering not only things, but technologies, strategems, blood and, most importantly, information. As a result, a new tribe rose in the Pacific, a powerful people with altered demands on the region's limited resources and with different responses to a changed world. Today's Pacific Islanders still grow sugar, cocoa, copra, coffee and timber – crops and stands very sensitive, especially on smaller islands, to storms, disease and fluctuating markets. Some Pacific island economies stave off bankruptcy only by selling offshore fishing rights to Japan, Russia, Korea or, increasingly, China. Or they host hordes of tourists. Many are rescued only by remittances, the 'blood of exiled sons': as it was this that kept old mothers from starvation in Ireland in the 1920s and in Crete in the 1970s, so it is still this that sustains extended families in Samoa and Tokelau, for example.

Some islanders believed bootlegging to be the key. This happened on St Pierre, France's Canadian isle. During Prohibition in the US in the 1920s the Canadian authorities forbade all transport of liquor over the US border – but still permitted the export of liquor to a foreign territory. St Pierre was neither Canadian nor US, but French. So a certain Mr McCoy was soon freighting 350,000 cases of whisky, gin and other spirits into St Pierre's harbour each month.[24] From here, island fishermen grew rich smuggling booze into all of New England, their bottles carefully wrapped in straw jackets to maintain silence. Still today many of St Pierre's houses reveal a spirited descendance: one residence – locals call it the 'Cutty Sark Villa' – is entirely constructed of whisky crates.

Other islands were exploited for their very substance. The Grasberg Pit in Indonesian Papua, New Guinea's western half, is currently the world's largest gold mine, third-largest copper mine and highest opencast mine: for many years now its tailings have simply been dumped into rivers flowing off the mountain range; down in the lowlands these coat the tropical forest with toxic sediment. Eight km south of Weymouth, the Isle of Portland – 'a white island lying out to sea like a great whale'[25] – became London's quarry after the Great Fire of 1666, when so much Portland stone was quarried that the rejects alone created a 150-m-high islet off the island's west end. Most of London's landmarks – from Bush House to the Cenotaph, from the Royal Exchange to the British Museum – originated on Portland, and it is reckoned there is still enough stone left there to rebuild the world for another five centuries.

Others manage to distil the most intoxicating solutions. In the early 1800s the principal exports from Islay, 'Queen of the Hebrides', were horses, cattle, sheep, pigs, poultry, cheese, butter, eggs and, in some years, potatoes. (Not fish, as this was only for local consumption.) Then it was discovered that Islay could produce some of the finest single malt whisky in the world. Today's population of about 3,000 profits from eight active distilleries (with another on the way) producing the famous, smoky, peaty malts treasured from Edinburgh to Auckland. Further islands have now entered the trade, too, earning enviable revenues and awards, especially Ireland and Japan. Even New Zealand boasts a whisky distillery, on South Island. Uniquely for the Pacific, New Zealand has become a chief wine exporter, the industry taking wing in the 1980s. The international demand for Kiwi wines saw the nation's vineyard plantings treble between 1995 and 2005. But dairy goods, wool and mutton still dominate New Zealand's economy, just after its king, Tourism. New Zealand is also the second largest exporter of logs to China.

'YO-HO-HO AND A BOTTLE OF RUM'

Pirates and privateers have been an island mainstay for millennia and these highwaymen of the oceans have rescued entire populations from starvation. When a nation or other agency authorizes piracy, then it is privateering, and through most of history privateering, not piracy, has been practised, as independent piracy is generally too ephemeral, disruptive and self-destructive. Privateering itself was only outlawed in the 1800s when most nations realized it impacted too rudely on the far greater profits issuing from colonial corporations.

The earliest known piracy – always a victim's label – was that of the Carians vandalizing the central Cyclades around 1600 BC; it took Minos of Crete and his multi-ethnic fleet to cast them out of the Ægean, perhaps in the 'Battle of Naxos' proclaimed on the Phaistos Disk. The later Sea Peoples, a loose confederation of Viking-like Hellenes led by the Danaans, tyrannized the Ægean and eastern Mediterranean as far as Egypt. The Tyrrhenians subsequently grew rich on sea plunder, as did the Phoenicians who also profited from targeting defenceless isles for the slave trade. Many Greek islands specialized in piracy, necessitating punitive expeditions by the wealthiest city-states. The Illyrians terrorized the isles of the Adriatic, while entire towns along the Anatolian coastline were dedicated to piracy, disrupting the Roman Empire's commerce. In 75 BC a young Julius Cæsar (100–44 BC) was captured by Cilician pirates and held captive on tiny Pharmacusa in the Dodecanese; his ransom of 50 talents of gold was dearly purchased – Cæsar afterwards raised a fleet, caught his former captors and executed each one.

The highly lucrative trade continued to wreak havoc in the Mediterranean isles. In the third century AD Goths descended on Crete and Cyprus, amassing a wealth of booty. Saxon and Frankish pirates were then raiding the isles and coasts of Armorica (modern Brittany and Normandy) and Belgic Gaul. Irish pirates attacked the Hebrides, Môn (Anglesey) and other isles and coastal settlements, often taking slaves (like young St Patrick around AD 403). In the Middle Ages, the Vikings were the world's privateers par excellence, turning the violent trade into a veritable industry as they created principal trade routes, founded cities and directed the course of Western Europe. Yet literally hundreds of other groups during the era terrorized isles, coasts and seaways in search of spoils and slaves. The entire Mediterranean was held to ransom by Saracens: Muslim pirates established centres in southern France and northern Italy, then based themselves in the Balearics as well as in the Emirate of Crete in order to ransack the sea.

In the Pacific, piracy was common to the Philippines and Malay Archipelago, as well as among Polynesian islanders who favoured swift attacks in small outriggers: this was not so much for plunder – portable wealth didn't exist as such in Pacific societies – as for

A seventeenth-century Song emperor shipping Chinese goods to offshore isles.

women and children as wives and slaves. East Asia's and South Asia's coasts and islands were plagued by privateering fleets for centuries. (Today, piracy still worries both regions.)

In the 1500s and 1600s the world's piracy capital lay in that curve between the Atlantic and Caribbean, the 'Spanish Main' – an erstwhile superhighway for galleons bulging with the gold and silver of South America. Francis Drake, Captain Kidd, Blackbeard and countless privateers and freebooters, several based on St Thomas in the Virgin Islands, plundered each Spanish vessel they encountered, then turned on all nations' shipping, including Britain's.

It is said that in the late 1600s a Captain James Misson established on Madagascar his own pirate kingdom called Libertalia.[26] His subjects allegedly grew so wealthy on their booty that they retired and began to live respectably. But their mountain of gold was of little avail when island neighbours refused to trade. Once their food grew scarce after about 25 years, most Libertalians reverted to piracy. (It is possible, however, that the entire tale is a fabrication.)

Other pirate isles flourished. Take the story of Hydra, for example, which lies only some 6 km off the Greek mainland and around 50 km from Athens. Though now a jet-set mecca, she once reigned as a piratical den.[27] Hydra's centuries of piracy – actually privateering, as it was authorized – generated the wealth for substantial mansions, indeed for entire dynasties. In fact, Greek independence took its spark from Hydra: the main thrust against the Ottoman Empire was facilitated by the island's swift corsairs. When the Greeks first declared war against their Turkish masters in 1770, Hydra's 4,000 families were swamped by 20,000 refugees from the north, and so the island began trading, alongside privateering. By the late 1790s, with Britain's economic blockade of Europe because of Napoleon, Hydra's shipping magnates had amassed vast fortunes. When the actual War of Independence was publicly declared in 1821, it was the patriotic Hydrans who ploughed their substantial fortunes into the Greek Navy, to do or die. They did, and profited doubly – in future markets and national renown. Each mansion today is like a small museum dedicated to the Greek Navy. And Hydra reigns still – as the capital of Greek national pride.

Today, seaborne piracy continues to plague international shipping, costing an estimated $13 to $16 billion worldwide in annual losses. Particularly troubled island locales include the Indian Ocean, the Gulf of Aden, Singapore, the Strait of Malacca, the South China Sea and the Niger Delta. Islanders themselves, however, are seldom targeted now, but rather the international crews of cargo vessels usually sailing under flags of convenience. Modern booty comprises crew, cargo and even vessels themselves which commonly fetch a ransom of many millions of dollars.

Wreckage also helped many islanders to survive in earlier centuries when goods of any kind were lifelines. In the Frisian Archipelago offshore from the Netherlands and Germany, such islands as Texel, Vlieland, Terschelling, Ameland, Schiermonnikoog and Rottumeroog survived times of need only by luring ships to founder in order to plunder their cargo. Mostly comprised of sand dunes, Ameland prevailed as a 'free lordship' independent of Holland from

1424 until her ruling family died out in 1708. This coast is so harsh that the sea sometimes froze over and goods had to be brought by sledge from the mainland. One might forgive these islanders their outrageous strategy, for it was ever life or death. Accidental plunder – jetsam, that is – is another matter altogether which, since the days of Jason and his Argonauts, has also secured survival on inhospitable isles. Sometimes serendipity reigns. In 1941 the ss *Politician*, carrying to the US a consignment of unbottled whisky in metal vats as well as 290,000 ten-shilling notes, wrecked at the Hebridean island of Barra, whereupon the Barrans had the devil's own time finding all the bottles, buckets and containers needed to haul the whisky away to their pantries, and many of the ten-shilling notes flew to the moon. The hilarious story inspired a novel of 1947 and the film *Whisky Galore!* (1949).

Smuggling remains a similar strategem, as we saw with St Pierre. Islands have hosted smugglers' dens ever since centralized governments began imposing excise taxation. When honest trade often meant penury and starvation, smuggling on occasion allowed smallholders to survive bleak island conditions. In the 1790s it was the Isle of Man that lay at the centre of the British Isles' smuggling, defying a rapacious London so far away. Unhappily, today's smuggling mostly involves not tobacco, wine or spirits but hard drugs, with the trade eliciting an island brutality not witnessed since the days of the Spanish Main.

'HE WOULD SELL US INTO ISLES'

Until fairly recently slaves always figured in any island economy – as chattel, labour or target – for islands lay in trade routes and all these routed slaves. Islanders themselves meant easy prey for slave raiders and many populations forever feared such attacks, with daughters failing to return from their washing on the shore and tribal numbers ever dwindling. In Homer's *Iliad*, for example, Poseidon reminds Apollo how Trojan king Laomedon had once threatened that 'he would bind together our feet and our hands above, and would sell us into isles that lie afar'.[28] Through the Greek isles slaves not only comprised a large percentage of the population but of trade as well, which situation was only exacerbated by the Roman Empire. Celts regularly traded in slaves in Ireland and Britain, and later Vikings fattened on the trade, too. In AD 987, for example, 2,000 men of Môn (Anglesey) were seized by Northmen – operating from their centres at Dublin and on the Isle of Man – and sold into slavery.[29] For centuries Saracen marauders thrived on the Mediterranean slave trade, many of their victims captured on Greek, Italian and Spanish island beaches. And the first gold of the Spanish Main was extracted by those doomed Caribbean islanders.

In the early part of the 1800s Danish (now US) St Thomas in the Virgin Islands was reckoned the largest slave market in the West Indies. African slaves were taken by the 'Danish West Indies and Guinea Company' first to St John to 'acclimatize' them after their nightmarish crossing of the Atlantic, then transferred to the slave market on nearby St Thomas. From here it was off to the sugar plantations on St Thomas, St John and St Croix. (Modern tourists visiting the ruins of St John's Annaberg estate often retch when they behold the grim slave quarters, dungeon and mill.) In November of 1733 the Africans rose up in brave defiance, but then a combined army of Danes, Britons and French – the three nations whose profligate profits were imperiled – mercilessly crushed them like so many stalks of sugar cane.

Though Britain abolished slavery throughout her Empire in 1833, the trade still thrived in the Indian Ocean. Indeed, most islands along the East African coast would go on selling slaves to American, Brazilian and Arab dealers, whereas the British chose to 'bond' or indenture Chinese and Indians as labourers while the French used similar pseudo-slaves in all their Indian Ocean plantations. Bahrain and Zanzibar, however, continued to make use of slaves well into the 1900s.

Inured to inter-valley and inter-island raiding for centuries, Pacific Islanders, too, experienced similar schemes. Labour 'recruitment' – often a euphemism for kidnapping – was yet another industry that fundamentally altered Pacific islands in the second half of the 1800s.[30] In search of cheap labour for Peru's plantations, haciendas and guano islands, for example, a small fleet of vessels belonging to international entrepreneurs, most of them Peruvian, sailed from Lima's port of Callao between 1862 and '64 into the Pacific and removed around 3,500 Polynesians (over 1,000 from Easter Island alone, the island closest to Peru) and Micronesians, most of them by deceit or violence. Human loss on some smaller islands, already decimated by Western diseases, ranged between 25 and 50 per cent. Outraged when they learned of the trade, foreign nations demanded that Peru return her 'slaves'. By the time Peru acquiesced, however, the worst had been done: by 1866 only 257 'blackbirded' islanders were still alive, the rest having succumbed to smallpox, 'nostalgia' and other diseases.[31] Only 37 finally returned to their home islands, some introducing devastating illnesses.

FRUITS DE MER

Shoreline and offshore fishing has always comprised an important part of island subsistence. Already in antiquity ocean harvests figured largely in international trade. But it was not until the end of the 1700s that certain species fostered entire industries. James Cook's third expedition had discovered fur seals along America's northwest coast; once news of this spread in the 1780s sealers began voyaging from Canton (modern Guangzhou) – the first Chinese port open to European trade – to hunt the seals, replenish and winter over in Hawai'i, then return to Canton to sell their sealskins for small fortunes. The trade changed Hawai'i forever, as on the islands the sealers sought water, provisions, alcohol and women, and the Hawaiians were happy to provide whatever and whomever they could in exchange for nails, hoop iron (for adzes) and cloth. These fur seals, in contrast to short-haired pinnipeds such as sea lions, possess lovely, thick, woolly coats beneath their matted upper hair, greatly prized by Chinese garment makers. (As a result, many species have been hunted to near-extinction.) Sealing stations were among the first semi-permanent European settlements in New Zealand.

Yet this was only the beginning. In the late 1700s and early 1800s King Coal and Queen Oil ruled the Industrial Revolution: coal for powering it, and whale oil for lighting and lubricating it. (New, improved lamps had just turned candlelit houses into bright centres of activity.) One can safely say that before modern tourism it was the whaling industry that cast islands' die – chiefly between the 1790s and 1850s and particularly in the Pacific – for generations of whalers in the North Atlantic had all but eradicated entire populations of sperm whales. With the demand for whale oil soaring as the populations of Atlantic sperm whales crashed, whalers descended on Pacific isles in droves and stayed for decades. Whaling didn't affect all Pacific islands: only those nearest major whaling grounds. (Islands and groups ignored by the whaling trade have generally remained in a backwater ever since.) Whaling poured the cast for the Europeanized Pacific. In many places this cast was New England American: 200 US whaling vessels ranged the Pacific in 1828, and 571 by 1844. In contrast, both Britain and France had only a few dozen whaling ships in the Pacific in the 1840s.[32] Each whaling voyage lasted an average of three years.

The industry not only fundamentally and permanently altered the lifestyles of all affected Pacific Islanders, it transformed US islanders as well. Off Massachusetts's coast, Nantucket, 20 km long by 8 km at her widest, was the world's whaling capital from around 1770 until 1850. The name Nantucket means 'faraway land' in the language of her earlier residents, the Wampanoag, a sub-tribe of the Algonquin. Englishman Thomas Mayhew purchased the island from the tribe, then sold her on 2 July 1659 to nine others seeking greater freedom from Massachusetts's religious intolerance, for £30 and two beaver hats.[33] Nantucket men – 'these naked Nantucketers, these sea-hermits, issuing from their anthill in the sea . . .' as Melville writes in *Moby-Dick* – were foremost farmers and sheep herders, but they had watched the Wampanoag drain precious oil from beached whales.[34] Soon they were out with the tribe catching whales offshore and hauling them back to the island, whereupon they developed deep-sea whaling, in competition to the French, Portuguese and Basques (who had been whaling commercially since the Middle Ages). With the Industrial Revolution's demand for whale oil, Nantucket boomed, as a cargo of oil worth $50,000 – then the price of a hundred houses – was not uncommon. Phenomenal personal fortunes were made. But then came the Quaker retribution for avarice: Nantucket Harbor's sandbar silted, blocking the entrance to heavier ships; these began deviating to New Bedford on the mainland. A conflagration then destroyed much of the town, warehouses and ships in the harbour. Finally, petroleum was discovered in Pennsylvania – far easier to find, extract and market than whale oil. When the whaling industry died, so did Nantucket.

Other islands had been compelled to diversify earlier. As of around 1670 St Pierre and Miquelon, the two French communes just off Canada's eastern coast, profited from whaling, but this was replaced by cod fishing when the Atlantic sperm whale populations plummeted a century later. Cod then became the blood of the islands' economies. In the 1900s frozen cod and fishmeal export came to dominate the islands' industry, which was small but sustainable. But when overfishing collapsed the Grand Banks' cod population, the Canadian government imposed on the cod industry a closure, which the French islands, by international agreement, had to observe, too. As a recourse, the islands have turned to tourism, agriculture, crab fishing and fish farming, none of which satisfies the communes' needs. Alone their strategic position, however, as France's last official bastion in North America – and as France's oldest overseas colony – still assures sustaining aid from the *mère patrie*.

Pacific islands' maritime resources remain vital to the world economy: over 50 per cent of the world's fish catch comes from the Pacific. But other important water-borne resources hail from there as well, such as pearls.[35] The chance of finding a pearl in an oyster is minute, which is why natural pearls were antiquity's greatest treasures. Cultured pearls enabled the modern pearl industry, and this was the achievement of Kōkichi Mikimoto of Japan in the late 1800s. Today the market annually produces over 100 tonnes of pearls, the main product being the Japanese Akoya pearl. However, the world's most prestigious are the white and black South Sea pearls. Whites are cultivated mostly along the shores of tropical western and northern Australia, but to a lesser extent also on the islands of Indonesia and the Philippines. Blacks were first produced in the early 1960s in the Tuamotus east of Tahiti, and production has since expanded throughout the Tuamotus and to the Gambiers (Mangareva) and Cooks. In Tahiti alone, the export value amounts to tens of millions of dollars each year.

On the world's largest island, Greenland, the tiny population of over 56,000 (est. 2010) still hunt and fish for a living, their wharves always slippery with fish scales and crushed ice. The local industry now focuses on salmon, halibut and shrimp (their cod is all but gone), with fish processing and limited mining recently supplementing the island's meagre economy.

THE LEADEN LIFELINE

Tourism: the blessing and the curse of nearly all islanders. Over the past 50 years no other industry on Earth has been as lucrative or as intrusive. Tourism has saved islands and it has damned islands.

The elite have always toured islands. That 'Oxford of the ancient world', Rhodes, was a veritable mecca for Greeks and Romans: a hub of learning, rhetoric and the fine arts. Cæsar, Brutus, Antony, Cassius and Cicero all studied in Rhodes; Tiberius spent one of his exiles there. Throughout the Middle Ages, too, other famous isles – Sicily, Venice, Crete, Cyprus – attracted the powerful and wealthy. In later centuries, voyagers' accounts of foreign isles, tailored to market tastes, created an 'island allure' that enticed many to emulation. With the technological and social changes of Western industrial countries in the late 1800s came the creation of a middle class and enrichment of the working class which then enabled mass-market tourism. Increased leisure, cash beyond necessity, improved steamship transport at reduced fares – all these led to ever more 'exotic' destinations: from the Isle of Wight to the Channel Islands; from Ibiza to Crete; from the Maldives to Hawai'i.

It was a protracted expansion. Consider Nantucket once again. When whale oil crashed, Nantucket's economy collapsed. Many islanders moved away, the burned ruins of the town were not restored, the cobbled streets grew thick with weeds. There was no trade, no visitors, and life was ebbing. By the 1880s Nantucket was moribund. How ironic, then, that a family named 'Coffin' – one of the island's oldest and largest – decided at this time on their clan reunion: 500 Coffins from throughout New England descended on their ancestral home, new accommodations were built to house them all, and it was these that were then used to host the island's first commercial tourists. It created an entirely new economy. In this fashion Nantucket became one of the world's first modern tourist islands and she has prospered from tourism ever since. In summer months tourists outnumber islanders five to one: a familiar statistic for easily accessible tourist isles.

The same had long been engaging Germany's Frisian and Baltic islands. Heligoland, two small isles lying 46 km off the northwestern German coastline, already in 1826 became a seaside spa and was soon expanding into a major tourist retreat for Germany's upper class, as well as a refuge for the revolutionaries of 1830 and '48 when Heligoland was still ruled by Britain. (However, when Britain ceded the two islands to Germany in the 1890 Heligoland–Zanzibar Treaty, the islands were militarized by the new German Empire which developed Heligoland into a key naval base; during the First World War the civilian population was evacuated to the mainland.) In the middle of the 1800s Norderney Island flourished when sea bathing became fashionable for the first time in Germany, and guest houses, hotels and resort spas opened, too, bringing sudden prosperity to this small island as well as to neighbouring Borkum, where the first tourists had arrived in 1834, eventually replacing whaling, fishing and trading as the mainstay of the local economy. In the Baltic Sea, Poel (part-Swedish until 1903) and Rügen (Germany's largest island, already a spa in 1794 and a bathing resort in 1818) followed a similar development and by the end of the nineteenth century both had become the new nation's most popular seaside resorts. Today all of these islands flourish from tourism, even more robust since Germany's reunification in 1990.

Once British middle- and working-class families had more leisure and ready money for short excursions, the Isle of Wight and the Channel Islands, with improved transport, were soon opening guest houses and, for wealthier visitors, larger hotels. Island travel became 'the thing to do', emulating the earlier Grand Tour which had opened up the isles of Italy and Greece. Slow ferries finally gave way to rapid hydrofoils at the same time that air travel not only brought tens of thousands to these islands but also had many islanders commuting to mainland jobs by air. In the early days before the Jersey airport, St Ouen's beach was the runway. Today the Channel Islands are linked with Dinard in France and Southampton in Britain and the longest flight is a little over half an hour; many small private planes access the islands too.

Especially after the Second World War, air travel revolutionized most island economies. Britain's General Charles George Gordon (1833–1885) had raved about the Seychelles in 1881: 'I think any requirement is fulfilled for deciding that the site of the district of Eden is near Seychelles.'[36] Yet it would take five days by slow steamer to get there from Mombasa, Kenya. Modern air travel opened up these islands, and so many more, to the rest of the world at last. Until 1964 Madeira was accessible only by ship and flying boat; when her mountainous terrain was planed to construct a modern airport, tourism boomed. Then there are Tenerife and Lanzerote in the Canary Islands, and Majorca, Minorca, Ibiza and Formentera in the Balearics – each virtually reinvented through modern jet travel in particular, with tourist numbers soaring beyond credence . . . and sustainability.

Increasingly since the 1980s wealthier citizens from the US and Canada, seeking tans and temperatures, have purchased and remodelled many old houses in Dunmore Town, for one, on Harbour Island in the Bahamas, and constructed new residences just outside.

This, together with modest tourism in half a dozen small hotels, has given the island's tiny economy a life-giving injection that does not intrude too onerously – the foreign owners are usually absent over the summer months. It's a familiar pattern in Puerto Rico, the Virgin Islands and Florida Keys, supplemented by financial investments, modern condominiums and timeshare schemes. Though many permanent islanders resent such island-hoppers, most recognize that their injection of capital and jobs buoys fragile economies.

Because of modern jet tourism the Greek isles are profiting and suffering like never before: visitation has become inundation and one is hard pressed to find an island which doesn't complain and cash in. But the reverse is also true, by virtue of modern commuting; from Greece's Saronic Islands – Ægina, Hydra, Poros, Spetses and others – white-collar workers ferry daily to office blocks in Piræus and Athens. (As do the commuters of Bainbridge Island near Seattle, Waiheke Island near Auckland, Phillip Island near Melbourne, North Stradbroke near Brisbane, and so many more.) In this way islanders turn 'day-mainlanders', melding into urbanites, as ferries conversely dump metropolitan hordes no island can reasonably sustain. Such commonplaces create their own 'commuting cultures' – exacerbating tourism, investment and absentee ownership. This is particularly felt near great metropolises. Lawrence Durrell was duly concerned about Greece's future in this regard, penning back in 1978:

> There is no doubt that Greece within the next decade will become the Florida of Europe, and one only hopes that good taste and good sense will prevent the atmosphere and the amenities from becoming totally unworthy of such a history and such a landscape. It is a matter of keeping one's fingers crossed.[37]

A generation later they remain crossed.

Just as in the Caribbean, Pacific island tourism is today the most important source of foreign exchange to balance trade deficits. It had been the earlier colonial system that enabled the economic and technological progress that made tourism viable: 'By 1900 every Pacific island was formally incorporated into someone's empire and painted the appropriate colour on maps.'[38] Plantation economies necessitated improved steamships, which then led to undersea cables, then radio (1920s), and finally oceanic air routes (1930s).

Pan Am pioneered the trans-Pacific route to China, using Honolulu, Midway, Wake and the Philippines as 'stepping-stones'.[39] But with improved access and communications, imperial nations adopted a psychological control over the Pacific world as well. (Indeed, one can now view the early to mid-1900s as the era when the Western hegemony – above all, Britain, France and the US – at last controlled most of the globe.)

> The Pacific islands in particular were now seen as a safe playground for recreational sailors, travellers, tourists. The Western body in nature was redefined. Nature itself could be redemptive. The island paradise was created.[40]

And with the new tourism, with this rapid influx of jobs and cash, with colonial government initiatives in health, housing and education, by the 1930s island populations began to grow once more.

Apart from the super-rich's retreats like privately owned Hamilton Island off Queenland's coast which caters only to tourism – enjoying non-stop profits with little injury – tourism will always remain a mixed blessing for the world's islands. Our planet's largest and fastest-growing industry, over the past 30 years tourism has been the proverbial lifeline for imperiled economies, to be sure. Even great New Zealand, this bastion of wool and mutton, finally saw tourism ($9.5 billion) topping dairy ($9 billion) as the nation's chief export earner in 2010. Tourism is the only industry that allows a net flow of wealth from richer to poorer countries, thus providing resource-poor island states with the foreign exchange needed to pay for imported goods and to service the borrowing bill. Yet this creates all sorts of problems. Up to 30 per cent of an island's employment may be tourism-linked, a fickle foundation at best. And only around 40 per cent of the net earnings from tourism remains in the host country; the other 60 per cent is lost to foreign wages, repatriated profits, commissions and other recipients. The maintenance of the infrastructure which modern competitive tourism demands burdens host governments. Most importantly, tourism's environmental and social effects in the main impact negatively on small and vulnerable island nations.[41] If tourism is a lifeline, then it is one of lead. At least for the time being, however, bulk tourism will doubtless continue to obsess the world's islands – its flowing funds a too-friendly fix.

ISLAND FINANCE

In the 1930s and '40s Montreal was the second most important city in the British Empire, the island seaport a mecca for international trade. And Manhattan, Hong Kong and Singapore are today financial centres of the first order, for such insular nodes not only foster commerce but focus its benefits, leading to the accumulation of immense wealth. So it was, too, in antiquity.

Take Delos, the focal point of Greece's Cyclades and the island that British historian Ernle Bradford (1922–1986) judged 'the last and best anchorage between Europe and Asia'.[42] Half bank and half shrine, Delos was the Wall Street of the ancient world.[43] One of Europe's most significant mythological, historical and archæological sites, in antiquity she was also revered as Apollo's birthplace and ritually purified through holy lustrations in 543 BC and again in 426 in a rite that endowed Delos with special magic. It was here that rich Levantines came to trade and bank – their deposits guaranteed by the tutelary security of sacred shrines – for Delos was the Ægean's capital of commercial magic, the isle a temple of a transcendent trust. In fact, so holy had Delos's soil become by the fifth century BC that all births and deaths had to occur only on neighbouring Rhenia. We must assume ancient Greeks were convinced their temple gods were sympathetic to material gain; so long as one shared one's wealth – in the form of gold, plate, statuary or precious stones – the gods of Delos brought good fortune and a fair breeze to one's enterprises. 'In this sense, the modern Americans, with their frank avowal that material gain is holy, are very like the ancient Greeks . . .'.[44] But the magic did not last: the Greek sophist Philostratus (c. AD 170–247) records that when Athens finally wished to sell Delos in her entirety, not a single buyer could be found.

Islands sometimes play financial hide-and-seek as well. At the end of 1910, to cite one notorious example, Jekyll Island off the Georgian coast of the US was the blind for five of North America's wealthiest financiers – representing, it is alleged, around one-fourth of the world's total wealth – and a senator and Assistant Secretary of the Treasury who, in insular secrecy, revolutionized the American financial system. They resolved to transform US banking, devised a new currency, and formulated what later would become the Federal Reserve Bank – a privately owned instrument to control and steer

America's finances to the gain of a select few. (In November 2010 the chairman of the Federal Reserve, Ben Bernanke, landed on Jekyll Island to commemorate the centennial of the historic event.) Tax havens – countries or territories where specific taxes are levied at reduced rates or not at all, attracting individuals and corporate entities wishing to avoid national obligations – have long been the purview of islands, where other forms of revenue (natural resources, trade, tourism, investment and so on) are wanting. Many islands make taxes more attractive, or eliminate them altogether, in order to elicit the capital that will then stimulate trade and encourage investment. In antiquity, Delos and other Greek isles functioned as just such tax havens, then to obviate Athens's 2 per cent tax on all imports. Today, the Isle of Man avers a tax haven status that originates from the first millennium AD, while the Channel Islands profess a tax independence from the Crown dating back to the Norman Conquest. Offshore company legislation in 1935 allowed Bermuda to become one of the first major, modern, corporate tax havens. Still, until the 1950s, it was mostly individuals who sought tax relief by moving their assets offshore to sympathetic islands. In the second half of the twentieth century ever more corporations then moved offshore as well, creating the newer phenomenon of offshore financial arenas.

Depositors need pay no personal income tax at all in the Bahamas, Bermuda (on foreign earnings), the Cayman Islands, the Channel Islands, and Nauru and Norfolk in the Pacific. Special individual and corporate tax benefits can be enjoyed – in a full array of competitive offers – in Anguilla, Antigua and Barbuda, Aruba, the Bahamas, Barbados, Bermuda, the British Virgin Islands, the Cayman Islands, the Channel Islands, the Cook Islands, Cyprus, Hong Kong, the Isle of Man, Labuan by Borneo, Mauritius, Nauru, the Netherlands Antilles, Nevis, New Zealand, Samoa, the Seychelles, St Kitts, St Vincent and the Grenadines, the Turks and Caicos Islands, the US Virgin Islands, the UK and Vanuatu. Many of these places – particularly in the Caribbean – have profited enormously from laundering drug money.

The Isle of Man has been accused in recent years of creating 'empty shells' – commercial companies existing only on paper – to avoid international sanctions with regard to the arms trade and to the smuggling of nuclear equipment. A disturbing new development is the money laundering which has occurred in the Cook

Islands, the Marshalls, Nauru, Niue, Western Samoa and Vanuatu whereby such shell companies pay large annual registration fees perceived by locals as essential to resuscitate struggling island budgets.

A recent enterprise that greatly benefits smaller islands in particular is philately. Collectors' postage stamps, providing a refreshing and artistic source of income that brings no infelicitous aspersions, have spawned entire industries on many islands that have vied with one another for the most colourful, appealing, exotic, rare or otherwise investible creations: the Solomons, the Faroes, Ascension Island, the British Virgin Islands, the Falklands, the Cayman Islands, the Turks and Caicos Islands, Christmas Island, all the British Leeward Islands (Antigua, Anguilla, Barbuda, Dominica, Montserrat, Nevis, St Kitts, the British Virgin Islands), Vanuatu, Norfolk Island, New Zealand and many more. Alone the Cook Islands Philatelic Bureau until recently long generated annual revenues of $1.4 million from the sale of collectors' postage stamps, and Tuvalu has recently introduced a similar scheme.

CRUSOE'S LEGACY

All the smaller Indian Ocean islands – except for Singapore (Malay Archipelago) and oil-rich Bahrain (Persian Gulf) – have stayed underdeveloped and disadvantaged.[45] Most acquire revenue chiefly from fishing and plantations, though tourist dollars have also significantly contributed, especially since the 1970s. Only fishermen and scientists seasonally frequent the ocean's isolated southern isles. Larger islands enjoy greater economic diversification – industry and a variety of agricultural pursuits – but still rely on tourism, fishing and plantations (tea, coffee, palm oil). Since the last quarter of the twentieth century coastal communities within new nation states – especially in Sri Lanka, Madagascar, Sumatra, Java and Luzon in the Philippines – have turned away from the sea and focused inland towards industrial and mining activities where regular, assured and more remunerative occupations are available, often with housing and health benefits. This is in fact a global trend and it cuts off an ancient island relationship with the sea: skills are lost, cultures are undone, and an entire psychology vanishes.

In the Caribbean tourist dollars or revenues from major crop exports like sugar or tobacco couldn't finance the prodigious population growth, so migration became a preferred recourse. This has led to shifting demographic and racial balances on many islands. Between 1900 and 1920, for example, many Bahamians sought Floridian jobs; others hied to other US ports. But then in the late 1920s tourism took off in the Bahamas themselves and so islanders from other Caribbean islands descended as construction labourers. Especially since the 1960s, émigré Haitians and guest workers from the Turks and Caicos Islands have regarded the Bahamas as their personal labour exchange and, as a result, social tensions have risen there. 'Bahamians First' campaigns have divided entire communities and strict immigration policies have had to be introduced.

Until recently, plantation (copra, sugar) and cash crops dictated Pacific islands' economies and many smaller nations there still rely on exports of passion fruit, papaya, pineapples, bananas, vanilla, citrus fruits and sweet potatoes, though this increasingly enthrals them to fluctuating and highly competitive markets quite beyond their control.[46] Yet Pacific islands' national planning no longer prioritizes agriculture, as more lucrative and reliable sources of revenue beckon. Like the Malay Archipelago and the Philippines, Melanesian islands have turned in a large way to timber, with Japan buying up most of their tropical hardwoods, but it is Melanesia's minerals (which account for some 46 per cent of all Pacific islands' annual income) that now tempt intemperate transactions. Fisheries and seafoods are second only to mining as Pacific islands' biggest export earner, and the sale of fishing rights generates handsome foreign revenues since many island states hold economic rights over immense tracts of ocean. Manufacturing in Pacific islands – apart from New Zealand and Hawai'i – has failed to achieve commensurate development, principally because of the restrictive costs of importing materials, the small volume of local markets, and difficulties of transport.

Where natural resources are wanting and manufacturing is impracticable, Pacific island nations have turned to service industries, like offshore banking, philately and other schemes. Rare revenues trickle in from online casinos and dot.com code sales – like Tonga's '.to' – for use in catchy domain names. Still, tourism reigns supreme for most islands within busier routes. Some tourist statistics are staggering: annual visitors to Guam outnumber locals by four to one, to the Northern Marianas (arriving mostly on cruise ships) by nine to one, and to Easter Island by twelve to one. In all, over 20 million tourists visit Pacific islands each year, and their numbers are rapidly increasing. Remittances – those monies islanders living and working abroad send back home – also contribute significantly to Pacific island economies. Even robust ones like Tonga's rely heavily on remittances, in this case primarily from Tongans living and working in New Zealand and Australia: these have accounted for over one-third of Tonga's foreign exchange earnings – more than the country's exports and tourism combined.[47]

'SAILING AN EMPTY SHIP'

Political independence for many island states has hardly brought economic independence. Sharing the burdens and troubles of international markets, island economies are additionally taxed by the 'high-low-less syndrome': high transport costs, low resident populations and less exploitable land. Fewer natural resources means increased dependence on one mineral or one agricultural product for the foreign revenue required to purchase essential imports and to service debt. Among these imports are most consumer goods, most food, and all fuel for nearly everything. Island economies usually lack technical and professional staff as well as managers, businessmen (businesswomen are still rare) and administrators who are trained and experienced. Natural disasters – typhoons, volcanic eruptions, earthquakes, tsunamis – are common to most islands and they kill, ruin crops, destroy villages, roads, ports and vessels and can reduce entire economies overnight.

Often only foreign aid can salvage a stricken island nation: one need only recall the tsunami that struck Aceh Province in Sumatra in 2004 and the earthquake that destroyed Haiti's Port au Prince in 2010. Because they are often little and alone, islands find infrastructure and communications (shipping, air travel and freight, telecommunications) too expensive to set up and maintain unless some foreign investment, profit-sharing or domination is involved. Ironically, colonials who once controlled indigenous islanders are regularly today, as independent nationals, themselves at the mercy of cosmopolitan powerbrokers in former homelands. Unhappily, too many island societies are 'sailing an empty ship' – that is, having nothing to offer and taking nothing on board, with the remittances and foreign aid proving to be false friends that briefly fill a sail to drive the dhow towards the doldrums.

All the same, some islands remain global powerhouses: Japan, the world's greatest island economy, is the third largest overall; the island of Great Britain, sixth. Of course in a world of over a million islands and islets, daunting economic extremes must obtain, so it is that poverty forces victims in every ocean to forsake their homeland daily. However, modern technology now comes to the rescue: a graphic designer on tiny Eigg in the Inner Hebrides, for example, can support himself and his family by working online at his portable laptop. 'Future-proofing' is the new catchword here: global connectivity through superfast broadband over fibre-optic cables. The innovation has drawn the young, trained and refreshingly enterprising back to otherwise derelict isles to enjoy a quality of life they know no polluted mainland could ever offer them and their children. Entire countries are taking this on board, too. At the time of writing, New Zealand is upgrading her entire telecommunications system, if merely to maintain international competitiveness.

Even the concept of 'island poverty' wants relativization. Such a statistic as '27 per cent of Micronesians live below the poverty line' has to be taken with a grain of the proverbial, as measurements of comparative wealth are fatuous exercises. In their perceived 'poverty' Developing World islanders often enjoy lives far richer, safer and more satisfying overall than those of most Developed World mainlanders.

One generation ago Lawrence Durrell had to sympathize with the people of Andros in the Cyclades who 'now turn their eyes to New York and Sydney where they hope to make a decent living, though it is sometimes difficult to persuade them that they will have to pay a high price for such a standard of life'.[48] Happily, this is now changing. While still remaining an islander one can migrate *online* instead. And when one assesses the new 200-mile economic zones, one can see 'small island nation-states' as rising to something – with their fishing rights and undersea mineral resources – as commanding as anything any modern European nation can own.

The verdict on island economies? Yes, there are islands phenomenally wealthy in natural resources that are pitifully exploited and impoverished by transnational corporations; and whole forests are being ravished in a mad attempt merely to maintain interest payments on World Bank loans – crippling these islands' future. This is especially true of Indonesia, the Philippines, New Guinea and the Solomon Islands. Still, subsistence economies have progressively thrived through trade; transformed themselves with changing markets; waxed wealthy through tin, slaves, sugar, gold; tanned in dollar tourism while flaunting offshore incentives; then embraced the twenty-first century with brave imagination by the megabyte. The 'benches of ivory, brought out of the isles of Chittim' so praised by Ezekiel (27:6) evidently still enthrone a fortunate few.

Especially those savouring the advantages of First World nationhood.

five

. . . of First Nations

Politics, according to the American journalist and historian Henry Brooks Adams (1838–1918), is nothing if not the 'systematic organization of hatreds'. Whether the cynical dictum applies to the politics of small islands is moot: certainly tiny Micronesian atolls could never have survived without cooperation and mutual respect. Then again, throughout history large islands appear to have been carnage's very crucible, while most mainlanders' dealings with islanders seem to have been little more than the 'systematic organization of extinction'.

It's no coincidence that Europe's first document heralds war. Crete's Phaistos Disk pithily demonstrates how islands are not only centres of trade but arenas of combat – at once powerhouses and victims. Such morbidity necessitated rigid regulation, fostering insular peace if only to survive. And so it's similarly no coincidence that Europe's earliest legal document hails from the same island but heralds order: Crete's Law of Gortys from the first half of the fifth century BC – engraved into (originally) twelve columns of five tiers, four tiers of which still dignify the ruins of the medieval St Titus church – comprises a series of laws fixing inheritance, land tenure, citizenship and marriage.

Island life *had* to cultivate cooperation: land was too scarce to squabble over. The ancient Greeks appreciated this, all Oceanians believed this, and as Western European society continued to advance all islanders there, too, bravely shouldered the belief: the world's oldest still-extant parliamentary institution is apparently Iceland's Althing, an outdoor assembly held at Thingvellir since about AD 930, and the Isle of Man's own Tynwald is a communal parliament in continuous existence since 979. To every islander, politics has been as essential as the sea, for the passionate practice has forever fended off that greatest foe of all.

War.

'DOWN TO THE SEA, EVERYONE!'

'War is nothing more than the continuation of politics by other means', intoned Prussian officer and military theorist Karl von Clausewitz (1780–1831). And islands have always figured among war's bloodiest stages. Internal island conflicts have erupted from ancient Crete to modern Bougainville, from Nuku Hiva's high-valley skirmishes to Sicily's hilltop free-for-alls. Inter-island warfare sporadically tore apart ancient blood ties between Tahiti and Mo'orea, between Hokkaidō and Honshū, between Java and Borneo, between Ireland and Britain. However, the greatest grievances were caused by invasion, colonial war, world war – those landings by Minoans and Phoenicians, Greeks and Romans, Saracens and Turks, British and French, Germans and Japanese.

For their situation at the interface of nations, islands have been exceptionally vulnerable, the quintessential showground for greed's biography. Second largest of the Ionian islands, Corfu, for one, was ravaged in turn by Corinthians, Persians, Lacedæmonians, Illyrians, Romans, Normans, Genoese, Epirus's Greek despots, Turks, Italians and Germans. It's a typical rap sheet, for history's strand is strewn with island corpses.

Around 1600 BC Minos of Crete 'was the first', you'll recall Pliny the Elder telling us, 'who fought a battle with a fleet', and from Thucydides we learned that Minos 'became lord of the Cyclades islands and first colonizer of most of them, driving out the Carians and establishing his own sons in them as governors'.[1] This was possibly the great Battle of Naxos whose name hails from the site of history's first documented island battle – illustrious Naxos in the Ægean.[2] The second occurred a thousand years later, in 665 BC, at Corfu when the Corfiot fleet fought the invading Corinthian fleet for control of the island. Then there were the townspeople of Phocæa, on the Ægean coast of Asia Minor, who established a colony at Alalia on Corsica's eastern coast around 565 BC; some 35 years earlier they had founded a Greek colony at Massalia (modern Marseille) and around 530 the Massalians fought and won a major naval battle against Etruscans and Carthaginians just off the Alalia colony – their historic victory emboldened Greek expansion into the central and western Mediterranean.

The celebrated Battle of Salamis in 480 BC was waged just off Piræus on the Greek mainland. By then all of Hellas had fallen to Xerxes's Persian army, but for Athens, the Peloponnese and her islands. Greece's leaders argued what to do. Mount a defensive retreat to the isthmus with all their forces? Or draw a line at Salamis – largest island in the Saronic Gulf – preventing the Persian Armada's manoeuvring in the difficult narrows? In desperation, Athenian politician and general Themistocles (*c.* 527–*c.* 460) chose to fight to the death at Salamis. Xerxes set up his throne of gold at Piræus to witness the certain annihilation of the Greeks: didn't his fleet boast some 1,200 triremes, while the Greeks could tally only around 380 smaller, albeit swifter vessels? But to Xerxes's horror the Persian fleet first foundered in the shallows, then over 300 triremes fell to the Greeks one by one or were wrecked when driven onto the cliffs below Xerxes's throne. In the end only 200 to 300 Persian vessels managed to escape while Xerxes fled with his invasion army. There was great rejoicing in Athens. A temple to the northeast wind rose on the banks of the Illysos. Hellas remained Greek and European civilization took wing.

During the Peloponnesian War (431–404 BC) – which Athens and her empire fought against the Sparta-led Peloponnesian League – island societies from Sicily to the northern Ægean (excluding neutral Crete) suffered bitterly. When Lesbos's ruling oligarchy, for example, revolted against Athens, for two years the city-state and her allies besieged the island. Finally, Cleon (*d.* 422 BC) persuaded Athens's Assembly to execute every man and enslave each woman and child on Lesbos and a vessel sailed off to accomplish just this, whereupon Demodotus eloquently addressed the Assembly, urging leniency, and so a second ship was sent countermanding the previous order. When this second ship arrived only Lesbos's ringleaders had been punished and a general bloodbath was thus avoided. Locked in a battle to the death with Sparta, Athens could well have used the revenue to be gained from Lesbos's enslavement – but for once rhetoric triumphed over force.

After the Greeks, it was the Romans who specialized in politics' practical extension. In the Battle of the Ægates Islands in 241 BC just off the northwest coast of Sicily the Romans defeated the Carthaginian fleet, ending the First Punic War and allowing Rome to seize Sicily, Corsica and Sardinia for the Republic. In 214 BC the Romans besieged Greek Syracuse on Sicily, which had broken an alliance and had sided with Carthage, and over the next two years the Sicilian Greeks met their attackers with new inventions by Archimedes (c. 287–212 BC): catapults, huge claws and even concave mirrors that ignited warships from afar, it was claimed; when Syracuse fell in 212 BC, Archimedes himself lay among the thousands slain.

In August of 55 BC Julius Cæsar landed 10,000 soldiers on Britannia's Kentish coast, but stayed less than a week; he returned briefly the following year, yet still failed to secure the island for the Republic. The Battle of Actium that Octavian fought in 31 BC against Marc Antony and Cleopatra just south of Corfu in the Ionian Sea – alongside the isles of Paxos and Antipaxos – was one of history's most decisive: it concluded the Roman Civil War, brought the Republic to a close, and ended the Greek Ptolemaic dynasty of Egypt. It also enabled Rome's annexation of Egypt, the rule of the Cæsars and the very creation of the Roman Empire: three years later Octavian was hailed as Augustus. In May of AD 43, the politician and general Aulus Plautius landed four legions and a host of auxiliaries – in total 40,000 legionnaires – on the island of Britannia and within four bloody years she, too, had finally been secured for the new Empire.

The island slaughter continued through the Middle Ages. Britain herself came to suffer invasions from various Germanic tribes, Irish, Vikings, Danes and then the Normans who attacked and settled also large parts of Cornwall, Wales, Scotland and Ireland. In the Mediterranean, Malta was the victim of the Byzantine–Arab Wars; Sicily was terrorized and ruled by the Vandals, Goths, Byzantine Greeks, Arabs and Normans; Crete fell to Iberian Muslims, was restored to the Byzantine Empire, then was lost again to Venice; and Cyprus, also part of the Byzantine Empire, was repeatedly ravaged for three centuries from the Levantine coast, then seized by Richard I of England (1157–1199) and sold a year later to the Knights Templar, whereupon bloody revolts forced her sale to France's Lusignan dynasty.

In the Indian Ocean, Sri Lanka's many kingdoms struggled with one another for centuries while also fighting off various invasions from the southern Indian mainland; the Srivijaya Empire (600s–1200s) spread the Malay culture through Sumatra and western Borneo

Marco Polo departing the island of Venice for East Asia in 1271.

mainly by conquest, only to fall to southern India's Chola Empire (300s BC–AD 1279) which, in turn, soon fell victim to rapacious Javanese kingdoms conquering large parts of the archipelago.

In the Far East, Japan of the late Heian period (794–1185) saw the rise of military clans which led to violent civil war, whereupon the subsequent feudal period – characterized by powerful families and military warlords – suffered intermittant warfare, two attempted Mongol invasions (1274 and 1281), and the turbulent period of the Warring Kingdoms from 1467 to 1573. Between Taiwan's central mountain range and coastal alluvial plains indigenous Austronesian tribes warred against one another continually, then, in the 1600s, found themselves battling invading Spaniards, Dutchmen and finally Han Chinese, who expelled the Dutch and seized the island for themselves, first establishing the short-lived Kingdom of Tungning (1662–83) then submitting to annexation by the mainland Qing Dynasty (1644–1912).

In the remote Pacific, the Tu'i Tonga conquered and ruled an enormous region for some 400 years. Cannibalistic raids bloodied the high valleys of the Marquesas Islands. The Māori of New

Zealand built large *pā* or hilltop defences as with swelling populations they increasingly contested tribal land claims. On Easter
Island the warrior clans of the *'urumanu* or 'commoners' wrested
control from traditional *'ariki* or nobles and erected ever more imposing stone busts to herald their supremacy. In Tahiti chiefs would
lead raids in swift war canoes over to neighbouring Mo'orea for
women and slaves. And Hawai'i's internecine warfare troubled the
group for centuries, retarding the formation of a strong centralized
monarchy.

By the eighteenth century Polynesian islanders were even fighting for King George III of England (1738–1820). At the Mitchell
Library in Sydney is a letter from Mary Hassall of Paramatta, Australia, penned to her brother living on Oxford Street, London, on 8
September 1818, telling of the recent arrival home of the Tahitian
christened 'John Henry Martin' who had lost his right arm at the
Battle of Waterloo: King George III had granted him a £20 annuity
for his sacrifice.[3] By this time, Britain and France were violently contesting many foreign isles: the Caribbean alone was the scene of
countless encounters that cost thousands of lives; enormous stone
bastions there, erected for insular defence and imperial intimida-
tion, still today stand silent sentinel.

Ireland, too, was awash with strife through the Middle Ages,
and by the 1600s the sieges and battles in proxy wars fought
between Louis XIV (1638–1715) and France's continental rivals saw
Irish Catholics and Protestants alike perish in large numbers.

The last battle to be fought on British soil – in contrast to the
Second World War's Battle of Britain which was fought in the air –
took place on Jersey in the Channel Islands early in 1781. The
French under Baron Phillipe de Rullecourt had invaded and the
British commander had given the order to surrender, but Major
Francis Peirson (1750–1781) ignored the order, counter-attacked
and repelled the invaders. Both he and Baron de Rullecourt fell in
the famous Battle of Jersey and today occupy neighbouring tombs
in a Jersey graveyard. Peirson never learned he had won the battle.

In the Seychelles, Anglo–French animosity achieved near-comi-
cal heights. In the mid-1700s French colonists from Mauritius –
around 1,400 km away to the south – landed and commenced construction and trade. During the Napoleonic Wars, when Britain
man-o'-warred into the Seychelles' main harbour, the French
Governor at once hoisted the Union Jack; satisfied, King George's

Royal Navy hove away again, and the Governor summarily rehoisted the newly adopted *tricolore*. Five further times was the farce re-enacted. Finally, in 1810, the British came to stay, yet retained the French Governor as His Majesty's administrator for the islands – for by then the French stamp there was indelible, something better to use than abuse.

The Spanish–American War of 1898 constituted a series of insular wars and occupations. The main point of contention between the US and Spain was Cuba, but the conflict also allowed America to incorporate within her sphere of influence a number of global isles at the very finale of this brass-band era of insular colonialism, in which Britain, France, Spain and the Netherlands had remained dominant. (It was in this same year that the US rudely seized the self-styled American-led 'Republic of Hawai'i' that had toppled the independent Kingdom of Hawai'i four years earlier.) In the end, after a series of bloody encounters on several islands, the Treaty of Paris (1898) granted the US temporary authority over Cuba as well as indefinite colonial control over the Philippines (including the Marianas), Guam and Puerto Rico. The war overthrew Spain's insular empire, leaving her only the Canary Islands – a great blow to Spanish pride.

Just before the First World War, US troops killed tens of thousands of Filipinos in a military seizure of Mindanao, second largest and easternmost island of the Philippines. At the same time, Dutch troops were slaying tens of thousands of islanders during their invasion of the Moluccas and Western New Guinea (modern Papua and West Papua). In the middle of 1915 the US invaded Haiti (Hispaniola's western half), which subsequently remained under US occupation for fifteen years; all Allied governments, then at war, said nothing. One year later, the US invaded the Dominican Republic (Hispaniola's eastern half), fought for two months, then conquered the defenders; whereupon the US proclaimed a military government, censored newspapers and locked up freedom fighters. What had earlier been a republic now became an involuntary American colony. Again the Allies – still mired in the trenches of the First World War – said nothing.

The First World War hardly touched the Pacific, Indian Ocean or Caribbean. But Atlantic and Mediterranean islands suffered grievous violence, exploitation and sudden deprivations. The magnificent bay of Milos in Greece's Cyclades, whence the 'Venus de' hailed, is so expansive that it was chosen to host the complete Allied Fleet. The Pacific did come to play a small part in the war. In September 1914 the Imperial German East Asian Cruiser Squadron, under the command of Admiral Maximilian Reichsgraf von Spee, shelled Pape'ete, Tahiti, and destroyed her marketplace; one month later, it assembled the German Pacific Fleet, twelve vessels in all, off Easter Island's Hanga Roa roadstead to acquire fresh fruit and living livestock and to refuel from arriving tenders. New Zealand sent mainly Niueans and Cook Islanders to war in the trenches of France; conscription was imposed for the Māori, many of whom then declined to appear. France sent New Caledonians and Polynesians from Tahiti (Society Islands) and the Marquesas. Most Pacific Islander deaths resulted from illness in the camps, but thousands were also slaughtered in the trenches. Britain didn't conscript Tongans, and only six Tongans volunteered for the Dominion army. Tonga also provided almost no funds for the war effort: Tonga's royal family announced they would 'pray'. Western Samoa was governed during all of the First World War as a military colony of New Zealand, which had seized the islands for Britain as soon as war had been declared on Germany.

The First World War in the Pacific, fought nominally to preserve and safeguard democracy, sadly saw the elimination and proscription of all democratic practices there. The hypocrisy wasn't lost on many. It gave birth to New Zealand's Labour Party, for one, where droves of socialists, union leaders and pacifists were also locked away: following the armistice of 11 November 1918 they emerged to change the face of New Zealand politics forever.

During the war, in 1916, the US, in a bid to safeguard its interests in the Panama Canal, purchased the Virgin Islands – St Thomas, St John, St Croix and many smaller islands situated some 60 km east of Puerto Rico and inhabited mostly by Afro-Caribbeans – for $25 million from Denmark, which had profitably held them since 1666. The Virgin Islands have remained an organized, unincorporated territory of the US ever since.

Despite the 'war to end all wars', island butchery only increased afterwards. Evoking the Athenian fleet's siege of ancient Syracuse, the Battle of Britain of summer and autumn 1940 was history's only decisive battle to be fought entirely in the air. (In this, London's defence was directed by another islander: Air Vice-Marshal Keith Park of Thames, New Zealand.) It thwarted Germany's planned annihilation of the Royal Air Force and so halted the prepared invasion. In the Siege of Malta the Axis nations attempted to bomb or starve Britain's Mediterranean island colony into submission from 1940 to 1942: Germans and Italians flew some 3,000 bombing raids against Malta's ports, towns and RAF defences, but failed to follow up with an amphibious landing. In 1941 the island of Crete experienced history's first major airborne assault, and within ten days the Germans prised the island from her British, Australian, New Zealand and Greek defenders; any resistance by native Cretans the occupying German forces then repaid with massacres and other atrocities. The German Navy and Wehrmacht suffocated Rhodes with mines and barbed wire; when the British tried to expel them the German defence proved impenetrable, so the British chose attrition: Germans and civilians alike – many of them Italians – starved, and all livestock disappeared, followed by dogs, cats, hamsters and rats. Only when 300 Germans were dying each day of starvation did their commander finally surrender. The Channel Islands also knew the cruelty of occupation. However, each suffered separately. Herm, for one, a small island east of Guernsey, during most of the Second World War hosted only two residents: the caretaker and his wife, whom the English car manufacturer Lord Percival Perry (1878–1956) had charged to look after his privately owned isle. When the Germans finally did invade, however, it was only to film. Since they regarded Herm to be militarily useless the Germans merely staged there a 'mock invasion' using Herm's beach as a replica for the invasion of the British mainland. The footage was actually screened later in Berlin.[4]

The War in the Pacific, on the other hand, was an island war. Japan had attempted to become Asia's dominant principal through the establishment of her 'Greater East Asia Co-Prosperity Sphere', but this plan was thwarted after Japan's military occupation of French Indochina in July 1941 when an embargo on iron from the US and on oil from the Dutch East Indies forced Japan to choose one of the three recourses left to her: submit, withdraw or fight.[5] Japan's dynamic expansion had been empowered by the doubling of her oil consumption between 1931 and 1937. Without oil and iron, Japan's military-industrial mill would grind to a halt. As much to stall the US's defence of Allied interests in the Pacific as to save face, Japan chose to seize the offensive. It was a fateful decision, for half a million Japanese soldiers and civilians were to lose their lives on

Micronesian and Melanesian islands. On Attu alone in the Aleutian Islands in 1943, the site of the war's only land battle fought on US territory, the Japanese lost 99.5 per cent of their force. Pacific islands had never known such carnage. During the conflict Japan's opponents were mainly US troops concentrated in four major bases: on New Caledonia's Grande Terre, Espiritu Santo in the New Hebrides (modern Vanuatu), Guadalcanal in the Solomons, and Bora Bora in Polynesia's Society Islands. War was prosecuted by the Allies with limited available resources, as Roosevelt and Churchill had agreed that the first priority was to defeat Hitler in Europe – even if this meant temporarily sacrificing Australia to Japan.

Unlike the Indians of Fiji, most Pacific Islanders didn't hesitate to don uniform. Over 2,000 native Fijians fought in the Solomons campaign, where also 680 Solomon Islanders served. Some 50 Tongans joined the Fiji Military Forces, too. Around 300 Polynesians and half-Polynesians volunteered in Tahiti to join the French Battalion of the Pacific, then fought valiantly in North Africa, Italy and Provence (southern France) alongside compatriot New Caledonians. New Zealand's famous Māori Battalion distinguished itself in North Africa, Greece and Italy. The Pacific Islands Regiment comprised more than 3,500 Papuan and New Guinean combatants, with a further 3,137 fighting police and 955 medical orderlies.

Then in Japan's own colonies of Pohnpei and Palau there were the Micronesians who served as non-combatants in the Emperor of Japan's volunteer units in New Guinea. When hostilities ceased there, Palau's 104th Construction Detachment, for one, was simply abandoned. It took them years to make it back home again to Palau.

War wreaked havoc on much of Melanesia and Micronesia, but perhaps its greatest victim of all was the very colonialism the Allies were so courageously defending. Still, it was not long after the Second World War that the US and France had created in Micronesia and French Polynesia their own Pacific islands, which were far removed from the independent, self-governing, autonomous bodies fostered, and then realized, elsewhere by Britain, Australia and New Zealand. This is because, for the US and France, the region represented merely a means to an end: the creation not of a freer Pacific, but of a *nuclear* Pacific. It was a war now waged against the very islands themselves.

The Pacific was 'reinvented' after 1945 as neo-colonial powers acted primarily for themselves and only secondarily for islanders.

The historically most challenging symbol of this posture: the two atomic bombs that exploded over Hiroshima and Nagasaki in August of that year, which may have ended the War in the Pacific but which also began an arms race that turned the region into a nuclear arena.[6] Over exactly half a century – between 1946 and 1996 – more than 250 nuclear bombs were detonated at Bikini, Enewetak, Johnston Atoll, Christmas Island, Malden, Moruroa and Fangataufa. The consequences of Pacific nuclear testing were devastating. The US destroyed whole islands and their societies, especially in Micronesia's Marshall Islands, still the subject of sensitive litigation. France ruined Moruroa and Fangataufa in the Tuamotus; as in the Marshalls, the economic dependence of the testing programme greatly crippled French Polynesia's political development.

The Bikini story is particularly poignant. The 167 inhabitants of one of Remote Oceania's earliest settled islands, a coral atoll of 26 islets, were informed in June 1946 by the US Navy that it wished to test the force of a new weapon against ships at sea.[7] The Bikini people, convinced they would be benefiting 'all mankind', allowed themselves to be transported to uninhabited Rongerik along with their 26 houses, dismantled church and community hall. The Navy promised them they would soon be back on Bikini; whereupon the US authorities positioned 80 obsolete target ships in Bikini's palm-fringed lagoon and, on 1 July 1946, detonated an atomic bomb in mid-air over the lagoon and ships. The destruction was appalling. Subsequently banned from their home, the Bikini people were shunted from island to island – the second island victims of the Atomic Age, after the Japanese. Between 1946 and 1958, 23 nuclear bombs were detonated at Bikini. The infamous Bravo test of 1954, the detonation of a hydrogen bomb 1,000 times the power of the bombs that obliterated Hiroshima and Nagasaki, pulverized Bikini's northwest. 'It has been said that the combined power of all the weapons fired in all the wars of history would fall short of that released by Bravo over the Bikini lagoon.'[8]

When decontamination of the vessels still afloat in Bikini lagoon failed, the highly radioactive ships were towed some 300 km to Kwajalein Atoll, one of the world's largest, to be cleaned there; but this also failed. So the vessels were used as target practice for missiles fired from Hawai'i and even California, some 6,600 km away. Kwajalein is still today off-limits to all but authorized US Army personnel. In 1992 the US government proposed decontaminating Bikini at last, intending to scrape a foot of topsoil from every inch of the island's 560 acres. But the plan proved far too dear and no one could explain how to dispose of Bikini's radioactive soil. In August 2010 Bikini Atoll was entered into the list of UNESCO World Heritage sites. Apart from intermittent visits by scientists for radioactive monitoring, she remains uninhabited.

Then there is Enewetak. Beginning in 1948 the US detonated some 43 nuclear bombs at this Marshall Islands atoll of 40 islands, a former Japanese colony that had been seized by the Americans in the Second World War and converted to a naval base. The base had been abandoned and the islanders forcibly evicted when the US decided to test there, safely away from any US contamination, and in late 1952 the first hydrogen bomb test was conducted: the small islet of Elugelab was vaporized. After testing ceased in 1958, the islet of Runit was burdened with 84,100 cubic metres of Enewetak's radioactive topsoil, which was then buried under an enormous concrete mound. In 1980 the people of Enewetak were allowed by the Americans to resettle, but the first crops were radioactive and so they were once again evicted. Permanent wards of the US government, the Enewetakans remain in exile.

Such abuse of islands by the US and France – Britain had also been involved, but only marginally – led in the 1970s to the 'Nuclear-Free Pacific' movement, which became a crusade uniting island peoples in unprecedented numbers for the first time and contributing further to the creation of a shared Pacific identity. By 1996 twelve of the sixteen member countries of the South Pacific Forum had signed the South Pacific Nuclear-Free Zone Treaty. Its protocols had been presented to the world's nuclear powers, and China and the former Soviet Union had signed; but the US, Britain and France refused. Only after France finally bowed to international pressure and ceased her nuclear testing in the Pacific islands did Paris finally sign the Treaty, as did Washington and London. Nonetheless, the 'nuclear Pacific' is not a finished story. Its legacy will continue to haunt all Pacific islands and her peoples – for tens of thousands of years.

Another insular tragedy indicts humankind. The greatest island carnage in history was the Suharto regime's slaughter in the 1960s of over one million Indonesian islanders. And the greatest atrocity perpetrated by one island nation against another occurred in East Timor, when Indonesia murdered at least 183,000 men, women and children. It is true that the British and, later, Australians committed a protracted genocide against the Aborigines – among the world's oldest islanders – from the eighteenth to twentieth centuries. And the War in the Pacific from 1941 to 1945 brought the greatest island carnage, mostly of Japanese and Americans: one US bombing raid on Tokyo – that of 10 March 1945 – killed 140,000 Japanese and left one million homeless. But Indonesia has caused the greatest civilian suffering and mortality between islanders. Nothing can ever justify – or erase – this crime.

The madness began in the 1950s and '60s when Indonesia's first president Sukarno (1901–1970) targeted all opposition to his concept of a unified and autocratic Indonesia. When he began courting the Soviet Union and her allies he was overthrown in 1967 in a military putsch led by Suharto (1921–2008), whereupon the mindless violence became about 'fighting communism' – which hypocrisy targeted Chinese and other ethnic groups opposing the new US-centred regime. It was an internal war waged with US funds, advisors, weapons and aircraft, as well as with increasing assistance from Britain and Australia. *The New York Times* tellingly called this eventual slaughter of over one million Indonesians 'a gleam of light in Asia'.

One of the worst holocausts of the twentieth century, it led to the Indonesian islands being handed over to alien corporations: it was, in effect, the new gold rush that set the foundation for globalization. The overall result was 'transnational neo-colonialism', with Indonesia's sweatshops producing incredible profits for more incredible exploitation: achieving the modern equivalent of a slave plantation on a national scale. Today, disease and overcrowding make these new labour camps veritable 'killing fields' for foreign investors – chiefly prestige labels from the US and Europe. Indonesia has since become the world's most egregious exemplar of the post-colonial poverty trap, with the foreign debt repayment, which addresses mostly interest, tantamount to modern tribute. Yet even an ancient Rhodesian or Lesbian held in thrall to Athens never suffered such wretchedness: as a reward of modern globalization, Indonesians are by and large poorer, sicker and younger than any of the world's islanders. No fresh breezes sighing in island palms here: only the roar of rumbling dumper trucks and the rasp of coughing children. Pre-Second World War islands never knew the like.

East Timor soon became a target of Suharto's expansionist policy.[9] Situated in the Lesser Sunda group, Timor is 480 km long and 100 km wide at its widest point; what was still then Portuguese Timor comprised the island's eastern end, 620 km northwest of Australia. When the Japanese had invaded Portuguese Timor in the Second World War, Australia had sent in troops but then withdrew in 1943, leaving the Timorese at the mercy of the Japanese army. Executions, torture, forced labour and starvation are alleged to have cost around 40,000 Timorese lives up until the end of 1945.[10] In October 1975, five international journalists – two Australians, one Englishman, one Scot and one New Zealander – were slain by Indonesian forces at Balibo on Timor's northern coast as they were filming the start of Indonesia's invasion for two Australian TV channels. Several weeks later, US President Gerald Ford and Secretary of State Henry Kissinger were in Jakarta consulting with Suharto, declaring that the US would not oppose Indonesia's violent annexation of Timor's eastern half, from which, after centuries of colonial rule, Portugal was finally withdrawing. The new country of Timor-Leste – East Timor – enjoyed just nine days of official independence. Then Indonesia struck. The invasion of the capital of Dili on 7 December 1975 saw hundreds slaughtered, including senior Australian newsman Roger East, the only journalist left in East Timor. The US had supplied the matériel and advisors; Britain, the funds; Australia, the intelligence. Indonesia remained in East Timor for 24 years, formally annexing the land in July 1976.

It was a quarter of a century of bloodshed and terror in the former East Timor. In September 1983, for example, 181 unarmed civilians were executed by the Indonesian Army on the bank of the Bi-Tuku River in the Kraras jungle.[11] Forced sterilization and infanticide were common. Countless Timorese disappeared and each town and village dreaded its contingent of Indonesian military, spies and informers. Even Portugal's president was moved to publicly declare Indonesia's rule there a 'genocide'. Officially representing an independent East Timor overseas, José Manuel Ramos-Horta (*b.* 1949) led the United Nation's first Nation in Exile; for their 'work towards a just and peaceful solution to the conflict in East Timor' both he and Carlos Filipe Ximenes Belo were awarded the 1996 Nobel Peace Prize.

Three years later the global opposition to Indonesia's reign of terror in East Timor had finally forced Jakarta to withdraw. Throughout 1999, as the Indonesian Army was pulling out, it destroyed most of the country's infrastructure and, after a vote on autonomy was rejected in a referendum on 30 August 1999, murder, arson and destruction once again ruled East Timor. From September well into October of that year the Indonesian Army and its militia proxies, using Indonesian trucks, seized mostly women and children, some 250,000 in total, and forcibly transported them to West Timor – an Indonesian province – into camps controlled by militia gangs. It was the greatest human relocation – kidnapping, in fact – of a civilian island population by a foreign power in human history. At last, Indonesia formally quit Dili on 1 November 1999. East Timor was free. In 1975 there had been 600,000 East Timorese; by the year 2000 only around 150,000 were left within the country's new borders. One seeks in vain anything comparable in modern island history.

Did the insular madness then cease? Already in 1974 Turkey had invaded Cyprus. In 1982 Britain and Argentina waged war over the Falkland Islands. The US invaded Grenada in 1983 in 'Operation Urgent Fury', which the UN General Assembly condemned as a 'flagrant violation of international law'.[12] On Sri Lanka – where many centuries of relative peace between Hindus, Buddhists, Muslims and Christians had ended at independence from Britain in 1948, when the Buddhist Sinhalese majority began reconstituting the island into a Sinhalese nation-state to the detriment of her Hindu Tamil minority – civil war raged from 1983 to 2009; the crushing of the Tamil Tigers (Liberation Tigers of Tamil Eelam) and the annihilation of any designs for a separate Tamil state followed the deaths of as many as 100,000 in savage battles, mass executions and suicide bombings; over 300,000 Tamils still remain displaced. In late 1998 militants on the island of Guadalcanal in the Solomons initiated a campaign of violence against settlers from the neighbouring island of Malaita, which then erupted into open civil war; by 2003, Australia, New Zealand and some twenty further Pacific island nations rushed in troops to contain the violence; many of these remain on Guadalcanal today to police the tenuous truce that was finally brokered.

MANIFESTATIONS

Just about every conceivable political construct will describe the world's islands: single-state islands, dual-state islands, single-state multiple islands (and archipelagos), dual-state multiple islands (and archipelagos), single-island territories, multiple-island territories, incorporated islands, private islands under state control, private sovereign islands, ad infinitum. The list is as rich as one's imagination.

Take Sark in the Channel Islands, often called 'the last feudal state in Western Europe' (though this no longer obtains). Her enclosed harbour is the smallest registered port in the world. To get to the isle's interior, a visitor leaves the quay and proceeds directly into a tunnel carved back in the 1500s out of rock. With a population of around 600, Sark is still nominally 'ruled' by the respective Seigneur or Dame – whose family has held fealty there for 400 years; who possesses the sole right to keep a duck, dove or bitch; and to whom each householder must pay the annual levy of one chicken – though it is Sark's 40 tenant farmers who actually control her parliament now. Defence and foreign representation, however, lie with London, and ultimate allegiance is owed to the Crown.

Somewhat similar is the status of modest Brecqhou just west of Sark, purchased in 1993 by British twins David and Frederick Barclay (b. 1934) who, declaring themselves tax exiles, erected there a neo-Gothic castle from where they rule a private fiefdom. Brecqhou finds a historical precedent in St Michael's Mount, 366 m off the southern Cornish coast, from whose castle eyrie the St Aubyn family has reigned locally since 1659 (subject, of course, to British taxes and law). Accessible by a man-made causeway only at low tide, St Michael's Mount hosts 40 staff and their families in a small village nested at sea level below the commanding castle.

Today, most islanders reside in communities that do not comprise their own political state. This commonly causes resentment towards ruling mainland governments that typically neither understand island life nor appreciate island needs. A Cretan, for example, 'feels about Athens very much what a Sicilian feels about Rome'.[13]

From the other perspective, cosmopolitan nations have seldom identified with those islands they hold and mould, but view them as something exotic, alien. It is mostly a legacy of nineteenth-century colonialism, a still-open wound from the Age of Imperialism when newly discovered isles were ripe for plunder and domination.

The moral and civic imperative was to impose the unquestioned superiority of Western civilization on new lands and peoples. That mind-set in itself assumed a juxtaposition and conflict of opposites –

civilization versus savagery and a tamed, pastoral nature versus an untamed wilderness.[14]

As late as the 1940s it was being heralded in the Pacific, for example, that the cosmopolitan 'white peoples' would forge the island world of the future:

> The European is strategically placed in the Pacific for political, economic, and cultural influence. If the white peoples of the Americas, of Australia and New Zealand follow their interests . . . some measure of politico-economic union amongst them will appear in the early future; and their variety of civilization will control the cultural and social formation of the new races.[15]

Yet perhaps the Pacific was a special cauldron. Centralized bureaucracies were established there by colonial governments to control, not to develop. With independence, mainly in the 1960s and '70s, these same systems were maintained by the islanders themselves – to the new nations' detriment, as it happened, for they were too expensive to operate and too unwieldly to help. From the Solomons to Easter Island the old colonial systems needed, and still need, dismantling and decentralizing, devolving more control to the local community who would then require adequate training and financing. Colonial political structures were also adversarial – one party versus another, as in European politics – and not hierarchical, where island clans are led by family chiefs. On small islands of contesting clans adversarial politics in particular invariably leads to violence. More appropriate for nearly all smaller islands of the world, and not just the Pacific, is the fostering of consensus governance, one that embraces coalition formation. On most islands, the Western mainland model doesn't work.

This is acutely felt in nearly all 'half-island nations' – those states forced to share an island with another state or territory, which usually denotes an unresolved problem. Hispaniola is divided between Haiti and the Dominican Republic. Indonesia's West Timor separates the island from independent Timor-Leste; just as Indonesia's Papua and West Papua (Western New Guinea) is alienated from Papua New Guinea. Turkish Northern Cyprus is partitioned from Greek Cyprus. Northern Ireland weighs heavily on the Republic of Ireland. For a generation the Tamils attempted to achieve a similar division on the northern half of Sri Lanka, but failed disastrously. Borneo is even more complex: the island's lower two-thirds is the territory of Kalimantan, belonging to Indonesia; the top third is the state of Sarawak, Malaysia; and the state of Brunei Darussalam – ranked the fourth wealthiest nation in the world per capita at purchasing power parity – sits within Sarawak.

An equal sting is felt when such division stretches over an archipelago. Many Samoans, citizens of their own country since 1962 when their isles became the first Pacific island nation to re-establish its independence in the twentieth century, still lament the fact that they are cut off from their fellow Samoans in American Samoa, the US's only territory south of the equator. Some nations consist of innumerable islands of one people in one sovereign state – Denmark and Japan are prime examples. In other cases the reverse is true: several sovereign states, overseas departments, territories and dependencies all within one small archipelago – such as in the Caribbean.

The 'British Isles' is an unofficial, traditional designation for over 1,000 islands and island groups that include five discrete nations: England (50 million inhabitants), Ireland (5.2), Scotland (5), Wales (3) and the Isle of Man (80,000). (Like the Channel Islands of Jersey and Guernsey, the Isle of Man is a self-governing British Crown Dependency and not part of the United Kingdom.) Some will argue that England, Scotland and Wales are countries within the nation of the United Kingdom, but this is merely sophistry: each is a nation of different peoples with their own unique history, traditions and tongue. And then there is the psycho-political Great Britain, to suggest an even more convoluted complex. Most English wish to maintain control in London. Most of the island's Scots and Welsh would prefer a federalistic Europe. All Manx celebrate their uniqueness, as does each Channel Islander. And on Ireland, northern Protestants cling tenaciously to Britain while northern Catholics cherish the Emerald Isle alone as 'Home'. Britain's ethnic and religious divisions of ancient provenance sometimes defy insularity's very definition. With recent devolution the United Kingdom is now a multinational state spread over not two but many islands, a fact perhaps soon to be formalized.

The political state that remains the United Kingdom, however, still wields authority over a large number of the world's islands in the form of an Overseas Territory, a legacy of the British Empire.

In the Pacific, only the four Pitcairn Islands – Pitcairn, Henderson, Ducie and Oeno (47 sq km in total) – remain British. In the Atlantic, Bermuda, the Falklands, St Helena, Ascension, Tristan da Cunha, South Georgia and the South Sandwich Islands are similarly all British Overseas Territories. The same status is enjoyed in the Caribbean by Anguilla, the British Virgin Islands, the Cayman Islands, Montserrat, and the Turks and Caicos Islands. The British Indian Ocean Territory comprises the six atolls of the Chagos Islands, purchased from Mauritius by the UK in 1965 for £3 million, whose main island of Diego Garcia (44 sq km) is now a joint British–American military facility which is almost exclusively American. On the island of Cyprus in the Mediterranean, the two Sovereign Base Areas of Akrotiri and Dhekelia – not Overseas Territories and without permanent populations – are still officially maintained by the UK.

Of the more than 2,000 islands in the Mediterranean (Croatia's Kornati archipelago alone counts more than 152) only Malta and Cyprus are nations. Malta is a single-nation island and member of the European Union, Cyprus a dual-nation island shared by the Republic of Cyprus – a member of the European Union since 2004 – and by the Turkish Republic of Northern Cyprus that only Turkey recognizes. All other Mediterranean islands are members of mainland nations.

The largest island in the world, Greenland, is an autonomous country within the Kingdom of Denmark. Having been granted home rule in 1979 as a Danish 'Commonwealth of the Realm', the more than 56,000 Greenlanders yield to Denmark only their defence, foreign representation and financial oversight.

Independence came for most islands of the Indian Ocean and Persian Gulf in the twentieth century: Singapore, Sri Lanka, Bahrain, Mauritius, the Seychelles, Madagascar, the Maldives, the Comoros (except Mayotte), Indonesia and also the Philippines. (By the time Mauritius had won independence in 1968, she had been ruled by 18 Dutch, 21 French and 31 British Governors.) France has politically absorbed as overseas *départements* the islands of La Réunion, Crozet, Kerguélen, Amsterdam, Saint Paul and also Mayotte in the Comoros. (Like the US, Indonesia and Chile, France still endorses and practises colonialism; self-rule and nationhood are not tolerated.) Coastal East African islands were claimed by their closest liberated state: Zanzibar and Pemba, for example, now belong to Tanzania. India inherited from the departing British Raj the Nicobar, Lakshadweep and Andaman Islands. Australia accepted sovereignty over Heard and McDonald, the Cocos group and Christmas Island. South Africa now claims Prince Edward Island. And as we have seen, Britain retains a presence here only in the Chagos Islands.

The Caribbean has always been a storm-tossed political sea, the result of historical claims by the British, French, Dutch, Danes, Spanish, Russians and Americans. Cuba was Spanish for 400 years until violently wrested away by the US in 1898, yet gained formal independence in 1902. Jamaica, in the Greater Antilles, achieved independence from Britain in 1962. North of Cuba, the Bahamas remained a British Crown Colony from 1718 until 1973 when independence was finally achieved. The Windward Islands of the Dutch Antilles lie nearly in the middle of what the British call the Leeward Islands (Antigua, St Kitts, Nevis and Anguilla). The Dutch Leeward Islands (Aruba, Curaçao and Bonaire) perch on South America's shoulder; only a few kilometres southeast lie what the British themselves call the Windward Islands. St Maarten/St Martin in the Netherlands Antilles is the smallest territory in the world governed by two different nations, the Netherlands and France. French St Martin, the other half of Dutch St Maarten, has not been made a nation but is still an 'overseas collectivity' of France. The Dutch Antilles were reconstituted in 2010 when Curaçao and St Maarten joined Aruba in becoming separate nations within the Kingdom of the Netherlands, while Bonaire, St Eustatius (which had 'enjoyed' 22 changes of flag within a few turbulent years) and Saba became autonomous special municipalities of the Kingdom. The Dutch government remains responsible for defence and foreign policy, and still retains initial oversight over Curaçao's finances under a debt-relief deal.

Though Dutch, Saba (pronounced by the locals *say-ber*) is home chiefly to descendants of settlers from Shetland off Scotland – and possibly also from Jersey in the Channel Islands – who arrived in the 1600s. The language is English and always has been. It's an unlikely isle: 'a slab of rock rising 3,000 feet to meet a cloth of cloud, its houses clinging like seabirds to its ledges'.[16]

New Zealand ranks as the Pacific's oldest internationally recognized sovereign state; self-governing as of 1852, she was declared a Commonwealth realm in 1947. In the 1960s and '70s seven further

Pacific colonies under British, Australian and New Zealand administration would gain independence and become full and equal members of the comity of nations: Western Samoa, Fiji, Tonga, Papua New Guinea, the Solomon Islands, Vanuatu (formerly the New Hebrides), and Kiribati and Tuvalu (both formerly the Gilbert and Ellice Islands Colony). In the Pacific only the Pitcairn Islands remain a British Overseas Territory. Cook Islanders and Niueans enjoy independence only in 'free association' with New Zealand, while Tokelauans still prefer New Zealand citizenship over independence.

American Samoa is an unincorporated territory of the US, as is Guam, both with an established civilian government; Hawai'i, however, is a state of the union. All French territories in the Pacific – New Caledonia, Wallis and Futuna, and French Polynesia – possess internal autonomy under local French officials not answerable to the respective Territorial Assemblies. Easter Island remains a special territory of Chile. Papua and West Papua (Western New Guinea) are Indonesia's largest provinces. Since the 1980s the Federated States of Micronesia and the Republic of the Marshall Islands have been in 'free association' with the US, which is allowed to wield considerable authority. In 1993 the Republic of Palau voted also to enter into 'free association' with the US on special terms, including military jurisdiction in times of 'crisis or hostilities', and one year later independence was declared.

Occasionally, frustrated, eccentric and/or admirably shrewd British have announced their own 'independent' isle – the UK government invariably frowning on the folly as local councils grin in eloquent sympathy. In 2008 the sole occasional occupant of Shetland's one-hectare Forewick Holm publicly declared the 'Crown Dependency of Forvik'; he is now offering different classes of citizenship while hawking 'oil exploration rights'. Piel Island, 20 ha situated 1 km off Cumbria's Furness Peninsula, presents a slightly different picture: gifted by the Duke of Buccleuch in the early 1900s to the people of Barrow-in-Furness, these latter crown as 'King of Piel' whoever runs the island's public house, the Ship Inn, since the publican and his family are this tidal isle's only permanent residents. It's all in good fun.

Little fun is had, however, from post-colonial independents who, usually comprising social elites, 'have tended to repeat, sometimes even more crudely and brutally, the arrogant environmental mistakes made by their colonial predecessors'.[17] On many of the world's islands, one finds attending newly gained independence the same disdain and disrespect for local island ways and traditional island knowledge that alien colonial powers had displayed. Everywhere, it's avarice alone cutting ribbons to open grand harbours and airports to mainly Western transnationals who disembark or descend to despoil and plunder more intensely than before. Islanders can seek redress, but with what authority? Even language is not proof. In 2010 the Tahitians, for example, appealed to the European Parliament to make the majority Tahitian language – rather than the French of the minority – the official tongue of the Parliament of French Polynesia; however, the European Parliament resolved there was no legislation in place to adjudicate the question. With their own unique grievances Easter Islanders have turned to the United Nations, native Hawaiians to Washington, Tuvaluans to Australia and New Zealand; but seldom are there international instruments or jurisdictions in place to arbitrate not only adequately but lawfully in such abstruse insular matters.

So islanders had to plait their own political lifelines.

ISLAND ORGANIZATIONS

Most island territories and colonies rejoiced at their independence in the second half of the twentieth century. The fireworks soon died, however. Economic inviability worried many fledgling island nations. Defence infrastructure crumbled; markets withered for such export staples as sugar, copra and tobacco; and islands without a good harbour or airport simply wilted. The problem remains that relatively small populations with few economic resources wield little political influence – they also daunt foreign investment. It was hoped by many in 1982 that ratification of the 200-nautical-mile Exclusive Economic Zone by the Law of the Sea Convention would furnish small island nations with an enormous territory of oceanic jurisdiction – several orders of magnitude larger than their actual land areas – that would prove to be 'money in the bank'. But even this helped little. Most islands lacked the resources not only to exploit the zone but to guard it from foreign infringement. So, especially since the 1980s, many islands have joined together to form political and economic affiliations. It is a promising resort that must only enrich the twenty-first century.

The Pacific was the modern pioneer in regional island planning and affiliation. Two major organizations have dominated Pacific islands for a number of decades now: the cosmopolitan South Pacific Commission, founded in 1947 and renamed the Secretariat of the Pacific Community in 1997; and the indigenous South Pacific Forum. Based in Noumea, New Caledonia, and originally founded to promote regional economic and social development, the Secretariat of the Pacific Community today comprises 22 Pacific states and territories and the vested nations of Australia, New Zealand, Britain, France and the US. Ongoing programmes address rural development, fisheries, agriculture, health, education, women's and family development, training, statistical services and environmental management. Dissatisfaction with the Commission's political steerage by its non-Pacific members eventually led to the foundation of the wholly separate South Pacific Forum in 1971; based in Suva, Fiji, the Forum is smaller and does not include Britain, France and the US among its sixteen self-governing members, who are led by Australia and New Zealand (which provide two-thirds of the annual budget). The Forum focuses on regional trade, investment, sustainable development and international affairs. In 1982, the Commission, the Forum and the United Nations established the South Pacific Regional Environment Programme, based in 'Apia, Western Samoa; made autonomous in 1993 with 26 member states, the Programme undertakes initiatives in species conservation, nature reserves, environmental and pollution management, and actively oversees international coordination and educational initiatives on many Pacific islands.[18] In 1994 the Forum was granted observer status at the United Nations.

The growing importance and political weight of the South Pacific Forum, in particular, resulted in mounting tension between it and the then South Pacific Commission which was still dominated by Britain, France and the US. So many inter-governmental agencies created by both organizations had led to redundancy, friction and confusion. To resolve this and to cope with the sudden proliferation of regional bodies in the 1980s, the South Pacific Organizations Coordinating Committee was founded in 1988. In 1999, the South Pacific Forum changed its name to the Pacific Islands Forum.

Elsewhere in the world organizations such as the Pacific Islands Forum are often nascent federations, in that they unite, regulate and protect a given region sharing like identities and goals. In recent years, the Forum Secretariat began investigating a possible free trade agreement between member island countries. If realized, this agreement would make the Forum the South Pacific pendant to the European Union, a prelude to potential political union. It is from such beginnings that a 'United States of the Pacific' or some similarly named political entity might emerge during the twenty-first century: one federation embracing all the free peoples of the Pacific.[19]

The rest of the island world was watching. In 1992 the UN Conference on Environment and Development officially recognized an altogether novel entity – the Small Island Developing States (SIDS). These independent states, dependent territories or confederated lands (some with UN membership) that, as political identities, all share the difficulties of island survival, find that their greatest challenges include: too heavy a dependence on international trade, remoteness, small population base, vulnerability to natural disasters (typhoons, volcanos, earthquakes, tsunamis), limited resources and fragile native cultures and environments. In 2010 the UN Department of Economic and Social Affairs listed 52 such SIDS, in three designated regions: the Pacific, Caribbean and AIMS (Africa, Indian Ocean, Mediterranean and South China Sea). Each of these three regions now commands its own cooperation organization, hence there is the Pacific Islands Forum, the Caribbean Community and the Indian Ocean Commission. Many, but not all, SIDS are members, associate members or observers of one of these three organizations. And most are also members of the AOSIS, the Alliance of Small Island States.

Founded in 1990, the AOSIS, with 42 members and four official observers (three American, one Dutch), is an inter-governmental organization of small island countries and low-lying coastal countries. It includes 28 per cent of the world's developing countries and one-fifth of the UN's members, its charter declaring its primary purpose to be the confrontation of the present climate change threatening many of these states' very existence (Maldives, Seychelles, Tuvalu, Kiribati, Tuamotus and so on). The AOSIS drafted in 1994 the first text of the Kyoto Protocol negotiations. And it is the AOSIS that lobbies and negotiates for the SIDS at the UN.

Islands First is another body only recently created by and for the world's islanders. It is an NGO (non-governmental organization) that represents SIDS primarily to address the effects of climate change and to halt the ill-advised exploitation of ocean resources mainly by large developed countries. It advocates on behalf of the small island states themselves, linking the environmental and scientific communities in direct, non-governmental ways in order to effect immediate island solutions. Working together with UN missions in this regard, it nonetheless remains independent and island-focused. Environmental justice tops the list of Islands First's priorities.

One also discovers a wealth of island research centres, institutes and reserves providing a focus for island and marine studies, offering expert advice and consultation on island problems, and fostering future leaders in island governance, management and ecological protection. The Bellairs Research Institute, for example, was founded in 1954 in Barbados as a field station for Canada's McGill University; among other things it now specializes in development studies, environmental engineering and marine biology. The University of the West of Scotland maintains the Scottish Centre for Island Studies, dedicated to the study of sustainable island communities – in particular those of the Scottish isles – and to the sharing of the results of fundamental research in this regard internationally. In the Orkneys there is the International Centre for Island Technology, providing since 1989 teaching and research facilities focusing on renewable energy, marine resources, biodiversity, waste and coastal zone management, island mapping and many other subjects. The University of Prince Edward Island in Canada maintains the Institute of Island Studies, which is a research, education and public policy institute specializing in the culture, environment and economy of small islands. The School of Pacific and Asian Studies at the University of Hawai'i at Mānoa manages the Center for Pacific Islands Studies, which offers courses on many diverse subjects relating to Pacific societies, traditions and governance, and also initiates programmes handling issues of insular importance in the region. Many similar public and private institutes and centres can be found around the globe.

FROM PANDATARIA TO DEVIL'S ISLAND

Criminals, political foes and innocent victims of authorities' bungling and neighbours' malice and greed have always been banished to islands. It would be no exaggeration to say that nearly every island close to a population centre has, at one time or another, served as a penal island – each worthy of the adjective 'notorious'. As early as 46 BC China's Han rulers were exiling political foes to Hainan where the imperial forces maintained a military garrison. The Roman emperor Augustus banished his daughter Julia the Elder to 175-ha Pandataria (modern Ventotene) in the Tyrrhenian Sea just off Campania, accompanied by her mother Scribonia; he also deported his grandson and adopted heir Postumus to the island of Planasia (modern Pianosa) in the Tuscan Archipelago for a suspected plot (where he was killed by his guards upon Augustus's death), and Postumus's sister Julia to the island of Trimerus (modern Isole Tremiti) in the Adriatic for having becoming pregnant by a Senator. Augustus's successor Tiberius (42 BC–AD 37), who personally enjoyed island isolation (Rhodes, Capri), exiled Augustus's granddaughter Agrippina the Elder, daughter of Julia the Elder and mother of Caligula, to Pandataria, the same island to which her mother had been banished; there she starved herself to death. Tiberius also deported her son Nero, accused of treason, to Ponza, largest of the Pontine Islands, where he either committed suicide or starved himself to death, too. Sometime between AD 161 and 168, Marcus Aurelius (AD 121–180) promulgated a law that, among other things, ordered banishment to an island for anyone who attempted to fill the minds of simple people with terror of the gods – Christians seem here to have been his main target. In 187 his son and successor, the venal Commodus, exiled his wife Crispina to Capri and then had her put to death. The prolific early Christian author Tertullian (*c.* 160–*c.* 220) noted that some of his fellow believers were languishing in exile on islands.[20]

Japan's legendary twelfth-century archer Tametomo was exiled to the island of Ōshima in the Izu Islands; he escaped, however, to the Ryūkyū Islands in the south, married a princess, and lived happily ever after in wealth and honour, so they say.

Beginning in 1830, Spain exploited Santa Cruz in California's Channel Islands as a penal colony: malefactors from Spain's California colony were transported to what is now called Prisoners' Harbor 'naked and in a filthy condition', as one report described, where they heard the camp commandant exhorting them to 'improve their morals' so as better to colonize California. And colonize they did. They soon constructed small boats and rafts and stole back to the mainland: it is their many descendants there who relate the tale today.[21] Catalina Island, south of Los Angeles, was being considered in 1886 as a potential penal colony for captured Apaches, but there were too many protests – not from friends of the Apaches or the morally indignant, but from land developers: the *Los Angeles Herald* proclaimed that the island was 'too good for the proposed occupants'.[22]

The British Empire used islands throughout the world much as the Romans did: as rubbish tips for human jetsam. Uncomfortable colonials were sometimes sent to the Seychelles: such luminaries as the Sultan of Perak, Malaya; an African ruler who insisted on butchering people; and even the ancient tortoise that once bit Cyprus's exiled Archbishop Makarios. From 1803 to 1853 Tasmania – originally named Van Diemen's Land – was home to some 75,000 transported convicts. Norfolk Island, east of the Australian mainland, from 1824 to '55 housed the 'twice-convicted' of New South Wales and became infamous worldwide as one of the worst hellholes. Melbourne built a prison on the southeastern coast of French Island; today it's used as guest accommodation. As of 1858 the Andamans and Nicobars in the Indian Ocean were partially developed as penal colonies for the British Raj in India, on which members of the Indian independence movement were incarcerated; when the islands became territories of the new Indian nation in 1950 both groups continued to be used as penal colonies. Today, any number of prisons and remand centres speckle the British Isles, including the Isle of Man, the Channel Islands and the Isle of Wight – Parkhurst Prison on the Isle of Wight, for example, began as a military hospital in 1805 before becoming a holding prison for boys awaiting transportation overseas, mainly to Australia; besides local remands it now holds long-term and life-sentence prisoners.

The Treaty of Fontainebleau in 1814 saw Napoleon Bonaparte (1769–1821) exiled to the island of Elba 20 km off the Tuscan coast, where he retained his title of emperor and could rule as he wished; but he escaped and when he lost for good at Waterloo he was transported in 1815 to St Helena in the South Atlantic, where he eventually died under British supervision, apparently of arsenic poisoning.

During the American Civil War, the Confederacy maintained a prison on 21-ha Bell Isle in the James River at Richmond, Virginia, where from 1862 to 1865 some 30,000 Union soldiers were incarcerated: perhaps as many as 1,000 perished. In 1861 the French colonial government began detaining political prisoners on Côn So'n Island off the coast of southern Vietnam, handing it over to the South Vietnamese government when the Geneva Accords brought independence with partition in 1954; during the Vietnam War, Côn So'n was one of the nation's cruellest prisons, closed only once the North Vietnamese assumed total control in 1975.

As of the middle of the nineteenth century Sweden preferred to transport her more hardened criminals to the island of Gotland, where they resided in a large stone prison dominating the port of Visby; closed in 1996, the prison was converted into a popular back-packers' hotel . . . and the author can attest to the therapeutic effect of a week of solitary there.

During the Second Anglo–Boer War (1899–1902), Britain trans-ported Boer prisoners from South Africa to Bermuda, abandoning them on various smaller isles in the Great Sound. With nothing to do, the Boers spent their days whittling wooden carvings which they then advertised for sale in the local newspaper; it brought in a modest income. (Today these are collectors' rareties.) More than 1,000 Boers were detained on Darrell's Island, for one, where they laid out a tennis court and croquet lawn. Indeed, life was so good there that in 1902, when the war ended, some Boers refused repa-triation and had to be returned to South Africa at gunpoint.

In the Pacific, between 1864 and 1897 around 20,000 French con-victs sentenced to more than eight years' hard labour arrived on the Grande Terre of New Caledonia; from 1871 to 1879 these included political prisoners from the Paris Commune, many of them cul-tured intellectuals. East Timor, as 'the most remote and neglected of all Lisbon's colonies', became a dumping ground for Portugal's political dissidents, the *deportados*.[23] (As of 1980 Indonesia – East Timor's new occupying power – held thousands of suspected Tim-orese nationals on the island of Ataúro north of East Timor: untold numbers died there of hunger and disease.) In New Zealand, military resisters just before and during the First World War were locked into cells on Ripapa Island in Lyttelton Harbour south of Christchurch. When New Zealand invaded Samoa in 1914, German officials were rounded up and sent either to prison or to prisoner-of-war camps at Motuihe Island in the Hauraki Gulf just offshore from Auckland, and also to Somes Island in Wellington Harbour.[24] In the 1920s Chile began using her territory of Easter Island as her own Devil's Island, though only infrequently, as transport was so dear; each 'guest of the Republic' was a political prisoner and during the dictatorship of 1928 eleven were landed. The Chilean Republic's political upheaval of 1931 saw another group arrive but these quickly managed to escape on a private yacht.[25]

During the Second World War many labour, internment and prisoner-of-war camps were situated on islands. In the Channel Islands, for example, Alderney held a German labour camp where mostly Eastern European prisoners suffered and died in their thousands; the Germans' concrete blockhouses and bunkers still remain as a grim and silent memorial to the horror. Surely one of the most notorious island POW camps was Changi at the eastern tip of Singapore, where from late 1941 to 1945 tens of thousands of British, Australian, New Zealand, Dutch and other Allied soldiers and civilians as well as many Malay non-combatants endured appalling treatment at the Selerang military base and Changi's prison.

Five-sq-km Robben Island – around 7 km west of Cape Town, South Africa – was used since the middle of the 1600s not only as a leper colony and quarantine station but also to isolate criminals and political opponents. Among her luminaries were Nelson Mandela (*b.* 1918) and Jacob Zuma (*b.* 1942), whose former cells are now tourist destinations.

The smallest and northernmost of the three Îles du Salut – only 11 km from French Guiana, South America – is a 14-ha, rocky, palm-bedecked isle whose name is today a byword for human cruelty: Devil's Island. Functioning from 1852 to 1952 as a dumping ground for France's undesirables, she hosted more than 80,000 victims – including the framed Jewish artillery officer Captain Alfred Dreyfus (1859–1935) – many thousands of whom never saw the mainland again.

Originally a military fortress, Alcatraz Island in San Francisco Bay housed Civil War prisoners as early as 1861, then after the war became a main US military prison until its deactivation in 1933 when it was converted into a federal penitentiary housing some of America's most notorious gangsters. Closed in 1963, Alcatraz became a popular tourist attraction and in 1986 was declared a National Historic Landmark. Even more notorious is the Guantánamo Bay 'detainment facility' on Cuba, established by America's Bush administration in 2002 to isolate and interrogate alleged opponents from Afghanistan and, later, from Iraq – perhaps more repugnant than

Devil's Island, since the 'facility' incarcerates both political and 'non-judicious' foes following extra-national military procedures above and beyond the jurisdiction of a democratic state.

And the register overflows. The new Greek nation's capital of Athens preferred to exile her political prisoners to 32-sq-km, sparsely populated Folegandros in the southern Cyclades. Ecuador exploited San Cristóbal as a penal colony from 1869 to 1904. Mexico still sends convicts to the federal prison established in 1905 on the Isla de María Madre in the Pacific's Islas Marías 100 km off her western coast. From the 1920s to '60s Australia's Queensland government maintained the infamous Palm Island Aboriginal Settlement: this incarcerated up to 1,630 native Australians for such 'crimes' as bearing a white man's baby or being born of 'mixed' blood; on landing, children were separated from their parents and no one was allowed to speak their native language or enter a 'white zone'. Initially to silence political opponents of his late 1930s right-wing regime, Portugal's dictator António de Oliveira Salazar (1889–1970) opened his iniquitous Tarrafal – the 'Camp of the Slow Death' – on the northwestern coast of Santiago Island in the (now independent) Cape Verde islands 570 km west of Africa; closed in 1954, the prison was reopened in the 1970s to detain Africans challenging Portuguese colonialism. Chiang Kai-shek's Taiwan incarcerated political dissidents in several different prisons on 15-sq-km Green Island 33 km off Taiwan's eastern coast; the Green Island Prison is still functioning. In the 1950s Colombia declared all of 26-sq-km Gorgona Island – some 50 km offshore in the Pacific Ocean – a high-security prison in apparent imitation of Alcatraz; the notorious penal complex was closed in 1985 and is now almost entirely jungle as the island reinvents itself as an important National Natural Reserve. Australia is currently using both Christmas Island and Nauru as convenient, long-term 'detention centres' to confine asylum seekers arriving illegally by way of Indonesia.

And who could possibly forget the fabulous Count of Monte Cristo imprisoned in the Château d'If on the isle of If, the smallest of the four islands in the Frioul Archipelago just 4 km from Marseille – or his extraordinary escape?

The politics of islands is not just about land. By international law sovereign countries can now claim a respective 'maritime zone' extending from any owned island(s), not just from mainland coast(s).[26] For this reason Britain has exercised her right to claim and enforce an Exclusive Economic Zone around the Falkland Islands as sovereign territory, and the US does the same with the Hawaiian Islands, Guam, American Samoa, Puerto Rico and many others. India follows suit with the Andamans and Nicobars. However, sand doesn't count here: 'There is a rule by which claims to territorial seas are allowed only from rocks. It is imprecise because it provides no way of distinguishing a small island from a large rock.'[27] Furthermore, under the Law of the Sea Convention as signed in 1982, archipelagic nations enjoy special provisions. According to these, a nation comprising one or more archipelagos – but no continental or other mainland territory – is allowed to project straight lines connecting her outermost islands and to measure her maritime claims from these. However, enormously discrete archipelagos like Kiribati or highly compact groups like New Zealand fall under rules disallowing such projected lines. (New Zealand would be the world's seventh largest nation if the Ross Dependency – a region of Antarctica – were included within her Exclusive Economic Zone.) Yet such diverse countries as Fiji, São Tomé and Príncipe, and Indonesia have indeed drawn huge archipelagic baselines whose maritime magnitude has been established and guaranteed by international law. Only one island lacks maritime claims: continental Antarctica, which falls under the special Antarctic Treaty that protects marine fish and animals as well as fuels, minerals and other resources.

It's little wonder, then, that at the second decade of the twenty-first century political conflict over island title and scope still causes strife nearly everywhere. In 2010 North Korea shelled Yeonpyeong Island – 12 km south of North Korea's coast, 80 km west of South Korea's – killing four and injuring nineteen South Koreans, in protest to South Korea's claim to the island; it has been one of the most egregious incidents in the region since the Korean War ended in 1953. China, Japan and Taiwan all lay claim to the East China Sea's Senkaku Islands (Chinese, Diaoyu Islands) – five uninhabited isles and three barren rocks that abut strategic shipping lanes, offer rich fishing grounds and are thought to include oil deposits; the US had held these islands from 1945 to 1972, then had reverted them to Japan. (The dispute recently prompted anti-Chinese protests in seven Japanese cities.) Taiwan herself is the focus of longstanding claims by the People's Republic of China; at present the situation there is perhaps Earth's most politically volatile. Turkey has finally allowed Armenians to visit Akdamar Island so that they may hold a mass at the Armenian Church of the Holy Cross from which they had been banned for 95 years; the tiny church, restored by Turkey in 2007, had only just been converted into a state museum; for over 1,000 years the island and church had been an Armenian pilgrimage site, and Armenians greatly long to regain uninhibited access. Both Tonga and Fiji claim possession of Minerva Reef – two submerged atolls lying south of both countries, a favourite anchorage for yachts sailing to New Zealand.

And traditionally inhabited by Japan's Ainu people, the Kuril Islands – a 1,300-km-long archipelago of 56 islands between Japan's Hokkaidō and Russia's Kamchatka totaling 15,600 sq km and currently home to about 17,000 Russians, Ukrainians, Belarusians, Tatars and others who live mostly on fishing – were seized by Russia in the final days of the Second World War. Japan is now insisting on return of the archipelago's 'Northern Territories' – the islands of Kunashiri-tō (Ainu 'Black Island'), Iturup (Ainu 'Place of Capes'), Shikotan (Ainu 'Land with Towns') and the Habomai Rocks – a recourse which, in 2005, the European Parliament recommended. But Russia has recently reaffirmed sovereignty over all the Kuril Islands: in 2010 President Medvedev declared the Southern Kurils (Japan's 'Northern Territories') to be 'an important region of our country' then shortly thereafter announced increased military deployment in the isles – an 'inseparable' part of Russia, he maintained.[28]

Small islands have turned against cosmopolitan states, too, at least against those accused of the most menacing abuse of all, as shown early in 2010 when the Federated States of Micronesia issued a legal challenge to the Czech Republic. This involved the Czechs' declared plan to extend the working life of the infamous Prunéřov Power Station, one of the world's most polluting, the Micronesians arguing that Prunéřov's emissions are ultimately contributing to sea-level rise and thus threatening the Federated States' existence. Though the legal challenge came to naught, one surely has not heard the last from now desperate islanders.

But others seek solace in moons and sixpence instead.

. . . of Moons and Sixpence

'Now would I give a thousand furlongs of sea', cries counsellor Gonzalo at the conclusion of Act I, Scene i of Shakespeare's *Tempest* when the King of Naples's vessel threatens to wreck, 'for an acre of barren ground, long heath, brown furze, any thing. The wills above be done! but I would fain die a dry death.' The island so central to the play is neither seen nor mentioned: for all that is sought is safety. And throughout, the island never truly appears – unnamed, immaterial, she remains magical scenery, a silent spark of stage and stagecraft to concentrate plot and character, acting as tool and archetype.

Such has been the literary fate of the island for almost 3,000 years, above all the creative mainlander's metaphor. Landscapes in general fail to enchant the peoples of this planet: 'Artists enchant them'.[1] And those many literati who have leavened and lauded islands since time immemorial in song, tales, histories, studies, poems, novels, plays and screenplays, only too seldom actually touched the sands and strode the strands.

Because their islands were chiefly those of the mind.

There is no 'island literature'. There is the prehistoric oral and historical written literature of indigenous islanders in their own and intruders' languages and scripts. And there is the islanders' literature about non-islanders on islands and on topics having nothing to do with islands. Some modern islanders attempt through literature to deconstruct island life, rejecting perceived Western contamination as they invent an imaginary 'new island literature'. But, relative to islands, filling the world's libraries and screens are above all the works of mainlanders who tell of isles imagined, visited, studied or otherwise artistically exploited in the words and ways of their own cultures and values. For the 'true' literature of islands is not about islands at all, really – it's about non-islanders' troubled encounters with unacceptable or misunderstood island demands and cultures. The conceit of 'moons and sixpence' – the artistic exploitation of the literary island – reflects historical attitude changes and reveals to a large degree the retarded maturation of Western accommodation to the foreign and unknown.

The literature of islands was born in the embrace of the insular ideal, lands lying in secret seas where the sun always sets or rises: the Greeks' Isles of the Blessed, abode of fallen heroes; Avalon of Welsh legend; Antilla, or the Portuguese's Isles of Seven Cities; and the Irish's Isle of St Brendan, whose tale thrilled Europe more than a millennium ago. Very similar are those barnacled fancies, too: Atlantis; Homer's island of the Phæacians, Odysseus's last destination before hailing his home island of Ithaca; the Island of Brazil, reputed to lie under the ocean off Cornwall; Kêr-Is, the lost Breton city that was swallowed by the sea. With such mirages one is tempted to agree with A. A. Milne:

> It really isn't anywhere!
> It's somewhere else instead.[2]

And in the end one is perhaps led to conclude that as there is no 'island literature' there is no real 'island' at all either, at least not in the magical worlds of ink, stage and screens, electronic or otherwise, where 'land surrounded by liquid' is rather something conjured up out of the mental and intestinal reaction to the stones and sands, ferns and feathers of that geological and biological reality.

'THE ISLE IS FULL OF NOISES'

For most of humankind's story literature meant oral literature: only a small fraction of original tribal songs, tales, genealogies, histories, pæans, eulogies and much more were ever entrusted to papyrus, parchment or paper. This oral literature also changed constantly, transformed by each new generation in reaction to perceived demands, for constantly remoulded in all societies, old and new, 'tradition' is not stone but clay. Island tales would take on new meanings, respond to natural disasters and local wars, accommodate foreign gods and goods, even adopt new tongues and technologies to tell the 'ancient' myths. This has happened with the Rapa Nui of Easter Island, with the Māori of New Zealand, with the Ainu of Japan, with the Corsicans, Irish, Greenlanders and Jamaicans. The articulation of island identity remains strong through chant, song, theatre and now, in the past few decades, through Western-influenced poetry, screenplays, rap – any oral expression of the indigenous franchise, exemplifying *The Tempest*'s

> Be not afeard: the isle is full of noises,
> Sounds and sweet airs, that give delight and hurt not. (III: ii)

Unhappily, lost forever are the tales of the Carib, Arawak and Ciboney peoples of the Caribbean. Gone are those early genealogies of the Marquesans, Tuamotuans and Ra'ivavaeans of the Pacific. Unknown are the hearth-told histories of the Sicani, Elymians and Sicels of ancient Sicily. Tossed to the winds are the haunting songs of the first Greenlanders, Britons, Cypriots and Filipinos. Insular literature was living literature – of the tongue and moment. Until writing arrived, that is.

FROM PHAISTOS TO ZORBA

Composed around 1600 BC, Crete's Phaistos Disk is the earliest island text – the document that turned European prehistory into history (see chapter Three). It also founded a tradition of island writing that would inspire the globe. Around one century later Cypriots began using an adapted borrowing, the Cypro-Minoan script, and then, from the seventh century BC until around 220 BC they used a daughter script, Linear C, to produce monumental inscriptions, legends on coins and contracts on bronze tablets. In the first millennium BC Lesbos excelled in her poets and musicians, the birthplace of antiquity's most famous poetess, Sappho (*c.* 612–*c.* 570 BC), who invented her own small version of the lyre to whose accompaniment she sang her ageless poems. Though in time hers became the female voice of all Greek islands, Sappho never once used the word *nēsos* ('island'); there was no need, for to an ancient Greek an island was life itself. (Hers was a sad fate: according to legend she pursued her lover, Phaon, through the islands and, because he rejected her love when she was around 50, she threw herself off the White Cliff on the Ionian isle of Lefkada.)

The Germanic peoples who settled in Britain brought with them the runic writing which had developed around the first century AD in northern Germany and Scandinavia; with these revered runes they composed brief texts on memorial stones, rings, brooches, clasps, weapons, ivory containers and other treasured objects; such runes were also popular on the isles of Denmark and Sweden. The Celts of Ireland, Scotland, the Isle of Man and Wales used the ogham (pronounced *ohm*) alphabet – one probably inspired by the runes – from the early fifth to seventh century AD, primarily on tombs and memorial stones.

As Greek writing had inspired Etruscan and Latin writing and the runes, Latin in turn inspired the later literatures which were written on the isles of Britain and Ireland, generating that long and magnificent history of indigenous written literature there, from the Germanic peoples' earliest saga *Beowulf* to the Welsh medieval *Mabinogion* and from this to Chaucer to Shakespeare to Milton to Dickens to Shaw to Harry Potter. The same occurred when Chinese inspired Japanese to write using Chinese characters, then to innovate their own unique katakana and hiragana scripts and create a glorious literature of their own, by the early eleventh century culminating in the splendid *Genji Monogatari* of Lady Murasaki Shikibu, that masterpiece of Heian fiction. In Iceland, hearth-told sagas of sailing and settlement, local battles and bloody family tragedies eventually produced a prose literature that excelled anything similar in Europe in the 1200s and 1300s when they were penned on parchment in Old Icelandic by anonymous authors.

On Sri Lanka the Tamils for centuries used their own form of Brahmi and Prakrit scripts, whereas the Sinhalese developed their own Sinhala script, an offshoot from mainland Brahmi which was conveying Sinhalese literature as early as the ninth century. In the Malay Archipelago several new scripts were being used in the wake of prolonged religious and cultural influences from India: Kavi, a Pali script, prevailed in Java between the 800s and 1400s; modelled after Siamese, it chiefly served Javanese speakers, the islands' largest linguistic community. Kavi also generated the only scripts used for writing in precontact Oceania: the Macassar-Buginese scripts in Celebes (perhaps through the Batak script of Sumatra), and the now-extinct Tagala and Bisaya scripts of the Philippines which were first encountered by Westerners in 1521.

Smaller islands knew lesser achievements that left scant trace in the outside world. In the late 1700s the Polynesian Rapa Nui of Easter Island in the southeast Pacific were demonstrated writing by Spanish visitors, whereupon these islanders innovated their own logographic *rongorongo* script – the only non-borrowed writing in Oceania before the twentieth century – in order to prompt priests' chanting of traditional repertoires; subsequently incised into hundreds of battle staffs and driftwood tablets, the *rongorongo* was then appropriated by the paramount chief in an attempt to thwart upstart contenders and secure the island's sacral mandate.[3] At the start of the 1900s in the western Pacific just north of New Guinea, Caroline Islanders imitated missionaries' Latin letters and Japanese syllabic signs to create two types of a syllabary in order to convey their Woleaian language.

The writings of other islanders, however, have widely inspired. Greece's most celebrated writer and philosopher of the twentieth century, Nikos Kazantsakis (1883–1957) is today considered second only to Shakespeare as the world's greatest island writer. A Cretan through and through, he painted in an island prose that was, as Lawrence Durrell remarked, 'well-fashioned, economical, shorn of excessive riches, powerful and controlled'.[4] His *Zorba*, for one, presents 'a sketch of a temperament as validly Greek as that of Odysseus himself'. Nominated in 1957 for the Nobel Prize for Literature, Kazantsakis lost to Albert Camus (1913–1960) by one vote. (Camus later declared that Kazantsakis deserved the tribute 'a hundred times more' than himself.)

Winner of the Nobel Prize in 2001 was V. S. Naipaul (*b.* 1932), the Trinidadian British writer who was also knighted for his contributions to literature; the Nobel Committee called Naipaul 'Conrad's heir' for his having narrated the fates of the colonial empires' vanquished, 'what they do to human beings' – though Naipaul himself has always stressed the realistic portrayal of Developing World existence, with all its convoluted contradictions and hypocrisies, often to the detriment of island sensitivities (particularly those in Trinidad). Naipaul's books are required reading in much of the Developing World. Caribbean writer, poet, playwright and visual artist Derek Walcott (*b.* 1930) from St Lucia, also writing in English, has celebrated the symbolism of island myth and its relation to culture, indicting the long-lasting effects of colonialism; he was honoured with the Nobel Prize for Literature in 1992. Mauritius's J.M.G. Le Clézio (*b.* 1940), who holds dual French-Mauritian citizenship – he calls Mauritius his 'little fatherland' – received the Nobel Prize in 2008 as an 'explorer of a humanity beyond and below the reigning civilization'.

Further islanders who have won the Nobel Prize for Literature include Britain's Rudyard Kipling (1907), John Galsworthy (1932), T. S. Eliot (1948), Bertrand Russell (1950), Winston Churchill (1953), William Golding (1983), Harold Pinter (2005) and Doris Lessing (2007); Japan's Yasunari Kawabata (1968) and Kenzaburō Ōe (1994); Ireland's William Butler Yeats (1923), George Bernard Shaw (1925), Samuel Beckett (1969) and Seamus Heaney (1995); Iceland's Halldór Laxness (1955); and Crete's Odysseas Elytis (1979).

Remarkably, the Nobel Committee has yet to acknowledge the incredibly rich and insightful Taiwanese literary production. Long dominated by the sophisticated and complex classical Chinese tradition, Taiwanese literature has finally found its own cultural footing and speaks out in a rare voice of insular strength and self-realization. Mainland-born and Hong Kong-educated Pai Hsien-yung (*b.* 1937), who spent his career teaching in the US, has imbued his short stories and novels – written in a unique mixture of literary Chinese and experimental modernism – with an underlying melancholy he feels pervading modern Taiwanese society. Chen Ruoxi (*b.* 1938), also now living in the US, is famous for her short stories that examine the 1960s and '70s Cultural Revolution on mainland China, based on personal experience. Mainland-born novelist and short-story writer Wang Wenxing (*b.* 1939) has confronted Taiwanese social issues with perceptive sensitivity. Principally a short-story writer, Huang Chunming (*b.* 1935) has focused on the lives of rural Taiwanese, but also has illuminated both the tragic and humorous struggles of urban life there.

Many other islanders – most writing in Western mode with Western genres in a Western tongue (usually English) – have also boldly stood forth: Samoa's Albert Wendt (*b.* 1939); New Zealand's Witi Ihimaera (*b.* 1944) and Alan Duff (*b.* 1950); Hawai'i's Kiana Davenport; Cuba's Alejo Carpentier (1904–1980) and Dulce María Loynaz (1902–1997); Sri Lanka's Gunadasa Amarasekera (*b.* 1929) in Sinhala, Varadar in Tamil, and Romesh Gunesekera (*b.* 1954) in

English. And there are so many more fine and sensitive island voices in print, far too many, alas, to pay homage to in a short survey.

But where is the Maltese Kazantsakis? Where is the Tahitian Naipaul? Tahiti, for one, has a splendid second-hand literary legacy from visiting luminaries: Herman Melville (1819–1891) was once incarcerated in Pape'ete for mutiny; Zane Grey (1875–1939) still holds the island's big-fish record; Somerset Maugham (1874–1965) pinched Gauguin's three painted glass doors there; Rupert Brooke (1887–1915) moved to Tahiti and fell in love with his landlady's daughter. But one still waits for the Great Tahitian Novel.

On many islands, the colonial legacy yet obscures budding brilliance. Often elders were not allowed to recite, their language banned, their story blistered by the white man's perceived sun. As one Grenadian from the southeastern Caribbean has related:

> The history we did, apart from Columbus and his voyages, was about English adventurers: Drake, Hawkins, Raleigh, Morgan the Pirate. We were told nothing about the Negroes – ourselves. And so we lived in ignorance of who we were and how we came to be where we were.
> Singing consisted mainly of old English, Scottish and Irish ballads. If we were heard singing calypsoes we were ordered to go and wash out our mouths because those were 'devil songs'.[5]

Islanders who wished to represent their past in some alternative way, however, still found means to do so – though many isles in equatorial latitudes prove perhaps too warm and sultry for that 'splinter of ice' that islander Graham Greene (1904–1991) claimed all writers must have, keeping one part of them cold and detached enough to transform experience into literature. It was both laudable and telling that Tasmanian-born Edith Lyttleton (1873–1945), novelist daughter of a landed family who had been reared on a sheep station in Canterbury, New Zealand – in the first half of the 1900s the country's most widely read author – as early as 1908 could publish a critique of imperialism, *The Altar Stairs*, revealing how capitalists from Britain, the US and France were earning from tropical islands by stealing tribal lands and kidnapping tribesmen for indentured plantation work. Hers was the dawn call that, by the end of the century, had become a veritable typhoon of islander writing – in so many languages and genres – that fairly swept away the cosmopolitan mirage, if not for good at least for better.

ATLANTIS AND BEYOND

That island mirage has been claimed to be 'essentially an English construct developed in the Pacific'.[6] In truth, it's far older. The palm-fringed lagoon, the radiant sandy beach and idyllic nature that spelled out, in most recent times, Tahiti in the public reverie were only the latest incarnations of a fancy 'at the end of a very long imaginative tradition, one that long predated the Enlightenment, and even the Renaissance. Indeed it goes back to the very beginnings of Western civilization.'[7]

Such as Atlantis herself, that earliest isle of literary renown. In his two dialogues *Timæus* and *Critias*, Plato (*c.* 427–*c.* 347 BC) tells of a legendary island in the Atlantic west of the Pillars of Hercules that once hosted a rich, powerful and advanced civilization 9,000 years 'before Solon', one that perished in earthquake and flood 'in a single day and night of misfortune'. The tale, allegedly related by Egyptian priests to lawgiver and poet Solon of Athens in the sixth century BC, fascinated Plato two centuries later. As Athenians purportedly had adopted Solon's laws in 549 BC, Atlantis, some 9,000 years earlier, would have been destroyed around 11,600 years ago. There were in fact enormous climatic and geological changes occurring between 12,000 and 11,000 years ago when the last ice age came to an end: the climate ocillated greatly; ice walls were in retreat; ocean plates rose when freed from thick ice; earthquakes and giant floods from natural dam-bursts would have been frequent. When sea levels rose dramatically islands did sink in their tens of thousands and those remaining assumed the shape we know today.

But did Atlantis exist? It is humankind's oldest island story, forever giving voice to an era's insular ideal: perfect climate; egalitarianism; protection from invasion; fertility; abundance of food, wood and metals; gold and silver statues; luxurious temples, palaces and harbour facilities; written language, with decisions and laws inscribed on temple walls and golden tablets. Symbolizing everyone's ideal society ever since Plato, Atlantis has led humankind down many paths – but not to where the human capacity for social cooperation, equity and justice actually lay.

Atlantis was always metaphor – like Wales's Avalon of Arthurian lore. Perhaps her *inspiration* lay in an actual island with a volatile past, however. Since 1960 Greek historian Angelos Galanopoulos has been arguing that Atlantis was in fact Santorini (Thera) north of Crete, as all the dates, distances, figures and measurements in Plato's account had been in error by a factor of ten due to a misunderstanding of ancient Egyptian numeracy.[8] The Minoan society of Crete and Santorini's volcanic eruption of the middle of the second millennium BC would match well with the description of Atlantis's erstwhile glory and alleged demise. Still, this was not west of the Pillars of Hercules. And Santorini, Crete and her Minoan society did not sink and die but survived the cataclysm and flourished for several centuries afterwards.

All societies appear to create their own literary islands and then set out to find them. Born to Greek parents in Egypt's Alexandria, the poet C. P. Cavafy (1863–1933) captured this paradox perfectly in his poem 'Ithaca':

> Lestrygonians, Cyclops and rough Poseidon
> You won't encounter them unless your thought
> Has harboured them and sets them up.[9]

Such tales as Homer's *Odyssey* or Pytheas's *Ocean* (see chapter Three) enthused generations of mariners to seek like wonders. Much later, medieval and Renaissance readers were inspired and informed just as enthusiastically and longingly by the travel accounts of Marco Polo (*c.* 1254–1324), 'Jehan de Mandeville' (1300s), Christopher Columbus and others. Indeed, it was Marco Polo who first reported to the Western world the great insular array of the Malay Archipelago and points east when, accompanying a Mongol expedition from Quanzhou on the Taiwan Strait to Sumatra, he learned that out in the China Sea lay '7,448 islands, most of them inhabited'.[10]

Such accounts, while awakening Europe's geographical and ethnological expectations, actually created a new genre, one highlighting islands.

> This early travel literature was important: successive generations of travelers relied upon it and so went with a sense of the expected. What characterized this 'knowing' was not just what to us is the rather absurd nature of the 'information', but a pre-Enlightenment 'cognitive apparatus' and a classification system that was convincingly 'derived from utterly fabulous authorities'.[11]

One now sought not a heavenly but an earthly Eden or Arcadia, a botanical paradise just over the horizon – 'a place offering the prospect of Christian domination, and, it was hoped, it would be littered with gold'.[12]

Particularly with the Portuguese and Spanish discoveries and the opening up of the West and East Indies, followed by the voyages across the wide expanse of the Pacific beginning in the 1500s and continuing unabated into the 1600s, scores of utopian conjectures and titillating tales about island bays and beauties appeared in print, culminating in the most famous and fabulous of them all: *Gulliver's Travels* by Anglo-Irish writer Jonathan Swift (1667–1745) – itself a satire on the very genre that so thrilled all of Europe.[13] By the end of the 1700s, particularly after Cook's three voyages, travel books featuring encounters with island cultures and peoples – like meeting men from Mars – were selling better than the Bible. Nor did an author-adventurer have to travel all that far: a masterpiece of the epoch is Samuel Johnson's brief *A Journey to the Western Isles of Scotland* from 1775, which enjoyed formidable sales.

The 1800s saw writers increasingly specializing in exotic isles, intentionally setting out, notebook in hand, to document and delight – with royalties, not research, foremost in mind. Herman Melville drew from Pacific experiences as a whaler to produce *Typee* (1846) and *Omoo* (1847). French naval officer and novelist Pierre Loti (Julien Viaud, 1850–1923) similarly used personal exploits to pen a potpourri of romantic, pseudo-autobiographical works – such as *Le Mariage de Loti* (1880) – that often combined real and idealized island settings and encounters in a thrilling 'faction' that found enduring fame. Even celebrated English textile designer William Morris (1834–1896) immortalized in his posthumous *Icelandic Journals* (1911) horseback trips he made on the island in 1871 and 1873.

Island travel books have remained a robust genre, with Italian and Greek isles the favourites. British novelist D. H. Lawrence (1885–1930), for example, celebrated his Sicilian adventures in *Sea and Sardinia* (1921) and American novelist Henry Miller (1891–1980) unbuttoned a Greek travel book, *Greece* (1964), that made love to island realities. Truly enamoured of islands was Indian-born novelist, poet and dramatist Lawrence Durrell who lived in the Greek isles for eight years before and after the Second World War. Famous are Durrell's travel books *Prospero's Cell* (1945) about

Corfu and *Bitter Lemons* (1957) about Cyprus, while *The Greek Islands* (1978) is his personal pæan, crafted cornucopia and passionate parade of island lore. Durrell also penned *Reflections on a Marine Venus* (1953) about Rhodes, as well as *Sicilian Carousel* (1977).

IMAGINED ISLANDS

From discovering islands of the world to creating islands of the mind was merely one small step. In the late fourth century BC Greek mythographer Euhemerus – perhaps from Messina, Sicily – in his *Sacred History* describes the fictional island of Panchæa, an earthly paradise in the Indian Ocean whose description owes more to Plato's Atlantis than Pytheas's Britain. The enduring significance of such pseudo-traveller's accounts lies in their inspiration of more consciously literary works, the most important and influential of these being Sir Thomas More's *Utopia* (1516). A name More coined from Greek *ou* ('not') and *topos* ('place') to describe an ideal island in the New World, *Utopia* is More's supercharged rendering of Plato's *Republic* in that it elaborates an insular society that knows no private ownership, no lawyers, no gender inequality, but thrives as a welfare state with free education, free medical care, common meals, legal divorce, a married priesthood, with all gambling, astrology, hunting and women's make-up discouraged. It is the purest socialism, of course, and this penned under that most ravenous of monarchs, Henry VIII. While the veiled satire remained a humanist's dream, its allegorical vehicle sped others on even greater literary flights.

By William Shakespeare's era, the end of the 1500s, islands had become the commonplace of cannibals and castaways, of pirates and privateers, of rollicking adventures and romances and wealth beyond one's wildest dreams.[14] Mixed together with Euhemerus's Panchæa and More's Utopia, the island of the mind took precedence over any substantial one of stone and sand. Now the island was the ultimate stage, the dramatist's blank foolscap. It was the season of *The Tempest*.

Old Icelandic sagas had introduced to Europe the first literary colonials on remote isles. The store was augmented by Portuguese and Spanish accounts, narratives and fabulations that were soon appearing in most European languages then supplemented by

Shipwreck on Prospero's magical isle in William Shakespeare's *The Tempest*.

original Italian, French and English contributions. Shakespeare now exploited the tradition to create his own island. Penned in 1610–11 and published in 1623, *The Tempest* was also inspired in part by Michel de Montaigne's (1533–1592) essay on cannibals as well as by several travel narratives, including an account by a castaway in the Bermudas – then the terminus of an educated European's geographical knowledge. (This was a century and a half before Cook would be uncloaking the Pacific.) *The Tempest* would address an array of contemporary concerns: 'the natural and the supernatural, nature and art, the savage and the civilized, the colonizer and the colonized, and engaged in debate about ideal sociopolitical organization'.[15]

Mainland cosmopolitan Gonzalo, the 'honest old counsellor of the right Duke of Milan', has been shipwrecked on an unnamed island where, like a Sir Thomas More incarnate, he forthwith ventures to his master and fellow castaways:

> Had I plantation of this isle, my lord . . .
> And were the king on't, what would I do? . . .
> I' the commonwealth I would by contraries
> Execute all things; for no kind of traffic
> Would I admit; no name of magistrate;
> Letters should not be known; riches, poverty,
> And use of service, none; contract, succession,
> Bourn, bound of land, tilth, vineyard, none;
> No use of metal, corn, or wine, or oil;
> No occupation; all men idle, all;
> And women too, but innocent and pure;
> No sovereignty . . . (II: i)

In a place apart Caliban, a 'savage and deformed slave', son of the wicked witch Sycorax and seeming specimen of island indigenes everywhere but Europe, is deceiving jester Trinculo and drunken butler Stephano with Arcadian reveries straight from travel pulp:

> Sometimes a thousand twangling instruments
> Will hum about mine ears; and sometime voices,
> That, if I then had waked after long sleep,
> Will make me sleep again: and then, in dreaming,
> The clouds methought would open, and show riches

Ready to drop upon me; that, when I waked,
I cried to dream again. (III: ii)

Playing the 'harpy' on Prospero's command goodly Ariel, chief
of the spirits and embodiment of the isle's inherent powers,
confronts the main party of castaways – those 'three men of sin'
whom Destiny forced the 'never-surfeited sea' to belch up – with
their grave misdeed of twelve years earlier when they had cast out
Prospero and his young daughter from Milan. For this crime alone
they are stranded, Ariel insists, on an island

Where man does not inhabit, – you 'mongst men
Being most unfit to live. I have made you mad;
And even with such-like valour men hang and drown
Their proper selves. (III: iii)

The tension is released when Prospero himself, with daughter
Miranda, addresses the King of Naples's son Ferdinand, her fresh
fiancé, and assures him that the 'revels' are now over and that any
perceived misadventure has been only a vision:

And, like the baseless fabric of this vision,
The cloud-capp'd towers, the gorgeous palaces,
The solemn temples, the great globe itself,
Yea, all which it inherit, shall dissolve,
And, like this insubstantial pageant faded,
Leave not a rack behind. We are such stuff
As dreams are made on; and our little life
Is rounded with a sleep . . . (IV: i)

Island as wish, island as enchantment, island as threat, island
as dissolving and resolving life. The setting of *The Tempest* is not
once named because it is never real, it is only dream. The tangible
fulfilment – the safe return to Naples and Milan, the restoration of
Prospero's dukedom, the marriage of Miranda and Ferdinand who
becomes the new King of Naples – occurs on the mainland, for only
there does one find real life. The island? – only stage, 'the great
globe itself', indeed the famous Globe. And her islanders? A
deceased witch, her deformed monster of a son and airy spirits who
are, one and all, left behind on something that never really existed.

MAINLANDERS' ISLES

It was on Lesbos in the northern Ægean that Greek writer Longus situated his second-century AD bucolic romance *Daphnis and Chloe*: Lesbos was a favourite *locus amoenus*, a 'pleasant place', indeed even a commonplace by then in Roman-era literature. For everyone recalled how Terpander, Alcæus of Mytilene and, above all, Sappho had composed there; Aristotle had taught for two years on Lesbos, while his contemporary and successor in the Peripatetic school, Theophrastus, was himself a native of Lesbos. The ancients loved such island settings – perfect for pastorals and romances, a popular genre with female readers.[16] Hence the island stage for *Daphnis and Chloe*.

The *mise en scène* was revived in the 1500s and 1600s, then elevated to new heights in the 1700s, above all when British writer, journalist and pamphleteer Daniel Defoe published his novel *Robinson Crusoe* (1719), now regarded as the founding monument of European Realism.[17] *Crusoe* is the archetypal island story, most likely based on the published account of Scots castaway Alexander Selkirk's (1676–1721) four years of survival alone in the then-uninhabited Juan Fernández Islands, 667 km west of Chile. Defoe puts his island in the Caribbean and doesn't shy from making it a soapbox to promulgate 'one of Western capitalism's more influential manuals for individual self-effort and economic progress and domination. It is also about personal salvation, imperial energy, and racial master-servant relationships.'[18] In his depiction of the castaway Crusoe – alone at first, destitute of any succour, lacking all means to practise society's arts yet still able to procure food, save his life and even attain to a modicum of human comfort and leisure – Defoe defines good adventure and better instruction. This is the stuff that fascinates people of all ages and that teaches children best of all. In his *Émile*, Swiss philosopher and writer Jean-Jacques Rousseau (1712–1778) recommended *Robinson Crusoe* as 'the best treatise on education according to nature'.[19]

Crusoe's island is quite the *tabula rasa*, Defoe's own empty stage but this time one on which to reconstruct the ideal human and the ideal society. This is no Panchæa or Utopia awaiting European discovery and emulation, but Christian Europe herself incorporated in a solitary man who knows to recreate the elevated, erudite, sophisticated, moral, indeed the hierarchical in all their evangelistic glory. One can view *Robinson Crusoe* as a rewriting of *The Tempest* only inasmuch as Defoe attempts to 'provide a resolution to the problem of the relationship between master and slave so hesitantly worked through in Shakespeare's text a century before'.[20] But Defoe sidesteps both sovereignty and savage per se for the greater goal of justifying the civilization of what Europeans then believed to be the savage in all men – here represented by the restrained savage in Crusoe and by the unrestrained savage in his man Friday.

The constant that would later come to dominate colonial insular writing – whereby cultural contact would be represented as 'a conflict between active, superior Westerners and passive, inferior islanders' – prevails already here in *Robinson Crusoe*.[21] Islanders are not subjects of integral worth but objects of Western manipulation; and islands themselves, just as in Shakespeare's *Tempest*, are stage scenery to enhance or contrast protagonists' otherworldly experience. Though *Robinson Crusoe* is probably the world's most famous 'island book' it could just as well have taken place in the Sahara. To be sure, there is a sprinkling of descriptive passages about 'a delicious vale' that 'looked like a planted garden'.[22] But for Crusoe it's a 'dismal unfortunate island . . . the Island of Despair'.[23] It is not the island that aids and preserves Crusoe: it's his Western education, discipline and perseverance; and foremost it's his caring God pitted in a victorious battle against indifferent Nature. In this Crusoe became the prototype of the British colonist.

Such a self-serving salvo inspired generations. Innumerable imitations – so-called 'Robinsonades', a label first used in Germany in 1731 – created their own genre. Most famous was perhaps *The Swiss Family Robinson* (1812) by Swiss pastor Johann David Wyss (1743–1818); this, too, inspired scores of imitations. The Robinsonades and all similar literature about isles – invariably centred on white castaways – were soon the most widely read works of the 1800s. They fitted the authoritarian English curriculum of the era, hierarchical and imperialistic, like a school cap. For the literary island zealously propagandized the evident: weren't white Christians the ones after all destined to inherit and civilize the rest of the world? Yet it was a reward that demanded effort.

> The island is presented as a land of plenty which promises to supply all their wants but for which they must necessarily toil: the crucial image, a corporate ideology, is of all striving for a single goal, the smooth and productive functioning of the body politic . . . .[24]

Nor was it only Britain and Switzerland. While living for two years on Île de France (modern Mauritius) Rousseau's novelist friend Jacques-Henri Bernardin de Saint-Pierre (1737–1814) learned the true story of the wreck of *Le Saint Géran* and, from this, fashioned a fanciful tearjerker at whose conclusion the fair heroine is returning to the island in a storm while her manly, faithful chevalier watches anxiously from the shore, only to witness her ship foundering and his beloved washing up, dead, almost at his feet – at which instant he of course expires from a broken heart. The novel *Paul et Virginie* (1787) was an immediate bestseller and has since experienced over 500 editions.

Islands beckoned and hosted innumerable mainland literati, many seeking not only refuge or isolation but also inspiration. George Sand (1804–1876) spent the winter of 1838–9 with her children and Frédéric Chopin (1810–1849) at the Carthusian monastery of Valldemossa on Majorca; Sand later described the adventure in *A Winter in Majorca* (1855). Banished from France for his criticism of Napoleon III, Victor Hugo (1802–1885) lived for many years in the Channel Islands, settling in Jersey; he was banished from Jersey in turn – this time for having published a pamphlet libelling Queen Victoria for her support of the corrupt French regime – and fled to Guernsey in 1855 where he remained for fifteen years. It was here on Guernsey that he penned the immortal *Les Misérables* (1862). Despite all his years in the islands Hugo never spoke or wrote a word of English, it is claimed. Today a French flag flies above the house where he lived on Guernsey.[25]

It was the 1800s that aired so many diverse and fantastic notions about islanders' origins. For their part, Pacific Islanders were thought to be descendants of the 'single, original family' of humankind – Noah's sons and their wives – who had somehow become separated from the Middle East and then degenerated as they wandered and sailed the globe for millennia to end up on distant isles: 'This notion of degeneracy is a critical one. It underlies eighteenth-century and later Western assumptions of the inherent inferiority and passivity of Pacific cultures, *and* of their fundamental fragility.'[26] It was the duty of 'superior and undegenerate' Christians to save and civilize the islanders before they perished, imparting a twofold profit – colonial wealth and Christian souls. However, many still held islanders superior to corrupted Westerners – the 'noble savages' one needed not to save and civilize, but emulate.[27]

The discovery of new island peoples and cultures fuelled Enlightenment enquiry and debate. What is the real meaning of 'civilized'? Who is the true 'savage'? Can the civilized tame a savage society? Conversely, can a civilized society turn savage itself? Many great minds investigated the influence of environment and climate on insular societies, seeking the answers there. French social commentator and political thinker Montesquieu (1689–1755), for one, had revived the ancient Greek theory that Europe's climate had produced an intelligent, vigorous people, while warmer climes fostered 'laziness, superstition, weakness and intellectual stupor'.[28] Soon a racial and moral geography was being promoted that was both arrogant and imperialistic, professing that all Europeans had the moral right to subdue and subject for the explicit reason that all foreign natives were victims of an inherently malignant Nature.

Yet the conceit was short-lived. European literature as of the mid-1800s began chronicling the newly founded disciplines of ethnography, sociology, anthropology and psychology, all of these acknowledging with their growing body of evidence the supremacy of natural laws controlling humankind universally. Perhaps a European way of life couldn't be justified on a foreign island, some were writing. Perhaps an 'inferior' culture was in fact superior *in situ* for its greater respective viability. Darwin's theory of evolution by natural selection only came as the final nail to paradise's coffin. Nature herself was perceived to 'favour the fittest' and the fittest were definitely not transplanted Europeans.

South Sea islands, including Tahiti and her neighbouring isles, were now the last possible place for an earthly heaven, one could clearly see. 'Since paradise was not there, it was nowhere on earth. Thus was paradise lost.'[29] The theme shed insular gloom throughout Melville's *Typee* (1846). It poisoned the pen of Joseph Conrad (1857–1924) in *Almayer's Folly* (1895), *An Outcast of the Islands* (1896) and *Victory* (1915); and of Jack London (1876–1916) in *The Sea-Wolf* (1904), *South Sea Tales* (1911) and *Jerry of the Islands* (1917). The noble savage turned back into the wild savage; the missionary stations dark dens of fear, harm and death; the islands themselves bare larders of privation and want. Hell was on Earth and its name was Island. 'For some, hate turned to fascination and with it sometimes the fall into temptation with island women. For others there was the mixed horror and glory of martyrdom.'[30]

In British literary history the expression of this island discourse that channelled colonialism and imperialism with waxing and waning enthusiasm was not *a* theme: it became '*the* theme of British colonialism'.[31] In the end the new literature was heralding that island cultures were no opponent to European and American ascendancy. As one contemporary proclaimed:

> There seems to be a certain incompatibility between the tastes of the savage and the pursuits of civilized man, which, by a process more easily marked than explained, leads in the end to the extinction of the former; and nowhere has this shown itself more visibly than in Polynesia.[32]

Yet there were those who refused to relinquish the 'paradise lost' theme, and this well into the 1900s. Sunken continents were now alleged to be humankind's cradle. The eminent German naturalist, biologist and philosopher Ernst Haeckel (1834–1919) held that Paradise – 'the *single primæval home* for mankind' – was a now-submerged land in the Indian Ocean called Lemuria.[33] In the twentieth century books on Lemuria (or Mu) proliferated, such as the very popular *The Children of Mu* and *The Lost Continent of Mu* by British cult writer James Churchward (1851–1936).[34] Easter Island, for example, was seen as the final 'vestige' of Mu, a claim modern geology has disproved.

Educational appropriation of island adventure books now became a major tool of British expansion. Those exciting yarns that comprised the light reading of English, Scots, Welsh and Irish for the 200 years and more after *Robinson Crusoe* were in fact the 'energizing myth' of British imperialism, which was fully English capitalism:

> They were, collectively, the story England told itself as it went to sleep at night; and in the form of its dreams, they charged England's will with the energy to go out into the world and explore, conquer, and rule.[35]

Only the European – and in particular the Englishman – was the supreme bearer of civilization, so read the message that dominated this literary market: 'Yet what this story most importantly omits is the inevitable and prolonged *dis*inheritance and *dis*possession of those who are to be "humanised".'[36]

ISLANDS

At the same time, the encounter with islanders and their islands opened the eyes of European scholars and scientists to contrasting cultures, climates, topographies and biota and allowed an objectification that by the middle of the 1800s was transforming every realm of investigation. A founding figure in the science of social anthropology, Edward Burnett Tylor (1832–1917) stressed, for one, that the 'study of the lower races is capable of furnishing most important knowledge about ourselves, about our own habits, customs, laws, principles, prejudices'.[37] Similar insights were filling Europe's journals and proceedings, much of this issuing from remote islands.

The scientific approach electrified the works of the extremely popular French author Jules Verne, who seized the island adventure tale and married it to sober science. A number of Verne's books reiterate – with specific reference to *Robinson Crusoe* and *Swiss Family Robinson* – the motif of educated, cultured Westerners coping with island existence: *The Children of Captain Grant* (1867–8), *The Mysterious Island* (1874–5), *The School for Robinsons* (1882), *Two Years' Holiday* (1888) and *The Second Fatherland* (1900). Verne's core theme is always that of *Crusoe*, yet he modernizes this in his attempt to show that island possession will only truly occur according to a series of scientific and technical laws 'constituted and inscribed elsewhere, but already known to the inhabitants' of Verne's imaginary island.[38] In *The Mysterious Island*, for example, Verne converts Defoe's eighteenth-century pseudo-sermon into a 'modern' nineteenth-century scientism that drives and flatters a new technological age: fantastic Lincoln Island thus becomes an enormous laboratory 'in which knowledges acquired elsewhere are resubmitted to nature, results carefully observed and, finally, re-documented'.[39] It is the island as the ultimate mental experiment – and it was fantastically profitable for its author.

Many readers still preferred sheer adventure though and Robert Louis Stevenson (1850–1894) now distilled the genre's archetype, perhaps the world's all-time favourite: *Treasure Island* (1883). Who could forget the novel's opening when Jack Hawkins evokes the image of Long John Silver? –

On stormy nights, when the wind shook the four corners of the house, and the surf roared along the cove and up the cliffs, I would see him in a thousand forms, and with a thousand diabolical expressions.[40]

One of the greatest adventure stories of all time, the book today enjoys its largest audience. Yet it, too, trumpets British imperialism. It was conceived and worded to sell as many copies as possible and in order to achieve this it had to be politically correct. So it fairly belabours the single, focused theme of self-righteous colonialism. However, there is no settlement here, no transposition of Western culture; one experiences a journey of acquisition, an exploration for portable wealth. 'Island' is equal to 'bank', in other words, a place to be plundered by those with a map and a ship. Stevenson's island is not even locatable, so ambiguous is its description, for it's merely the model for all treasure islands in one's imagination. In this way Jack Hawkins's story is as true and enduring as Crusoe's, since it exists in that most real of realms: timeless myth. In the same stroke it exploits myth to achieve myth: for *Treasure Island* is not so much a boy's daydream as it is a capitalist's dream. This reverie was consciously and masterfully fashioned by Stevenson into a high art form by neutralizing the environment, ignoring nature and submerging place to prioritize psychology, action and style. The ultimate irony is that *Treasure Island* has everything but an island.

However, Stevenson was too good a writer and too sensitive and perceptive a human being to abandon all islands to this oblivion in his works. His is perhaps the rarest balance of all. The physical Pacific does comprise 'waving palms and glowing sands', yes. However, the social Pacific that Stevenson describes clearly illuminates 'as a persistent literary undercurrent the potential moral turpitude of white men in the tropics', especially as read in his travel narrative *In the South Seas* (1896).[41] Stevenson insightfully describes here how the Pacific's imperial history was foremost an empowerment of Western intruders and disempowerment of ancient islanders, the region's culture a dying one of subservient survivors and appreciative supplicants beneficently yoked to colonial teams. Particularly moved by the many respective depopulations, Stevenson was wondering: was it disease, firearms, alcohol, European clothing, new diet, repressive regulations? The verdict was pure Stevenson: 'The unaccustomed race will sometimes die of pin-pricks.'[42]

Stevenson had arrived with his family in Tahiti in 1888 in search of a favourable climate to relieve his tuberculosis and, while residing temporarily in the chief's house at Tautira, fell in love with the locale and people. It was here he penned *The Master of Ballantrae*

(1889), set in Scotland, America and India, and the very antithesis of his bright and joyful island life. But because Tahiti was then virtually incommunicado, melting into obscurity under France's brutal ennui, Stevenson's publishers suggested that he move to Samoa so that he could post his manuscripts with the mail ships regularly steaming from Australia to England; so Stevenson left for Samoa. He died there at Vailima in 1894 and was buried atop nearby Mount Vaea. His former residence at Vailima became the German governor's, then the New Zealand administrator's, then the Samoan prime minister's; today it's a museum dedicated to Stevenson's memory.

Yet island disillusionment now had the upper hand, peaking in the 1920s. 'If I had been content with reading Stevenson', wrote British chemist Robert James Fletcher (1877–1965),

> I should still believe in the paradisiacal charm of a coral reef and a coconut tree. Now the one is a thing that stinks like Billingsgate market and knocks nasty holes in expensive boats, while the other is the produce of 1/100th of a ton of copra which also stinks.[43]

Fletcher took an Oxford chemistry degree, then quit England in 1912 to spend ten-odd years in the Pacific, having been enticed there by Stevenson's writings. He lived mostly in the New Hebrides (Vanuatu) working for plantations and his letters from there to a friend in England later comprised *Isles of Illusion* (1923). For Fletcher, the romantic islanders in the literature he had devoured were – in the reality he encountered – 'hideous, mis-shapen, lice-stricken savages'.[44] At the same time the literature predicting the imminent extinction of Pacific Islanders was at its height of popularity and authority.[45] Modern British anthropology came of age in the Melanesian isles of the early 1900s (before moving to Africa in the 1930s because fieldwork there was cheaper), whence emanated the era's anthropological revelation, that 'the difference between the savage and the civilized . . . was no longer considered one of evolutionary distance, but merely one of different social and physical environments'.[46] It is the attitude we embrace today.

The new outlook was beginning to influence popular literature directly following the First World War. Two American Lafayette Escadrille veterans – James Norman Hall (1887–1951) and London-born Charles Nordhoff (1887–1947) – co-authored in Paris a book on the air squadron, moved to the island of Martha's Vineyard in the US, then received a commission from *Harper's Magazine* to write a series of articles about the South Pacific and left for Pape'ete, Tahiti. Nordhoff stayed twenty years, Hall the rest of his life. (Hall lived at Matavai Bay, where Captain Bligh's *Bounty* had anchored.) There they published a number of bestselling works about the islands, most famously their 'Bounty Trilogy': *Mutiny on the Bounty* (1932), *Men Against the Sea* (1933) and *Pitcairn's Island* (1934). Especially in the last work, the differences between the British exiles and their Polynesian partners and opponents are described as social and physical extremes, pitting the learned (and often perverse) resources of the one against the immediately experienced (and prejudiced) stores of the other, until the reader finds solace in the voice of human reason alone, whether white or brown.

A similar distanced admission of social and physical relativization can be found in the many island works of English playwright, novelist and short-story writer W. Somerset Maugham – in the 1930s perhaps the world's highest-paid author. In 1916, at the height of the First World War, Maugham fled to the South Pacific to research a novel very loosely based on the Tahitian experience of French painter Paul Gauguin: it resulted in *The Moon and Sixpence* (1919), a dark and tormented work about art, civilization, Polynesian redemption and ultimate destruction of the Euro-Pacific dream – his protagonist's magnum opus is torched by his Tahitian widow on the artist's death. As Maugham explained in a letter of 1956: 'If you look on the ground in search of a sixpence, you don't look up, and so miss the moon.' In the 1920s and '30s Maugham and his partner Frederick Haxton toured the centres of Empire in India, Southeast Asia, China and the Pacific, and Maugham wrote many stories about the islands he encountered in these regions, almost invariably through the eyes of a sensitive, but utterly colonial-hackled, upper-class visitor cum narrator. Maugham was aware of the social and physical criteria of the nature–culture debate, as perhaps best exemplified in his short story 'Rain' in which an island missionary attempts to reform the prostitute Sadie Thompson; but Maugham failed to take this one step further, either by reconciling the extremes or by elevating the perception. His protagonists usually die on the foreign isle, forgotten by their landsmen, loved only by the naive native paramours who never understand the exiles' torment.

Such literary encounters – Melville, Stevenson, London, Maugham and so many others in a host of languages – have spawned their own vast deconstructionist literature: works seeking meaning in the differences between relational qualities.[47] Following the horrors of the Second World War historians began decolonizing history itself as the imperial agenda was universally jettisoned. An 'island-centred' arena replaced the aloof colonial observatory. Both in scholarship and in creative writing, authors began examining events 'in an indigenous cultural context'.[48] More recently, this new approach has been supplemented by an appreciation of the processes of globalization – defence, trade, investment – which have tended to relegate the island mandate. In their island creations historians and novelists alike now prioritize global conditions and political situations.

One writer who made islands themselves his chief protagonists was the American James A. Michener. In such unforgettable books as *Tales of the South Pacific* (1947), *Return to Paradise* (1950), *Hawaii* (1959) and *Caribbean* (1989) Michener combined sweeping saga with fastidious research, imaginative romance with historical diligence, very often sandwiching historical exposition between captivating epic in order to illuminate entire epochs of island life. Stationed on Espiritu Santo in the New Hebrides during the Second World War, Michener was inspired by his view of Ambae on the horizon to create his imaginary 'Bali Ha'i' in his first novel, *Tales of the South Pacific* – later turned into a New York musical and Hollywood film (*South Pacific*) which did much to promote tourism and modern Pacific myths after the war.

His contemporary, British novelist, poet, playwright and Nobel laureate William Golding (1911–1993) in his first novel *Lord of the Flies* (1954) revived the deserted isle theme in order to strip humanity bare of the trappings of civilization and show how, on a paradisiacal island, even the 'superior white' can degenerate into brutal savagery when brought to an extreme pass. It is an 'anti-Crusoe' tale of dark pessimism, pleading that there is no true refuge that will save human flotsam from the effects of a nuclear holocaust. When the superficial rules of society confront humankind's innate drive for power and survival, there appears in the end to be only one winner: one 'island morality', Golding is telling us, which inhabits all of us.

History, love, war and reconciliation with life itself in all its myriad splendours and tragedies, all occurring on Kefalonia, largest of the Ionian islands in western Greece, imbue *Captain Corelli's Mandolin* (1994) by British novelist and short-story writer Louis de Bernières (*b.* 1954) with Michener epic and Maugham romance. The novel captures the garlic-and-goat's-milk essence of a Greek isle as it portrays amid bloody war the rude charm of an outsider's – the Italian Captain Corelli's – love affair with the local doctor's daughter, gradual understanding of a special island people, and creation of a transcendent music to give heartfelt expression to both. In contrast to Golding's dark indictment of humankind in which island is again stage, de Bernières's glowing encomium addresses, indeed ennobles, a real island that knows both evil and good yet can still celebrate man's essential dignity through true love, selfless activity and eternal music. Unhappily, as de Bernières's book continues to commemorate Kefalonia, hordes of tourists have flocked there in search of Captain Corelli's world, despoiling through sheer numbers what they had come in search of – to the author's own dismay.

*F*rom *Sappho on Lesbos* to Bashō (1644–1694) on Honshū, from Shakespeare in Britain to John F. Deane (*b.* 1943) in Ireland, poets of all periods have praised islands and islanders, have word-walked them, like John Keats in his 'On First Looking into Chapman's Homer':

> Round many western islands have I been
> Which bards in fealty to Apollo hold.

Greeks and Romans proclaimed island passions, Celtic chieftains in Hebridean haunts arrayed wreaths over eloquent bards, Germanic lords on Baltic isles heaped gold on runesmiths, Byzantine monarchs rejoiced to poems of island conquests, Javanese kings bestowed estates on eloquent minstrels, Hawaiian *ali'i* regaled inspired chanters with fish and whales' teeth. And we, too, still smile today when we hear a particularly inspired islander intone:

> Willows whiten, aspens quiver,
> Little breezes dusk and shiver
> Thro' the wave that runs for ever
> By the island in the river.[49]

Alfred, Lord Tennyson (1809–1892) was a 'double islander', actually. Resident on the Isle of Wight, he found he 'got so rusty' there that he was compelled to remove for a month or two each year to London – capital of another isle.

English poet Rupert Brooke (1887–1915) was also an islander who loved islands and who, during his convalescent tour of 1913–14, spent many months in Tahiti searching for 'lost Gauguins'. Immediately falling in love with his landlady's young daughter, he soon immortalized her in the poem 'Tiara Tahiti'. A little over one year later and now a temporary Sub-Lieutenant in the Royal Navy Volunteer Reserve, Rupert Brooke was dead, having developed sepsis from a mosquito bite and succumbing on a French hospital ship anchored off the Greek isle of Skyros while en route to Gallipoli. (On the other side of the world, his Tahitian love – who allegedly bore Brooke a daughter after his departure – perished around the same time.) Since April 1915 Brooke has lain buried in an olive grove over a kilometre from Skyros's shore; the tomb was tidied up by the Royal Navy in 1960 and enclosed with four, monolithic, white cornerposts and dark metal railing and only recently it has again been whitewashed and cleaned for the many lovers of timeless poetry coming to pay their respects to the genius gracing this island shrine.

Chile's immortal poet Pablo Neruda (1904–1973), winner of the Nobel Prize for Literature in 1971, in this same year paid a short visit to Easter Island, a territory of Chile, which he celebrated in his poem 'La rosa separada' that commences:

A la Isla de Pascua y sus presencias
salgo, saciado de puertas et calles,
a buscar algo que allí no perdí.

To Easter Island and her figures
I set out, sated of doors and streets,
to seek something I hadn't lost there.

And there on that infinitely remote, tiny island, surrounded by these grey figures of ancestral *moai*, the celebrated stone busts, by the spacial whiteness, by the azure stirring, coastal water, clouds, stone . . . 'I recommence the lives of my life'. It is the faraway island, that enduring dream, perceived as a personal *rebirth*. (Sadly, only two years later – in the very month of Chile's brutal military *golpe de estado* – Pablo Neruda was lost to us forever.)

Rousseau held that there will be 'no book but the world, no teaching but that of fact'.[50] Perhaps the world does indeed demand that we view it as text, if merely in order to give structure to the diverse discourses. The empirical island, for one – that bold and brutal encounter between man and nature, between mainlander and islander – fairly shouts for a textual decipherment so as to achieve the 'legibility of the literary island'.[51] The spoken or written word, the oral and fixed literature about and coming from islands – still overwhemingly proffered by mainlanders – provides not only the means to approach insular knowledge but also the mechanism to validate island realities. Too long, however, has the 'desert isle literature' à la Crusoe held sway, where the stage glorifies the vehicle but ignores the road. The imperial legacy still lingers.

seven

. . . of Palettes and Pipes

One gazes in wonder at Minoan Crete's spirited murals, Scotland's bold tartans, Ireland's brilliant Book of Kells, Gauguin's Polynesian palette. One touches in awe Easter Island's mute megaliths, Nantucket's whale-tooth scrimshaw, Henry Moore's abstract bronzes. Women and men shimmer and shine in Javanese jewels, Sri Lankan saris, Japanese pearls, Māori facial tattoos, Manhattan musicals. Ears delight to Highland pipes, the Japanese *koto*, West Indian reggae, Tahitian drums, the Cretan lyra, the Philippine gong. And feet and hips, hands and arms rejoice to Celtic reels, the Hawaiian hula, the Tahitian *tāmūrē*, the Balinese *legong*, Japanese *odori*, Cypriot *tatsia*.

Island manifestations, all. Cultural creations that have thrilled, entertained, adorned and inspired since canoe first touched shore. Some of the world's finest painters, sculptors and composers were born, flourished and died on islands. Most of the rest? – seduced by islands. Masters of carving in amber, ivory, greenstone, wood and volcanic tuff knew the clouds of Gotland, the winds of ancient Malta, the rains of Hainan, the snows of New Zealand's Southern Alps and the sea spray of distant Easter Island. It's the indomitable and inventive human spirit that speaks through hands and bodies, mouths and minds of those island dwellers fearing the sea and revering the land. The voice is as varied as Earth's islands themselves. And as resonant. For island art is the quintessence of island man.

THE ATLANTIC

Greenlandic figurines in soapstone, ivory and wood; British cave murals and grave carvings – these were humankind's first expressions in the Atlantic, long before the settlement of the Faroes, Orkneys, Iceland, Azores and Canaries. In early Atlantic societies tattooing was common and private adornment included multicoloured beads and rare feathers. Song and dance enlivened evening entertainment. No rich tradition, this. But it enabled primitive peoples to survive. Breath was given to inner dreams and desires.

Earth's earliest island art hails from Nottingham's Creswell Crags: bird and animal drawings discovered in 2003, then pictures of dancing women and animals and geometric patterns found one year later. They had been painted onto limestone walls of caves around 13,000 years ago. However, Britain wasn't an island then. In the later Neolithic, once sea surrounded Ireland and Britain, enormous landscape architecture adorned such ritual centres as Stonehenge, Avebury, Marden and so many others.[1] From the third millennium BC the isles' Beaker people were fashioning figurines, vessels, jewellery and other works of tin, gold and silver. Well into the Roman period indigenous Irish and Britons excelled in intricate crafts exploiting metal, stone and wood equally. A special feature of Celtic art was intricate geometrics, with decorative curving lines, plants, zoomorphs and a high degree of symbolism. With the Romans came mosaics and glasswork and the indigenous insular voice increasingly copied Continental manifestations.

Christian motifs arrived in the fourth century AD, yet often still maintained a Celtic essence. Long-resident Anglo-Saxons had introduced Germanic traditions and Celtic passion was seemingly preserved only in Wales, Scotland, the Isle of Man and Ireland: some of the most beautiful manifestations being the illuminated manuscripts of remote isle monasteries. At this time England's Germanic peoples were producing some of Europe's finest ivory and bone sculptures, as well as creating breathtaking illuminations similar in style to Continental creations. Throughout the Middle Ages the isles excelled in Christian paintings, intricate wood panelling and stained-glass windows. Elizabethan portrait miniatures were lauded throughout Europe and by the 1600s full-size portraits and landscapes from the British Isles were competing equally with Continental works.

By the 1700s the islands dominated portrait art in particular, led by such luminaries as Thomas Gainsborough (1727–1788), Sir Joshua Reynolds (1723–1792) and George Romney (1734–1802). The 1800s saw landscape artists John Constable (1776–1837) and J.M.W. Turner (1775–1851) transform the genre into iconography's very veneration.[2] Whereupon England's Pre-Raphaelite movement introduced an almost photographic realism to religious, literary and historical themes; English painter and illustrator Sir John Everett Millais (1829–1896), one of the founders of the Pre-Raphaelite Brotherhood, hailed from a Channel Islands family. Well into the twentieth century – with such artists as English sculptor Henry Moore (1898–1986), Scots painter John Duncan Fergusson (1874–1961) and Irish portraitist John Butler Yeats (1839–1922) – the British Isles not only equalled anything the Continent was producing but often inspired directions that the entire world followed, the perquisite of Empire. Characteristic of much art here is the proximity of the sea and atmosphere of coastal landscapes: these distinguish and colour even urban themes.[3]

Who cannot hear surf crashing and gulls crying and wind soughing in the Irish fiddle, Scottish *clàrsach*, Welsh *crwth* and *telyn*? The pipes have forever raised goosebumps throughout the isles, then went on to kittle the world. England's shanties, hornpipes and jigs charmed the naturalized Georg Friedrich Handel (1685–1759) who singlehandedly tempered the timbre of Northern Europe. Acclaimed among world composers in the 1800s and 1900s were Britain's Edward Elgar (1857–1934), William Walton (1902–1983) and Benjamin Britten (1913–1976). And of course the Beatles. Islanders all. Nor will the British Isles' dances ever halt: the Irish *céilí* that can be so swift and intricate; Scotland's strathspeys, jigs and reels that fill dance evenings; Wales's clog dancing that features at each National Eisteddfod; and the English morris dance that animated manuscripts as early as the 1400s.

Icelandic art found its own voice only in the twentieth century.[4] In the 1800s artists there still imitated Northern European celebrities, but by the 1900s such landscape artists as Þórarinn Þorláksson (1867–1924) and Ásgrímur Jónsson (1876–1958) were expressing the unique topography and lighting of their native island, bringing her to life pictorially for the first time in a naturalistic style. Landscapes have remained the most popular theme in Icelandic painting, despite a wave of abstraction, pop and expressionism in the mid-1900s. An 'abstract expressionism' that often incorporated the Icelandic landscape informed the hybrid creations of Louisa Matthíasdóttir (1917–2000), for one, who had moved to New York in 1942 but never entirely forsaken her island's captivating ambience.

The two main hubs of the Canary Islands – Las Palmas de Gran Canaria and Santa Cruz de Tenerife – dominate artistic life there. Much like that of Iceland, the art of the Canary Islands was for many centuries a continental import politely respected for its religious traditionalism. Only in the twentieth century did such innovative and creative artists as painter, sculptor and architect César Manrique (1919–1992) of Lanzarote introduce indigenous themes, involve themselves in local architectural design and regulation, and successfully commercialize Canary Island subjects for the new tourist market. Among the most characteristic of Canary Islands dances are the graceful *isas*, some of which form ever more intricate chains led by a vocal dance captain.

The nine islands of the Azores similarly genuflected before a Roman Catholic iconography, after the style of the ruling Portuguese mainland. Again, only as of the 1900s did local artists attempt to express a unique Azorean voice in painting and sculpture, and many island works now attract a robust tourist clientele. Horta on the island of Faial houses one of the world's finest collections of scrimshaw, of both whale's tooth and jawbone. Among the traditional dances of Santa María in the eastern Azores, often performed to the *viola de arame* among other instruments, are the *moda do moinho de mão* ('dance of the hand mill') and the *balão* ('balloon').

THE CARIBBEAN

The visual, sculptural, musical and terpsichorean arts of the Caribbean were, until recently, all but dominated by great Cuba.[5] A complex amalgam of European, North American and African motifs, themes, traditions and rhythms, Cuban art and music were, like those of so many islands of the world, initially a borrowing of and innovation on the colonial import. For too many centuries it was not Cuban invention but Roman Catholic convention that dictated subject-matter, form and style. This rendered most, but not all, Cuban artists and musicians humble imitators of perceived superiors. With the late 1800s the Cuban landscape came to the fore, and then with the 1900s such modernist pioneers of the local 'Vanguardia' movement as Victor Manuel García Valdés (1897–1969), Carlos Enríquez Gómez (1900–1957) and Antonio Gattorno (1904–1980) distilled through innate genius a national identity for the first time. The blend of Europe and Africa came to characterize the best of Cuban art, and naive and 'Afrocubanismo' productions grew in popularity and profundity, as testified by the works of such contemporary exponents as Manuel Mendive (*b.* 1944) and José Rodríguez Fuster (*b.* 1946).

The creolized style of Cuban music has, since the end of the 1800s, been hugely popular and influential, with frequent use of bongos, congas, comparsa and batá drums; both jazz and salsa are direct heirs of the Cuban sound and Cuban classical composers and pianists have thrilled international stages as well. The 'rumba craze' of the 1930s and '40s was a speciality of such Cuban band personalities as Xavier Cugat (1900–1990) and Desi Arnaz (1917–1986). Among the many popular dances of Cuba which spread throughout the world, the favourites will always be the cha-cha-chá, rumba, mambo and conga.

Caribbean art is a blazing blend of sights, sounds and movements of widely diverse peoples and cultures over many centuries.[6] As with Cuba, virtually nothing remains of the artistic genius of the islands' earliest inhabitants; but all the richer, then, are the mutually enriching traditions which, from the 1400s to the 1800s, were introduced by Spanish, Dutch, British and French colonial masters and their West African victims. Over so many centuries visiting or settling European artists also contributed what wealthy patrons demanded – chiefly imitations of religious or secular masterpieces from home, or conventional portraits. An individual 'Caribbean art' came into existence only long after Cuba's emancipation from foreign domination. It was not until the mid-twentieth century – just after the Second World War – that Caribbean artists discovered their own voice and, in turn, came to merit international attention and acclaim.

One finds that on most of the world's islands artistic production is distinctly divided between foreign-trained and/or -influenced experts and indigenous amateurs. In the Caribbean, however, an immediately recognizable blend between mainstream stylism and self-taught ritualism empowers artists whose prime concerns remain *vodou* (voodoo), *santería* (the syncretic West African and local religion) and Christian revivalism.[7] In the last few decades European imposture has here yielded to insular authenticity, in that postmodernism's search for defining identity has meant the Caribbean artist finding self in the process of self-expression. The fortuitous response to this special hybrid of West African and European-influenced passion is a robust and highly lucrative tourist market.

Caribbean music is no less complex. It, too, is an incredibly rich mixture of European, African, Indian and local traditions, the most piquant element wafting from Africa. Immediately recognizable internationally: the calypso that originated in Trinidad and Tobago; the salsa, a modern way of playing Cuban *son, son montuno* and *guaracha* with other elements; the *zouk* ('party') from Guadeloupe and Martinique, based on the Polish *mazurka* that had been introduced to the French Caribbean in the 1800s; and of course the reggae that first developed in Jamaica in the 1960s – here Bob Marley (1945–1981) gave voice not only to island culture but to the hunger of an entire age. Reggae in particular has made multi-millionaires of many Caribbean artists and the genre still contributes and inspires everywhere.[8] Traditional and modern Caribbean dances include the calinda, palo de mayo ('Maypole'), Jamaican 'daggering', the *zouk*, limbo, kwadril and many more – exciting, sensuous, insular mayhem.

THE MEDITERRANEAN

Wealthy nodes of ancient trade routes that generated luxury and leisure, the Mediterranean isles were cultural crucibles: here we find some of humankind's earliest and most profound works of art. As early as 3800 BC Cypriots at Lempa were carving female figurines of stone, while Malta's Neolithic geniuses were adorning temples with complex bas-reliefs and anthropomorphic sculptures. Cycladic sculptors working in approximately 2500 BC fashioned flat female figures and rounded, faceless harpists and pipers, haunting spirits of a once-ebullient Ægean society.

But it was Minoan art, above all, that – taking wing on Crete then blessing vassal islands and trading ports between 2000 and 1500 BC – gave expression to that primordial sea of heroes: indeed, the *dæmon* of island art personified.[9] Knossos's palace would have exemplified the epoch's majesterial architecture. It was the Minoans who created the greatest murals of the ancient world and frescos were evidently this rare people's most cherished art, as they apparently so adorned each room of each dwelling. Yet Minoans excelled, too, in sculpture and carving in wood, stone and ivory; lost-wax bronzes of all shapes and sizes; intricately incised intaglios and sealstones; and exquisite pottery flaunting spirals, curves, crosses, then later more naturalistic lilies, birds, fishes and squid.[10] Motion quickened all animates – a gaggle of maiden saffron gatherers, a trio of bull springers, two naked boxing boys, birds in flight, lions on the run. Even the Phaistos Disk brings its few glyphs to life: a bird aloft, a striding man, two punching fists. Would that our ears could ring to their lyra and kithara, cymbal and panpipes; that our eyes could behold those young initiates at Knossos in their long skirts and high bared bodices as they glided, twisted, dipped – a sound and sight for island gods.

A thousand years later and it was still the Hellenes who coloured the Mediterranean. Yet mainland and island art were one now: the magnificent temples, marble statuary, elaborate mosaics, paintings on walls and wooden boards, the portable art of gold, silver and ivory were the expression of a single folk, citizens of city-states who identified with the 'ethnic nation' of all Greeks. Certain islands were still distinguished for their art, however. Because of Protogenes's painting of Ialysus, King Demetrius of Macedon, for example, as Pliny the Elder tells us, 'in order to avoid burning a picture, abstained [in 305–4 BC] from setting fire to Rhodes when the city could only be taken from the side where the picture was stored, and thru consideration for the safety of a picture lost the chance of a victory!'[11] And the Winged Victory of Samothrace that now blesses the Louvre once graced the ancient Samothrace temple complex in the northern Ægean, commanding an altar in view of the ship monument sculpted on commission of this same King Demetrius (who also commissioned the Colossus of Rhodes) to celebrate his naval victory over Ptolemy II in 305 BC. The white Parian marble of goddess Nike was then hidden in a rock niche close to Palæopolis where it lay for over a thousand years until discovered by the local French consul in 1863.

Sicily was all but alone in developing her own special ceramics that borrowed heavily from an earlier Sicanian tradition. Otherwise the island art of Magna Græcia (Sicily, Malta, Corsica) and the later Roman Empire (now including Cyprus, Sardinia, the Balearics) comprised import and imitation. And so it remained through the Middle Ages when the ecclesiastical dictate determined form and style which remained indistinguishable whether on mainland or isle – notably with a preference in Malta and in the western Mediterranean for Romanesque and southern Gothic styles. Icon painting achieved new heights in the Greek isles, including Cyprus. In the early Renaissance, Sicilian painter Antonello da Messina (*c.* 1430–1479) introduced Flemish realism to the Mediterranean, influencing not only northern Italian but also Maltese painting. Italian and Flemish Mannerism then flourished on Malta under such geniuses as Matteo Perez d'Aleccio (1547–1616), who had studied under Michelangelo, and Filippo Paladini (1544–1614), that great master of Tuscan Mannerism. Caravaggio (1571–1610) lived on Malta for fifteen months and painted at least seven works there. The Cretan School (Post-Byzantine) of icon painting – the main occupation of Greek art from the fifteenth to seventeenth centuries – found a worthy disciple in El Greco (Doménikos Theotokópoulos, 1541–1614), one of the immortals among island-born painters.[12]

During the Baroque period, Malta's Melchior Gafà (1639–1667) developed into one of Rome's leading sculptors. Rococco, Neoclassicism and Romanticism then swept over the islands of the Mediterranean as wealthy patrons sought to keep up with the latest trends in mainland art. Rarely did a native voice emerge above the foreign inundation. Themes and styles followed the purses of increasing numbers of tourists from Italy, France, Germany and especially Britain – island landscapes became the era's 'picture postcards'.

A modern and independent insular song rang out only as of the 1900s, as happened on so many other islands of the world. Malta's 'Modern Art Group' reinvented the indigenous voice after the Second World War under such leading exponents as Josef Kalleya (1898–1998), George Preca (1909–1984) and Emvin Cremona (1919–1986). Sardinian Eugenio Tavolara (1901–1963) won fame for his terracotta statuettes in traditional Sardinian costume. Others found fame only far from their islands. Sicilian painter and set designer Renato Guttuso (1911–1987), for example, based himself in Rome in order to develop an Expressionistic idiosyncrasy in landscapes and social commentaries that evoked raw Palermo roots. Corsican-born painter François Lanzi (1916–1988) pursued abstract landscape collages, Christ-like figurines, equine heads and stained-glass productions while living most of his life in England. In the Balearics, however, internationally acclaimed Miquel Barceló (*b*. 1957) of Majorca, for one, though often exhibiting overseas remains fixed on his native island, which he continually invokes in sea paintings, ceramics and sculptures.

Mediterranean island music is as varied as it is ancient. First islanders dreamed to the tunes of bone pipes and skin drums; classical islanders sang and danced to the lyre, kithara, phorminx and panpipes; medieval performers took to the lute and dulcimer, psaltery and gemshorn; and every possible instrument under the sun has since been introduced, mastered and exploited. Characteristic of Mediterranean isles is a rich mixture of ancient Greek and Roman, North African and Middle Eastern, medieval and subsequent French and Italian influences. All can be experienced on Cyprus, which was heavily influenced by French court music from the mid-fourteenth to -fifteenth centuries; Byzantine chant still thrived there during the Ottoman Empire when Constantinople's compositions were preferred; today there thrives an array of classical, folk and modern genres, including since the late 1970s Cypriot rock and heavy metal. With a similar tradition, Crete's favourite instrument remains the lyra, often accompanied by the lute: folk groups still dance the *hasapiko* or 'butcher's dance' which is performed armed with any sort of knife. Lawrence Durrell raved: 'Advancing and retreating, the dancers clash knives until the sparks strike, and they utter roars and snarls which suggest that their enmity is not imitated but real.'[13] A new type of Cretan popular music that mixed folk with classical techniques was favoured by such stars as the 'Archangel of Crete', Nikos Xilouris (1936–1980). Sicily's intoxicating music was distilled from Greek, Roman, Norman, French, Spanish and Arab grains: from the *ciaramedda* (Sicilian bagpipe) to the unforgettable bel canto operas of Catania-born Vincenzo Bellini (1801–1835), Sicily today abounds in music festivals, concerts, operas and special performances in Siracusa's ancient Roman amphitheatre. Sardinia is famous for her *launedda*, an instrument of three single-reed pipes blown simultaneously, as well as her *gozos* or sacred songs. The polyphonic choral tradition that characterizes Corsican song is always sung a capella; this has now become a fountainhead of Corsican national identity. Spanish Baroque composers Francisco Guerau (1649–1722) and Antonio de Literes (1673–1747) both hailed from Majorca. In another age and dimension, the celebrated 'Balearic Beat' is an assorted blend of DJ-moderated electronic dance music that exploded in the 1980s among club and beach rave goers in tourist-inundated Ibiza.

INDIAN OCEAN AND MALAY ARCHIPELAGO

Since around the third century BC the island of Sri Lanka has enjoyed a rich Buddhist tradition, her painting and sculpture both spiritual longing and celebration, her architectural wonders regal declarations of wealth and power.[14] Sinhalese art was a Buddhist import from India that followed strict conventions then developed its own indigenous dynamic. Sculptures and carvings, wall paintings and spectacular furnishings adorned such incredibly wealthy shrine complexes as Anuradhapura. Despite waves of Hindu Tamil destruction, by the eleventh and twelfth centuries AD the Kingdom of Polonnaruwa, for one, was able to cast sophisticated bronzes of Hindu gods and goddesses. A classical naturalism soon developed that prevailed for centuries, in the eighteenth and nineteenth centuries culminating in a greatly stylized form still embracing archaic tradition as a fundamental theme.

By 1815, when Sri Lanka became a British colony, the central Kandyan tradition enhancing the capital's temples had discarded all naturalism to adopt strict, simple, illustrative stereotypes. The 'Southern School' had developed in the same direction, yet was far more expressive and detailed. Through the 1800s British-imposed European archetypes came to dominate. However, by the 1900s a hybrid voice rose to the fore, a felicitous marriage of the indigenous and Western import: neoclassicist Solias Mendis (1897–1975), for example, specialized in temple murals combining Indian-Buddhist style with the indigenous Sinhalese-classical as imbued in Anuradhapura's naturalism – amalgamating, but limiting, imposed European strictures. Another luminary was Maligawage Sarlis (1880–1955), master of Buddhist oils and litho prints as well as a gifted writer and poet. Over the last generation the civil war between Buddhist Sinhalese and Hindu Tamils has fairly shouted the necessity for a new, harmonious hybrid.

Common to many islands close to the African coast is the blend of artistic traditions from Africa, the Arab nations, India, Southern Asia and Europe, each island flaunting her dominant legacy. Zanzibar, for one, though highly influenced by nearby Tanzania still wears her centuries of Arab sway splendidly. In the 1800s many Zanzibar artists began specializing in the carving of wooden doors – many studded with brass spikes – exploiting a unique blend of western Indian and Islamic themes. Carved chests parading individual symbols were another island speciality. Popular among today's tourists is the primitive, colourful *tingatinga* art introduced from Tanzania in the latter half of the 1900s. Nor has Zanzibar's musical contribution been negligible: Freddie Mercury (1946–1991) of legendary British rock band Queen was born there.

Madagascar's art was imported from the Malay Archipelago by Austronesian settlers in the first few centuries AD.[15] Nothing separated art from religion – one was simply the expression of the other, in wood, weaving, basketwork and pottery. The individual artist dissolved within the communal chorus, as all art was the anonymous solo of the whole tribe. Traditional art then altered with the arrival of African Bantu migrants around 1,000 years ago, then with Arab traders and further East African migrants in subsequent centuries, whereupon this distinctive blend of cultures attracted European notice in the 1800s. By the twentieth century the plundering of Malagasy graves fed a growing artefactual trade, and the island's ancient art was being regarded as something predominantly funereal. As Madagascar was ruled by France from 1890 until 1960 the French influence started overwhelming all genres. Today each of these developments is reflected in the local statement, as some artists prefer traditional, some European, many a hybrid between the two. Traditional Malagasy music is equally hybrid, characterized foremost by the *valiha* or bamboo tube zither and by polyharmonic choral singing; a wide range of traditional, contemporary and popular music can today be heard, exploiting a variety of local and introduced instruments. Music still accompanies the induction into the trance state of ritual *tromba* practices, but much more common are the folk and soft-rock blends of highland bands or popular coastal styles of *salegy* and *tsapika* dance music.

Mauritius, Réunion, the Seychelles, Comoros, Laccadives, Maldives and other islands of the Indian Ocean all flaunt the art of immigrant peoples who have come to terms with new cultures, with mainland neighbours and with distant trading partners and colonial masters. Since most were settled under Europeans, they embrace an artistic statement more Euro-centred and less 'indigenous' than that of Sri Lanka or Madagascar; their music, too, appears more eclectic, popular and commercial. In the Seychelles, for example, a former colony of both France and Britain, music is a giddy blend of *sega* (the erstwhile 'dance-and-trance music' of imported slaves) from Mauritius and Réunion, French folk, *taarab* from Kenya and Tanzania, the sensuous *moutya*, the English *contradanse*, mazurka, as well as Polynesian, Arcadian, Indian and some African styles – a merry melange actually quite typical of the more remote islands and archipelagos of the Indian Ocean.

The art of the Malay Archipelago – that of the islands of Singapore, Indonesia, Malaysia, Brunei and East Timor – draws deeply from the well of archaic Austronesian tradition.[16] Heavily influenced through trade, especially with India, the Arab nations, Southeast Asia and China, Malay art has experienced waves of individualizing Buddhist and Hindu, later Muslim, stimuli on the bedrock of Austronesian communal articulation. In a later era, Portugal and then the Netherlands added their own cloves and nutmeg to the local bouillabaisse, concocting one of the planet's most piquant regions. Indeed, 'there is hardly any other area in the whole world which has experienced so many cultural and religious impulses of such diverse kind and force and of such enduring effect'.[17] Underlying all art in this phenomenally fertile archipelago is the relationship between human and divine, its confession differing in each epoch. Even court art – in earlier eras *the* patron – was religious art.

Woodcarving ornamentation in the archipelago's Indian-influenced architecture and furnishings astounds. Silversmith work and intricate engraving bring honour to Sumatra and Java's Yogyakarta province. South Sulawesi is known for her filigree, Bali for her various styles of wood, sandstone and clay sculpture. Primarily focused on Islamic themes – while Hindu themes occupy Bali and some other islands – the archipelago's visual arts follow very much the traditional statement, even when imitating European exemplars. Java, as the original home of batik – a method of producing coloured designs on textiles using wax to resist dye – boasts of several famous centres; Bali competes with her own local designs. Gold- and silver-threaded handwoven cloths distinguish some island locales, and richly designed cottons and silks beautify other regions. An art form in itself are Java's leather or wooden puppets, often re-enacting celebrated stories from Hindu epics. Similar are Java's and Bali's dance dramas which animate Hindu mythology and tales from the Mahabharata and Ramayana. Such dance dramas delight to full *gamelan* orchestras of gongs, drums, xylophones, flutes and strings. North Sulawesi favours the xylophone whereas West Java's bamboo *angklung* charms with melodic tinkles.

The Malay Archipelago's modern scene is among the richest in the world, from traditional carving to avant-garde oils and acrylics. The depth and breadth of this island art simply overwhelm. Among the more prominent of recent luminaries: Affandi (1907–1990) of West Java, the expressionist painter who taught the world to 'squeeze from the tube'; Basuki Abdullah (1915–1993) of Central Java, the realist painter tragically beaten to death by robbers in his Jakarta home; Ida Bagus Made (1915–1999), traditional Balinese painter; and Sudjana Kerton (1922–1994) also of West Java, the artistic journalist and revolutionary painter who in his final years celebrated colourful commonplaces.

The Malay Archipelago's musical legacy is no less impressive, famous not only for its *gamelan* ensemble but also for the modern *dangdut*, complex *jaipongan* and Java's *campusari*. In Singapore, *peranakan* folk music mixes Malay-derived melodies with English texts, while more traditional music is inspired by ethnic Malay, Chinese and Tamil tunes; the metropolis is also a vibrant centre for pop, rock, heavy metal and other styles as well as for the Singapore Symphony Orchestra that rivals the world's best. Though Brunei's strict Islamic observance limits some musical expressions, this small nation within Borneo preserves her Kedayan *aduk-aduk* percussion-accompanied ceremonial dance and her Malay *jipin* dance performed to the traditional stringed *gambus dan biola*, *dombak* goblet drum and *rebana* tambourine, among other folk styles and idioms; Brunei also fosters, like Singapore, Western classical music of the highest order. East Timor's *likurai* dance, performed to a small drum by women welcoming home their warriors, was once the country's most common folk music; modern rhythms still preserve some Portuguese fado strains, but mixed with the Indonesian *gamelan*; in more recent years rock, pop, reggae, hip hop and other styles sung in Tetum or Portuguese – usually to guitar accompaniment – have seduced the young, with local bands proliferating like palms on the strand.

THE PHILIPPINES AND EAST ASIA

Carving, weaving and pottery fascinated Filipino artists before the arrival of the Spaniards: southern islanders favouring intricate carving in various woods, northern islanders ornate geometrical patterns woven into various fabrics. All islanders would decorate their pottery with a wide variety of styles. Islam imbued *okir* wood-carving and metalworking (such as weapons) that favoured curved lines, and also timbred those geometric tapestries that were women's work. On Samar from the early 1600s to the late 1800s a unique style known as *kut-kut* enthralled: a flat wooden panel with lightly flowing, multilayered textures telling four individual 'stories'. As of the 1600s, though, European-style biblical scenes in oils was the taste of Spanish colonials and many indigenous Filipinos learned this new art quickly and came to excel in its production. Sculpture, engraving and then lithography followed, all in European-inspired styles. In time, Filipino painting came to figure among the world's most distinctive, with such notables as historical impressionist Félix Hidalgo (1855–1913), Ilocano realist painter and sculptor Juan Luna (1857–1899), and portraitist and landscape artist Fernando Amorsolo (1892–1972).

Each Philippine island cherished her own musical tradition, one subsequently influenced and altered with each new intrusion and colonization by Muslim Malays or Roman Catholic Spaniards. Because of this independent evolution and because of the archipelago's many discrete languages, never did there develop a national musical consciousness. In the Philippines children's songs are believed to be the true traditional songs. Vocal and dance music now comprises most of what is regarded as time-honoured, separated in the public consciousness into Muslim and Christian music, though other influences also resonate: the Thai *piphat*, Indonesian *gamelan*, Malay *caklempong*, Okinawan *min'yō*. 'Christian' dance music – the fandango, polka, *jota*, *curacha*, *habanera* and others – is recreational. But 'Muslim' dance music is narrative, commonly re-enacting like Indonesian and Indian music a story taken from Indian saga in order to edify and inspire. Instrumentation includes gongs (the *gangsa* flat gong of the northern isles and bossed gong of the southern isles), *banduria* mandolins, and guitars. Modern Philippine music embraces, too, the 'original pinoy', developed in the 1970s and borrowing heavily from indigenous traditions;

American rock, sung in English, Tagalog and any number of local languages and dialects; local folk-rock and hip hop; as well as jazz, reggae, Latino and the recent bossa nova revival. The Philippines enjoy an extremely dynamic youth culture, while older generations prefer the music that primarily celebrates the islands' ethnic marquetry.

Taiwan's artistic province demands a tripartite regard: that of her eleven indigenous peoples; that of the Chinese Fukienese-speaking mainlanders whose ancestors arrived in the 1600s; and that of the two to three million Mandarin speakers who landed as of 1949 with the mainland Kuomintang government. Among early Taiwanese, knotting, dough-figure sculpture and paper cutting were popular expressions; southern Taiwan's Rukai and Paiwan special-ized in stylized anthropomorphic, serpentine and geometric wood-carvings; the Atayal wove fabric designs in diamonds, squares and triangles. The characteristic walking-and-stomping lion and dragon dances favoured accompaniment by vocal chorus, simple strings and woodwinds, drums and various rattles. The native art of Taiwan is still popular and celebrated in many local festivals throughout the island.

In the 1600s styles, tastes and entire genres were introduced from mainland China and have since come to dominate Taiwanese culture, though altered by many foreign influences. Puppetry has always been eagerly practised on the island, with richly garbed glove puppets, marionettes and fanciful shadow puppets telling local legends or drawing from classical Chinese literature. Temple sculp-ture repeated the ornateness of mainland models, and ceramics reproduced mainland demands. Painting, calligraphy and intricate seal carvings all followed mainland archetypes as well. Only during the period of Japanese rule (1895–1945) did Taiwanese painters break free from the mainland dictate and begin to focus on native landscapes and everyday Taiwanese life, copying Japanese impres-sionism. At the peak of the 'nativist art movement' in the middle of the 1900s many painters specialized in traditional ink painting.

With the arrival of the Kuomintang government from mainland China in 1949 – when the *Guóyǔ* ('National Language') was im-posed on the non-Mandarin majority as the only language of edu-cation and civil service – indigenous Taiwanese expressions were robustly suppressed. Perhaps unsurprisingly, abstract Western art was embraced in the late 1950s and '60s, whereupon a 'neo-nativist movement' encouraged a return to folk themes, local landscapes and architectures, as well as depicting daily life under the Kuomintang. All these movements are evident in the works of such renowned Taiwanese artists as impressionistic painter Chen Cheng-po (1895–1947); Tokyo- and Paris-trained painter and sculptor Yen Shui-long (1903–1997); and London-based Suling Wang (*b.* 1968), famous worldwide for her large-scale, multilayered, calligraphic and cartoon-like abstracts.[18]

Taiwanese music has echoed the influences and trends and the current scene is a rich fusion of traditional Taiwanese, Chinese folk and classical, Western classical, and Western popular. Classical Chinese orchestras using traditional instruments are popular on the island still, but there is renewed interest in Taiwanese allegro *beiguan* and andante *nanguan* music. All the same, Western classical music predominates and Taiwan's several symphonic orchestras rank among the world's most professional. Of course, like with the Philippines all forms of modern Western popular music now resonate on Taiwan, too, and – especially since the lifting of martial law in 1989 – are the favourites of young Taiwanese.

The general isolation of Korea's largest island, Jeju-do, has allowed a separate culture to evolve there that has left an indelible mark on the regional canvas. The most obvious icon of her separateness? – those ubiquitous, mushroom-like, basalt *dol hareubang* or 'stone grandfather figures', centuries-old deity statues up to three metres in height (so reminiscent of Easter Island's *moai*) that stand sentinel at temple and residential gates as protection from passing demons. The island's more mirthful feature surely must be the 'Jeju Love Land', an outdoor sculpture park and exhibition centre dedicated to sexual art and instruction. It was that the island had become a popular honeymoon destination after the Korean War, but those young couples of arranged marriages had had no knowledge of sex and therefore this sculpture park was created to 'inspire' them. Today some 140 sculptures reproduce couples in different sexual positions, stone phalli and labia and other relevant topics, with rotating exhibits by international artists eager to contribute to the celebrated scheme. The park draws tourists from throughout the world.

Like the islands of Britain, Sri Lanka, the Malay Archipelago and the Philippines, Japan can look back over several millennia of artistic inspiration.[19] Long periods of isolation punctuated by brief foreign contact have engendered genres and styles that are at once both uniquely Japanese and curiously hybrid. The Jōmon era (around 11,000–300 BC) featured clay figurines, vessels decorated with cord markings, and crystal jewels. Subsequent Yayoi immigrants excelled in ceramics, bronze bells and copperwork. *Haniwa* clay sculptures and bronze mirrors characterize the art of the Kofun period (AD 250–552). The following Asuka and Nara periods (552–784) delighted in Buddhist mainland traditions of temple decoration, large bronze and clay statuary, lacquered woodwork and intricately ornamented utensils. Heian art celebrated the *emaki* or picture scroll, and Kamakuran art introduced a new realism to Buddhist sculpture and *emaki* illustrations. An artistic revolution occurred during the Muromachi period (1338–1573) when all cultural expression adopted an elitist exclusionism: imported Chinese paintings introduced a preference for monochromes with a minimum of brushstroke detail, screen painting became popular, and landscapes were a favoured theme. During the Edo period (1603–1868) artists ceaselessly tried to break the strictures of the repressive shogunate, from Sōtatsu's (*c.* 1600–1640) natural motifs on gold-leaf backgrounds to Enkū's (1632–1695) 120,000 crude Buddhist images, yielding over time to the 'floating world' *ukiyo-e* paintings and woodblock prints, as well as to other landscape, historical, theatrical and pleasure-quarter themes; here, woodblock printing experienced its apogee.

The subsequent Meiji period (1868–1912) saw Japan opening up to Western influences, with a simultaneous integration, assimilation and confrontation with Western art: some demanding wholly new styles, others wishing to retain traditional art, and those seeking an artistic synthesis. From this contest emerged the two Japanese styles which still command: the traditional *nihonga* and synthetical *yōga*. Alone in pottery and porcelain, the depth of historical development and breadth of styles – from Sue stoneware to copper-glazed Oribe ware, from Ko-Kutane enamelware to Imari porcelain, Satsuma earthenware, Kakiemon ware, and Fukugawa and Kutani ceramics – distinguish the Japanese kiln as perhaps the world's most sophisticated.[20]

As of the 1950s Japanese artists were either creating or participating in such avant-garde movements as installation art, performance art, wearable art and conceptual art. Anime cartooning, inspired by American illustrators, transcended to high art under

Japanese disciples. Such contemporary artistic icons as surrealistic photographer and poet Kansuke Yamamoto (1914–1987), manga artist and film director Hayao Miyazaki (*b.* 1941), avant-garde artist and musician, activist and philanthropist Yoko Ono (*b.* 1933, a 'tri-islander', as she was also based in London before settling in New York), or painter and sculptor Takashi Murakami (*b.* 1963) illustrate that Japanese artists share art's summit whether on Honshū, Britain or Manhattan.

Japanese music, dance and theatre have similarly fascinated the world. Surviving from the Jōmon era are clay and stone flutes as well as original stringed zithers; as of the Yayoi period metal gongs and bells joined these to form ensembles. Already some 1,400 years ago Japanese orchestras featured flutes and stringed instruments, chimes, gongs and drums: *gagaku* ceremonial courtly music and *bugaku* courtly dance music are still performed before the emperor and at Buddhist temples and Shintō shrines. Buddhism had introduced the rhythmic chanting that accompanies *shigin* performance poetry and that linked with folk forms to create such new vocal expressions as that found in the classical Noh musical drama performed since the fourteenth century.[21] Many of these traditions continue to inspire thousands of contemporary composers and performers. Folk, Buddhist and Shintō influences converge not only in Noh but also in kabuki and *bunraku* dramatic performances. Western music was popularized as of the Meiji period, and following the Second World War – with the American occupation – all forms of Western popular music were imitated and came to dominate the market, but with Japanese lyrics. Classical Western symphonic music also resurged and Japanese orchestras and choral ensembles now count among the finest in the world. Today, all forms of popular music thrive in Japan, especially among the young. A musical phenomenon – karaoke, created in Kobe in 1971 – soon became an international fad and now figures as a recognized genre of performance art.

THE PACIFIC ISLANDS

Art everywhere in the Pacific islands expressed the indigenous belief system, immediately supporting, legitimizing and maintaining those in authority.[22] Artistic creation often focused on religious ritual and social ceremony. It was invariably anonymous, for all

Oceanic art was the creation of the community, not of the individual. On the 30,000-odd islands of Oceania artistic expression varied widely according to region and culture. However, certain constants are clear: thematically, in the stress on both fertility – human, animal and terrene – and the supernatural; and substantially, in the all but ubiquitous tattooing, rock art, woodcarving, stone carving, and textile fabrication and decoration.

Melanesian art emphasized ritual.[23] Decoration both beautified and dignified cult houses. Spirit paintings that depicted deities of the Abelam people of the Sepik region of Papua New Guinea, for example, covered elevated facades of structures connected with the *tambaran* cult. Colourful headdresses of bright feathers and elaborate body paintings and ornamentation as well as vivid costumes empowered all Melanesian ceremonial meetings and exchanges, even warfare. Ritual canoes were brightly painted and decorated. Carved slit-gong drums, brilliantly painted wooden masks and costumes highlighted song and dance festivals, some of these items to be purposefully destroyed at the festival's conclusion, their ephemerality an integral part of the artistic purpose – they would then be recreated for the next festival. Melanesia still enjoys hundreds of regional art styles, many characterized by their use of indigenous materials: feathers, wood, barkcloth, plaited rattan and other specialities.

In contrast, Micronesian art has always seemed sober utilitarianism, born of an attitude reflecting the sparse resources of this island world.[24] None of Melanesian art's flamboyant colours, headdresses and body paintings, this; none of Polynesia's complex carvings in stone and wood. Bodily ornamentation – necklaces, bracelets, gorgets, belts – often consisted of simple shells, sharks' teeth, flowers, coconut leaves and other perishables. Yet Micronesian basket and mat weavers are still celebrated for their intricate geometric designs, achieving a felicitous marriage of controlled uniformity and resourceful creativity.

All Polynesian art was likewise an impersonal expression upholding the sacredness of the ruling authority. In this, it was 'political art'. No names attached to Polynesian productions, as the individual was insignificant: art was not the expression of one person but of an entire community. Free creativity was discouraged, rigid conformity demanded. Even the accidental slip of an obsidian cutter or stone adze could result in an artist's severe punishment.

Religion, art, politics – all occupied the same space in the prehistoric Polynesian psyche, which was yet spared the West's compartmentalization and personalization.

Here artwork often involved carving images of ancestors or deities in wood or, less frequently, stone. These were erected as highly stylized torsos or squat phallus-bearing likenesses on a ceremonial platform or along its wings. An internationally recognized icon of ancient Polynesia is the Rapanui (Easter Island) *moai* or ancestral figure of volcanic tuff which evolved from the same tradition. Similar statuary adorned the *marae* of the Society and Austral Islands, the *tohua* of the Marquesas, and the *heiau* of Hawai'i. Wood and stone carving features prominently in all Polynesian art, particularly in eastern Polynesia. Such carvings can even relate clan history, as the Māori 'read' in the intricate architectural carvings of the *whare runanga* or public meeting houses of New Zealand.

Samoans were expert mat weavers. Hawaiians excelled in fashioning cloaks of thousands of red and yellow feathers worn by high chiefs. Rarotongans carved intricate genealogical staffs, similar to the abstract, phallus-like genealogical *ti'i* (tiki 'figurine') of Rurutu in the Austral Islands. The South Island greenstone or nephrite jade of New Zealand was fashioned into powerful symbols of authority (Māori chiefs' ceremonial adzes and clubs) as well as elaborate personal ornaments like small *hei tiki* figures, *hei matau* hooks, *pekapeka* ornaments and other things. Possession of such portables increased one's *mana* in ancient Polynesian societies. In time certain objects came to be identified as necessary paraphernalia of rank, such as the Māori chiefs' *mere pounamu* club or the Rapanui orators' *'ua* staff. Such pieces now grace the world's museums, acknowledged to rank among the finest indigenous artwork on Earth.

A special domain of Oceanic art is the *tatau* or tattoo.[25] Islanders have forever practised the *tatau*, that wonderfully versatile bodily decoration encompassing a portable art that can be 'pinched but not stolen'. (This fact held great significance in small island societies where communal possession was the rule and personal possession had few safeguards.) It is assumed that the Lapita people were already wearing *tatau* over 3,500 years ago, who then carried the practice with them wherever they settled in Oceania. Melanesian tattooing was known from Papua New Guinea to Fiji. Micronesia's Caroline and Marshall islanders tattooed themselves. Pacific islands' most elaborate *tatau*, however, occurred in Polynesia, where over time each island developed characteristic designs. A *tatau* in itself never signalled rank, but brought great status to those who bore especially elaborate, high-quality designs covering much of their body. Men's tattoos covered more bodily area than women's, which sometimes were traditionally located on one spot only – such as Māori women's *moko* on the chin and lips. Marquesan women, in contrast, were tattooed on the arms, hands, stomach and lower back; Marquesan men often had full-body tattoos, including the face. Indeed, Marquesan women thought it shameful to have sex with a man who was 'naked' – that is, without a tattoo. Rapanui experts of Easter Island's *rongorongo* writing in the first half of the 1800s sometimes had chest and both cheeks tattooed with inscriptions in Oceania's only indigenous script.

The West's incursion into Pacific islands changed everything: old practices were abandoned or forbidden, old values discarded, foreign imports imitated and adapted. Notable landscape artists from Europe recorded what they saw in the exotic isles: London-born painters William Hodges (1744–1797), who accompanied Cook's second voyage; John Webber (1751–1793), who was on Cook's third voyage; and Augustus Earle (1793–1838), who travelled widely and best captured the early New Zealand landscape. Some European artists came and stayed, 'discovering themselves' in the Pacific. Among these, Paris-born Paul Gauguin (1848–1903) must figure as the most illustrious, who developed a 'Tahitian style' that was utterly French Post-Impressionist and had little to do with the Pacific islands but much to do with vibrant colour, flowing nature and lithe Polynesian beauty; his island themes inspired hundreds of painters to South Sea emulation. Tyneside-born lawyer William Fox (1812–1893) emigrated to New Zealand in 1842 where he became not only a prolific artist but also the country's premier. Pilsen-born and Viennese-trained Gottfried Lindauer (1839–1926) emigrated to New Zealand in 1874 where he won everlasting fame for his Māori portraits. French painter and illustrator Jean Charlot (1898–1979) discovered his art in Mexico which he subsequently fleshed out in Hawai'i, where he finally settled and evolved a unique voice among avant-garde island painters and woodcarvers. Other Pacific artists abandoned the islands altogether to seek fame and fortune abroad: Dunedin-born Frances Hodgkins (1869–1947), for example, left New Zealand in the early years of the twentieth century for England, where she became one of the leading figures in British Modernism.

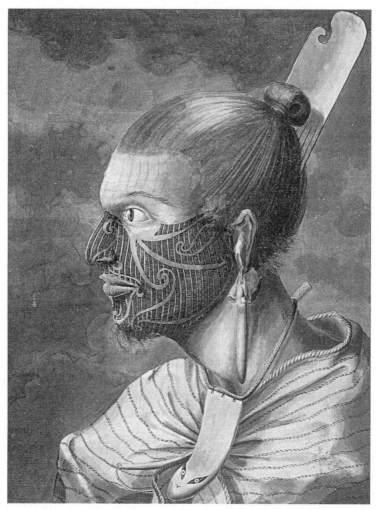

Male facial tattoo of a New Zealand Māori.

Best-loved, of course, are the islanders who remained to celebrate in art their native isles and who, through this, attained to
international recognition. In New Zealand this includes, among
many others, portraitist and landscapist Rita Angus (1908–1970),
abstract artist Gordon Walters (1919–1995), modernist Colin
McCahon (1919–1987) and Māori minimalist Ralph Hotere
(*b.* 1931). Honouring Polynesian themes and motifs, Fatu Feu'u
(*b.* 1946) is an award-winning Samoan painter based in New
Zealand since 1966. Hawaiian-born Joseph Nāwahī (1842–1896)

245

was the first Native Hawaiian to win recognition as a painter – quite apart from his career as newspaper publisher, lawyer and legislator. Hawaiian painter and bestselling author Herb Kawainui Kane (1928–2011), elected a 'Living Treasure of Hawai'i' in 1984, specialized in Hawaiian and other Polynesian historical paintings.

The traditional music of Pacific islands comprised many different types of wooden and earthen drums, nose flutes, small and large flutes (of wood, soapstone or bone), conch shells and a wide array of choral configurations.[26] Other instruments featured as well: availability of resources often dictated what could be produced. Only once the horse was introduced to Easter Island in the late 1800s, for example, could its jaw bone be 'played' as an instrument. Panpipes and 'bamboo bands' were popular in the Solomon Islands. Traditional Pacific song was usually accompanied by dance of some kind, either solo or perambulating, standing or sitting in group formations. Later, Western hymns greatly influenced Pacific music: those striking polyphonic choirs so admired from New Caledonia to the Tuamotus actually trace their roots back to early nineteenth-century Protestant hymns reverberating from Welsh chapels and New England churches. Today, 'traditional' (or semi-traditional/ reinvented) musical performances enliven ethnic centres and tourist hotels, annual insular festivals and the quadrennial Festival of Pacific Arts. Among more familiar styles are Hawai'i's hula, Tahiti's *tāmūrē* and New Zealand's *kapa haka*. Throughout Oceania but for rarely visited isles and for most of New Guinea, nearly everyone's favourite music is adapted American country and western and African American soul sung in the local language(s), as well as rock, hip hop, reggae and many other modern trends.

And what of the artists of Ireland and of the hundreds of Dutch, German, Danish and Swedish isles? What of the contemporary scene on Vancouver, Montreal, Paris's Île de la Cité? Art, its studios, its galleries and exhibition centres seem to gravitate to islands: where the traditional has all but yielded to the modern hybrid – painters and potters, weavers and jewellers who are working their magic from upmarket Bainbridge in Washington State to teeming Rhodes in the Ægean, from the aristocratic Isle of Wight to humble Waiheke Island. Like bees to honey, curious visitors are drawn to islands and invest there in creations that allow local artists to remain islanders. Installations, festivals and similar events attract

even greater numbers: Easter Island's annual Tāpati Festival, for
example, is a joyous self-celebration that lures thousands from
abroad, with local Rapanui artists competing in stone and wood-
carving, tattooing, weaving, song and dance. A salute to island life
and a much-needed injection of foreign cash, such a festival can
now be enjoyed on isles throughout the world. Waiheke's 'Art on
the Gulf', for one, every other year inspires tens of thousands to
stroll our island's sea cliffs and admire a parade of temporary
installations, some of which go on to grace museums, parks and
private estates. Here, the island herself *becomes* art.

Which brings us to Christo and Jeanne-Claude. Born on the
same day – 13 June 1935 – Bulgarian artist Christo Javacheff and
his Casablanca-born French wife Jeanne-Claude Denat de Guille-
bon (*d.* 2009) targeted the immediate impact of huge outdoor
installations, launching new and unique artificial landscapes. Like
the art of Melanesia, that of Christo and Jeanne-Claude has
exploited the magic of ephemerality, 'wrapping time' in the
moment, constructing to deconstruct. And this includes islands. For
over a fortnight in 1983, after three years of preparation, they and
hundreds of assistants surrounded eleven uninhabited islets in
Miami's Biscayne Bay with more than half a million square metres
of luminous pink polypropylene fabric. Titled *Surrounded Islands*,
the 11.3-km contour-shaped wrapping could be viewed by the
public from shore, causeway and water- and airborne traffic. (The
display was monitored day and night by 120 guards in inflatables.)
Never before had islands experienced the like, or been experienced
this way: exposed, accentuated, elevated beyond mere topography
to 'live' as art themselves – exactly the effect that Christo and
Jeanne-Claude sought.[27]

Hollywood's earliest films were also offering a unique take on
islands, unfortunately one hardly an islander could recognize.
Though delivering some quite credible re-enactments of pre-mis-
sionary island society, before national censorship descended directors favoured bare-breasted maidens in sundry pseudo-Polynesian
(mis)adventures. By the mid-1930s, however, with breasts now
hidden behind flowing tresses or Mother Hubbards, films based on
the adventure novels of Nordhoff and Hall – such as *Mutiny on the
Bounty* and *The Hurricane* – were rewarded with remarkably
robust ticket sales; the film of *The Hurricane* (1937) paired Hall's
nephew Jon Hall with Dorothy Lamour. By 1939 it seems that

islands were solidly stereotyped and clichéd in the public cine-imagination and, ever since then, every possible island scenario has featured on film, some admirable, most incredible. Among the more memorable experiences: *Jurassic Park*, the *Pirates of the Caribbean* franchise, *The Truman Show*, *Zorba the Greek*, *Stromboli*, *Balibo*, *King Kong*, *Castaway*, *Jaws*, *Lord of the Flies*, *Treasure Island*, *Swiss Family Robinson*, *Shutter Island*, *From Here to Eternity* and many many more. Television series (*Gilligan's Island*, *Fantasy Island*) reinforced the conceit of palmed isolation. Islands appear to encourage such extravagances. Indeed, the motion picture camera itself was co-developed on an island: it was in 1889 that Bristol-born William Friese-Greene (1855–1921) was awarded a patent for his 'chronophotographic' camera that could take up to ten photographs per second.

Yet as we prize islands of palettes and pipes, of song and silver screen, so do we value just such islands of the mind, too.

eight

. . . *of the Mind*

What would become Earth's most isolated inhabited archipelago was sighted for the first time in 1509 by Portuguese navigator Tristão da Cunha, whose name eventually graced the lead island of this South Atlantic group. Three centuries of neglect followed. Then in 1816 Britain established a small garrison on Tristan da Cunha – still like occupying the far side of the Moon – to safeguard St Helena where Napoleon was exiled under British guard. One year later the garrison was recalled, but three Britons chose to remain. Over subsequent years various whalers, sealers and castaways, some bringing women from St Helena, managed to establish a lasting community, constructing British-style cottages of stone and thatch, growing vegetables, raising livestock and fishing. Trade comprised bartering meat, vegetables and fresh water with the occasional passing ship for manufactured goods and such luxury items as soap, flour, sugar and tobacco.

However, when the whaling days ended and shipping routes changed – whale oil surrendered to petroleum, sail to steam, and the Suez Canal beckoned in 1869 – vessels called only rarely. Tristanians were now fleeing on these and by 1892 only 50 were left. Those who refused to quit the island experienced three generations of the same bitter isolation and hard subsistence known to Easter Islanders in the Pacific. In 1942 the United Kingdom established a naval base there that encouraged radio communication and more frequent callings. In 1950 a cannery opened, processing a commercial crayfishing catch. By 1961 the population was back up to 264 and growing, but then a volcanic eruption near the single settlement of Edinburgh threatened and the islanders were evacuated to Britain where they became depressed and ill, unable to cope with exile. An advance party made the return voyage to Tristan in September 1962 and nearly all the other exiles followed in November 1963 after over two years' absence. Immediately their health improved.

Since then, the British government has provided funds for the construction of a new harbour, financed modern homes, built administrative facilities, modernized local farming techniques, erected a school and hospital, installed water and sewerage systems and electrical generation, and provided a new source of income in philately. Today's population – 80 families descended from fifteen original settlers – matches in size that of 50 years ago and each Tristanian, though a British citizen, is first an islander and proud of it.

These were the lucky ones, it seems. Clinical depression – what used to be called 'nostalgia' – was the inevitable affliction that resulted from the removal of Caribs and Lucayans to Hispaniola (1500s); Pitcairn Islanders to Norfolk (1856); Easter Islanders to Peru (1862–3), Mangareva and Tahiti (1871); Makateans to Tahiti (as of 1908); Banabans to Rabi Island, Fiji (as of 1945); Bikinians to Rongerik Atoll (1946); Enewetakans to Ujelang Atoll (1947); and Chagossians of Diego Garcia to the Seychelles and Mauritius (1966–71). Some returned. But most died in exile, their hearts broken.

What creates smitten islanders? What cerebral miracle converts a mainland genus into insular species whose ultimate welfare depends on occupying a specific pimple of land surrounded by sea? Mainlanders seek out islands for a purpose (holiday, refuge, exploitation), linger a while, then leave again; for them, island is locus. Islanders, on the other hand, are home; island is focus. For them there's no other place on Earth that can satisfy certain innate needs. If forced to live on a mainland, islanders become disconnected: life's essence is sapped. Hence 'nostalgia'. It's something only too familiar to Tahitians in Paris, Greenlanders in Copenhagen, Kiwis in London.

An insular fancy forever fascinates the British public, too, where schoolchildren learn that they dwell on a 'fortress built by nature' – no recent conceit, this, but gifted the folk by Shakespeare in *Richard II* only seven years after her insularity saved Britain from Spain's Armada: 'This royal throne of kings, this sceptered isle, / This earth of majesty, this seat of Mars . . .' (ii, i). Alfred, Lord Tennyson could confidently remind co-islanders in his 'Ode on the Death of the Duke of Wellington' (1852): 'Not once or twice in our rough island-story, / The path of duty was the way to glory'. In addressing the

House of Commons on 4 June 1940, Sir Winston Churchill pledged
'We shall defend our island, whatever the cost may be . . .'. And
Prime Minister Edward Heath (1916–2005) declared in 1970: 'We
may be a small island, but we are not a small people.'[1] It was a bind-
ing bromide that survived even the Channel Tunnel.

Each of us cherishes an island 'image' and each image differs.
With some, New Zealand, for example, might evoke the vision of
fern forests and performing Māoris; Cuba, cigars; Iceland, steaming geysers; Ibiza, browning bodies. And who counts as an 'islander'
is subject to size and location, both then super-subject to attitude:
a resident of minute Manhattan might challenge being called an
'islander', yet a native of gargantuan Greenland wouldn't think of
denying it.

> There's an island deep down in my sleep
> A lost land I long to find
> But I wake 'ere I reach the island
> So it must only live in my mind.[2]

Continentals and 'Big Islanders' (Australians, Britons, Japanese, Sri Lankans and so on) commonly hold an island to be only a
small speck of land and remain blind to the sea that defines it. But
a natural islander understands sea as part and parcel of island
existence; sea is forever the fund of resources, treasure-house of
ancestral myth. That is, sea is 'island territory', too. It is not to be
wondered that several Western-trained island scholars are now rein-
terpreting the cultural mapping of Oceania, for one, redefining in
the process what 'island' truly means to island peoples themselves.[3]

Non-islanders – and even islanders from Britain and Japan –
find magic in the island world mostly because they believe it to be
missing at home. What other reason could have compelled
Lawrence Durrell to laud his beloved Greek isles so:

> Never will you go to sleep so soundly as you will in Mykonos – and
> it is the deep sleep of early infancy. In the morning, when you push
> back your shutters, the whiteness comes up to meet you again like
> the caress of wet eyelashes.[4]

'Centers of isolation invariably used in descriptions of the first
human discovery and colonization of the islands', eminent Pacific

A medieval Fool weighed down by islands of the mind.

historian Kerry Howe (*b*. 1947) tells us, 'are . . . culturally loaded: isolated from what? The distance is invariably measured from continental centers of assumed "civilization".'[5] It's time we see islands for what they really are to our species: cultural artefacts. Islands of the mind.

And it is here that we meet perhaps the greatest constant in this general nesology, at least in cultural terms: islands are attitude. It is in this fashion that the disconnected and remote – the very 'insular' – become the connected and close, where 'every man is an island'. Hence, a petite holm called Manhattan can metamorphose into New York, a civilization. With these islands of the mind it's really not about pimples of land at all – but mountains of meaning . . .

Subjectification, Objectification, Identification, Mediation and *Idealization*.

'WOULDN'T IT BE WONDERFUL IF . . .'

It is subjectification – the assessment of external stimuli based on individual criteria – that allows most of us, on hearing the word 'island', at once to call to mind an image. The simple noun bears a heavy semantic load, whether *île, Insel, isla, isola, ynys, eyja, ostrov, jima, motu* and so many more, each evoking something dependent on our personal relationship to the generic. Most often this something is analogous to ancient Arcadia, that domain of Pan piping any one of his modern melodies – Treasure Island, Fantasy Island, Majorca or Hawai'i. It may well be a realm we should wish to visit but never could reach, as we know it's something too different, too far. We appreciate that Latin *insula* also engendered the cognates 'insular' and 'isolated', evoking this remote realm of the recluse:

I am a rock, I am an island . . .

Essential apartness has ever been the mainlander's prime perception of island existence, a confusion immortalized in John Donne's 'No man is an island'. In Europe, Southern Asia and the Far East it was the hermit above all who sought out an isle to purge himself in solitude and dearth, to perform penance. It was the isle as ablution, chastening, even self-realization. To most non-islanders, 'island' was synonymous with 'cell', its perceived reality a dangerous and ill-stocked incarceration.

Until the eighteenth century no one wanted to touch an island. Then a major perception shift occurred. Mostly as a result of the great voyages of Roggeveen, Wallis, Bougainville, Cook, La Pérouse and Vancouver, islands became subjectified into personal exploitables: they were not merely for escape, it was widely realized, not just for the profit of King and country, for the promotion of Christianity or Islam; they could also be for personal advancement, adventure, fun. That is, the island became a *psychological space*. The subjectification persists. Islands still offer an immediately measurable difference to non-islanders: sun, sand, lagoon, indolence, non-responsibility, no survival or career pressures (if but for a few days). An island? It's warmth bathed in surfeit and wrapped in security. No matter that this only exists in the mind: the tourist who imports these notions invariably 'discovers' them.

Just like the 'Desert Island Syndrome'. This is also subjectification. The vision of an uninhabited tropical isle appeals to most, being again often equated with Arcadia or an 'earthly paradise'. The reality of the castaway is, of course, anything but paradisiacal. One need only read the genuine Robinson Crusoe story – that of Alexander Selkirk who survived from 1704 to 1709 on an uninhabited island in the Juan Fernández archipelago west of Chile – in order to appreciate the mindnumbing monotony and desperate battle such a purgatory entails, where only ingenious resourcefulness and remarkable mental vigour ensure personal survival.[6] Yet many still seek out 'desert islands' in order to fulfil some internal screenplay only they can see and understand.

Norwegian explorer Thor Heyerdahl (1914–2002) and his bride Liv ran off to the South Seas in 1937 with no intention of returning to Europe, seeking Rousseau's 'return to nature'. Eventually landing at the sparsely inhabited Ui'a valley of eastern Fatu Iva in the Marquesas, they built a thatched hut on stilts then nearly expired from the incessant rain, disease-bearing mosquitoes, inundating mud and poor relations with the locals. In the end Thor and Liv were discovered hunkering in a cave waiting only to be rescued, then hied back to Norway cured forever of their desert island dream.[7]

Very soon afterwards, in 1939, a certain wealthy American sought a sanctuary for himself and his family because he feared America's probable involvement in a second world war. Soon he found a peaceful island as far from America and Europe as possible in order to live out his Robinsonesque dream. The island lay in the western Pacific, in the Solomon Islands. Its name? – Guadalcanal.[8]

Sometimes the dream is so near. From 1930 to 1942, newlyweds Herbert and Elizabeth Sherman (she a New York librarian) moved to California's San Miguel Island seeking an alternative lifestyle in seclusion, and lived there with their subsequent children in a house they built from shore debris. They fished and farmed for their food, erected a schoolhouse for their children, and had a Model T Ford shipped over to tour the farm in. Herbert became ill, then disabled. One day he asked Elizabeth for some paper, then disappeared. It was for his suicide note. Herbert lies buried in a homemade coffin at San Miguel's Harris Point.

And then there was New Zealander Tom Neale (1902–1977) who, after 30 years roaming the Pacific, at age 50 went to live alone on Suwarrow in the Cook Islands. Not even 1 km long and only 100 m wide, Suwarrow lies some 300 km from the nearest inhabited island.

> I chose to live in the Pacific islands because life there moves at the sort of pace which you feel God must have had in mind originally when He made the sun to keep us warm and provided the fruits of the earth for the taking.[9]

One day, while working alone on Mo'orea 17 km from Tahiti, Tom had told himself: "'Neale," (I always call myself Neale when I talk to myself), "this is the nearest thing on earth to paradise".'[10] It had been American author and Pacific expert Robert Dean Frisbie (1896–1948) who had put Tom on to Suwarrow and, while store-keeping on Pukapuka, Tom found he always had at the back of his mind: "'What a bore life is! Wouldn't it be wonderful if for once I could see what life is like on an uninhabited island".'[11]

He finally made it to Suwarrow in 1952 – where he survived alone until 1954 – and then again from 1960 to 1963. Tom's hardships there were hardly to be borne: not only did he suffer hard labour from dawn to dusk, but pests, violent storms and arthritis also took their bitter toll. He mastered these courageously, but nearly died several times. It was the periodic presence of pearl divers that finally drove him off the island. The success of his autobiography *An Island to Oneself* (1966) gave Tom the funds for even a third sojourn on Suwarrow, where he lived alone from 1967 to 1977 when a visiting yacht found the solitary 75-year-old ill with stomach cancer.

Rushed to Rarotonga, Tom died there eight months later. Had it all been worth it? It is more than difficult to glean personal introspection from the New Zealander's gruff prose. All the same, once, after an old friend had called on his island, Tom had solilo-quized he wouldn't mind returning to cosmopolitan Rarotonga for a fortnight's holiday at least: '"Don't be a sentimental old fool, Neale," I said severely. "You know damned well you'd hate it after a week".'[12]

With many the *idea* of a beautiful island had become a cultural commodity, reconstituted over centuries to reflect Western expectations. Age-old Indo-European and Arabic themes of 'paradise' had metamorphosed into exploitable plunder under Portuguese and Spanish tutelage, only to be replaced by British and French notions of tropical wonderlands sprinkled with warm gardens and heavy with easy sex – the antithesis to Europe's cold, squalor, misery and prudery. Soon, with more Europeans arriving in Pacific waters in particular, obvious dangers (both natural and human) were encountered and islands came to signify savagery and brutality again, as in the Middle Ages – something to be avoided. Colonists now thought twice before entrusting families' welfare to New Zealand farms or New Caledonian plantations. With the twentieth century, paradise intruded yet again once calloused colonies had softened into successful nations, whereupon capitalistic tourism rebranded islands as profitable merchandise. A novel international mobility through improved technology enthusiastically embraced islands' most recent incarnation.

The greater process cuts much deeper than the private subjectification. For well over the past 200 years now islands have comprised an 'ideological testing ground' for Western nations:

> Ideas and questions about human 'civilization', the relationships between nature and culture, racial classification and culture contact, cultural and biological survival and destiny have all been extensively tested and examined using Pacific case studies. Thus the islands of the Pacific Ocean have not only been economically and politically colonized by the West, but, perhaps more profoundly, they have been intellectually occupied and conceptually shaped by the West. And, in turn, experiences in and observations of the Pacific have sometimes influenced Western understandings of itself.[13]

A major psychological focus has been sex. Ever since Cook's three voyages insular sex has fascinated European readers, and this well into the 1960s when general liberalization finally rendered the theme all but irrelevant. It was not the Polynesians' 'free raw sex' as such that mattered – since strumpets could be found on every London corner for a shilling – but the open, profligate, ritually vindicated sex that was not only condoned but actually encouraged by island society at large. Cook himself had been rather shocked by it all:

> There is a scale in dissolute sensuality, which these people have ascended, wholly unknown to every other nation whose manners have been recorded from the beginning of the world to the present hour, and which no imagination could possibly conceive.[14]

Indeed, all of Europe and America was shocked . . . and fascinated. Soon the Pacific lured Europeans and Americans of all stations, as the subjectification of islands included their transformation into biding bordellos. Here, insular sexuality became a Western male construct.

And women's islands, one might well enquire? Missionary demotion of women's central role in Pacific societies and the conversion of every exploitable female into the chastened, submissive, wedded wife saw the creation of the new Western woman of the Pacific, a central theme in Pacific women's studies since the 1970s.[15] 'Male colonialism' is today often touted as a cause of the now unacceptable sexism and domestic oppression that one finds in many Pacific societies.[16]

Subjectification of islands involves children, too. Children are attracted to society's packaging of islands, perhaps because they recognize here the adventure and protection of the tree hut or hideaway. German philosopher Ernst Bloch (1885–1977) held that the child's 'wishful land is an island'.[17] Again it's all in the mind: for children don't comprehend the concrete speciality of an island. What they understand is the adult garment which they then don on their own terms, attracted foremost by the travel and adventure, not by any island reality. In fact, most small children in Britain, Japan, New Zealand, Sri Lanka or Madagascar don't even realize they are already islanders.

At their deepest level of understanding islands offer all non-islanders a 'psychological no-man's land'. The very idea of being abandoned on a desert island – so universally imagined yet so rarely experienced – poses that most fundamental of challenges: 'Why am I in the world and what am I here for?' Yet it is the shallow daydream, not the deep introspection, that wins in the end, subjectifying the fantasy with mindless extravagance. Hawai'i profits enormously from just this: the 'Polynesian Disneyland' of Brigham Young University's

Polynesian Cultural Center, featuring a grinning cast of colourfully garbed and gracefully hulaing islander students from throughout the Pacific; the Kodak Hula Show; tourist hotel pageants; seasonal festivals – a pre-packaged *luau*-bord as fertile as plastic bananas and as hollow as coconut breasts.[18] Many regard this capitalistic side of island subjectification as the prostitution of island peoples.

Yet islanders subjectify, too, especially those confined to smaller and/or politico-economically subordinate isles. In this inverse situation islanders compare their fate with that of wealthy visitors and invariably discover a distinct disadvantage, indeed a 'racial' subordination whose almost universal consequence is a feeling of inferiority. Their island thus becomes something intrinsically negative: a place where one fails; fails to achieve recognition, wealth and status; fails to find personal happiness. Especially since the importation of Western materialism to the world's islands, this fundamentally false perception of inferiority has prompted entire generations of young island wage earners to migrate to neighbouring metropolises. And the psychological upshot of the exodus? – island societies now betray a hitherto unwonted polarization: those who passionately cling to and those who dismissively deny their island home. Here, subjectification has led to re-identification, obliging a false need to invent the self.

'IN THE DEEP WIDE SEA OF MISERY'

It is objectification – reducing something to a concrete reality – that allows many people to encounter islands as microcosms of the perceived 'larger battle of life'. We've seen that islands have enormous appeal to people who don't live on one. Yet the daily reality of island life is something altogether different from the mainlanders' subjectification. One need not go so far as Shelley (1792–1822) who lamented in 'Lines Written Among the Euganean Hills':

> Many a green isle must be
> In the deep wide sea of Misery.

But an 'island reality' does exist, all the same, and it can be as hard, brutal and unforgiving as any mainland life – even more so in view of geological vulnerabilities and biological constraints. Yet the *'interpretation* of "reality" is likely to be a product of the observer's cultural positioning, whose depiction of it will be in culturally specific language. There is no neutral or value-free observation post.'[19] What we appreciate as 'knowledge' is merely a creation – by diverse cultures and for diverse ends. In this sense, then, the objectification of islands cannot really be something to be empirically determined, 'fixed and true for all times and all observers'.[20] Even the 'concrete reality' of objectification, in other words, is really a form of subjectification in the end. It is Marcus Aurelius's 'The universe is mutation, life is opinion'; it is Shakespeare's 'There is nothing either good or bad but thinking makes it so'; it is Tennyson's 'All things are as they seem to all'.[21] In the view of modern quantum physics, one could well add, we should question whether matter possesses an objective existence at all.

Sometimes the objectification is itself a chimera, or simple fear. The Flannan Isles, 30 km west of the Isle of Lewis in the Hebrides, had always been feared by Scots fisherfolk. On coming ashore they always observed many ancient rituals and carefully avoided the usual names of things and places, practising 'sea taboo' or name substitution to ward off evil. Only one habitation marked the Flannans: the lighthouse. Overseeing it at the end of the nineteenth century were three full-time keepers. One night in December 1900, the light failed. A mainland party was sent over to investigate and they discovered to their horror that no trace of the three keepers could be found. Ever since then, no one has been able to explain their disappearance and the island mystery has been a cornucopia of speculation. The Flannans were objectified to 'isles of death'; others were convinced they were the 'isles of alien abduction'.

As earlier remarked, Thor Heyerdahl and his bride Liv, fleeing civilization for Fatu Iva in the Marquesas in their subjectification of the island dream, experienced only a nightmare reality instead: insects tormented them, locals irritated them, their food ran low, it never stopped raining, and everything moulded or rotted away. Heyerdahl's verdict: 'There is nothing for modern man to return to; one can't buy a ticket to Paradise.'[22] Yet it is symptomatic that, all the same, the objectification continues to lose out everywhere to the subjectification. That is, most continue to seek the 'island paradise'. This must surely signal society's continued failure to satisfy some basic psychological need.

The eighteenth-century Pacific island dream was certainly shattered soon enough: Cook murdered in Hawai'i; Marion du Fresne

(1724–1772) and 26 of his crew butchered and eaten in New Zealand; the Comte de Lapérouse (1741–c. 1788) and his two crews vanished in Melanesia. Subsequent sealers, missionaries, traders, colonists and whalers found in the Pacific – the new measure of island life – no paradise but to a man the daily reality of brutal existence. What violence that took place there was then exaggerated in European and American print media; the metaphor of the 'savage island' was born, itself having as little to do with reality as the metaphor of the island paradise. 'By the end of the eighteenth century and right through the nineteenth century, Westerners commonly regarded the Pacific with fear and loathing; it was a place of both cultural and natural dangers.'[23] Usually shipboard deserters or escaped convicts from New South Wales, so-called beachcombers came to know islander reality by 'crossing the beach'. Their experiences were generally brutal and often downright harrowing – one need only recall sailor Toby's four months with Marquesans in Melville's *Typee* – and almost all fled within one year.[24]

Polish anthropologist Bronisław Malinowski (1884–1942) met in Melanesia a similar disillusionment. He noted in his diary

> the picturesque landscape, the poetic quality of the island set on the ocean, and the wretchedness of life here . . . I would imagine life amid palm groves as a perpetual holiday. That was how it struck me looking from the ship. I had a feeling of joy, freedom, happiness. Yet only a few days of it and I was escaping from it to the company of Thackeray's London snobs.[25]

An island objectification informing world opinion between 1820 and 1920 held that these palmed places were quite horrid sites denoting danger, disease, degeneration and white men's demise. And the myth continued long after. The author remembers well how in 1956, when his parents told neighbours the family was moving to Okinawa, everyone was shocked we should dare to venture to a 'God-forsaken island'.

Once the early-twentieth-century nature movement took hold in Europe and North America, however, a new island image competed for mainlanders' indulgence. Nature was not intrinsically brutal or dangerous after all, said the fresh creed, but a neutral territory easily tamed by technology; nature could also be most therapeutic. For the first time the middle classes pursued all sorts of outdoor pleasures away from cities: youth and nature clubs, mixed bathing, naturist colonies. The less endowed enjoyed not only fishing and hunting, too, but family tramping and camping – something hitherto unimaginable. No longer Satan, but God himself was found in nature. And since islands were natural places, so God had to be in island life, too. The Union Steam Ship Company of New Zealand was extolling Hawai'i as early as 1912:

> Here perpetual summer reigns, and the fragrance of flowers unceasingly fills the air. The wealth of tropical vegetation, the abundance of fruit, the waving palms, the wide acres of sugar cane, the happy natives, and the sea breaking in long rolling waves over the coral reefs . . . all these make up a picture that combine to emphasize the novelty and augment the charms of this Paradise of the Pacific.[26]

No mention of Honolulu's open sewerage, of course. Not a word about her squalid housing, daily knifings, sweatshops, opium dens, rampant child prostitution or violent racism. The objectification had come full circle: Western 'civilization' itself had tamed the savage islands.

Perhaps even more potent than islands' advertised therapeutics was their perceived power of 'salvation'. So many shattered victims of First World War trenches ended up in the quayside bars of Key West, Florida, or Pape'ete, Tahiti. English veteran officer, poet and novelist Robert Graves (1895–1985) finally found nearly 40 years' solace on Majorca. Even the great Pacific itself was so 'tamed'.

> By the mid-twentieth century, the Pacific islands had certainly become a major playground for the recreational sailor, traveler, and tourist, most of whom cavorted in sea and sand and wrote books around the theme of adventures in paradise.[27]

Culture was no longer subservient to nature, in other words, but nature herself became the product of a predominately Western, homogeneous, capitalist culture. The islands of the Pacific, Mediterranean and Caribbean, the Seychelles, Maldives and Canaries became the new playgrounds for the wealthy, free and abysmally bored.

And so the objectification – now the imagined fancy of an island 'reality' – continues in this no less blinkered twenty-first century. According to a survey by US bi-monthly *Psychology Today* the ideal 'dream holiday' for the heterosexual male involves being 'marooned on a tropical island with several members of the opposite sex'.[28] Otherwise intelligent, educated writers still succumb, too, to the fantasy, seeking and indeed finding a 'reality' that they themselves have simply imported. More recently it was American travel writer and novelist Paul Theroux (*b.* 1941) who complained:

> My soul hurt, my heart was damaged, I was lonely. I did not want to see another big city . . . I wanted to be purified by water and wilderness . . . The image came to me again, of the Pacific as a universe, and the islands like stars in all that space.[29]

'Pacific tourism', asserts Kerry Howe, 'is not about discovery, it is about confirmation of what we expect to find.'[30] One might say the same about all island dreams.

For it is the creation of a landscape, it's the objectification of one's inner desires. In just this way the small, uninhabited island in New York Harbor – first, part of the three Dutch Oyster Islands; later, Bedloe's Island of the English; later still, Fort Wood – became as of 1885 the site of France's gift to the US to mark the country's centennial: the Statue of Liberty. Called Liberty Island as of the turn of the twentieth century, she stands for the island as symbol of freedom, as innate potential, as boundless possibility to those shipboard immigrants straining the rails at their first glimpse of the New Land. Liberty Island's towering statue is also one of history's great icons of political propaganda, evoking the Colossus of Rhodes and Pharos of Alexandria.

We all objectify our islands, even those of us who live on one. Writing on behalf of the Greek isles Lawrence Durrell, for one, had to query:

> To what point are we the dupes of history and of fashion? After all, there are islands every bit as beautiful as Greek islands off the coast of Yugoslavia, off Scotland, in the Caribbean. Is one just a prey to a facile, poetic self-indulgence? The question will not hang in the air for long, and the answer will be an almost certain 'No'. There is a special kind of presence here in this land, in this light; it

is not uncommon for visitors of sensibility to have the almost uncomfortable feeling that the ancient world is still there, at their elbows, just out of sight.[31]

The objectification can smart. We accept that islands are not in general the peaceful, docile, romantic places touted by the tourist trade. Fiji's coups of 1987, 2000 and 2006 were a slap in the face for all of the world's islanders, for example, highlighting as they did the extremes of those artificial constructs of 'indigenous tradition' and 'Western democracy'. This contentious issue of island realities and identities has engendered in the past two decades a robust scholarly discussion – one that still seeks satisfactory, objective answers.[32]

'US VERSUS THEM'

Shifting from major to minor like Addinsell's 'Warsaw Concerto' – yet another island creation – the psychological process of identification can include a transference of self-image to location. Like with subjectification and objectification, this fascinating mind-play, too, dons diverse robes on the islands of the world.

Take exclusivity. Island peoples can identify with site to such a degree that all outsiders meet the fiercest resistance. Many Pacific Islanders, for example, were long inimical towards any callers, resulting in exaggerated tales of missionaries boiling in oversized kettles. For several centuries the Japanese closed their islands to all foreigners; even today they often display an amplified exclusivity and resist the creation of a multicultural society. 'Sons of Heaven', Japanese were indoctrinated to consider themselves racially superior to non-Japanese (including Okinawans), which explains their treatment of Allied soldiers during the Second World War – though many Japanese were also ashamed of this insular pride. Historical precedents of similar extremes are legion in the Greek isles, New Guinea, Micronesia and many Polynesian islands.

For an islander, the world is seldom elsewhere. Just like with many religious communities, those of islands often cultivate an 'us versus them' mentality with most long-settled families taking decades to accept outsiders. After seventeen years here on Waiheke, the author appreciates he must wait another thirteen or so to be a 'true Waihekean'. On Nantucket Island, some 50 km south of Cape

Cod, Massachusetts, one can read on the tombstone of a man who had arrived as a small child and died at 91: 'Farewell, Stranger'.[33]

On 10-sq-km Capri, which has ever preserved her village character, atmosphere and loyalty, it is abundantly clear who is 'us' and who is 'them'. For Capri actually has three distinct levels and two towns: the Marina Grande, Capri town and Anacapri. Earlier only a rock ladder – the 'Phoenician Staircase' – connected the three, so communication between the two towns, one above the other, was rather limited: townspeople regarded the other with suspicion and dislike, as if two separate principalities. Finally in 1874 a proper road was built and centuries of enmity vanished overnight. Capri town is the tourist mecca – loud, busy, crowded. Higher up, Anacapri is more sedate, mellower, closer to the Capri that once was, before the circus began. All townspeople are inured to tourists and their foibles; they simply no longer bother – tourists are transient ghosts here – and the Capriots will ever shout, sing, haggle, sip wine and make deliveries and love, for they know this is their island.

Communal solidarity of smaller islands is quite akin to that of ancient tribal society. For this reason holiday-home islanders aren't really 'at home'. Countless mainlanders want to 'rent a cottage on the Isle of Wight if it's not too dear', but these recreational home, flat and condominium owners seldom integrate or make a contribution: like Capri tourists they are only passing spectres. All the same, in today's mobile world such ghosts overwhelm some islands – a situation often resented by those who permanently live there. The latter must witness the homes empty over long months, experience the shops' lost revenue, pay the inflated rates and taxes to maintain the phantoms' imported living standards. Islanders can always identify the mainlanders: they're the ones who don't smile and wish you a good day.

Islanders are invariably partial to other islanders, however. It's apparently genetic magnetism: all home in on other islands as if somehow 'hard-wired' to do this. Islander James Cook was perhaps history's greatest island-finder. Nantucket whalers knew the Pacific like the back of their hand; their most prominent family named Starbuck Island in Kiribati and survive today among the descendants of the *Bounty* mutineers. Irish sought out Iceland; they now flock to Manhattan. Shetlanders first settled Saba in the West Indies. New Zealanders target the Cooks, Fiji, Samoa and Tonga.

Japanese increasingly 'invade' Hawai'i. Britons love the Hebrides, Tenerife and Ibiza. And nearly all Polynesians now want to move to New Zealand, it seems.

Joe Frahm of Great Barrier Island – on the horizon just 40 km north of the author's window – coined the word *insulatilia* to describe just that condition afflicting the island-haunted of the world.[34] Those so stricken also appreciate the deeper value of brief visits to the mainland. As Capri-born writer, historian, engineer and botanist Edwin Cerio (1875–1960) penned so acutely, 'Only by coming back to the island people can understand what rewards life grants to those who stay.'[35]

Self-identification is stronger the smaller the island. The British are 'weak islanders' but this certainly doesn't include the proud residents of Môn (Anglesey), Man, Mull, Wight or Jersey. New Zealanders seem not so insouciant, yet are manifestly surpassed in zeal by those of Waiheke, Great Barrier or Stewart Island. Yet even such larger places as Hawai'i, Crete, Malta, Gotland, Cuba, Okinawa, Guam or Newfoundland engender intense identities that cling and mould, too. All lie within some mental zone one is able to exploit as a mobile extension of self. It's the complex histories and cultures of such islands – with their diverse socio-economic, political and now especially environmental challenges – that oblige locals for survival to acknowledge a shared peril, a protective identity, a common fate. The 'smallest islanders' of all of course know no such qualification as small: for their space always includes the sea.

Does island identity fade when one's 'islandness' disappears with the building of a bridge or causeway? A certain intimacy and perceived isolation was lost in 1826 when one could finally cross from Môn over the Menai Strait to the Welsh mainland on Thomas Telford's (1757–1834) suspension bridge. A Scot walking the new Skye Bridge from Kyleakin to the Kyle of Lochalsh's supermarket on the mainland 3 km away must certainly query whether he's still an 'islander'. Yet in the Outer Hebrides a series of causeways linking islands from Eriskay north all the way to Benneray has failed to efface community spirit. On some isles identification arches higher than any bridge. Accessible from Scotland's west coast since 1792 via lovely stone Clachan Bridge, Seil hosts an inn where island men used to change their kilts for trousers before hazarding a mainland visit.

Mediterranean islanders par excellence, Cretans can turn insular self-identification into a religion. They've experienced it all: the rise and fall of the Minoan Empire, Phoenician pirates, the waxing and waning of Athens and Sparta, Roman legions, Arab marauders, Venetian galleons, Turkish slave bazaars, German parachutists and Californian hippies – nothing has escaped the Cretans' purview. Yet they remained island Cretans throughout. St Paul informed Titus, first Bishop of Crete, that, as Lawrence Durrell relates,

> to quote a poet, the islanders were 'always liars, evil beasts, and slow bellies'. It is clear that he had gone into a bar in Chanea for an *ouzo*, with a mass of contentious epistles under his arm . . . The truth is that the Cretans are the Scots of Greece; they have lived through countless crises to emerge always just as truly themselves – indomitable friends or deadly enemies.[36]

Until relatively recently there were only two permissable topics for Cretan men: guns and boots. As on Sicily, a man was someone who had reached rifle-bearing age. Cretans have belonged to Greece only since 1913. Most still don't really regard themselves as Greeks. About what mainlander could one ever relate:

> During a parachute course in the Middle East, the instructor, jump-training a group of commandos from various islands, saw one of them fumble with his harness and hesitate to advance into the bay [of the aircraft] for the jump. Incautiously, he made a pleasantry – asking if the novice was scared? The response was unexpected. 'Scared?', cried the young man, 'You dare to tell a Cretan that he is scared? I'll show you who is scared.' He unhooked his safety harness altogether and jumped to his certain death.[37]

This story was related to Durrell by a Cretan. Only a Japanese – plunging from a cliff at the order of his shōgun – might have reciprocated.

Such fanatic loyalty is just the stuff of island self-identification. We have heard of those of Tristan da Cunha and Diego Garcia who took ill and even died when wrenched away: the Tristanians at least made it back after two miserable years but the Chagossians were barred a return by the British and still languish in exile. One can imagine that islanders who abandoned the 'Mystery Islands' (see chapter Four) felt the same wrench.

One of the North Frisian Islands, Heligoland – 1.7 sq km situated 46 km off the German coastline and ceded by Britain to Germany in 1890 in exchange for Zanzibar – bred such a fiercely loyal folk. Bombed and mined during the Second World War, the Heiligolanders were finally forced from their island only the day after a particularly savage attack by 969 British aircraft in April 1945. For seven years the uninhabited island became the Royal Air Force's chief target range for ordinances, the site in 1947 of one of history's largest non-nuclear detonations: it even altered the island's shape. Heligolanders were only allowed back to their isle in 1952 when Britain reverted her sovereignty to the new German Federal Republic. Though the island the Heligolanders once knew had been pummelled beyond recognition, they raised a new, picturesque Heligoland from the rubble, today one of Germany's most popular tourist sites. It is now next to impossible to get a Heligolander to leave.

Difficult islands also breed extreme loyalty. The pride and passion of the people of the Outer Hebrides, Orkneys and Shetland – more Norway than Scotland – where the seas are more perilous and the isles more far-flung than near-mainland islands, distinguish special islanders who exult in their difference and inspire their children to emulation. Such are also the approximately 3,100 (est. 2007) Falkland Islanders – also known as 'Kelpers' for the enormous kelp beds surrounding their islands in the South Atlantic – who are descendants of South American gauchos, British colonists, English and American sealers, several European nationals and, more recently, Chileans, Australians, New Zealanders and Saint Helenians. Fiercely loyal first and foremost to their island home – not to any distant capital or flag – they enjoy British citizenship but nevertheless aver that recent moves towards self-determination cannot be halted. They insist on the continued development of a separate Falklands identity while acknowledging their political link to Britain, wishing to foster closer ties with Chile and Uruguay but ardently rejecting Argentina and her sovereignty claims. Falkland Islanders believe they live in their own nation as a separate and unique people.

Of late, the sensitive islander's 'hula-nausea' has been relieved by an ideological tonic that now privileges the indigenous mandate: 'Notions of indigenous culture and custom have been reified.'[38] Though that ludicrous fanatic, the 'noble savage', may still embarrass popular entertainment of the twenty-first century, a much more mature islander poise than that known in the past actually obtains in most places. Identification heralds liberation.

THE 'CRITICAL PERCEPTUAL SHIFT'

Mediation – the fashioning of interventional modes or interceding conceptions – also plays a leading role in the islands of the mind. What psychologists call a 'critical perceptual shift' occurs when conscious mind seeks and finds new strategies for coping with transitional dynamics: moving from mainland to island, island to mainland, island to island.

Quitting the mainland for an island has one adjusting despite oneself. For most this involves stress reduction – from congested to isolated, from hazardous to safe, from noisy to quiet, from challenging to calm. The beehive is exchanged for the nest. Multi-tasking and serial prioritization are at once reduced to focused acquiescence. Of course this depends on circumstance. The holiday visit occasions only superficial mediation, and the daily commute home to the island is simple routine. A mainlander's move to a new island home, however, is a major life commitment, never gone into lightly and engaging a plethora of mediational mechanisms. Everything mainland life demanded is often brought along on the ferry, ship or plane: all must be jettisoned consciously through a succession of mediational confrontations and arbitrations. This often requires painful concessions and sacrifices: unaccustomed isolation, disconnection from social activities, loss of treasured friendships, inaccessibility to habitual amenities and so much more.

The reverse is true for the islander leaving for the mainland, whether for the day or forever. Just as with the mainlander moving to the island, respective motivation usually determines the mediational strategy: the mainlander seeks the peace of escape, the islander the rush of a modern megalopolis, career, money, advancement.

Mediation also takes place in the gradation of insularity: proximity to land, frequency of visit or commute, situation of the islander (is she only visiting her holiday home?), or respective political circumstance (privately owned, autonomous, incorporated with a local council, without a local council?). An intriguing mediation occurs with islanders off islands off islands: the 125 residents of 854-ha Iona, for example, perceive their own 'greater islandness' when contemplating their 2,667 neighbours on 87,535-ha Mull 1.6 km away; whereas those of Mull are confident of their own 'greater islandness' when regarding the Scottish coast – the British mainland, eighth largest island in the world – only 2 km away, with its 60 millions (est. 2009). When the Ionans go to 'the mainland', they mean Mull; when those of Mull go to 'the mainland', they mean Britain. And Britons themselves go to 'the Continent'.

Whether islanders cope well when moving to other islands depends on many things. Big Islanders seem to thrive on all islands. The island-based British Empire never had a problem with island life: her emissaries, merchants, colonists, missionaries and prisoners simply recreated Home abroad and the indigenous islanders there had to assimilate or perish. Aberdeen merchant Thomas Glover (1838–1911) even opened Japan's first coal mines and developed at Nagasaki the nation's first dry dock. Many of these 'new islanders', or their children, thrived on returning Home as well: Ernest Rutherford (1871–1937) became the 'father of nuclear physics' only after quitting the South Island of New Zealand for Britain in 1895, and Katherine Mansfield (1888–1923) achieved literary greatness after leaving Wellington, New Zealand, for the second time for Britain in 1908. Hundreds of thousands of impoverished West Indian islanders found safety, relative affluence and a new home in Britain after the Second World War; among their descendants are some of Britain's most prominent personalities. In almost each case – from the cultured Rutherford to the struggling Jamaican labourer – the mediation process was protracted, difficult, often painful, yet successfully achieved.

Some people regard the most exotic place in Britain to be the Isles of Scilly, an archipelago of five inhabited islands (pop. 2,100 in 2008) and some 140 rocky islets situated 45 km west of Land's End, Cornwall. Even here mediation rules, for the 72 residents of 148-ha St Agnes celebrate that they inhabit Britain's southernmost situation and are therefore the 'true islanders' – as they will forever tell each 'Scilly mainlander' in the island's only pub, The Turk's Head.

Mediation also attends that abrupt transition when bridge, causeway or tunnel joins one bit of land to another: the instant one is 'back on the isle' will be invariably registered as a return to the womb.

Perhaps it is mediation that explains the remarkable resilience of some islanders, often tolerating the intolerable to continue their special identity. This surely occurred in the Dodecanese, twelve large and 150 smaller islands in the southeastern Ægean where, from 1919 to 1947, Italy did everything in her power to destroy local Hellenism. The Greek islanders replied, however, with phenomenal resilience, though as Lawrence Durrell noted, 'the Italians were much tougher even than the Turks . . .'.[39] Such is the character trait that also ennobles the Maltese, East Timorese, Easter Islanders and many more. Like that 'damned spot', island culture will not out. For a true islander mediates to survive.

IDEALIZATION

Idealization, that cerebral gymnastics whereby in some circumstances one can regard something as better, more attractive or preferable than 'objective reality' would otherwise justify, is of course inherent in subjectification. But idealization seems to go further – proffering an internalized framework of values synergistically validating the respective conceit. Particularly for palm-eyed mainlanders but also for inveterate islanders 'lands surrounded by liquid' have always provoked exaggerated musings, their inherent apartness prompting an impression of security, serenity, seclusion, slowness, a sense of social divestiture: the emancipated man, the liberated woman. Water is one's only warden.

The notion is perhaps more acutely perceived by those who have lived elsewhere than by native islanders – from Napoleon Bonaparte (1769–1821) of Corsica to Lilly Langtree (1853–1929) of Jersey – who exchange island demons for mainland mayhem. For the 'happiest' islanders are often transplanted mainlanders who have entrusted their fates to the idealization and consented to reality nicely disenchanting them. Living on an island is wholly different from visiting an island: most of us derive pleasure from the fleeting dreamscape, yet those who do stay often discover that the idealization hadn't been too far from the truth after all.

It all depends on delivery. The 'perfect island' – at least for the normal Westerner from a Developed World nation – should really lie in the Goldilocks Zone that places it

> Within a comfortable and affordable commute of a metropolitan centre (for culture, entertainment, purchases, employment, brief 'escape')

Beyond mass access (to discourage crowding and crime), and
in a temperate or subtropical climate, avoiding extremes.

In addition, the 'perfect island' should

Not be too large or small, but roughly 100 sq km
Enjoy a population between 500 and 10,000
Possess a selection of smaller, discrete villages
Be affordable
Be subject to stable governance
Display a mature community spirit
Be ecologically manageable and, most importantly, sustainable.

Bonuses would be a positive and harmonious ethnic and age
diversity; a plentiful ration of artists, musicians and writers; and
such specialities as vineyards, olive groves, orchards, nature reserves
and trails, bays for boating, fishing and diving. Diminishing any of
these features would of course be: the intrusion of a well-travelled
bridge, causeway or tunnel connecting to the mainland; the rash of
holiday homes; the imposition of large corporate or private
landowners; the impudence of a metropolis on the island; or the
shock of any polluting industry.

Money helps, but it certainly isn't everything. 'It is partly
poverty', Durrell felt, 'that keeps the Greeks so happy, so spare
and in tune with things.'[40] Most islanders sincerely contented with
their isolation tend to be non-capitalist, non-materialist and non-
Western. Of course, contented colonials during the Age of Empire
had simply transplanted their ideal, as it was always Home that
held the dream. On British Ceylon (modern Sri Lanka) at the end
of the 1800s, for example:

Planters nearly always married into one another's families when
they returned from their education in England, and they lived a
well-ordered country gentry's life. People were normally At Home
once each week, and there were frequent calls, and dances at the
Queen's in Kandy, and golfing weekends at Nuwara Eiya, and the
bungalows were lofty and cool and lapped in lawns, and there was
an English vicar at the church up the road, and all seemed change-
less, useful and very agreeable.[41]

Whether for British, French, Spanish, Portuguese, German, Danish, Dutch or American colonial masters, this was indeed the likeness of island life in times gone by: the recreation at second remove of the childhood turf. It was in fact no insular world many were wanting, but the idealization of Home abroad.

Indigenous islanders can nurture a similar chimera. Māori and Hawaiian youths, for example, now emulate African American speech, dress, gesture, song and dance in an apparent identity crisis that rejects traditional realities yet devours media fantasies. (For devotees of island cultures, it is something profoundly sad to witness.) Yet seeing oneself as an 'islander' is not so much identification – recall what was mentioned above about this – as it is state of mind. Since islands are no longer places of isolation, being 'an islander' no longer means, at least psychologically, what it used to mean. First distance was eroded by steamship, then by radio, telephone and aeroplane. Jet-age tourism was followed by fax, television and video. And with the World Wide Web any remaining vestiges of remoteness have vanished. Most islanders electronically touch the world, instantly and constantly. Isolation is now choice, not necessity. And one major victim of this development has been that idealization which mainlander and islander alike once practised.

Today, if there is one thing that defines what island existence is truly about, it is *water*. Every islander, from the briefest visitor to the most obstinate hermit, is forever aware of being water-bound, of staying water-focused. The insular consciousness bathes in sea, lake or river. So many activities revolve around marine factuality – fishing, boating, swimming, diving, shelling – that an idealized constant must be this natural girdle that defines the place. 'Real' islanders not only sense the water, they bask in it: 'The regular pounding of waves on the shore is deeply reassuring, like the beating heart an infant feels in his mother's arms.'[42] The ultimate idealization would have to be the successful marriage of land and water.

When does an island cease being 'insular' in the human imagination? – When land or culture overwhelms water. Big Islanders do this naturally: Britons and Japanese might appreciate they are surrounded by sea, but they value more being citizens of great and powerful nations. Metropolitan islanders do this unnaturally: Manhattan, Montreal, Hong Kong, Singapore and central Stockholm have swallowed insularity with skyscrapers, high-rise apartments, congestion and confusion of activity.

In the end, perhaps the 'ideal island' is one's own. You can leisurely walk around tiny Herm in the Channel Islands in a single hour. Major Peter Wood and his wife Jenny arrived there shortly after the Second World War and after over 30 years of island seclusion Major Wood could confess, 'People ask us what we get from it, don't we get bored with it? The answer is that we get tranquillity – and that is something we could never be bored with.'[43]

*L*ike *music or wine*, an island is different for each person. Psychological diversity is greater now than before. Some imperial myths still hold, as does the question: who 'owns' what? (This would touch particularly the US, France and Chile.) But such outmoded rudenesses regularly fade – the Netherlands, for example, has just divested herself of two Caribbean colonies – not only in the political consciousness but also in popular imagination. And psychological isolation is probably gone for good, what with mobile phones, laptops and the internet. Only rare isolates remain, fossils of an age that once was. Of course geographical isolation remains to plague and impoverish small distant islands: restricted supplies and visitor numbers, limited health services, reduced educational possibilities, inadequate governance by central authorities and the like. All the same, even isolated islanders think differently now, weaned from their seclusion by technology to become hybrid, mobile, cosmopolitan denizens of the wired world – yet still identifiable as a people 'apart'.

The metaphor of the remote island as a 'Westerner's playground paradise' has enthused ancients and moderns alike. It was frequent with Greeks and Romans, and history's dialectic saw the notion repackaged (1700s), rejected (1800s), then repackaged again (1900s).

The real continuity between old and new paradises . . . lies more in the fact that they remain predicated upon colonialist assumptions and realities and are places wherein nature is reformulated to meet the changing expectations and requirements of Western culture.[44]

And so the fancy fades once again in the twenty-first century, as a consequence of global warming, oil depletion, economic vagaries, international terrorism and shrinking tourist numbers. That each age recreates its own islands of the mind is the greater lesson here. For islands exist for humankind only when they are imagined.

Beyond culture's touch islands are but stone and sand, ferns and feathers.

Is there an island mentality? For many, indeed – and to several degrees and in diverse categories. The 'islandness' of Britain, Ireland, Japan, Taiwan and New Zealand cannot be denied, but perhaps rather as 'national insular consciousness'. The folk island is still immediately perceived on Hainan, Malta, Iceland, Easter Island, Tahiti, Nassau, the Isle of Man or several of the Channel Islands. The community island is most strongly felt on Lindau in Lake Constance, Yell in Shetland, Sark, Catalina, Martha's Vineyard and the like. A critical difference lies in the fact that Britons do not feel like islanders, whereas New Zealanders – who inhabit two main islands of roughly the same size as Britain and who share a similar national insular consciousness – do feel like islanders: it's about remoteness, ethnic composition, the juniority of nationhood, the invented 'culture of islandness' itself. Japanese feel like islanders, too, but chiefly by reason of ethnic exclusivity, something neither Britons nor New Zealanders share or understand.

A perceived 'island mentality' is particularly distinct in such places as Rarotonga, the Outer Hebrides, the Chathams or the remoter Dalmatian isles where time seems to have stood still and the most important task of the day is that natter with the neighbour. Durrell discovered in the Greek isles that 'a Sicilean exuberance reigns, and it is customary to leave the courtyard door ajar so that strangers can peek in and admire what they see. This is also a way of getting into a free chat and gossip, which is so very dear to the Greek heart, particularly on the remoter islands.'[45] This is no modern surveillance society but simply a community holding together, defined by shore and sea. If anything, islands are a paranoid's paradise, since one is liberated from the uncaring eye of the nameless observer. On smaller islands, *everyone* cares.

Globalization and mass tourism have most recently bruised island life with Western clichés, decadence and wealth. Still, island life nearly everywhere survives and rewards. Some claim that in today's shrinking world islands can no longer be those special refuges we so valued. But they can. Just not in the same way as before, as Wordsworth already divined two centuries ago, who found this refuge

Not in Utopia, – subterranean fields, –
Or some secreted island, Heaven knows where!
But in the very world, which is the world
Of all of us, – the place where, in the end,
We find our happiness, or not at all![46]

Since we're all survivors of the last isle now.

nine

The Last Isle

On 4 June 1629 the Dutch ship *Batavia* sank in the coral atolls of Western Australia's Abrolhos group. On the same day 334 years later, visitors who discovered the wreck could soon tell that the crew had murdered their 125 castaway passengers, ostensibly to better their own chances for survival – several skulls still contained bullets. Today, the *Batavia* incident counts as Australia's earliest known atrocity.

In 1835 the Mexican government sent the *Peor es Nada* to forcibly evict from California's Channel Island of San Nicolas the native Tongva tribespeople and resettle them on the mainland. During the embarkation in foul weather, one woman protested that in the confusion her baby had not been brought down from the hills and off she ran to fetch it. Refusing to wait, the Spanish captain sailed without her. For eighteen years the Tongva woman remained marooned alone on her ancestral island, only occasionally seen by sailors and hunters – always she fled in panic. Finally two sealers found her clothed in feathers in a whalebone hut and managed to convey her to the Santa Barbara Mission on the mainland. There, where no one could understand her Tongvan tongue, she perished within a few days.

And one of the saddest tales of all must be that of 9-sq-km barren Clipperton Island in the eastern Pacific, southwest of Mexico. In the early 1900s about 100 men, women and children were sent there to mine phosphate, with a supply ship arriving with sustenance only twice a year from Acapulco. But in 1914 – because of the Mexican Revolution and because the British Pacific Island Company financing the venture with the Mexican government had declared bankruptcy – the supply ship didn't come. No one called until 1915. After this, some of the stranded miners built a boat and set off for the mainland but vanished. By 1917 scurvy and starvation had scythed down the rest until only the lighthouse keeper and fifteen women and children were left. When the keeper began raping and killing them, the governor's widow, who had been his frequent victim, slew him. Only four women and seven children were finally rescued by USS *Yorktown* on 18 July 1917. To this day, Clipperton Island has remained uncolonized.

Castaways and derelicts fascinate, perhaps because we all intuit that we, too, are in a similar circumstance. Might our fate also be similar? we ask ourselves. For the past two decades Easter Island, for example, has been invoked as a warning of how a society can destroy its sustaining ecosystem; it is a chilling tale to read.[1] Yet something is often forgotten here: that the Rapanui people of Easter Island time and again adapted to often cruelly changed circumstances, accepted their altered island in the end, and not only survived but prospered. Perhaps we can all tap this resilence.

Yet only once we accept that we all ride Earth Island.

The first two chapters of this book adequately defined islands geologically and biologically. But when islands were approached culturally each concrete attempt at a comprehensive definition seemed to crumble. Confronted by a similar perplexity Welsh novelist and travel writer Leslie Thomas (*b.* 1931), for one, had to conclude: '. . . in the end, it is people who make an island'.[2] It's all about meaning, what islands *mean* to us as human beings. Humankind's islands survive and thrive – that is, live for us – only when ostensible weaknesses are turned into strengths, when seeming disadvantages are forged into advantages. In earlier chapters we have seen how islanders have profited from smuggling, piracy, offering refuge, exchanging rare plants and minerals, providing singular foodstuffs like spices. And the disadvantage of isolation has become the advantage of prosperous tourism, offshore banking, commercial conveniences. Once-feared island waters are now havens for diving, fishing, cruising. Island remoteness encourages scientific discovery. Small island populations foster stable communities and encourage personal integration – just what is sought by so many disenchanted mainlanders. Through history islands have meant all these things to us, these are the cultural constants that define the word and embrace the reality we recognize. For us islands exist because we imagine them, and what Durrell wrote about the Greek isles can epitomize so many others:

> This small country, so repeatedly raped and shattered and ground to powder, and then reduced to the bare calc of its desolate capes and headlands, never had any fixed geographical borders. It was a state of mind.[3]

Even the island of the mind, however, demands her toll and this cultural meaning claims the highest price of all. To maintain their pleasures and continue their bounties, island ecosystems must be maturely – that is, sustainably – managed: not just for humankind but for all life forms, if only to validate our purported humanity. Unhappily, long-term resource depletion and pollution for short-term capital gain worry island societies even more now than in the past.[4] And islanders and islands appear more vulnerable than ever before as a new Global Society imposes manifestly non-insular demands.

CONSTANTS

Throughout this insular cruise we have tried to image an ocean through a wealth of bays: in other words, to recognize those constants that – above latitude and longitude, beyond coral and granite – appear to connect island existences and/or define something that mainland life just doesn't share. For example, each island grows into a cultural limb of the nearest, or politically or financially dominant, body, as with the Isle of Wight, Gotland, Capri, Hainan, even Hawai'i and Easter Island. Rare island cultures managing to retain a unique identity are those isolates that are away from major trade routes and were spared foreign settlement: Nukuoro, Kapingamarangi, Taku'u, Nukumanu and several more of these fascinating Pacific outliers.

Another constant. Islands generally do not breed historical personages. So Lesbian Sappho, Samian Pythagoras, Cretan El Greco, Corsican Napoleon or New Zealander Ernest Rutherford are the grand exceptions, not the rule. However, this constant defers to size of population: consider such Big Islanders as Shakespeare and Bashō, Isaac Newton and Charles Darwin.

A further constant. Humankind has always transformed islands. This can entail altering, like adding a breakwater or artifical harbour. It can engage identity, such as building a causeway to the mainland. Or it can even encompass reinvention: Manhattan, Hong Kong and Paris's Île de la Cité, for example, have been so transformed that they barely seem islands anymore.

It also holds as a constant that in their infinite variety and forms 'islands provide microcosms of all the world's environments. They represent, therefore, laboratories where we can study every natural interaction.'[5] For islands are 'small, encapsulated units that can be studied and understood in a way that is not possible when we are dealing with the complex interwoven relationships of life on a large continental land mass'.[6] We have seen how Charles Darwin had been inspired by the Galápagos Islands, among others, to develop his theory of evolution by natural selection. Lesser-known cases of similar island contributions are legion.

On 29 May 1919 English astrophysicist Arthur Eddington (1888–1944), for example, photographed on Principe Island off Africa's west coast the Hyades star cluster as it lay almost directly behind the sun during a total eclipse, confirming that the apparent shift of about 1/2000th of a degree in position was due to the lensing of light as predicted in Albert Einstein's 1916 theory of general relativity. In more recent times, simian immunodeficiency virus (SIV) from drills – close relatives of baboons – living on Bioko Island off Cameroon's coast were compared with virus samples from the mainland, as since the last ice age there had been 10,000 years of evolutionary divergence; this allowed scientists to determine that 'it must have taken at least 32,000 years to generate the diversity seen in SIV throughout Africa' – an important insight into the longevity of the related HIV virus which may be relevant to attempts to control its spread.[7] Innumerable island nature reserves, conservation centres and scientific stations are now furnishing essential data to better understand our planet.

The greater her isolation, the more an island progresses as a closed system: 'sensitive to even the smallest interference'.[8] It's for this reason that all the world's remote small islands are the most vulnerable to current global warming. This includes barrier islands – on which anyone who builds does so at her peril. In the early Middle Ages the Low Germans, for example, began developing barrier islands off the Frisian coastline.[9] Countless settlements, churches, even entire towns were then lost: local folk tales overflow with stories of church bells tolling undersea. Germans responded by building ever larger dykes – 10 to 20 m in height, 20 to 30 m thick – as sea walls. Isles became enwalled fortresses: Texel in Holland, Borkum and Nordeney in Germany, and many others.

Yet all such barrier islands are naturally shrinking and it is folly to build on any. In 1968 a US government insurance programme subsidized coastal property owners up to 80 per cent and made barrier-island construction financially attractive. Thousands of homes were built over the next twenty years until the programme was halted in the 1980s – not because of safety or conservation but to save federal funds. By then the harm was done, though, and all along the US coastlines today barrier island communities either lie in ruin or face imminent annihilation from global warming's fiercer and more frequent hurricanes and storm surges.

Another island constant is the more recent 'human laboratory'. These were spawned by the Age of Colonialism and are now to be found – in their more developed stage – throughout the world. Take Mauritius, where in the 1800s indentured Indian labourers and freed slaves from Madagascar and Africa mixed and proliferated. Other migrants arrived – from Asia, India, France – and a diverse, peaceful, stratified island culture developed through the succeeding 1900s. Filling an assortment of occupations on Mauritius today are the Creoles of mixed French and African heritage. Chinese are the merchants, just as one finds in much of French Polynesia. Most politics, however, is controlled by the Indians. And the white upper class, chiefly French, still manage the (now transnationally owned) sugar plantations. There is no segregation. Religious tolerance and even ecumenical enthusiasm abound. Still, there is little social mixing (which makes this different from Polynesia). By the last quarter of the 1900s Mauritius was suffering runaway population growth and massive unemployment. Since then, government family planning measures have lowered the population growth rate to 1 per cent, while unemployment fell from 20 to 3 per cent. Per capita income has doubled. A few have attributed much of this improvement to the 'emancipation' of Mauritius's women: freed from continuous childbearing and -rearing and from household incarceration, Mauritian women for the first time can get a higher education and create and fill new jobs. Jet-age tourism also brought new wealth and employment (Mauritius is particularly popular with the French). At the start of the twenty-first century Mauritius's is not an uncommon story.

Another insular constant is ethnic continuity. In the middle of the 1800s, for example, Paris handed over St Barthélemy in the Virgin Islands to Sweden, whereupon the French families there, resident for many generations, fled en masse to nearby St Thomas where they were welcomed by resident Danes. The French are still there – an important and distinct minority on St Thomas who fish, sell straw work to tourists and even now speak an archaic Norman French.

Then there's Lord Howe between Australia and New Zealand, the world's most southerly coral island. Home to only around 347 (2006) permanent residents, her 16.5 sq km of English-like fields bristle with Norfolk pines. It used to take five days to boat there from the Australian mainland, but in 1974 an airport was constructed. First visited by Europeans in the 1700s, by the early 1800s Lord Howe was welcoming whalers who purchased fruit and vegetables from temporary settlers. The first permanent colonists were Thomas and Margaret Andrews who arrived in 1842 and brought up a family in perilous isolation. In 1853 American whaler Nathan Chase Thompson arrived with a 12-year-old Gilbertese 'princess' named Bogue and her two maidservants Boranga and Bogaroo, which trio Thompson had found cast adrift: Bogue had fled an arranged marriage, she had claimed. Thompson settled with the three girls on Lord Howe, constructing a house to accommodate them all and wedding the servant Boranga 'to keep things proper'. When Boranga died in 1865, Thompson then took to wife Bogue herself. Still today their descendants remain on Lord Howe. It's a tale all too common to more remote isles.

The constant of island abandonment will probably never cease, for a sad palette of reasons. The St Kilda archipelago – 64 km west-northwest of Scotland in the Outer Hebrides – consists of four rock-pinnacle isles (Hirta, Soay, Dun, Boreray) and numerous islets and stacks. Permanently inhabited for at least 2,000 years, the archipelago boasted the village of St Kilda on Hirta, with Britain's highest sea cliffs – her residents, never numbering more than about 200 souls, living mostly on seabirds and eggs and isolated for most of the year from the rest of the world. As of the 1800s St Kilda's population steadily declined. Many newborns succumbed to tetanus due to the erstwhile rite of smearing their navel upon birth with fulmar oil from contaminated gannet-stomach pouches; adults were scythed down by TB and pneumonia. There was no doctor.

After the terrible winter of 1929–30 the resident missionary appealed to London to rescue the 36 surviving inhabitants. On 29 August 1930 all the St Kildans abandoned their ancestral isle on the cruiser HMS *Harebell*. Still deserted through the Second World War, the archipelago only received permanent residents again as of 1957 when various Ministry of Defence installations were constructed. Today, a small army contingent tracks the Hebridean missile range from Village Bay, and occasional National Trust parties, including St Kildan descendants, arrive in summer to restore houses and maintain the church and school museum. In 1986, for its remarkable prehistoric and medieval ruins and unique topography the archipelago was made Scotland's first UNESCO World Heritage Site. A similar biography has haunted islands throughout the world.

A further insular constant is accelerated change, particularly in the last 40 years. Because of their small population, generally retarded infrastructure and technology, and centuries of relative or real isolation, as a result of the unprecedented influx of tourists, capital investment and new technology many islands have experienced a pace of change that sees each year bringing what mainland communities experience in five. That backward, quaint Easter Island that the author discovered in 1993 – unpaved roads, difficult telephone access, most transport by horseback, only 400 vehicles, two flights weekly and 4,000 tourists a year – rapidly vanished over the subsequent two decades, with each near-annual visit shockingly revelational: paved roads, internet, the horses all but gone, 4,000 vehicles, two flights daily, cruise ships arriving and over 50,000 tourists annually. Modern jet tourism, international investment and the advent of an insular middle class have transformed hundreds of isles. As a result, everything that made these places so special is disappearing fast – a universal complaint.

Another constant is language change. As with Darwin's finches, human languages always evolve into separate 'species' – we call them daughter languages – with separation and time. In this way, Norse became Norn in Shetland, Faroese in the Faroe Islands, and Icelandic in Iceland. Eastern Polynesian became over many centuries of colonization and change Marquesan, Tuamotuan, Mangarevan, Rapanui, Hawaiian, Tahitian, Māori and many more. But separation – over a long period of time – is the key point here. Otherwise you merely have that dialect variation so common to the British Isles, the Greek isles, Japan's many islands, the Caribbean, the Hawaiian archipelago and elsewhere. Creolization is typical on islands where several diverse ethnic communities have come together, requiring a common tongue for interaction. Indians, Arabs and Africans in the Seychelles, for example, developed as their first language a Seychelles Creole; many also speak French as a second language, the original colonial tongue.

Pacific island languages are simply astounding. Between them, Pacific Islanders speak more than 1,200 distinct tongues – about one-fourth of Earth's total. Papua New Guinea alone claims more than 500 languages, the planet's greatest concentration. There were once only two language families in the Pacific: Papuan (New Guinea) and Austronesian (with its origins on Taiwan). The most numerous languages are Papuan, the most widely spread Austronesian. English is widely spoken in all island groups except where French is the official language (mostly in East Polynesia but also in New Caledonia and the Loyalty Islands). Several versions of pidgin (a language made up of elements of two or more other languages) are used in Melanesia, in some cases as a speaker's first tongue.

Indonesia's island world holds over 300 ethnic peoples, each speaking their own language. Second in linguistic diversity only to New Guinea, Indonesia was using Malay as a widely spoken lingua franca already by the early 1500s when the first Europeans arrived. A dialect of Malay, Bahasa was first put forward as a national language in 1926 by those agitating for independence from the Netherlands. (Dutch was never widely spoken there and would never unify the ethnic peoples as English had done in India.) After independence in 1945 Indonesia formally adopted Bahasa as the national tongue for use in officialdom, broadcasting, the press and education. To most Indonesians it remains a second language, however; many still cannot speak or read it.[10] Such linguistic diversity as well as attempts towards a national tongue are characteristic of many larger islands.

Nesonomastics – the study of island names – is a beguiling branch of nesology. It is a science unto itself, as islands have known naming, renaming, triple and quadruple naming through millennia of discovery, conquest, colonization and reinvention. Many island nations and groups bear a generic name (New Zealand, Japan, Hawai'i, the Galápagos) but consist of up to hundreds of separate islands each of which sports her own nesonym. Since antiquity, these names have been donned and shed like old coats, or piled on top of one another like epithetic carpets. Samos in the Northern Sporades, for example, whose fertility was so prized by comic dramatist Menander (*c.* 342–*c.* 292 BC) that he announced that Samos's fowls produced not only eggs but milk as well, bore as her epithet 'Watery' from Homer. But she was also known as *Anthemis* for her flowers, *Phylis* for her greenery, *Pityoussa* for her pines, *Dryoussa* for her oaks and so on. (They say the loveliest of all Greek folk songs is 'Samiotissa' or 'Girl of Samos'.) Where island names are concerned, Rhodes must rank as the most protean: *Stadia* for her ellipsoid shape (like a maple leaf); *Atabyros* after her main mountain; *Olyessa* for her earthquakes; *Poeissa* denoting her bounty; *Makaria*, the blessed one; *Asteria*, of the stars; and Snake Isle, for unclear reasons.

Tiny Iona off Mull in the Inner Hebrides has, at one time or another, been known as Gælic *Iovava* or 'Yew Place'; Norse *Hiōe*, perhaps 'Island of the Cave'; and Middle English *Icolmkill* and its variants; the modern name Iona came from a 1700s misreading of the manuscript variant *Iova*, by which the *v* was mistakenly read as an *n*. Sri Lanka was called by ancient Chinese *Ssu Cheng Pu* or 'Land Without Sorrow', by medieval Arabs *Serendib* or 'Fortunate', and by later Portuguese *Ceilão* or 'Celestial'; when Britain annexed the island in 1796 she anglicized the Portuguese name to Ceylon. But with independence in 1948 the Sinhalese changed their island name to Sri Lanka or 'Resplendent Land'. Mauritius, also in the Indian Ocean, was named after Prince Maurice of the Netherlands when five ships of the Dutch Second Fleet were blown off course there in 1598. After the Dutch abandoned the island in 1710, the French arrived in 1715 and later named her *Île de France*. But then the French formally surrendered the island to the British in 1810 and the island reverted to her historic name Mauritius.

What the British called the Sandwich Islands became in time better known by the indigenous name, Hawai'i, through the influence of the House of Kāmehameha. The earliest known nesonym south of Australia is Van Diemen's Land, which Abel Tasman (1603–1659) immortalized on discovery in 1642 to honour the then Governor General of the Dutch East Indies; in 1856, however, the island was renamed Tasmania ostensibly to honour Tasman himself but actually to remove the 'demon' connotation that hung over this former penal colony.

Today there are nearly as many island names as there are islands, and if one should include all the historical name changes and epithets there are surely tens of thousands more. Naming must be one of islands' most enduring cultural constants.

ASYLUM

Islands' cultural meaning also lies in their identity as essential or convenient places of asylum. This has many origins. One of the most common and unfortunate is the fear of contagion, so that, like with penal islands (see below), quarantine islands apparently have existed since the beginning of time. Leper islands were already known in antiquity, but waxed ubiquitous in medieval Europe and India. The idea eventually spread to the Pacific: the Kalawao and Kalaupapa communities on Moloka'i in Hawai'i were infamous leper colonies in the 1800s, the former where Father Damien (1840–1889) selflessly sacrificed himself and the latter still accommodating around fourteen former sufferers of Hansen's disease. Other leper islands include Viringili Atoll in the Maldives, 'Ei'a'o in the Marquesas (late 1800s), Chacachacare in the Bocas Islands between Trinidad and Venezuela, D'Arcy Island east of Vancouver Island, Canada (1894–1924), Penikese off the coast of Massachusetts (1905–21), Ambae in Vanuatu (1900s), Peel Island east of Brisbane, Australia (1907–59), Hei Ling Chau in the Islands District of Hong Kong (1950–74), Round Island in the Seychelles, Robben Island off Cape Town, South Africa, and many more. One of Europe's last leper colonies, tiny Spinalonga off Crete's northern coast, operated from 1903 to 1957.

Rehabilitation islands have been popular since the 1800s, most frequently to isolate and cure alcohol and drug abusers. It is hoped that such enforced or voluntary 'insulation' will remove temptation and access, facilitate monitoring and create an environment of positive social reintegration. Osea Island, for example, a 1.6-sq-km isle in Essex's River Blackwater estuary, housed until 2010 an elite alcohol and drug treatment centre. In the early 1900s the Salvation Army purchased 24-ha Pakatoa Island and 82-ha Rotoroa Island in the Hauraki Gulf just off Auckland, New Zealand, as alcohol and drug treatment facilities: Pakatoa housed women until its closure in 1964, while neighbouring Rotoroa accommodated men until it was closed in 2005. The 40-ha hilly island of St John's just 6.5 km south of Singapore hosted a drug rehabilitation centre in the mid-1900s until it was converted in 1975 to a 'getaway isle' resort. Sunshine Island in the Islands District of Hong Kong as of 1952 offered a successful treatment centre for opium addicts; she now lies deserted. There have been many such islands. In the same context one should mention the numerous nature rehabilitation islands set aside to protect rare birds and mammals – such as the several closed island reserves in The Gambia's River Gambia National Park, asylum for several chimpanzee groups.

A special type of asylum is the 'nudist isle'. Many naturists find insular isolation the only remedy to escape curious non-participants while enjoying activities with the like-minded in an open environment offering immediate beach access. Among the more famous naturist isles is France's 8-km-long and 2-km-wide Île du Levant off the Riviera: 90 per cent of the island is a restricted missile testing zone, but the rest is dedicated to naturism and includes Europe's first naturist village, Héliopolis, established in 1931. Sea Island Sanctuary on Cat Island, South Carolina, was America's first naturist camp, purchased in 1932 and accessible only to naturists; economic constraints, however, forced its closure in 1936. In the Adriatic the island of Koversada – linked by a bridge to the Istrian mainland – is Europe's largest naturist resort, one of many Croatian islands dedicated to naturism such as Cres, Krk and Losinj. Several naturist beaches adorn the Donauinsel, the 21-km-long holm in the Danube that runs right through Vienna. Though Asia possesses many naturist beaches – most of which are illegal – no island is wholly dedicated to nudity. Some Caribbean islands tolerate a small number of naturist beaches: Curaçao, Aruba and both French and Dutch Saint Martin/Sint Maarten, for example. Individual naturists in North America seek out Knight Island in Lake Champlain, Vermont; Bird Island, North Carolina; Sauvie Island (at 105 sq km the largest holm in the US) and Glassbar Island, Oregon; Mercer Island, Washington; and Steveston Island, British Columbia. In Australia, Queensland's Bribie Island used to attract naturists; and in New Zealand, Little Palm Beach on Waiheke Island is ever a popular naturist retreat.

Island refuges are often also ethnic asylums. The West Indies, for example, once hosted a sizable colony of refugee Jews, most having fled persecution in Catholic Brazil in the late 1600s and early 1700s. In Philipsburg, Dutch capital of Sint Maarten, one can still see the remains of what is believed to be a 300-year-old synagogue. Many of the islands – especially Nevis and the Netherlands' Sint Eustatius – maintain cemeteries with large tombstones bearing Hebraic epitaphs, some of the stones having arrived as ballast in ships' holds. Though the Jewish colonies have long disappeared after most Jews migrated in the late 1800s to New York or Europe, they are now being replaced by new colonies of their great-grand-children seeking holiday or retirement homes away from New York's winter and Miami's overcrowding. At one time as many as one-fifth of Nevis's inhabitants were Jews, most labourers in the sugar plantations. In 1830 in the St Thomas town of Charlotte Amalie in then-Danish Virgin Islands, Camille Pissarro (1830–1903) – father of Impressionist painting – was born to Spanish Jews who regularly worshipped at the town's synagogue, second oldest in the Western hemisphere. Pissarro's parents still lie buried in its Jewish cemetery.

'SAPPHIC JUMPERS' AND BIRDMEN

Island meaning literally takes wing in island sports. Some sparked and died overnight, others fired the imaginations of generations. One has gone on to conquer the world.

Humankind's earliest known team sport was Minoan Crete's bull-leaping. According to the depiction in surviving frescos from the mid-second millennium BC, a mixed trio – two girls and a boy – would time successive somersaults over a steer's horns to coincide with diversionary manoeuvres. It was highly dangerous. Perfect timing was vital. The Minoan bull cult was later borrowed by Mediterranean trading partners and developed over many centuries into the blood sport of bullfighting that is only now experiencing its finishing *estocada*.

The White Cliffs of 335.8-sq-km Lefkada in the Ionian Sea on Greece's west coast – 'from which the poetess Sappho made her ill-fated leap into eternity' – offer a 72-m plunge into the sea from a deeply undercut cliff.[11] Several recorded legends indicate that ancient Greeks believed a person could dive from the cliff edge straight down into Hades (much like the 'Leap of Empedocles' into Etna's crater on Sicily). The 'Sapphic Jump' became the ancient world's version of Acapulco's famed La Quebrada cliff divers: many young Hellenes performed the dive and survived and the sport was apparently still popular at the time of Cicero (106–43 BC) and Strabo (63 BC–*c*. AD 24), who both mention it. It was claimed that Apollo's priests performed the dive regularly without harm, some wearing wings and plumes attached to their shoulders. Known anciently as the *katapontismos*, the Sapphic Jump was perhaps some sort of propitiatory act of cultic significance.

Ancient Easter Islanders rocketed down the grass of a volcanic cone on a banana-trunk sled in a hair-raising ride that meant bruises, breaks or worse; the time-honoured *hakape'i* competition is still re-enacted each year, to the delight of locals and tourists. Easter Island's Birdman contest – whereby young men would race down a 300-m, near-perpendicular cliff face, paddle on a reed float out to an offshore isle to await, then seize, the first egg of the sooty tern, paddle back and ascend the cliff to hand the egg to their clan leader who would then be hailed as the new paramount chief for one year – is one of those rare instances in human history when competitive sport determined local governance.

First mentioned by European visitors to the Pacific islands in the second half of the 1700s, surfing has always featured as a prominent sport of the Polynesians.[12] It was greatly enjoyed in pre-contact Tonga, Samoa and Hawai'i and could have been taken even to distant Easter Island nearly 1,500 years ago. In modern times the sport spread from Hawai'i to California and Australia and from there to the world, especially as of the 1960s when surfing developed into a major sport. Out of this came an entire culture – surfing competitions, safaris, dress, music, films – which enthuses devotees throughout the world. For millennia other Pacific Islanders similarly enjoyed canoe racing, kite-flying, spear- and dart-throwing, archery, wrestling, footracing, sham battles and many more organized activities. Bungee jumping, to name only one, began on Pentacost Island in Vanuatu as a test of courage and rite of passage long before its technological re-invention in Bristol, England, in 1979 and universal proliferation.

Everyone knows that the world's most popular sport – football (soccer) – began on an island, too. Various football games enlivened Britain's public schools, but it was not until 1848 that the Cambridge Rules were drawn up to distinguish this one particular practice. In similar fashion Britain was also home in the 1700s to baseball, which later became the national sport of the US (and its many island territories and former Trust Territory) and Japan; in the 1800s to rugby, which was to become so popular in Wales, France, South Africa, Australia, New Zealand and many Polynesian islands; and at the same time perhaps also to cricket, which came to dominate the Commonwealth nations, including the islands of the Indian Ocean and British Caribbean, though this sport might actually have come to England much earlier from Flanders.

L. J. SILVER'S LEGACY

Treasure islands are not just the stuff of literature and films, feeding fancied meaning to those islands of the mind. They exist for real, as we saw earlier when discussing the wealth of Bronze Age Greece and Caria submerged just off the southwest isles of modern Turkey. Many a hoard of gold and silver awaits discovery on or near islands the world over, rendering isolated isles the hunting fields of bold adventurers and pinstriped holding companies. Canada's privately owned, 57-ha Oak Island near Nova Scotia, for example, is supposed to be concealing in her fabled 'Money Pit' the alleged billions of Scots pirate (or privateer) Captain William Kidd (1645–1701). Real treasure was found off the island of Terschelling in the Dutch Frisian Islands, where in 1799 HMS *Lutine* sank with gold bullion and coin; most of her cargo remains unsalvaged.

Spanish galleons wrecked off Caribbean isles have attracted treasure hunters for centuries. *Nuestra Señora de Atocha* was the most famous vessel of a fleet lost in 1622 in the Dry Tortugas west of Key West, Florida, while carrying the wealth of the New World back to Spain; rediscovered in 1985 after a search of more than sixteen years, her cargo of gold, silver and emeralds was one of the richest undersea hauls ever made. In 1822 the three-masted Chinese junk *Tek Sing* ran aground on a reef in the Bangka-Belitung Islands of Indonesia and sank with 1,600 passengers and 200 crew members; known as 'the *Titanic* of the East', the shipwreck was rediscovered by a British marine salvor in 1999 along with its cargo of Chinese porcelain – at 350,000 pieces the largest ever found. Off Costa Rica lies the treasure haven of 23.8-sq-km, uninhabited Cocos Island, where the government has forbidden access to treasure hunters; the island is rumoured to conceal 350 tonnes of gold bullion pirated in the early 1800s from Spanish galleons by British naval officer Captain Bennett Graham, who was later arrested and executed for his unauthorized activities. Also on Cocos Island is supposed to lie the cache of Portuguese pirate Benito Bonito who is alleged to have buried there the fabulous 'Treasure of Lima'.

MATTERS OF QUALITY

The true significance of what we mean by 'islands' lies in the living locales we know daily, where real people experience real lives of thrill and monotony, of compromise and heartbreak. Take North Haven, Maine, a 213.7-sq-km retreat that over 5,000 years ago hosted the Red Paint People but now is home to a permanent population of around 380 Americans of mostly Anglo-Saxon descent who enjoy ferry access to the mainland three times a day. North Haven includes many holiday homes that are occupied only at summertime and there are few young families. The islanders would like to build a new schoolhouse to attract more couples with children. Most residents are fishers and farmers, simply getting by. In a BBC report in 2010 North Haven was praised as 'small town America'. Her story is universal, really. It at once reminded the author of 1.5-sq-km Rākino Island just off Auckland. Rākino counts sixteen permanent residents who would never think of abandoning their quiet isle, but includes as well 68 holiday homes which know life and noise only during a handful of summer weeks.

Some island communities are actively working to reverse this depressing trend. Rathlin, the only inhabited isle off the coast of Northern Ireland, is one such. In the 1800s Rathlin hosted a proud population of over 1,000 souls who spoke their own unique dialect of Irish. In the 2001 census only 71 were left. Ten years later there are over 100. The increase is easily explained: Rathlin is now connected to Ballycastle on the mainland, 10 km distant, by two ferries – one a vehicle-and-passenger ferry when weather allows, and the other a fast passenger-only ferry for daily commuters to mainland jobs. A more rapid population increase is hoped from young families now planning to move to the island.

And move they probably will. Because island life holds special value. Mercer's Quality of Living Survey annually assesses 221 cities of the world based on 39 criteria such as level of crime, limits on personal freedom, hospital services, schools, public transport, housing, recreational facilities and more. In 2010 island cities ranked especially high in the Survey, with Auckland tying with Vancouver in fourth place. In the Survey's eco-ranking – judging water availability and potability, waste removal, sewerage, air pollution, traffic congestion and so forth – Honolulu ranked second, Wellington fifth, Copenhagen eighth and Stockholm ninth (shared with Oslo and Kobe). But it was an island city that also featured as worst: Port-au-Prince on Haiti. In the 2008 judging of *Monacle*'s annual list of the world's most livable cities, Copenhagen ranked first; in *Monacle*'s 2010 assessment Copenhagen placed second, Tokyo fourth, Stockholm sixth, Honolulu thirteenth, Fukuoka fourteenth, Montreal nineteenth and Auckland twentieth. In a 2010 United Nations survey on the best places to live, New Zealand ranked third (just after Australia). The 2011 Global Peace Index ranked island nations as the world's first, second and third most peaceful: Iceland, New Zealand and Japan.

Such appraisals shouldn't surprise. Islands are a byword for shelter, with smaller populations mostly, but not always, adhering to time-honoured ethical and moral codes. Hence there is less crime, reduced violence, fewer external disruptions by virtue of remoteness. Certainly there are environments with heightened danger: some Indonesian, Philippine and Muslim islands might better be avoided. Certain statistics do shock: Greenland's and Manhattan's murder rate, Japan's and New Zealand's suicide rate, Haiti's crime rate and other things. But islands are certainly among the safest destinations for young backpackers in an era when thousands are kidnapped each year for ransom (a statistic rarely revealed by the media). Even during political coups – such as the most recent on Fiji in 2006 – tourists remain not only unharmed but ceaselessly pampered, most of them unaware that anything is amiss.

Island metropolises will long continue as havens, with good reason. Sitka in Alaska is exemplary. The unified city-borough is located on Baranof Island and extends northwards onto the southern half of Chichagof Island, both of them in the Alexander Archipelago, a 500-km-long scatter of around 1,100 isles. Sitka's population of approximately 9,000 (2005) makes her Alaska's fourth largest city. 'Downtown' Sitka is considered to be the part of the city situated on the western side of Baranof Island, an imposing giant of 4,162 sq km – actually, the 137th largest island in the world. Here life centres on government employment and the health industries, fishing, seafood processing and tourism, while on the smaller offshore isles – each hosting about five to ten families – mothers boat their kids over to the waiting schoolbus on the larger mainland island. Sitka herself has two high schools while neigh-bouring Japonski Island has one state-run Native boarding high school; Japonski also houses the Southeast-Sitka Campus of the University of Alaska. It's a solid life in this difficult-to-access environment. Many seek out just such substance, far away from mainland noise.

On the downside, one must accept crowding and concomitant health risks. On smaller isles congested populations negatively im-pact on fresh water. Fæcal clearance is ever a concern, too: human waste is often deposited straight into the sea, for tides and currents to flush. Over many centuries in Japan, cultural customs evolved for contamination avoidance – long before Pasteur's warnings – in this mountainous topography with highly congested shorelines: bowing, not touching; face-masks; hot communal baths; stigma-tizing wet kerchiefs in pockets; disposing human waste on fields from 'honeybuckets', far from any water source; eating with *hashi* or chopsticks, never one's fingers. And many more – such as the celebrated 'Japanese smile' which hides more than it reveals – much of which the rest of the world could do well to emulate. Population concentration on small islands in tropical latitudes exacerbates all common illnesses. This fact was realized early in island history and inspired most further voyages of discovery.

Despite increased exposure to health risks, some islanders bask in longevity. Discounting Cretan Epimenides's claimed 154 sum-mers, we concede those confirmed cases that must only catch one's curiosity. It was no coincidence that Spanish explorer Juan Ponce de Léon (1474–1521) sought in Bimini's waters a cure for aging. Today one seeks the same in Okinawa's foodstuffs – a nutrient-rich, low-calorie diet favoured by many in the Ryūkyū Islands. Here one can encounter one of the largest concentrations of centenarians on the planet, though their high age – several have lived beyond 110 – probably has more to do with genes, a quiet lifestyle and a special environment than with diet. The same can be said of island Japan in general, which, like Puerto Rico, shares a high proportion of supercentenarians. On the other hand Pacific Islanders – chiefly because of diet and lifestyle – display an inordinate propensity towards obesity, diabetes, hypertension and heart disease, and must admit of one of the shortest longevities even when residing on larger, developed islands like New Zealand and Hawai'i. Whenever one can avoid stress and limit access to modern diets, pesticides or other chlorine compounds, it seems that one can live a more traditional life and prolong human longevity, something certain islanders have demonstrated.

Because of restricted partner choice, island inbreeding can cause disabilities in descendants, whereby otherwise recessive mutations are allowed a statistically more frequent expression.[13] Colour blindness dominates Micronesia's Pingelap and Pohnpei and also Denmark's Fuur Island. A cleft palate and cleft lip trouble many on Spanish Wells in the Bahamas. And half of Tristan da Cunha suffers chronic asthma. Extremely small island populations – of around 50 or so – teeter on the cusp of extinction, alone for genetic reasons. (It might explain the Pacific's so-called 'Mystery Islands'.)

The case of Pingelap in the Federated States of Micronesia is extremely telling. She comprises three islets that form a broken ring about a central lagoon nearly 3 km in diameter. Each islet is hardly 3 m above sea level, yet Pingelap has been occupied for well over a millennium, growing to some 1,000 souls. In 1775 a typhoon struck, washing a storm surge over Pingelap that claimed the lives of nine out of ten islanders. The 100-odd who survived, among them the chief and his household, had only fish for sustenance. Soon only twenty were left alive, yet these bred and restored the population. But of the 700 islanders alive today, 57 are colour-blind, the highest incidence on Earth. It's that a genetic mutation in one of the typhoon survivors was allowed to duplicate over and over among the severely limited breeding population of only twenty persons. 'Elsewhere in the world, the incidence of achromatopsia is less than one in 30,000 – here on Pingelap it is one in 12.'[14]

But island existence is painted with a broad brush. Malta is now Europe's most congested and car-dense country. Polynesian Tikopia? – she still has no electricity, no telephone, no roads, no cars or bicycles, no airstrip. One has always travelled on Tikopia by foot on footpaths. The island has always supported only around 1,200 persons; no more than this number is sustainable. So infanticide was common in the past: whenever starvation threatened, newborns were taken out in canoes and thrown overboard. Living close to nature can be too close for some.

When one can gear down and truly make do with less, then in general island life awards everyone healthier and better-quality years. Advantages do outweigh disadvantages. When living on modest islands each person should be resourceful, satisfied and content with basics, world-wise in the simpler life. But if there one is looking for fame, fortune, career, high culture and nightlife, the small island is not for her.

It's clearly not enough for many Pacific islanders either, whose populations are swelling more rapidly than the Developed World's. Within New Guinea, Fiji, New Zealand, even Samoa and Tahiti, thousands migrate to their largest cities. At the same time, Cook Islanders, Niueans, Tokelauans, Samoans and Tongans flood into Auckland; Guam's Chamorros have relocated to Honolulu and Los Angeles; Marquesans flee to Pape'ete; Loyalty Islanders to Noumea on New Caledonia. At once, life is even harder there: with job competition, loss of extended family, unfamiliar customs and languages, exploitation, urban crowding, squalor, and finally drugs and crime. And still they quit their natal isles in droves. More Cook Islanders, Niueans and American Samoans, for example, live and work abroad than are left at home.

At present the greatest island problem is economic sustainability. Development is normally too costly, yet standing still means sliding back. Nearly all islands are dependent on foreign aid of some kind. Certainly islanders prefer trade over aid, but many have only white sandy beaches and palm-fringed lagoons to pander. Still, most islands lie too remote and remain too poor to develop a resort, port or landing strip. Ancient subsistence modes ever grip too many small islands. And most larger ones are finding it all but impossible to join the global economy.

To stand at the interface of a cosmopolitan and an island life is the 'ideal' for many who have given the topic serious thought – isolation with proximity, nature with culture – and an array of islands can indeed offer this: North Stradbroke, Waiheke, Jersey, Bainbridge, Gotland and so many more. One doesn't really need a Manhattan (which vies with Hong Kong as the world's most crowded island) to find insular life rewarding. Yet many are destroying this important balance to pamper an imported chimera or to redress the cost of World Bank debt servicing: Madagascar, Indonesia and the Philippines are even razing entire forests, well on their way to imitating the ancient Easter Islanders. In this they are dooming themselves and their descendants and taking countless innocent species with them.

Islands everywhere continue to suffer the human onslaught, now even from under the seas. In January 1993 the Liberian-registered supertanker *Braer* wrecked off Shetland, leaking almost 600,000 barrels of crude oil that then devastated bird and sea life, polluted pristine strands and necessitated an outrageously expensive clean-up. Only a few days later, in the Andaman Sea, the *Sanco Honour*'s collision with the *Maersk Navigator* released nearly 2 million barrels of crude which then polluted Nicobar and Sumatran shores. Worst of all was the collision between two supertankers off Tobago in 1979 that polluted the Caribbean with 2,200,000 barrels.

Yet our future holds man-made threats even greater than this. Twenty times the amount of oil that leaked from the Deepwater Horizon disaster of 2010 in the Gulf of Mexico will soon be escaping from submerged wrecks of oil tankers, most of them dating from the Second World War and many of them near islands: more than 8,500 'submarine time bombs'.[15] In 2010 the British tanker *Darkdale*, sunk by the Germans in 1941 off St Helena in the South Atlantic, began releasing her 4,000 tonnes of oil at last. Over 50 Japanese wrecks litter Chuuk Lagoon in the Federated States of Micronesia. About 1,700 wrecks threaten US coastal waters. Perhaps their poisonous cargo amounts to 2,500,000, perhaps 20 million tonnes. All will soon be revealed, that much is certain.

Most wrecks lie between Europe and North America/Caribbean and in the western Pacific. A 2001 typhoon broke open the military tanker USS *Mississinewa* – sunk by the Japanese in 1944 while carrying 20,000 tonnes of oil – in Ulithi Lagoon, Yap state, in the Federated States of Micronesia, polluting the shoreline. The British tanker *Coimbra*, carrying 11,000 tonnes of lubricating oil, was sunk by a U-boat in 1942 off Long Island, New York; for years the submarine wreck has been polluting the area's beaches. In the Pacific, 85 per cent of the wrecks are Japanese, the rest mostly American. In the Mediterranean, half are British, 16 per cent American. By international law, wrecks are the responsibility of their owners. In many cases the military wrecks belong to political entities – Germany, Japan and Italy during the Second World War – that no longer exist. Small island nations in particular could never afford the clean-up.

Though humankind appears to be islands' greatest threat, there looms one infinitely greater.

Nature herself.

THE PRICE

Vulnerability. This is surely the most painful insular constant. One cannot even hope to postpone the inevitable.

Hurricanes, volcanos, earthquakes, tsunamis – the Four Horsemen of the Islands. These formed them originally and they form them still. And a Fifth has now arrived: global warming, which is changing weather patterns, raising sea levels and putting new pressure on Earth's plates. Global warming creates 'thermal expansion' in that warm water takes up more room than cooler water. So the seas weigh more and press down harder on geological plates that fracture at the edges – just where isles abound.

Hurricanes (cyclones, typhoons) have forever plagued island societies, whose local architecture as a result eschewed permanent dwellings for lighter, ephemeral constructions. The most destructive Atlantic hurricane on record occurred in 1780 and killed some 22,000 in the Lesser Antilles. Now, with global warming, the frequency and intensity of such events have increased, bringing greater destruction, especially in the western Pacific and Caribbean. Thousands died in the Philippines when tropical storm Thelma struck in 1991. The following year hurricane Iniki caused $3 billion damage on Kaua'i in the Hawaiian Islands. Hurricane Ivan destroyed 90 per cent of Granada's homes in 2004. In 2008, hurricanes Gustav, Hanna and Ike took the lives of nearly 800 in Haiti. A horrible price to pay for island life – terror, destruction, death – the toll is ancient, one that most islanders have simply become inured to.

Volcanos frighten most, but damage least. Occasional exceptions, whereby an entire island can tremble like Keats's 'god in pain', do provide however quite spectacular statistics. By their geological nature most islands are located in major zones of volcanic activity and so eruptions might be expected: Japan, for one, currently registers 120 active volcanos. Nevertheless, eruptions are only fractionally as common as hurricanes or earthquakes. Nearly 2,000 years ago Pliny the Elder reported: 'During the Allies' War, Holy Island and Lipari among the Æolian Islands near Italy burnt in mid sea for several days, as did the sea itself, till a deputation from the senate performed a propitiatory ceremony.'[16] If only such a ceremony had saved the Indonesians centuries later. For on 15 April 1815 the volcano Tambora on Sumbawa, east of Lombok in the Malay Archipelago, erupted for five days, ejecting 160 cubic kilometres of material, spewing ash over 900 km, and killing 10,000 at once. (An estimated 66,000 died later from disease and starvation.) Up to one-fifth of the sun's heat and light was lost over the globe; Britain and Scandinavia had incessant rain from May until October; and the northeastern US suffered frost and snow through June. There was no summer in 1815.

And then there was Krakatoa (Indonesian Krakatau), 1,400 km to the west of Sumbawa. A small mountainous isle in the Sunda Strait between Sumatra and Java, for many centuries Krakatoa had been a navigational landmark. Her volcano had erupted in the 1600s, but re-vegetation had masked all evidence of this and everyone believed it extinct. For three months prior to 26 August 1883, inhabitants of neighbouring islands felt rumblings and frowned at plumes of smoke. Suddenly at one in the afternoon on this day loud explosions rent the air which then grew in intensity. A British sea captain 40 km away wrote: 'The ear-drums of over half my crew have been shattered.'[17] An hour later a giant black cloud shrouded the strait. As the world turned dark, a series of tsunamis struck Java's and Sumatra's coastal villages. All night long the sky was 'one second intense blackness, the next a blaze of fire'. At 10 am on 27 August 1883, Krakatoa incandesced, blasting fire, rock and ash heavenwards. A series of frightful tsunamis – some with waves up to 40 m in height – annihilated all life on adjacent isles. The blast reverberated on Rodrigues Island east of Mauritius over 4,500 km away. Ash fell on ships 6,000 km away. For one entire day the Sunda Strait brooded in black oblivion. 165 villages had disappeared from the face of the earth.

Some 36,400 people had died, mostly from the tsunamis. Only one-third of Krakatoa remained. Just to her north, new islands had surfaced. The eruption had driven a massive plume of gas and ash into the upper atmosphere, reddening sunsets worldwide and cooling Earth by more than one degree. Later, Krakatoa rose again. A fishing crew reported in 1927 that they had seen smoke rising from her crater, and two years later Anak Krakatau ('Child of Krakatoa') announced her presence in the Sunda Strait. In 1953 eruptions enhanced the cone to 60 m above sea level. Since the 1950s Anak Krakatau has been growing 13 cm per week and recent eruptions have caused growing anxiety in the region.

Island volcanos have since demanded an exorbitant toll in many places. The worst such event of the twentieth century was Mount

Pelée's 1902 eruption on Martinique in the eastern Caribbean, claiming around 30,000 lives in the city of Saint Pierre. The Philippines' Mount Taal erupted in 1911, costing 1,340 lives. Indonesia's Mount Kelud in East Java erupted in 1912, killing over 5,000. In 1951 New Guinea's Mount Lamington erupted, with 3,000 lives lost. The eruption of New Zealand's Mount Ruapehu in 1953 claimed 152. Bali's Agung erupted in 1963, killing 1,500 and destroying the homes of thousands. Mount Laki on Iceland erupted in 1973, resulting in terrible floods that took more than 9,000 lives, destroyed around 80 per cent of Iceland's livestock, and ruined great swathes of arable land. The Philippines' Mount Pinatubo erupted in 1991 and killed over 800; it has remained quite active ever since. Dormant for centuries, the Soufrière Hills volcano on Montserrat in the Caribbean's Lesser Antilles erupted in 1995 and buried the island's capital, Plymouth, under more than 12 m of mud; a protracted series of eruptions followed, among which one, in 1997, killed nineteen islanders in a pyroclastic flow; the volcano again burst to life in 2009–10, raining down ash on nearby Guadeloupe and Antigua. In 2010 Java's Mount Merapi erupted, costing 353 lives. The explosive eruption of Iceland's Eyjafjallajökull, also in 2010, caused no deaths but resulted in the closure of airspace over Europe for the first time in history and seriously disrupted international air travel; in May 2011 a different Icelandic volcano, Grimsvötn, shut airspace again over Ireland, Scotland and northern Germany in an eruption that released ten to a hundred times as much ash. In the same month Europe's most active volcano, Etna on Sicily, began erupting again for the first time since 1992.

Island earthquakes exact terrible tolls, too, especially when coupled with tsunamis that can sweep away tens of thousands of lives. Pliny the Elder documented how 'the sea suddenly snatched away more than 30,000 paces together with most of the human beings from the Island of Ceos, and half the city of Tyndaris in Sicily'.[18] A 1692 earthquake that struck Port Royal in Jamaica, one of the wealthiest and busiest ports in the West Indies, caused two-thirds of the town (13 ha) to sink into the sea; this and the subsequent tsunami claimed around 2,000 lives, with a further 3,000 perishing of injuries and disease shortly afterwards. In more recent times, the 1995 earthquake in Kōbe, Japan, cost more than 6,000 lives. The earthquake and tsunami which struck the Indian Ocean in 2004 killed more than 230,000, the earthquake's magnitude of between 9.1 and 9.3 making it the third largest ever recorded; it is regarded as one of the ten worst in history in regard to loss of human life – the islands of Indonesia alone lost more than 200,000, with further 500,000 displaced. The two near-simultaneous Samoan earthquakes of 2009, the largest of the year at magnitude 8, caused a tsunami that resulted in nearly 200 deaths in Samoa, American Samoa and Tonga. The Haitian earthquake of January 2010 cost the lives of between 92,000 and 220,000 and left as many as 1,800,000 homeless. In February 2010 a magnitude 8.8 earthquake struck off Concepción, Chile, and sent a tsunami towards Robinson Crusoe Island in the Juan Fernández archipelago, some 600 km to the west: the wave, estimated by some as 6 m high, was funnelled into Cumberland Bay where the island's only village, San Juan Bautista, is located; the tsunami destroyed the small settlement and swept away several villagers – there had been no warning. The Sumatran earthquake of October 2010 caused a tsunami that struck the Mentawai Islands, resulting in nearly 500 deaths and leaving around 20,000 homeless.

During the writing of this book Christchurch, New Zealand, has suffered grievously from innumerable earthquakes: from September 2010 till May 2011 there were no fewer than five and a half thousand aftershocks. And then, in June 2011, within a little over an hour of one another a 5.7- then a 6.3-magnitude quake struck. Though the protracted succession of aftershocks – New Zealand's greatest natural disaster – is revolutionizing seismologists' understanding of fault interaction, the people of Christchurch are asking whether they have a future. One thing is certain: more shocks will come. It is an unprecedented disaster-in-progress.

Then came Japan. The quake that struck Honshū's northeast on 11 March 2011, now officially known as the Great East Japan Earthquake, was the most powerful to have occurred in the country since AD 869, ravaging also the 260 pine-covered islands of Matsushima Bay. Because of an extremely destructive tsunami more than 20,000 died and over 10,000 are unaccounted for. With a potential cost of over $300 billion, it is already regarded as the world's most expensive natural disaster.

Such is the price of island life. Islanders are more exposed than mainlanders to nature's most violent forces, and plants and animals suffer in greater numbers than humans. Worst is the combination of earthquake and tsunami. Such catastrophes ruin more than individual villages, farms, towns, existences: they can destroy national economies and obliterate entire habitats.

Since time immemorial, it seems, a boat-shaped island of hope has graced the Tiber in central Rome. Situated at the fabled river's southern bend, the Isola Tiberina – a 270-m-long and 67-m-wide holm – has been sailing History herself, one might say, her two bridges linking the Eternal City to her special power of healing. For here was erected in the third century BC the Temple of Æsculapius, the Roman god of medicine. After the second century BC several other temples rose. In the Middle Ages the Basilica of S. Bartolomeo dominated the erstwhile site of Æsculapius's temple. In 1584, on the western half of the island, a hospital opened whose doors have never shut. Thus, amid the cosmopolitan crush, Tiber Island yet dispenses physical and spiritual renewal.

As do many islands, for those who learn them and care.

In an age when isolation of any sort is disappearing, social responsibility has become the universal imperative. We accept we must grow more aware of our surroundings, then act according to increased understanding if we wish to survive as a species and to assist thousands of fellow creatures to do the same. Islands are benchmarks for all of us in this process, helping to heal a wounded planet.

Bermuda, for example, has begun one of the most robust conservation programmes in the Atlantic.[19] It was high time, for by the early 1900s little native vegetation had been left there and Bermuda's cedar forests were decimated in 1942 by a scale blight introduced from California. In one such programme 5.7-ha Nonsuch – in the 1800s a yellow fever quarantine islet – has been designated a national treasure reserve that features the Nonsuch Island Living Museum pioneered and led by David Wingate (*b.* 1935), who removed most foreign flora and fauna and reintroduced native biota. Nonsuch now impresses select visitors with a recreated Bermuda as she once flourished before human impact.

A similar 'Tiberinan hope' echoes on Codfish Island (off Stewart Island) and Anchor Island (in Dusky Sound, Fiordland National Park) in New Zealand's extreme south. That icon of insular bio-survival, the kakapo (*Strigops habroptila*), a large, flightless, nocturnal parrot endemic to New Zealand – one of the world's longest living birds and perhaps the world's most endangered bird

The Isola Tiberina, oasis of hope in the midst of Imperial Rome,
with the Temple of Æsculapius at the far end.

species – has responded well to managed isolation on these two
islets controlled by the Department of Conservation. Safe from all
predators, kakapo have finally attained a breeding minimum of 131,
suggesting species survival. For many years it had been touch-and-
go. Each bird is given a name and monitored individually, something only an islet control programme can achieve.

Recalling Haiti and Christchurch and Japan; seeing the dangers
and consoling with victims; conceding the ubiquitous suburban-
ization now obliterating one's traditions and quality of life in this
twenty-first century, one welcomes any such 'Tiberinan hope'
intimating sustained viability. Greater ecological care is paramount.
Modern coral monitoring, for example, can aid defenceless
islanders and force polluters to assume responsibility. In 2002 a
cargo ship wrecked outside Yap's main lagoon, releasing 200,000
litres of oil that harmed the coral reef.[20] Four years later a judge
awarded the Yap people $861,600 in damages, a judgment based on
a new scientific technique measuring genetic coding of proteins in

coral. Most importantly, the case publicized coral reefs' ability to rally against warming oceans – so long as they remain healthy. It's really our call, in other words.

But simple geography of isolation, lack of resources and a small labour force overwhelm even a modest advancement for most islands. When modern demands intrude, most small islands simply cannot keep up. Also, climate change impacts on islanders more egregiously than on continentals:

> The smaller landmass and proportionately longer coastline indicates that a large component of their most productive land could be adversely affected. Moreover, the environmental management strategies of small island communities, including resource and social planning capacities, are less well developed than those of larger nations.[21]

Unhappily, islanders' traditional conservation practices fell to centuries of rabid European and American exploitation that knew no limits. Ancient securities were lost. But today many are being found again through re-awakened awareness, responsible legislation and modern science. In the Pacific, for example, Papua New Guinea and the Cook Islands are now fusing traditional law with modern democratic legislation; Hawai'i, Tahiti and New Zealand would like to do the same, but are often thwarted by commercial interests and/or governmental obstruction. Lack of enforcement still remains a serious issue, as many islands stay weak and vulnerable targets of foreign governments and transnational corporations. Still, one must try to overcome the odds.

> It is generally agreed that whatever the future holds, the return of island ecosystems to as near a pristine condition as is possible will be important, not only in allowing the ecosystems to have the most beneficial response to global change, but for maintaining the sustainability of the most important economic activities of the islands.[22]

One serious problem is global warming's heating of the oceans, leading to a measurable rise in sea level. Around 2.4 per cent of Earth's water is currently ice. Pushing hurricanes, cyclones and typhoons further north and south, tropical climates might soon expand towards the poles, melting glacial ice. Over the last century the sea level rose between 1 and 2 cm and the rate of rise now appears to be accelerating.[23] If emissions are allowed to grow at current rates the sea level will rise between 0.9 and 1.6 m by 2100 – perhaps even sooner, given Antarctica's and Greenland's accelerated melting. Many coastal cities and plains would of course disappear. So would some 200,000 low-lying islands, many of them nations. Conversely, perhaps an equal number of islands would also be 'calved' as coastal hills and ranges isolate from mainlands. Such is the give and take of our planet's island history.

Global warming will increasingly transform those islands and island cultures we currently know. Greater mortality, loss of crops and tourism, failed economies, increased emigration – 'ghost islands' will proliferate. Of course for many low-lying coral islands the sea-level rise will mean oblivion. Robust survivors, coral-reef islands might fare better than reefless islands – *if* they remain unpolluted and not too greatly challenged by rising temperatures. Increased storm intensities and frequencies will erode cays and damage protective reefs, however. All reef islands could erode in higher seas; more critically, small freshwater 'lenses' will be easily destroyed by saltwater pollution, ending any agriculture. Tuvalu's fresh water, for example, is even now disappearing: upwelling saltwater is making the cultivation of taro and other crops impossible. Most Tuvaluans now plant in plastic buckets and water gutters. Only increased rainfall through climate change might grant them a reprieve.

High islands – Tonga, Samoa, Hawai'i, Japan, Cuba, Sri Lanka and so on – will experience increased growth rate in vegetation due to CO_2's fertilizing affect, if their soils have sufficient water and nutrients for new growth. But they, too, will suffer more frequent and more powerful storms. Through erosion all islands will forfeit their low-lying lands to the sea, likely losing on low islands the best nurseries or habitats for local sea life, on high islands the best food-producing land.[24] On non-tropical islands increasing humidity and rainfall will raise the risk of pathogens: bacteria and fungi could well end all life there. Tourist beaches will wash away; wildfires will wipe clean entire nesoscapes. Maplecroft, a British risk analysis firm, produced in 2010 the Climate Change Vulnerability Index covering the next 30 years: the least negatively affected countries will be the Scandinavian nations and their islands, as well as the island nations of Ireland and Iceland; the most vulnerable include the Philippines and Madagascar.[25]

For some islands the sea level rise will come slowly: seas will simply wash higher each year, as already happened in the sixth and seventh centuries AD at ancient Heracleion and Eastern Canopus near Alexandria, both of which were gradually submerged. Or, like with the medieval Halligen or 'Holy Isles' of Germany's North Frisia, land may be eroded by wave action and washed away by currents. Other islands may frequently be inundated by storm surges – when tide, wind and waves can cause so much destruction that reconstruction might be pointless. Most islands will not submerge entirely, but simply suffer more frequent flooding events. This much is clear: our world is getting warmer, oceans are rising, the rise is accelerating, and islands stand at greatest risk.

Low-island life may cease altogether on our planet. It has happened before and will happen again, perhaps sooner than one imagines. And the most ingenious geo-engineering schemes to counter the inevitable – 'jacking-up' terrain and towns; cooling the seas with tiny bubbles; reining in the glaciers; somehow 'unplugging' the oceans themselves; 'up-pumping' Antarctic waters to freeze; spraying the stratosphere with sulphate droplets to cool the planet; building 'floating cities' – are not only science fiction but science *faux*, with the potential to cause more harm than good: the 'mongoose syndrome' all over again. Low-lying atolls really have only two practicable recourses: bulwarks or abandonment. The first is preferable, but unaffordable; the second is practicable, but devastating. Currently at greatest risk are, among others, the Maldives, Tuvalu, Tokelau, Kiribati, the Tuamotus and Anguilla.

Some islands seem geologically 'pre-programmed' to cope with the effects of climate change. As the sea rises, the most vulnerable coral reef islands, for example, can self-defend by producing more sediment, thus increasing mass, something pointed out as early as 1994 by Australian geomorphologist David Hopley (*b.* 1940).[26] In the most recent survey, the land surface of 27 Pacific islands was scanned from 1950 to 2010 using aerial photographs and high-resolution satellite images.[27] Most of the islands have remained stable over the past 60 years; some have even grown. Though local sea level rose by 120 mm, only four islands were smaller than they had been in the 1950s. It appears that coral debris of low-lying islands – eroding from surrounding reefs and accumulating through the combined actions of currents, waves and winds – will continuously 'feed' an island. Also causeways and other constructions linking islands boost growth by trapping sediment. When Pacific hurricane Bebe struck in 1972, depositing 140 hectares of debris onto Tuvalu's eastern reef, her main island grew 10 per cent. Tuvalu's trig point is 4.5 m above sea level. Since the 1950s seven islands in one of Tuvalu's nine atolls on average grew 3 per cent; alone Funamanu gained 0.44 hectares, almost 30 per cent of her earlier area. In Kiribati the three major urbanized islands all grew: Betio (36 ha, 30 per cent), Bairiki (5.8 ha, 16.3 per cent) and Nanikai (0.8 ha, 12.5 per cent).

Though islands can so 'respond' to rising seas, any acceleration to the rise might overtake sediment accumulation. Temperatures are now accelerating and the sea level rise rate is as unknown as island growth potential. The world's first climate change asylum seekers are apparently the residents of Papua New Guinea's isolated Carteret Islands: as the rising sea level is taking land, contaminating water supplies and inundating crops with saltwater the PNG government early in 2010 initiated a relocation programme, but so far only few families have resettled to Bougainville 86 km to the southwest. Experts predict the Carterets will soon be uninhabitable.

One must anticipate even more frequent and more intense volcanos, earthquakes and tsunamis in future with global warming causing heavier oceans and putting even more stress on submarine plates, effecting more frequent fracturing and movement. On 26 December 2004 came the Sumatran quake at 9.1 on the Richter scale; in the Kuril Islands on 15 November 2006, 8.3, then on 13 January 2007, 8.1; and finally on 11 March 2011 the Great East Japan Earthquake, 9.0. 'What is clear', warned Thorne Lay of the University of California, Santa Cruz, already in 2010, 'is that for the 6.2 years since 2004, there have been more great earthquakes around the world than in any 6.2-year period throughout the 110-year history of seismic recordings.'[28]

At the same time, global warming is altering island storm patterns. It appears that by the end of the twenty-first century the frequency of tropical cyclones will have fallen by 31 per cent over Southeast Asia but increased by 65 per cent over the north-central Pacific. As a result there will be fewer cyclones in the Philippines and southern China, but more in the Hawaiian Islands.[29] With stronger irradiation, greater evaporation will generate increased cloud cover, over time altering local weather patterns on islands throughout the world.[30]

That first, stunning 'Earthrise' photograph taken from the moon in 1968 by US astronaut William Anders (*b.* 1933) heralded above all that Earth herself is an island: isolated, nourishing many inter-dependent life forms, constantly in change, eroding, adapting, aging – and so utterly vulnerable to external threats: meteorite strikes, solar storms, asteroid collisions, gamma ray bursts. Perhaps Earth is living Gaia after all, as British environmentalist James Lovelock (*b.* 1919) proposed decades back: a self-regulating system that robustly manipulates the environment in order to maintain those conditions most favourable for her own survival.[31] But the story of all islands – metaphorical or real – is complex and obstinate and never ends in moral absolutes.

The final constant is surely time itself, as already divined by a Greek-speaking Sicilian back in the fifth century BC. For Empedocles knew

As long as water, islands;
As long as fire, islands.

We shall all go, but islands will endure. Then, in several hundred million years, the last continent, Novo-Pangæa, will be describing 70 per cent less coastline and far, far fewer islands. In 1.2 to 1.4 billion years the oceans will have evaporated away. And in seven billion years – æons after the dodo and kiwi, after Minoan Crete and Manhattan, after the Battle of Naxos and Hiroshima, after Atlantis and *Treasure Island* – a solitary feature will haunt a golden planet of molten rock roasting in the rays of a red giant Sun . . .

The last isle.

References

Preface

1 Quoted in Philip Dodd and Ben Donald, *The Book of Islands* (Wingfield, SA, 2008), inside jacket.

one: . . . of Stone and Sand

1 Jack Szostak, 'Out of a Harsh and Hostile Earth', *New Scientist*, 2772 (7 August 2010), p. 26.
2 Ovid, *Metamorphoses*, XV, quoted in Louise B. Young, *Islands: Portraits of Miniature Worlds* (New York, 1999), p. 181.
3 Frank H. Talbot, 'Introduction', in *Oceans and Islands*, ed. Frank H. Talbot and Robert E. Stevenson (London, 1991), p. 10.
4 David Hopley, 'Worlds Apart', in *Islands*, ed. Robert E. Stevenson and Frank H. Talbot (London, 1994), p. 14.
5 The definitions are taken from Judy Pearsall, ed., *The Concise Oxford Dictionary* (10th edn, Oxford, 1999).
6 C. T. Onions, ed., *The Shorter Oxford English Dictionary on Historical Principles* (3rd revd edn, Oxford, 1973), p. 268.
7 *New Scientist*, 2770 (24 July 2010), p. 10.
8 Robert E. Stevenson, 'Foreword', in *Islands*, ed. Stevenson and Talbot, p. 11.
9 Richard W. Grigg, 'The Formation of Coral Islands', in *Oceans and Islands*, ed. Talbot and Stevenson, pp. 144–5.
10 Pliny, *Natural History*, II, 87, trans. H. Rackham (Cambridge, MA, and London, 1949), vol. I, pp. 331–3.
11 Young, *Islands*, p. 7.
12 David Hopley, 'Continental Islands', in *Islands*, ed. Stevenson and Talbot, p. 24.
13 Ibid., p. 17.
14 John C. Yaldwyn, 'Land of the Moa', in *Islands*, ed. Stevenson and Talbot, pp. 74–5.
15 Hopley, 'Continental Islands', pp. 24–6.
16 Pliny, *Natural History*, II, 90, vol. I, p. 335.

17 Young, *Islands*, pp. 182–3.

18 Stevenson, Foreword, p. 11.

19 Graham Joyner, 'Crete: An Ancient Island State', in *Oceans and Islands*, ed. Talbot and Stevenson, pp. 175–7.

20 Lawrence Durrell, *The Greek Islands* (London, 1978), p. 266.

21 Terence Lindsey, 'Arctic Islands', in *Islands*, ed. Stevenson and Talbot, p. 104.

22 Knowles Kerry, 'The Subantarctic Islands', in *Oceans and Islands*, ed. Talbot and Stevenson, p. 171.

23 Bent Fredskild, 'Greenland', in *Islands*, ed. Stevenson and Talbot, p. 134.

24 Hopley, 'Continental Islands', pp. 26–7.

25 Young, *Islands*, p. 126.

26 Ibid., p. 6.

27 Alexander Malahoff, 'Oceanic Volcanoes', in *Oceans and Islands*, ed. Talbot and Stevenson, p. 127.

28 Ibid.

29 Sheena Coupe, 'Krakatoa: An Island Erupts', in *Oceans and Islands*, ed. Talbot and Stevenson, p. 128.

30 Paul Michael Taylor, 'The Indonesian Archipelago', in *Islands*, ed. Stevenson and Talbot, p. 110.

31 Malahoff, 'Oceanic Volcanoes', p. 131.

32 Alexander Malahoff, 'From Volcanoes to Islands', in *Islands*, ed. Stevenson and Talbot, pp. 38–9.

33 Young, *Islands*, p. 14.

34 Richard S. Fiske, 'Unstable Oceanic Volcanoes', in *Islands*, ed. Stevenson and Talbot, pp. 42–4.

35 Malahoff, 'Oceanic Volcanoes', p. 130.

36 Pliny, *Natural History*, II, 89, vol. I, pp. 333–5.

37 Young, *Islands*, p. 215.

38 Grigg, 'The Formation of Coral Islands', p. 141.

39 Ibid., p. 142.

40 Ibid., p. 143.

41 Hopley, 'Continental Islands', p. 19.

42 Richard S. Fiske, 'The Instability of Oceanic Volcanoes', in *Oceans and Islands*, ed. Talbot and Stevenson, p. 136.

43 *New Scientist*, 2774 (21 August 2010), p. 16.

44 Hopley, 'Continental Islands', pp. 27–8.

45 Ibid., pp. 29–30.

46 Grigg, 'The Formation of Coral Islands', pp. 143–4.

47 Hopley, 'Continental Islands', pp. 28–9.

48 Pliny, *Natural History*, II, 96, vol. I, pp. 339–41.

49 Ibid., II, 92, p. 337 and note *a* on p. 336.

50 Young, *Islands*, p. 170.

two: . . . of Ferns and Feathers

1 Mark F. Large and John E. Braggins, *Tree Ferns* (Cambridge, 2004), pp. 120–21.

2 Louise B. Young, *Islands: Portraits of Miniature Worlds* (New York, 1999), p. 7.

References

3 John C. Yaldwyn, 'Land of the Moa', in *Islands*, ed. Robert E. Stevenson and Frank H. Talbot (London, 1994), p. 75.

4 Young, *Islands*, p. 10.

5 Quoted ibid., p. 54.

6 David Quammen, *The Song of the Dodo: Island Biogeography in an Age of Extinctions* (New York, 1996), p. 436.

7 Quoted in Young, *Islands*, p. 70.

8 Ibid., p. 119.

9 Storrs L. Olson, 'The Atlantic Islands', in *Islands*, ed. Stevenson and Talbot, p. 87.

10 Quoted in E. Alison Kay, 'The Pacific Islands', in *Oceans and Islands*, ed. Frank H. Talbot and Robert E. Stevenson (London, 1991), p. 159.

11 Ibid.

12 Ibid., pp. 161–2.

13 Ibid., p. 161.

14 Ibid., pp. 162–3.

15 Ibid., p. 163.

16 Ibid., p. 164.

17 Ibid., p. 159.

18 Yaldwyn, 'Land of the Moa', pp. 74–5.

19 Kay, 'The Pacific Islands', pp. 164–5.

20 Ibid., p. 164.

21 G. M. Wellington, 'The Galapagos Islands', in *Oceans and Islands*, ed. Talbot and Stevenson, pp. 155–8.

22 Ibid., p. 157.

23 Ibid.

24 Richard W. Grigg, 'The Formation of Coral Islands', in *Islands*, ed. Stevenson and Talbot, p. 49.

25 Ibid., p. 146.

26 Ibid.

27 Harold Heatwole, 'The Colonization of Coral Islands', in *Oceans and Islands*, ed. Talbot and Stevenson, p. 147.

28 Ibid., p. 151.

29 Ibid., p. 153.

30 Storrs L. Olson, 'The Atlantic Islands', in *Oceans and Islands*, ed. Talbot and Stevenson, p. 166.

31 Olson, 'The Atlantic Islands', in *Islands*, ed. Stevenson and Talbot, pp. 84–5.

32 Olson, in *Oceans and Islands*, p. 168.

33 Olson, in *Islands*, ed. Stevenson and Talbot, p. 85.

34 *New Scientist*, 2770 (24 July 2010), p. 10.

35 Olson, 'The Atlantic Islands', in *Oceans and Islands*, p. 167.

36 Lawrence Durrell, *The Greek Islands* (London, 1978), p. 270.

37 Ibid., p. 274.

38 Ibid., p. 247.

39 Diana Walker, 'Islands of the Indian Ocean', in *Oceans and Islands*, ed. Talbot and Stevenson, p. 168.

40 David Hopley, 'Worlds Apart', in *Islands*, ed. Stevenson and Talbot, p. 17.

41 Young, *Islands*, pp. 97–8.

42 Walker, 'Islands of the Indian Ocean', p. 170.
43 Young, *Islands*, p. 109.
44 Quoted ibid., p. 127.
45 Walker, 'Islands of the Indian Ocean', p. 169.
46 Leslie Thomas, *A World of Islands* (London, 1983), p. 167.
47 Young, *Islands*, pp. 123–5.
48 Quoted in Thomas, *A World of Islands*, p. 181.
49 Walker, 'Islands of the Indian Ocean', p. 169.
50 Paul Michael Taylor, 'The Indonesian Archipelago', in *Islands*, ed. Stevenson and Talbot, p. 110.
51 Terence Lindsey, 'Arctic Islands', in *Islands*, ed. Stevenson and Talbot, p. 104.
52 Ibid., p. 106.
53 Knowles Kerry, 'The Subantarctic Islands', in *Oceans and Islands*, ed. Talbot and Stevenson, pp. 171–2.
54 Ibid., p. 172.
55 Alec C. Brown, 'Introduced Species', in *Oceans and Islands*, ed. Talbot and Stevenson, pp. 218–9.
56 Quoted ibid., p. 219.
57 Olson, 'The Atlantic Islands', in *Islands*, ed. Stevenson and Talbot, p. 87.
58 *New Scientist*, 2774 (21 August 2010), p. 16.
59 Terence Lindsey, 'Introduced Species', in *Islands*, ed. Stevenson and Talbot, p. 152.
60 James Fergusson, *The Vitamin Murders* (London, 2007), p. 111.
61 Young, *Islands*, p. 9.
62 Ibid., p. 91.

three: . . . of First Footprints

1 See Steven Roger Fischer, *Evidence for Hellenic Dialect in the Phaistos Disk* (Bern, Frankfurt am Main, New York, Paris, 1988), and also *Glyphbreaker* (New York, 1997), pp. 1–137. For his decipherments of Crete's Phaistos Disk (1984) and of Easter Island's *rongorongo* script (1993), the author was elected a Fellow of the Royal Society (NZ) on 6 October 2010, during the writing of this book.
2 Pliny, *Natural History*, VII, 57, trans. H. Rackham (Cambridge, MA, and London, 1947), vol. II , p. 647.
3 Thucydides, *History of the Peloponnesian War*, I, 4, trans. Charles Forster Smith (Cambridge, MA, and London, 1980), vol. I, p. 9.
4 Kerry R. Howe, *Nature, Culture, and History: The 'Knowing' of Oceania* (Honolulu, HI, 2000), pp. 74–5, and Clive Ponting, *A Green History of the World* (London, 1992).
5 Colin Martin, 'The First Explorers', in *Oceans and Islands*, ed. Frank H. Talbot and Robert E. Stevenson (London, 1991), pp. 95–6.
6 *New Scientist*, 2764 (12 June 2010), p. 16.
7 Kenneth McPherson, 'People of the Indian Ocean', in *Oceans and Islands*, ed. Talbot and Stevenson, p. 188.
8 Deborah and Peter Rowley-Conwy, 'A Fortress Built by Nature?', in *Islands*, ed. Robert E. Stevenson and Frank H. Talbot (London, 1994), p. 114.
9 *New Scientist*, 2777 (11 September 2010), pp. 6–7.

References

10 Steven Roger Fischer, *A History of the Pacific Islands* (Basingstoke, 2002), pp. 11–12.

11 John Davies, *A History of Wales* (revd edn, London, 2007), p. 13.

12 Quoted in Louise B. Young, *Islands: Portraits of Miniature Worlds* (New York, 1999), p. 160.

13 Barry Cunliffe, *The Extraordinary Voyage of Pytheas the Greek* (London, 2002), p. 85.

14 Ibid., p. 131.

15 Pliny, *Natural History*, IV, 16, vol. II, p. 199.

16 Ibid., pp. 102–4.

17 Pliny, *Natural History*, XXXVI, 18, trans. D. E. Eichholz (Cambridge, MA, and London, 1949), vol. X, pp. 65–7.

18 Lawrence Durrell, *The Greek Islands* (London, 1978), p. 272.

19 Ibid., p. 255.

20 Cunliffe, *The Extraordinary Voyage of Pytheas the Greek*, p. 30.

21 Durrell, *The Greek Islands*, p. 159.

22 Quoted in Young, *Islands*, p. 166.

23 Durrell, *The Greek Islands*, pp. 125–6.

24 Ibid., p. 9.

25 Leslie Thomas, *A World of Islands* (London, 1983), p. 112.

26 McPherson, 'People of the Indian Ocean', p. 188.

27 Martin, 'The First Explorers', in *Oceans and Islands*, ed. Talbot and Stevenson, p. 96.

28 Frank H. Talbot, 'Zanzibar', in *Islands*, ed. Stevenson and Talbot, p. 143.

29 Fischer, *A History of the Pacific Islands*, p. 35.

30 McPherson, 'People of the Indian Ocean', pp. 188–9.

31 Tim Severin, *The Brendan Voyage: Across the Atlantic in a Leather Boat* (Dublin, 2005).

32 Bent Fredskild, 'Greenland', in *Islands*, ed. Stevenson and Talbot, pp. 134–5.

33 George Gordon, Lord Byron, 'Childe Harold's Pilgrimage', IV, i.

34 Sidney W. Mintz, 'Three Atlantic Islands', in *Oceans and Islands*, ed. Talbot and Stevenson, p. 184.

35 Young, *Islands*, pp. 183–4.

36 Christopher Columbus, *The Journal of Christopher Columbus*, trans. Cecil Jane (London, 1960), p. 40.

37 Quoted in Thomas, *A World of Islands*, p. 70.

38 Quoted in Howe, *Nature, Culture, and History*, p. 9.

39 Richard H. Grove, *Green Imperialism: Colonial Expansion, Tropical Island Edens and the Origins of Environmentalism, 1600–1860* (Cambridge, 1995), p. 23.

40 McPherson, 'People of the Indian Ocean', p. 190.

41 Quoted in Thomas, *A World of Islands*, p. 25.

42 Mintz, 'Three Atlantic Islands', pp. 184–6.

43 Fredskild, 'Greenland', in *Islands*, ed. Stevenson and Talbot, pp. 135–6.

44 J. C. Beaglehole, ed., *The 'Endeavour' Journal of Joseph Banks, 1768–1771* (Sydney, 1963), vol. I, p. 252.

45 J. C. Beaglehole, ed., *The Voyage of the 'Endeavour', 1768–1771* (London, 1988), vol. I, p. 187.

46 Louis-Antoine de Bougainville, *A Voyage Round the World . . . in the Frigate 'La Boudeuse' and the Store Ship 'L'Étoile'*, trans. J. R. Forster (London, 1772), pp. 228–9.

47 Ibid., p. 257.

48 John Prest, *The Garden of Eden: The Botanic Garden and the Re-creation of Paradise* (New Haven, CT, 1981), pp. 27–9.

49 Ibid.

50 Howe, *Nature, Culture, and History*, p. 10.

51 Quoted in Thomas, *A World of Islands*, p. 201.

52 Philip Houghton, *People of the Great Ocean: Aspects of Human Biology of the Early Pacific* (Cambridge, 1996), and John Miles, *Infectious Diseases: Colonizing the Pacific?* (Dunedin, 1997).

53 Quoted in Beaglehole, ed., *The Voyage of the 'Endeavour', 1768–1771*, vol. I, p. 99.

54 Howe, *Nature, Culture, and History*, p. 43.

55 Ibid., p. 42.

56 Ibid. See also Roy MacLeod and Philip F. Rehbock, eds, *Nature in Its Greatest Extent: Western Science in the Pacific* (Honolulu, HI, 1988), and Roy MacLeod and Philip F. Rehbock, eds, *Evolutionary Theory and the Natural History of the Pacific: Darwin's Laboratory* (Honolulu, HI, 1994).

57 Quoted in Thomas, *A World of Islands*, p. 147.

58 McPherson, 'People of the Indian Ocean', pp. 190–91.

59 Fischer, *A History of the Pacific Islands*, pp. 95–120.

60 Norma McArthur, *Island Populations of the Pacific* (Canberra, 1967).

61 Howe, *Nature, Culture, and History*, p. 67.

62 T. R. St. Johnston, *The Islands of the Pacific, or the Children of the Sun* (New York, 1921), p. 12, quoted in Howe, *Nature, Culture, and History*, p. 53.

63 Translator's preface to J.J.H. de Labillardière, *Voyage in Search of La Pérouse, Performed by the Order of the Constituent Assembly during the Years 1791, 1792, 1793, and 1794* (London, 1800), p. vii, quoted in Howe, *Nature, Culture, and History*, p. 38.

64 Howe, *Nature, Culture, and History*, p. 38.

65 Ibid., p. 22.

66 Fischer, *A History of the Pacific Islands*, pp. 252–3.

67 Young, *Islands*, p. 214.

68 Paul Michael Taylor, 'The Indonesian Archipelago', in *Islands*, ed. Stevenson and Talbot, p. 113.

69 Ibid.

70 Fredskild, 'Greenland', pp. 135–6.

four: . . . of Tin and Tans

1 Steven Roger Fischer, *A History of the Pacific Islands* (Basingstoke, 2002), p. 44.

2 R. F. Willetts, *The Civilisation of Ancient Crete* (London, 1992).

3 Fischer, *A History of the Pacific Islands*, p. 20.

4 Barry Cunliffe, *The Extraordinary Voyage of Pytheas the Greek* (London, 2002), p. 120.

5 Malcolm H. Goyns, *Saffron* (Abingdon, Oxfordshire, 1999).

References

6 Colin Martin, 'The First Explorers', in *Oceans and Islands*, ed. Frank H. Talbot and Robert E. Stevenson (London, 1991), p. 96.

7 Ibid.

8 Lawrence Durrell, *The Greek Islands* (London, 1978), p. 126.

9 Ibid.

10 Ibid., p. 241.

11 Keith Hopkins, 'The Transport of Staples in the Roman Empire', in *Trade and Staples in Antiquity (Greece and Rome)*, ed. P. Garnsey and C. R. Whittaker (Budapest, 1987), p. 86.

12 Frank McLynn, *Marcus Aurelius: Warrior, Philosopher, Emperor* (London, 2010), p. 200.

13 Pliny, *Natural History*, IX, 58, trans. H. Rackham (Cambridge, MA, and London, 1956), vol. III, p. 243.

14 Leslie Thomas, *A World of Islands* (London, 1983), p. 80.

15 John Davies, *A History of Wales* (revd edn, London, 2007), p. 54.

16 Louise B. Young, *Islands: Portraits of Miniature Worlds* (New York, 1999), p. 86.

17 Ibid., p. 89.

18 Ibid., p. 91.

19 Kenneth McPherson, 'People of the Indian Ocean', in *Islands*, ed. Robert E. Stevenson and Frank H. Talbot (London, 1994), p. 140.

20 Sidney W. Mintz, 'Three Atlantic Islands', in *Oceans and Islands*, ed. Talbot and Stevenson, p. 187.

21 Young, *Islands*, p. 139.

22 William Lithgow, *The Total Discourse of the Rare Adventures of William Lithgow* (Glasgow, 1906), quoted in Durrell, *The Greek Islands*, p. 181.

23 Kerry R. Howe, *Nature, Culture, and History: The 'Knowing' of Oceania* (Honolulu, HI, 2000), p. 76.

24 Thomas, *A World of Islands*, pp. 6–7.

25 H. V. Morton, *In Search of England* (London, 1933), p. 62.

26 Captain Charles Johnson [Daniel Defoe?], *A General History of the Pyrates* (London, 1724).

27 Durrell, *The Greek Islands*, pp. 266–8.

28 Homer, *The Iliad*, XXI, 453–4, trans. A. T. Murray (Cambridge, MA, and London, 1985), vol. II, p. 441. In Book XXII, 44–5, Priam declares that Achilles 'hath made me bereft of sons many and valiant, slaying them and selling them into isles that lie afar'.

29 Davies, *A History of Wales*, p. 96.

30 Fischer, *A History of the Pacific Islands*, p. 122.

31 H. E. Maude, *Slavers in Paradise: The Peruvian Slave Trade in Polynesia, 1862–1864* (Canberra, 1981).

32 Fischer, *A History of the Pacific Islands*, pp. 100–1.

33 Thomas, *A World of Islands*, pp. 12–16.

34 Herman Melville, *Moby Dick*, quoted in Thomas, *A World of Islands*, p. 11.

35 William Reed, 'Pearls and Pearling', in *Oceans and Islands*, p. 205.

36 Quoted in Thomas, *A World of Islands*, p. 165.

37 Durrell, *The Greek Islands*, p. 258.

38 Howe, *Nature, Culture, and History*, p. 22.

39 Thomas, *A World of Islands*, pp. 36–7.

40 Howe, *Nature, Culture, and History*, p. 54.

41 Fischer, *A History of the Pacific Islands*, p. 274.

42 Quoted in Durrell, *The Greek Islands*, p. 237.

43 Ibid.

44 Ibid., p. 240.

45 McPherson, 'People of the Indian Ocean', p. 144.

46 Fischer, *A History of the Pacific Islands*, p. 269.

47 Ibid., p. 275.

48 Durrell, *The Greek Islands*, p. 250.

five: . . . of First Nations

1 Pliny, *Natural History*, VII, 57, trans. H. Rackham (Cambridge, MA, and London, 1947), vol. II, p. 647; Thucydides, *History of the Peloponnesian War*, I, 4, trans. Charles Forster Smith (Cambridge, MA, and London, 1980), vol. I, p. 9.

2 See the text of the Phaistos Disk commencing chapter Three.

3 Leslie Thomas, *A World of Islands* (London, 1983), p. 203.

4 Ibid., pp. 102–3.

5 Steven Roger Fischer, *A History of the Pacific Islands* (Basingstoke, 2002), pp. 210–11.

6 Ibid., p. 230.

7 Louise B. Young, *Islands: Portraits of Miniature Worlds* (New York, 1999), pp. 207–8.

8 Ibid., p. 209.

9 Jill Jolliffe, *Cover-up: The Inside Story of the Balibo Five* (Melbourne, 2001).

10 James Dunn, *Timor: A People Betrayed* (Brisbane, 1983), p. 26.

11 Jolliffe, *Cover-up*, p. 7.

12 'United Nations General Assembly Resolution 38/7', 2 November 1983.

13 Lawrence Durrell, *The Greek Islands* (London, 1978), p. 92.

14 Kerry R. Howe, *Nature, Culture, and History: The 'Knowing' of Oceania* (Honolulu, HI, 2000), p. 15.

15 Paul McGuire, *Westward the Course: The New World of Oceania* (Melbourne, 1942); quoted in Howe, *Nature, Culture, and History*, p. 23.

16 Thomas, *A World of Islands*, p. 47.

17 Richard H. Grove, *Ecology, Climate and Empire* (Cambridge, 1997), p. 3.

18 Fischer, *A History of the Pacific Islands*, pp. 283–4.

19 Ibid., p. 285.

20 Tertullian, *Digest* 48.19.30.

21 Thomas, *A World of Islands*, p. 25.

22 Ibid., p. 29.

23 Jolliffe, *Cover-up*, p. 42.

24 Stevan Eldred-Grigg, *The Great Wrong War: New Zealand Society in WWI* (Auckland, 2010), p. 101.

25 Steven Roger Fischer, *Island at the End of the World: The Turbulent History of Easter Island* (London, 2005), p. 185.

26 Victor Prescott, 'The Law of the Sea', in *Oceans and Islands*, ed. Frank H. Talbot

and Robert E. Stevenson (London, 1991), pp. 213–15.

27 Ibid., p. 215.

28 'Medvedev Vows to Visit Islands Claimed by Japan', Reuters release, 29 September 2010.

six: . . . *of Moons and Sixpence*

1 Michael Bartholomew, *In Search of H. V. Morton* (London, 2004), p. 124.

2 A. A. Milne, 'Halfway Down'.

3 Steven Roger Fischer, *A History of the Pacific Islands* (Basingstoke, 2002), pp. 63–4, and *Rongorongo: The Easter Island Script. History, Traditions, Texts* (Oxford, 1997).

4 Lawrence Durrell, *The Greek Islands* (London, 1978), p. 81.

5 Cited in the 'Ecumenical Program for Interamerican Communication and Action Task Force', in *Grenada, the Peaceful Revolution* (Washington, DC, 1982), p. 81.

6 Glyndwr Williams, *The Great South Sea: English Voyages and Encounters, 1570–1750* (New Haven, CT, 1997), pp. 182–3. In this regard, see also Gavan Daws, *A Dream of Islands: Voyages of Self-discovery in the South Seas* (Milton, Queensland, 1980).

7 Kerry R. Howe, *Nature, Culture, and History: The 'Knowing' of Oceania* (Honolulu, HI, 2000), p. 14.

8 Angelos Georgiou Galanopoulos and Edward Bacon, *Atlantis: The Truth Behind the Legend* (Indianapolis, IN, 1969).

9 Quoted in Durrell, *The Greek Islands*, pp. 45–6.

10 [Marco Polo], *The Travels of Marco Polo*, trans. Ronald Latham (Harmondsworth, 1958), p. 248.

11 Howe, *Nature, Culture, and History*, p. 11.

12 Ibid., p. 9.

13 David Fausett, *Images of the Antipodes in the Eighteenth Century: A Study in Stereotyping* (Amsterdam, 1995).

14 Neil Rennie, *Far-fetched Facts: The Literature of Travel and the Idea of the South Seas* (Oxford, 1995). See also Howe, *Nature, Culture, and History*, p. 11.

15 Howe, *Nature, Culture, and History*, pp. 11–12.

16 Steven Roger Fischer, *A History of Reading* (London, 2003), pp. 59–60.

17 Diana Loxley, *Problematic Shores: The Literature of Islands* (Basingstoke and London, 1990), p. 6.

18 Howe, *Nature, Culture, and History*, p. 12.

19 Loxley, *Problematic Shores*, p. 7.

20 Ibid., p. 6.

21 Howe, *Nature, Culture, and History*, p. 63.

22 Daniel Defoe, *Robinson Crusoe* (London, 1964), p. 74.

23 Ibid., p. 53.

24 Loxley, *Problematic Shores*, pp. 81–3.

25 Leslie Thomas, *A World of Islands* (London, 1983), p. 104.

26 Howe, *Nature, Culture, and History*, p. 43.

27 Henri Baudet, *Paradise on Earth: Some Thoughts on European Images of Non-European Man*, trans. Elizabeth Wentholt (New Haven, CT, 1965).

28 Quoted in Howe, *Nature, Culture, and History*, p. 20.

29 Ibid., p. 15.

30 Ibid.

31 Loxley, *Problematic Shores*, p. xi.

32 Michael Russell, *Polynesia: A History of the South Seas* (London, 1853), p. 469.

33 Ernst Haeckel, *History of Creation, Or the Development of the Earth and Its Inhabitants by the Action of Natural Causes*, trans. E. Ray Lankester (London, 1883), pp. 325–6.

34 James Churchward, *The Children of Mu* and *The Lost Continent of Mu* (London, 1931).

35 Martin Green, *Dreams of Adventure, Deeds of Empire* (London, 1980), p. 3.

36 Loxley, *Problematic Shores*, p. 2.

37 Edward B. Tylor, 'Phenomena of the Higher Civilisation Traceable to a Rudimental Origin Among Savage Tribes', in *Anthropological Review*, 5 (1867), pp. 304–5; quoted in Howe, *Nature, Culture, and History*, p. 63.

38 Loxley, *Problematic Shores*, p. 34.

39 Ibid., p. 47.

40 Robert Louis Stevenson, *Treasure Island* (London, 1977), p. 6.

41 Howe, *Nature, Culture, and History*, p. 18.

42 Robert Louis Stevenson, *In the South Seas* (London, 1896), p. 42.

43 Robert James Fletcher, *Isles of Illusion: Letters from the South Seas* (London, 1923), p. 108.

44 Ibid., p. 35.

45 See W.H.R. Rivers, ed., *Essays on the Depopulation of Melanesia* (Cambridge, 1922) and George Henry Lane Fox Pitt-Rivers, *The Clash of Culture and the Contact of Races* (London, 1927).

46 Howe, *Nature, Culture, and History*, p. 47.

47 See Rod Edmond, *Representing the South Pacific: Colonial Discourse from Cook to Gauguin* (Cambridge, 1997), and Vanessa Smith, *Literary Culture and the Pacific: Nineteenth Century Textual Encounters* (Cambridge, 1998).

48 Howe, *Nature, Culture, and History*, p. 68.

49 Alfred, Lord Tennyson, 'The Lady of Shalott'.

50 Jean-Jacques Rousseau, *Émile*, trans. Barbara Foxley (London, 1911), p. 131.

51 Loxley, *Problematic Shores*, p. 8.

seven: . . . of Palettes and Pipes

1 Tim Ayers, ed., *The History of British Art*, vol. I: *600–1600* (London, 2008).

2 William Gaunt, *The Great Century of British Painting: Hogarth to Turner* (London, 1971).

3 Nikolaus Pevsner, *The Englishness of English Art* (London, 1956).

4 Ólafur Kvaran and Karla Kristjánsdóttir, eds, *Confronting Nature: Icelandic Art of the 20th Century* (Reykjavik, 2001).

5 Juan Martínez, *Cuban Art and National Identity* (Gainesville, FL, 1994).

6 Veerle Poupeye, *Caribbean Art* (London, 1998), pp. 1–3.

7 Ibid., p. 4.

8 Dave Thompson, *Reggae and Caribbean Music* (San Francisco, CA, 2002).

9 Reynold Higgins, *Minoan and Mycenæan Art* (2nd revd edn, London, 1981).
10 Donald Preziosi and Louise A. Hitchcock, *Ægean Art and Architecture* (Oxford, 1999).
11 Pliny, *Natural History*, XXXV, 36, trans. H. Rackham (Cambridge, MA, and London, 1952), vol. IX, p. 339.
12 José Gudiol, *Doménikos Theotokópoulos, El Greco, 1541–1614* (New York, 1973).
13 Lawrence Durrell, *The Greek Islands* (London, 1978), p. 92.
14 Ananda Coomaraswamy, *The Arts and Crafts of India and Ceylon* (New York, 1964).
15 Anne Lavondès, *Art traditionnel Malgache: Introduction à une exposition* (Tananarive, 1961).
16 Frits A. Wagner, *Indonesia: The Art of an Island Group*, trans. Ann E. Keep (New York, 1959).
17 Ibid., p. 5.
18 Nicholas José and Yang Wen-i, eds, *Art Taiwan: The Contemporary Art of Taiwan* (Sydney, 1995).
19 Danielle and Vadime Elisseeff, *Art of Japan*, trans. I. Mark Paris (New York, 1985).
20 Tsugio Mikami, *The Art of Japanese Ceramics* (New York, 1972).
21 Ezra Pound and Ernest Fenollosa, *The Classical Noh Theatre of Japan* (New York, 1959).
22 Anne D'Alleva, *Art of the Pacific* (London, 1998), p. 3.
23 Steven Roger Fischer, *A History of the Pacific Islands* (Basingstoke, 2002), p. 71.
24 Adrienne Kaeppler, *The Pacific Arts of Polynesia and Micronesia* (Oxford, 2008).
25 Nicholas Thomas, Anna Cole and Bronwyn Douglas, eds, *Tattoo: Bodies, Art and Exchange in the Pacific and the West* (London, 2005).
26 Adrienne L. Kaeppler and J. W. Love, eds, *The Garland Encyclopedia of World Music*, vol. IX: *Australia and the Pacific Islands* (New York, 1998).
27 Werner Spies, *Christo: Surrounded Islands, Biscayne Bay, Greater Miami, Florida, 1980–83* (New York, 1985).

eight: . . . *of the Mind*

1 'Sayings of the Week', *The Observer* (21 June 1970).
2 Christopher Plummer, *In Spite of Myself* (New York and Toronto, 2008), p. 7, recalling 'Polly's Island' (Île Perrot on Lake of Two Mountains) southwest of Montreal.
3 See, for example Eric Waddell, Vijay Naidu and Epeli Hau'ofa, eds, *A New Oceania: Rediscovering Our Sea of Islands* (Suva, 1994). Cf. Kerry R. Howe, *Nature, Culture, and History: The 'Knowing' of Oceania* (Honolulu, HI, 2000), pp. 61 and 98.
4 Lawrence Durrell, *The Greek Islands* (London, 1978), p. 230.
5 Howe, *Nature, Culture, and History*, p. 61.
6 Robert Kraske, *Marooned: The Strange But True Adventures of Alexander Selkirk* (New York, 2005).
7 Thor Heyerdahl, *Fatu-Hiva: Back to Nature* (London, 1974).
8 Leslie Thomas, *A World of Islands* (London, 1983), p. xvi.
9 Tom Neale, *An Island to Oneself* (Auckland and London, 1975), p. 19.

10 Ibid., p. 23.

11 Ibid., p. 29.

12 Ibid., p. 227.

13 Howe, *Nature, Culture, and History*, p. 2.

14 James Cook, *An Account of a Voyage Round the World* (London, 1773), vol. I, p. 207.

15 For example, see Jocelyn Linnekin, *Sacred Queens and Women of Consequence: Rank, Gender and Colonialism in the Hawaiian Islands* (Ann Arbor, MI, 1990); and *Family and Gender in the Pacific: Domestic Contradictions and the Colonial Impact* (Cambridge, 1989).

16 Howe, *Nature, Culture, and History*, p. 78.

17 Ernst Bloch, *The Principle of Hope*, trans. Neville Plaice et al., 3 vols (Cambridge, MA, 1986), vol. I, p. 24; cited in Howe, *Nature, Culture, and History*, p. 12.

18 See in this regard Elizabeth Buck, *Paradise Remade: The Politics of Culture and History in Hawai'i* (Philadelphia, PA, 1993).

19 Howe, *Nature, Culture, and History*, p. 1.

20 Ibid.

21 Marcus Aurelius Antoninus, *Meditations*, Book IV, paragraph 3; William Shakespeare, *Hamlet*, Act II, Scene ii; Alfred, Lord Tennyson, 'We Are Free', I, 7.

22 Heyerdahl, *Fatu-Hiva*, p. 381.

23 Howe, *Nature, Culture, and History*, p. 15.

24 See Greg Dening, *Beach Crossings: Voyaging Across Times, Cultures and Self* (Philadelphia, PA, 2004).

25 Bronisław Malinowski, *A Diary in the Strict Sense of the Term* (London, 1967), pp. 161–2; quoted in Howe, *Nature, Culture, and History*, pp. 18–19.

26 T. W. Whitson, ed., *The Tourists' Vade Mecum (Illustrated), Being a Handbook to the Services of the Union Steamship Company . . . Together with an Index Guide* (Dunedin, 1912), p. 60; quoted in Howe, *Nature, Culture, and History*, p. 24.

27 Howe, *Nature, Culture, and History*, pp. 25–6.

28 Thurston Clarke, *Searching for Crusoe* (New York, 2001), p. 6.

29 Paul Theroux, *The Happy Isles of Oceania: Paddling the Pacific* (London, 1992), p. 6.

30 Howe, *Nature, Culture, and History*, p. 30.

31 Durrell, *The Greek Islands*, p. 41.

32 See Jocelyn Linnekin, 'The Ideological World Remade', in *The Cambridge History of the Pacific Islanders*, ed. Donald Denoon et al. (Cambridge, 1997), pp. 397–438.

33 Thomas, *A World of Islands*, p. 17.

34 Ibid., p. xv.

35 Edwin Cerio, *On Capri*, quoted in Thomas, *A World of Islands*, p. 108.

36 Durrell, *The Greek Islands*, pp. 59–60.

37 Ibid., p. 92.

38 Howe, *Nature, Culture, and History*, p. 70.

39 Durrell, *The Greek Islands*, p. 138.

40 Ibid., p. 128.

41 James Morris, *Pax Britannica* (London, 1968), pp. 222–3.

42 Louise B. Young, *Islands: Portraits of Miniature Worlds* (New York, 1999), p. 3.

43 Thomas, *A World of Islands*, p. 105.

44 Howe, *Nature, Culture, and History*, p. 30.

45 Durrell, *The Greek Islands*, p. 201.

46 William Wordsworth, 'The Prelude', Book XI ('Residence in France, Concluded'), lines 140–44.

nine: *The Last Isle*

1 Paul Bahn and John Flenley, *Easter Island, Earth Island* (London, 1992), and John Flenley and Paul Bahn, *The Enigmas of Easter Island* (London, 2002). See also Steven Roger Fischer, *Island at the End of the World: The Turbulent History of Easter Island* (London, 2005).

2 Leslie Thomas, *A World of Islands* (London, 1983), p. 147.

3 Lawrence Durrell, *The Greek Islands* (London, 1978), p. 272.

4 Kerry R. Howe, *Nature, Culture, and History: The 'Knowing' of Oceania* (Honolulu, HI, 2000), p. 76.

5 Robert E. Stevenson, 'Foreword', in *Islands*, ed. Robert E. Stevenson and Frank H. Talbot (London, 1994), p. 11.

6 Louise B. Young, *Islands: Portraits of Miniature Worlds* (New York, 1999), p. 250.

7 Bob Holmes, 'HIV May Remain Deadly for Millennia', *New Scientist*, 2779 (25 September 2010), p. 12.

8 David Hopley, 'The End of Isolation', in *Islands*, ed. Stevenson and Talbot, p. 196.

9 David Hopley, 'Continental Islands', in *Islands*, ed. Stevenson and Talbot, p. 30.

10 Paul Michael Taylor, 'The Indonesian Archipelago', in *Islands*, ed. Stevenson and Talbot, p. 112.

11 Durrell, *The Greek Islands*, p. 38.

12 Matt Warshaw, *The History of Surfing* (San Francisco, CA, 2010).

13 Young, *Islands*, p. 218.

14 Oliver Sacks, *The Island of the Colorblind* (New York, 1997), p. 38.

15 Mick Hamer, 'Disaster from the Deep', *New Scientist*, 2776 (4 September 2010), pp. 34–7.

16 Pliny, *Natural History*, II, 110, trans. H. Rackham (Cambridge, MA, and London, 1949), vol. I, pp. 363–5.

17 Sheena Coupe, 'Krakatoa: An Island Erupts', in *Oceans and Islands*, ed. Frank H. Talbot and Robert E. Stevenson (London, 1991), p. 128.

18 Pliny, *Natural History*, II, 94, vol. I, pp. 337.

19 Storrs L. Olson, 'The Atlantic Islands', in *Islands*, ed. Stevenson and Talbot, p. 89.

20 Sonia Van Gilder Cooke, 'Coral "Whisperers" Diagnose Reef Woes', *New Scientist*, 2801 (26 February 2011), p. 8.

21 Alistair J. Gilmour, 'The Implications of Global Climate Change', in *Oceans and Islands*, ed. Talbot and Stevenson, p. 227.

22 Hopley, 'Coral Reefs', in *Islands*, ed. Stevenson and Talbot, p. 151.

23 Gilmour, 'The Implications of Global Climate Change', p. 226.

24 Ibid., p. 227.

25 *New Scientist*, 2783 (23 October 2010), p. 7.

26 Hopley, 'Coral Reefs', in *Islands*, ed. Stevenson and Talbot, p. 151.

27 *New Scientist*, 2763 (5 June 2010), p. 10.

28 Quoted by Paul Marks, 'Megaquake Aftermath', *New Scientist*, 2804 (19 March

2011), p. 6.

29 *New Scientist*, 2780 (2 October 2010), p. 4.

30 Gilmour, 'The Implications of Global Climate Change', p. 226.

31 James Lovelock, *Gaia: A New Look at Life on Earth* (Oxford, 1979).

Select Bibliography

Ahlburg, D., and M. Levin, *The North-East Passage: A Study of Pacific Islander Migration to American Samoa and the United States* (Canberra, 1990)

Baudet, Henri, *Paradise on Earth: Some Thoughts on European Images of Non-European Man*, trans. Elizabeth Wentholt (New Haven, CT, 1965)

Beaglehole, J. C., ed., *The Journals of Captain James Cook on His Voyages of Discovery*, 3 vols (Cambridge, 1955–74)

—, *The Exploration of the Pacific* (3rd revd edn, London, 1966)

Bellwood, Peter S., *Man's Conquest of the Pacific* (Auckland, 1978)

—, *The Polynesians* (London, 1987)

Bensa, Alban, and Isabelle Leblic, eds, *En pays Kanak: Ethnologie, linguistique, archéologie, histoire de la Nouvelle-Calédonie* (Paris, 2000)

Brake, B., J. McNeish and D. Simmons, *Art of the Pacific* (Oxford, 1979)

Buck, Elizabeth, *Paradise Remade: The Politics of Culture and History in Hawai'i* (Philadelphia, PA, 1993)

Burt, Ben, and Christian Clerk, eds, *Environment and Development in the Pacific Islands*, Pacific Policy Paper 25 (Canberra and Port Moresby, 1997)

Campbell, Ian C., *Worlds Apart: A History of the Pacific Islands* (Christchurch, 2003)

Clarke, Thurston, *Searching for Crusoe* (New York, 2001)

Columbus, Christopher, *The Journal of Christopher Columbus*, trans. Cecil Jane (London, 1960)

Connell, John, ed., *Migration and Development in the South Pacific* (Canberra, 1990)

Coomaraswamy, Ananda, *The Arts and Crafts of India and Ceylon* (New York, 1964)

Crocombe, Ron, *The South Pacific: An Introduction* (2nd revd edn, Suva, 1989)

—, *The Pacific Islands and the USA* (Suva and Honolulu, 1995)

—, and Admed Ali, eds, *Foreign Forces in Pacific Politics* (Suva, 1983)

Cunliffe, Barry, *The Extraordinary Voyage of Pytheas the Greek* (London, 2002)

D'Alleva, Anne, *Art of the Pacific* (London, 1998)

Danielsson, Bengt, and Marie-Thérèse Danielsson, *Poisoned Reign: French Nuclear Colonialism in the Pacific* (Harmondsworth, 1986)

Davidson, J. M., *The Prehistory of New Zealand* (Auckland, 1984)

Daws, Gavan, *Shoal of Time: A History of the Hawaiian Islands* (Honolulu, HI, 1974)

—, *A Dream of Islands: Voyages of Self-discovery in the South Seas* (Milton, QLD, 1980)

Denoon, Donald, with Stewart Firth, Jocelyn Linnekin, Malama Meleisea and Karen
    Nero, *The Cambridge History of the Pacific Islanders* (Cambridge, 1997)
Dodd, Philip, and Ben Donald, *The Book of Islands* (Wingfield, SA, 2008)
Dodge, Ernest S., *Beyond the Capes: Pacific Exploration from Cook to the
    'Challenger' (1776–1877)* (London, 1971)
Douglas, Ngaire, *They Came for Savages: 100 Years of Tourism in Melanesia*
    (Lismore, NSW, 1996)
Dunn, James, *Timor: A People Betrayed* (Brisbane, 1983)
Durrell, Lawrence, *The Greek Islands* (London, 1978)
Edmond, Rod, *Representing the South Pacific: Colonial Discourse from Cook to
    Gauguin* (Cambridge, 1997)
Elisseeff, Danielle and Vadime, *Art of Japan*, trans. I. Mark Paris (New York, 1985)
Fausett, David, *Writing the New World: Imaginary Voyages and Utopias of the Great
    Southern Land* (Syracuse, NY, 1993)
—, *Images of the Antipodes in the Eighteenth Century: A Study in Stereotyping*
    (Amsterdam, 1995)
Firth, Stewart, *Nuclear Playground* (Sydney, 1987)
Fischer, Steven Roger, ed., *Easter Island Studies: Contributions to the History of
    Rapanui in Memory of William T. Mulloy* (Oxford, 1993)
—, *Rongorongo: The Easter Island Script. History, Traditions, Texts* (Oxford, 1997)
—, *Glyphbreaker* (New York, 1997)
—, *A History of the Pacific Islands* (Basingstoke, 2002)
—, *Island at the End of the World: The Turbulent History of Easter Island* (London,
    2005)
Goldman, Irving, *Ancient Polynesian Society* (Chicago, IL, 1970)
Green, Martin, *Dreams of Adventure, Deeds of Empire* (London, 1980)
Griffin, James, Hank Nelson and Stewart Firth, eds, *Papua New Guinea: A Political
    History* (Richmond, VIC, 1979)
Grove, Richard H., *Green Imperialism: Colonial Expansion, Tropical Island Edens
    and the Origins of Environmentalism, 1600–1860* (Cambridge, 1995)
—, *Ecology, Climate and Empire* (Cambridge, 1997)
Hanlon, David, *Remaking Micronesia: Discourses over Development in a Pacific
    Territory, 1944–1982* (Honolulu, HI, 1998)
Henningham, Stephen, *France and the South Pacific: A Contemporary History*
    (Sydney, 1992)
Hezel, Francis, *The First Taint of Civilization: A History of the Caroline and
    Marshall Islands in Pre-colonial Days, 1521–1885* (Honolulu, HI, 1983)
—, and Mark Berg, eds, *Micronesia: Winds of Change* (Saipan, 1979)
Hiery, Herman Joseph, *The Neglected War: The German South Pacific and the
    Influence of World War I* (Honolulu, HI, 1995)
Higgins, Reynold, *Minoan and Mycenaean Art* (2nd revd edn, London, 1981)
Hill, A.V.S., and S. W. Serjeantson, eds, *The Colonization of the Pacific: A Genetic
    Trail* (Oxford, 1989)
Holm, Bill, *Eccentric Islands: Travels Real and Imaginary* (Minneapolis, MN, 2000)
Hooper, Antony, ed., *Culture and Sustainable Development in the Pacific* (Canberra,
    2000)
—, and Judith Huntsman, eds, *Transformation of Polynesian Culture*, Memoir of the

Select Bibliography

Polynesian Society 45 (Auckland, 1985)

Houghton, Philip, *People of the Great Ocean: Aspects of Human Biology of the Early Pacific* (Cambridge, 1996)

Howe, Kerry R., *Where the Waves Fall: A New South Sea Islands History from First Settlement to Colonial Rule* (London and Sydney, 1984)

—, *Nature, Culture, and History: The 'Knowing' of Oceania* (Honolulu, HI, 2000)

—, Robert C. Kiste and Brij Lal, eds, *Tides of History: The Pacific Islands in the Twentieth Century* (London, 1994)

Howells, W. W., *The Pacific Islanders* (London, 1973)

Hughes, Helen, ed., *Women in Development in the Pacific* (Canberra, 1985)

Hunt, Colin, *Pacific Development Sustained: Policy for Pacific Environments* (Canberra, 1998)

Irwin, Geoffrey, *The Prehistoric Exploration and Colonisation of the Pacific* (Cambridge, 1992)

Ishikawa, E., ed., *Cultural Adaptation to Atolls in Micronesia and West Polynesia* (Tokyo, 1987)

Jennings, Jesse D., ed., *The Prehistory of Polynesia* (Cambridge, MA, and London, 1979)

Jolliffe, Jill, *Cover-up: The Inside Story of the Balibo Five* (Melbourne, 2001)

José, Nicholas, and Yang Wen-i, eds, *Art Taiwan: The Contemporary Art of Taiwan*, (Sydney, 1995)

Kaeppler, Adrienne, *The Pacific Arts of Polynesia and Micronesia* (Oxford, 2008)

King, Michael, *The Penguin History of New Zealand* (Auckland, 2003)

Kirch, Patrick V., *The Evolution of the Polynesian Chiefdoms* (Cambridge, 1984)

—, *The Lapita Peoples: Ancestors of the Oceanic World* (Oxford, 1997)

—, *On the Road of the Winds: An Archæological History of the Pacific Islands Before European Contact* (Los Angeles and Berkeley, CA, 2000)

—, and Roger C. Green, *Hawaiki, Ancestral Polynesia: An Essay in Historical Anthropology* (Cambridge, 2001)

Kiste, Robert, *The Bikinians: A Study in Forced Migration* (Menlo Park, CA, 1974)

Kvaran, Ólafur, and Karla Kristjánsdóttir, eds, *Confronting Nature: Icelandic Art of the 20th Century* (Reykjavik, 2001)

Lal, Brij V., *Broken Waves: A History of the Fiji Islands in the Twentieth Century* (Honolulu, HI, 1992)

—, ed., *Pacific Islands History: Journeys and Transformations* (Canberra, 1992)

—, and Kate Fortune, eds, *The Pacific Islands: An Encyclopedia* (Honolulu, HI, 2000)

Laracy, Hugh, *Marists and Melanesians: A History of Catholic Missions in the Solomon Islands* (Canberra, 1976)

Lavondès, Anne, *Art traditionnel Malgache: Introduction à une exposition* (Tananarive, 1961)

Lieber, Michael, ed., *Exiles and Migrants in Oceania* (Honolulu, HI, 1977)

Linnekin, Jocelyn, and Lyn Poyer, eds, *Cultural Identity and Ethnicity in the Pacific* (Honolulu, HI, 1990)

Lovelock, James, *Gaia: A New Look at Life on Earth* (Oxford, 1979)

Loxley, Diana, *Problematic Shores: The Literature of Islands* (Basingstoke and London, 1990)

McArthur, Norma, *Island Populations of the Pacific* (Canberra, 1967)

MacArthur, Robert, *The Theory of Island Biogeography* (Princeton, NJ, 1967)

McCall, Grant, and John Connell, eds, *A World Perspective on Pacific Islander Migration: Australia, New Zealand and the USA* (Sydney, 1993)

MacLeod, Roy, and Philip F. Rehbock, eds, *Nature in its Greatest Extent: Western Science in the Pacific* (Honolulu, HI, 1988)

—, eds, *Evolutionary Theory and the Natural History of the Pacific: Darwin's Laboratory* (Honolulu, HI, 1994)

Martínez, Juan, *Cuban Art and National Identity* (Gainesville, FL, 1994)

Maude, Harry, *Of Islands and Men: Studies in Pacific History* (Melbourne, 1968)

—, *Slavers in Paradise: The Peruvian Slave Trade in Polynesia, 1862–1864* (Canberra, 1981)

Mazellier, Philippe, *Tahiti autonome* (Pape'ete, 1990)

Meleisea, Malama, *Lagaga: A Short History of Western Samoa* (Suva, 1987)

Meller, Norman, *Constitutionalism in Micronesia* (Honolulu, HI, 1985)

Miles, John, *Infectious Diseases: Colonising the Pacific?* (Dunedin, 1997)

Moore, Clive, Jacqueline Leckie and Doug Munro, eds, *Labour in the South Pacific* (Townsville, QLD, 1990)

Morrell, W. P., *Britain in the Pacific Islands* (Oxford, 1960)

Narokobi, Bernard, *The Melanesian Way* (Boroko and Suva, 1980)

Nash, Dennison, *Anthropology of Tourism* (Oxford, 1996)

Neale, Tom, *An Island to Oneself* (Auckland and London, 1975)

Neemia, Uentabo Fakaofo, *Cooperation and Conflict: Costs, Benefits and National Interests in Pacific Regional Cooperation* (Suva, 1986)

Nicole, Robert, *The Word, the Pen, and the Pistol: Literature and Power in Tahiti* (Albany, NY, 2001)

Nile, Richard, and Christian Clerk, *Cultural Atlas of Australia, New Zealand and the South Pacific* (Surry Hills, NSW, 1996)

Oliver, Douglas L., *Ancient Tahitian Society*, 3 vols (Honolulu, HI, 1974)

—, *The Pacific Islands* (3rd edn, Honolulu, 1989)

Oliver, W. H., and B. R. Williams, eds, *The Oxford History of New Zealand* (Oxford, 1981)

Overton, John, and Regina Scheyvens, eds, *Strategies for Sustainable Development: Experiences from the Pacific* (Sydney, 1999)

Peattie, Mark R., *Nan'yo: The Rise and Fall of the Japanese in Micronesia, 1885–1945* (Honolulu, HI, 1988)

Ponting, Clive, *A Green History of the World* (London, 1992)

Poupeye, Veerle, *Caribbean Art* (London, 1998)

Poyer, Lin, Suzanne Falgout and Laurence Marshall Carucci, eds, *The Typhoon of War: Micronesian Experiences of the Pacific War* (Honolulu, HI, 2001)

Prest, John, *The Garden of Eden: The Botanic Garden and the Re-creation of Paradise* (New Haven, CT, 1981)

Preziosi, Donald, and Louise A. Hitchcock, *Ægean Art and Architecture* (Oxford, 1999)

Quammen, David, *The Song of the Dodo: Island Biogeography in an Age of Extinctions* (New York, 1996)

Rata, Elizabeth, *A Political Economy of Neotribal Capitalism* (Lanham, MD, 2000)

Rennie, Neil, *Far-fetched Facts: The Literature of Travel and the Idea of the South Seas* (Oxford, 1995)

Select Bibliography

Robie, D., *Blood on Their Banner: Nationalist Struggles in the South Pacific* (Leichhardt, NSW, 1989)

Sacks, Oliver, *The Island of the Colorblind* (New York, 1997)

Sahlins, Marshall, *Islands of History* (Chicago, IL, 1985)

Salmond, Anne, *Two Worlds: First Meetings Between Maori and Europeans, 1642–1772* (Auckland, 1993)

Samson, Jane, *Imperial Benevolence: Making British Authority in the Pacific Islands* (Honolulu, HI, 1998)

Scarr, Deryck, *Fiji: A Short History* (Sydney, 1984)

—, *A History of the Pacific Islands* (Richmond, VIC, 2001)

Schalansky, Judith, *Atlas der entlegenen Inseln* (Hamburg, 2009)

Smith, Bernard, *European Vision and the South Pacific* (New Haven, CT, 1990)

—, *Imagining the Pacific: In the Wake of the Cook Voyages* (New Haven, CT, 1992)

Smith, Gary, *Micronesia: Decolonisation and US Military Interests in the Trust Territory of the Pacific Islands* (Canberra, 1991)

Smith, M. A., M. Spriggs and B. Fankhauser, eds, *Sahul in Review: Pleistocene Archæology in Australia, New Guinea, and Island Melanesia*, ANU Prehistory Occasional Paper 24 (Canberra, 1993)

Smith, Valerie L., *Hosts and Guests: The Anthropology of Tourism* (2nd revd edn, Philadelphia, PA, 1989)

Smith, Vanessa, *Literary Culture and the Pacific: Nineteenth-Century Textual Encounters* (Cambridge, 1998)

Spanish Pacific from Magellan to Malaspina (Barcelona, 1988)

Spate, O.H.K., *The Pacific Since Magellan*, 3 vols (Canberra, 1988)

Spies, Werner, *Christo: Surrounded Islands, Biscayne Bay, Greater Miami, Florida, 1980–83* (New York, 1985)

Stanley, David, *South Pacific Handbook* (7th revd edn, Emeryville, CA, 2000)

Steven, Anna, ed., *Pirating the Pacific: Images of Travel, Trade and Tourism* (Sydney, 1993)

Stevenson, Robert E., and Frank H. Talbot, eds, *Islands* (Surry Hills, NSW, 1994)

Stewart, Pamela J., and Andrew Strathern, eds, *Identity Work: Constructing Pacific Lives* (Pittsburgh, PA, 2000)

Tagupa, William, *Politics in French Polynesia, 1945–1975* (Wellington, 1976)

Talbot, Frank H., and Robert E. Stevenson, eds, *Oceans and Islands* (London, 1991)

Terrell, J. E., *Prehistory in the Pacific Islands: A Study of Variation in Language, Custom, and Human Biology* (Cambridge, 1986)

Theroux, Paul, *The Happy Isles of Oceania: Paddling the Pacific* (London, 1992)

Thomas, Leslie, *A World of Islands* (London, 1983)

Thual, François, *Équations Polynésiennes* (Paris, 1992)

Urry, John, *The Tourist Gaze: Leisure and Travel in Contemporary Societies* (London, 1990)

Ushijima, Iwao, and Ken-ichi Sudo, eds, *Cultural Uniformity and Diversity in Micronesia*, Senri Ethnological Studies 21 (Osaka, 1987)

Waddell, Eric, Vijay Naidu and Epeli Hau'ofa, eds, *A New Oceania: Rediscovering Our Sea of Islands* (Suva, 1994)

Wagner, Frits A., *Indonesia: The Art of an Island Group*, trans. Ann E. Keep (New York, 1959)

Ward, R. Gerard, *Widening Worlds, Shrinking Worlds? The Reshaping of Oceania* (Canberra, 1999)

Weisgall, Jonathan M., *Operation Crossroads: The Atomic Tests at Bikini Atoll* (Annapolis, MD, 1994)

Weisler, Marshall I., ed., *Prehistoric Long-Distance Interaction in Oceania: An Interdisciplinary Approach*, New Zealand Archæological Association Monograph 21 (Auckland, 1997)

White, J. P., and J. F. O'Connell, *A Prehistory of Australia, New Guinea, and Sahul* (Sydney, 1982)

Williams, Glyndwr, *The Great South Sea: English Voyages and Encounters, 1570–1750* (New Haven, CT, 1997)

Young, Louise B., *Islands: Portraits of Miniature Worlds* (New York, 1999)

Acknowledgements

I would like to thank the following people: Paul Bahn; Rich and Nancy Byrne; Harriet Glan; Kennedy and Marilyn Graham; Robert and Audrey Gray; Susan Gray; Kate Hubbard; Joan Seaver Kurze; Mary Dell Lucas; Garry and Susan Mason; Julia Meek; Sid Orr; Arnold and Nancy Simon; Paul Spiekermann; Rose Marie Wallace; Terry Welbourn; and David Wheeler and Christine Hafermalz-Wheeler.

I have received valuable advice from Jeremy Black; John Charlot; Alastair and Adaline Christie-Johnston; Riet Delsing; John Flenley; Sonia Haoa; H.G.A. Hughes; Robert and Denise Koenig; Charles M. Love; Père André Mark sscc; Paul Monin; Peter Monin; Steve Pagel; Cristián Moreno Pakarati; and Thomas and Christel Stolz.

Especial thanks to Jill Jolliffe, for the true story about East Timor. To Michael Leaman of Reaktion Books in London, as ever my heartfelt appreciation. Undying gratitude and esteem go to the late Thomas Charles Lethbridge of Cambridge. My wife Dagmar has been, as always, my inspiration.

This book is dedicated to Georgia Lee and Frank Morin, selfless friends of islanders everywhere.

Photo Acknowledgements

The author and publisher wish to express their thanks to the following sources of illustrative material and/or permission to reproduce it.

page

17 Courtly vessel plying the Japanese isles during the Heian Period (794–1192); woodcut illustration by Shunshō Yamamoto from a 1650 Kyoto edition of Murasaki Shikibu's *Genji Monogatari*

49 Māori bird-woman Kurangaituku, with *koru* fronds and her pet birds and tuatara lizards; carved figure from a meeting house in Rotorua, New Zealand. Margaret Orbell, *The Illustrated Encyclopedia of Māori Myth and Legend* (Christchurch, 1995), p. 47

89 Shipwreck and armed warriors on an Ægean isle in the first half of the second millenium BC; contemporary miniature frieze from Akrotiri, Santorini. Christos Doumas, *The Wall Paintings of Thera* (Athens, 1992), p. 58

147 A seventeenth-century Song emperor shipping Chinese goods to offshore isles; contemporary watercolour on silk. Noel Grove, *National Geographic Atlas of World History* (Washington, DC, 1997), p. 117

169 Marco Polo departing the island of Venice for East Asia in 1271; illumination *c.* 1400, Bodleian Library, Oxford

208 Shipwreck on Prospero's magical isle in William Shakespeare's *The Tempest*; frontispiece from the 1709 London edition by Nicholas Rowe

245 Male facial tattoo of a New Zealand Māori; 1769 drawing by Sidney Parkinson aboard James Cook's *Endeavour*. Richard Nile and Christian Clerk, *Cultural Atlas of Australia, New Zealand & the South Pacific* (Surry Hills, NSW, 1995), p. 83

252 A medieval Fool weighed down by islands of the mind; Swiss woodblock print. Sebastian Brant, *Das Narrenschiff* (Basel, 1494), p. 24

301 The Isola Tiberina, oasis of hope in the midst of Imperial Rome, with the Temple of Æsculapius at the far end. *All of Ancient Rome* (Florence, 1988), p. 99

Index

Index